# The Digital Marketer's Playbook

How to Effectively Collaborate with Agencies, Freelancers, and Digital Marketing Experts

Diego Adolfo Carrasco Gubernatis

Apress®

*The Digital Marketer's Playbook: How to Effectively Collaborate with Agencies, Freelancers, and Digital Marketing Experts*

Diego Adolfo Carrasco Gubernatis
Essen, Nordrhein-Westfalen, Germany

ISBN-13 (pbk): 979-8-8688-0545-5  ISBN-13 (electronic): 979-8-8688-0546-2
https://doi.org/10.1007/979-8-8688-0546-2

Copyright © 2024 by Diego Adolfo Carrasco Gubernatis

This work is subject to copyright. All rights are reserved by the Publisher, whether the whole or part of the material is concerned, specifically the rights of translation, reprinting, reuse of illustrations, recitation, broadcasting, reproduction on microfilms or in any other physical way, and transmission or information storage and retrieval, electronic adaptation, computer software, or by similar or dissimilar methodology now known or hereafter developed.

Trademarked names, logos, and images may appear in this book. Rather than use a trademark symbol with every occurrence of a trademarked name, logo, or image we use the names, logos, and images only in an editorial fashion and to the benefit of the trademark owner, with no intention of infringement of the trademark.

The use in this publication of trade names, trademarks, service marks, and similar terms, even if they are not identified as such, is not to be taken as an expression of opinion as to whether or not they are subject to proprietary rights.

While the advice and information in this book are believed to be true and accurate at the date of publication, neither the authors nor the editors nor the publisher can accept any legal responsibility for any errors or omissions that may be made. The publisher makes no warranty, express or implied, with respect to the material contained herein.

>Managing Director, Apress Media LLC: Welmoed Spahr
>Acquisitions Editor: Shivangi Ramachandran
>Development Editor: James Markham
>Editorial Assistant: Jessica Vakili

Cover designed by eStudioCalamar

Distributed to the book trade worldwide by Springer Science+Business Media New York, 1 New York Plaza, Suite 4600, New York, NY 10004-1562, USA. Phone 1-800-SPRINGER, fax (201) 348-4505, e-mail orders-ny@springer-sbm.com, or visit www.springeronline.com. Apress Media, LLC is a California LLC and the sole member (owner) is Springer Science + Business Media Finance Inc (SSBM Finance Inc). SSBM Finance Inc is a **Delaware** corporation.

For information on translations, please e-mail booktranslations@springernature.com; for reprint, paperback, or audio rights, please e-mail bookpermissions@springernature.com.

Apress titles may be purchased in bulk for academic, corporate, or promotional use. eBook versions and licenses are also available for most titles. For more information, reference our Print and eBook Bulk Sales web page at http://www.apress.com/bulk-sales.

Any source code or other supplementary material referenced by the author in this book is available to readers on GitHub. For more detailed information, please visit https://www.apress.com/gp/services/source-code.

If disposing of this product, please recycle the paper

*To my wife, whose unwavering support and encouragement have been my greatest source of strength.*

*To my daughters, to show them that you have to overcome challenges and take advantage of opportunities, even if they are scary.*

*Thank you for being there for me.*

*To those who know me, I have not yet realized that there are limits and I still firmly believe that anything is possible.*

# Table of Contents

About the Author ................................................................................. xxix

Acknowledgments ................................................................................ xxxi

Introduction ........................................................................................ xxxiii

## Part I: Digital Marketing: Fundamentals, Concepts, and Actors .... 1

### Chapter 1: Defining Digital Marketing ....................................................... 3
Digital Marketing As Defined for This Book .......................................... 4
    A Closer Look at the Three Major Stages ....................................... 6
Why Digital Marketing Is Important ....................................................... 9
    Advantages and Disadvantages of Digital Marketing ..................... 10
Summary ............................................................................................. 13

### Chapter 2: Digital Assets and Why They Are Important ........................ 15
Brand Equity ........................................................................................ 16
Rule of Thumb for Handling Digital Assets .......................................... 17
Digital Assets and How to Save Them ................................................. 19
Summary ............................................................................................. 21

### Chapter 3: Structure of the Digital Advertising Ecosystem ................. 23
Understanding the Structure ................................................................ 24
Four Pillars .......................................................................................... 27
Summary ............................................................................................. 27

TABLE OF CONTENTS

## Chapter 4: Understanding Customer Awareness Levels in Digital Marketing ...........................................................................29
Comparing Awareness Levels: A Practical Example............................30
Visualizing Awareness Levels ..............................................................30
    Most Aware Customers................................................................33
    Product Aware Customers ..........................................................33
    Solution Aware Customers .........................................................33
    Pain or Problem Aware Customers ............................................34
    Completely Unaware Customers ................................................34
    Implementing Awareness in Strategy.........................................34
Incorporating Awareness Diagram with Customer Interactions..........35
Example Strategy Details for Each Awareness Level ..........................36
Summary.................................................................................................36

## Chapter 5: Understanding Walled Gardens and Open Internet ...........39
Walled Gardens in Digital Marketing....................................................39
The Open Web .......................................................................................40
Closing Thoughts...................................................................................40
Summary.................................................................................................40

## Chapter 6: The Essence of Targeting in Digital Marketing..................41
Delving Deeper: An In-Depth Look at Targeting..................................42
    Collection of Settings and Criteria..............................................42
    Messages and Creatives...............................................................42
Types of Targeting: Broad vs. Specific .................................................43
    Example Application ...................................................................43
Summary.................................................................................................44

TABLE OF CONTENTS

## Chapter 7: Understanding Cannibalization in Digital Marketing ........45
The Concept of Cannibalization ..................................................................... 45
Bidding Wars and Budget Impacts ................................................................ 46
Addressing Cannibalization ........................................................................... 47
    Strategies to Mitigate Cannibalization ..................................................... 47
Summary ........................................................................................................ 47

## Chapter 8: Understanding Placements and Inventory ...................... 49
What Are Placements and Inventory? ........................................................... 49
Advanced Concepts: Blocklisting, Allowlisting, and Managing URLs ................ 50
    Blocklisting and Allowlisting ..................................................................... 50
    Important Consideration ........................................................................... 51
    Role of URLs in Ad Placements ................................................................ 51
    Practical Example of URL Management .................................................. 51
The Importance of Monitoring Ad Placements ............................................. 52
    Accurately Monitoring .............................................................................. 52
Blocklisting and Analyzing URLs ................................................................... 52
Understanding Thumb-Clicks in Mobile Gaming Ads .................................. 53
    Thumb-Clicks ............................................................................................. 53
    Exploring the Impact ................................................................................. 54
    Why Monitoring Thumb-Clicks Makes Sense ......................................... 54
    Significance of Monitoring ........................................................................ 54
    Identifying Thumb-Clicks ......................................................................... 54
Evaluating Mobile Advertisement Strategy for Apps and Smartphone Games .... 55
    Ad Placement Strategy ............................................................................. 55
    User Experience Considerations ............................................................. 55
Summary ........................................................................................................ 55

## Chapter 9: Target Groups, Audiences, and Personas .........................57

Introduction to Target Groups and Audiences ................................................... 57
    Identify and Engage................................................................................. 58
    Example of Target Group Utilization......................................................... 58
    Ad Platforms and Targeting Options ........................................................ 59
    Understanding Who Sees Your Ads.......................................................... 59
    Understanding Audiences........................................................................ 59
    Audience Analysis.................................................................................... 60
Understanding the Difference: Target Group, Audience, and Persona ................ 60
Summary............................................................................................................ 61

## Chapter 10: Understanding Bids, Bid Strategies, and Their Impacts ....63

Bids in Digital Marketing.................................................................................... 63
Popular Bid Strategies ....................................................................................... 64
    Defining Risk in the Context of Bidding Strategies.................................... 65
Practical Definition of Risk................................................................................. 66
    Managing Risk......................................................................................... 66
    Choosing the Right Strategy .................................................................... 67
    Choosing the Right Strategy .................................................................... 70
Detailed Analysis of Bidding Strategies and Risk Allocation.............................. 70
    Cost per Click (CPC)................................................................................. 70
    CPC Risk Bearing..................................................................................... 70
    Use Case Example ................................................................................... 71
    Cost per Mille (CPM) ................................................................................ 71
    CPM Risk Bearing.................................................................................... 71
    Use Case Example ................................................................................... 71
    Cost per Action (CPA) .............................................................................. 71
    CPA Risk Bearing..................................................................................... 72

# TABLE OF CONTENTS

    Use Case Example ............................................................................. 72
    Cost per View (CPV) ........................................................................ 72
    CPV Risk Bearing ............................................................................. 72
    Use Case Example ............................................................................. 72
    Cost per Install (CPI) ....................................................................... 73
    CPI Risk Bearing .............................................................................. 73
    Use Case Example ............................................................................. 73
    Enhanced Cost per Click (eCPC) ..................................................... 73
    eCPC Risk Bearing .......................................................................... 73
    Use Case Example ............................................................................. 74
    Return on Ad Spend (ROAS) ........................................................... 74
    ROAS Risk Bearing ......................................................................... 74
    Use Case Example ............................................................................. 74
    How to Calculate ROAS ................................................................... 75
    Example of ROAS Calculation ......................................................... 75
    Importance of ROAS ....................................................................... 76
  Exploring Programmatic Buying ........................................................... 76
    What Programmatic Buying Is Not ................................................. 76
    Alternatives and Considerations ..................................................... 76
    Cons of Programmatic Buying ........................................................ 77
  Summary ................................................................................................ 77

## Chapter 11: Exploring Ad Quality from Multiple Perspectives ............ 79

  Defining Ad Quality .............................................................................. 80
    High-Quality Ads ............................................................................. 80
    Low-Quality Ads .............................................................................. 80
    Ad Quality Tracking ......................................................................... 80

TABLE OF CONTENTS

    The Customer's View on Ad Quality ................................................................ 81
        The Ad Provider's View on Ad Quality ........................................................... 82
        Provider's Practical Insights .......................................................................... 82
        The Advertiser's View on Ad Quality ............................................................. 82
        Advertiser's Example Scenario ..................................................................... 83
    Exploring Ad Quality Score and Ad Quality Ranking ........................................ 83
        Ad Quality Score: What It Is and Why It Matters ........................................ 84
        Ad Quality Score Explanation ....................................................................... 84
        Practical Example ......................................................................................... 84
        Effects of Ad Quality Score ........................................................................... 85
    Ad Quality Ranking: Determining Visibility and Auction Outcomes ..................... 85
        Ad Quality Ranking Explained ...................................................................... 85
        Ad Rank and Its Consequences .................................................................... 86
    Breaking Down Ad Relevance .......................................................................... 86
    Enhancing Landing Page Quality ...................................................................... 86
        Practical Example ......................................................................................... 87
    Diagrammatic Representation of Factors Influencing Ad Quality and
    Ad Position ....................................................................................................... 87
    Summary .......................................................................................................... 89

## Chapter 12: Understanding Digital Marketing Metrics ........................ 91

    Understanding Key Digital Marketing Metrics .................................................. 91
        Cost per Click (CPC) ..................................................................................... 91
        Cost per View (CPV) ..................................................................................... 94
        Clicks ............................................................................................................. 96
        Click-Through Rate (CTR) ............................................................................. 97
        Impressions ................................................................................................ 100
        Conversion Rate ......................................................................................... 102
        Reach .......................................................................................................... 104

TABLE OF CONTENTS

    Frequency ................................................................................................ 106

    Share of Impressions ............................................................................... 108

    Cost per Mille (CPM) ............................................................................... 110

    Comparing Digital and Traditional Marketing ............................................... 112

        Integrating Digital Tracking in Print ....................................................... 112

    Summary ................................................................................................ 113

## Chapter 13: Understanding the Customer/Buyer Journey ................ 115

    Defining Customer Journey ....................................................................... 115

    Detailed View of the Customer Journey with a Diagram ............................... 116

    Summary ................................................................................................ 118

## Chapter 14: Keywords in Digital Marketing: What They Are and Why They Matter ......................................................................... 119

    Keywords and How They're Used ............................................................. 120

    The Role of Keywords in Digital Advertising .............................................. 120

        Positive and Negative Keywords ......................................................... 120

    Keywords and Contextual Advertising ....................................................... 121

        How Contextual Targeting Works ........................................................ 121

    Integrating Keywords with Ad Copy and Landing Pages ............................. 122

    Understanding Keyword Match Types ....................................................... 122

        Types of Keyword Matches ................................................................ 123

        Strategic Use of Keyword Match Types .............................................. 124

    Keyword Selection, Costs, and Budgeting ................................................. 125

        Understanding Keyword Costs and CPC ............................................. 125

        Max CPC and Its Implications ............................................................ 125

        Budgeting for Keywords .................................................................... 126

    Keyword Research Tools and Techniques ................................................. 126

    Keyword Optimization Strategies .............................................................. 127

## TABLE OF CONTENTS

Long-Tail Keywords ............................................................... 128
Keyword Trends and Seasonality ......................................... 129
Local SEO and Local Keyword Targeting ............................ 130
Keyword Intent and User Behavior ...................................... 130
Summary ................................................................................ 131

### Chapter 15: Exploring Types of Digital Marketing Campaigns ......... 133

Additional Campaign Types to Consider ............................. 133
    Content Marketing ........................................................... 136
    Retargeting Campaigns ................................................... 136
    Referral Marketing .......................................................... 136
    Account-Based Marketing (ABM) ................................... 137
Summary ................................................................................ 137

### Chapter 16: Crafting Creatives, Messages, and Copy for Effective Digital Marketing Campaigns ........................................... 139

Understanding Creatives, Messages, and Copy ................ 140
Types of Creatives and Their Usage ................................... 140
Collaboration with Service Partners ................................... 141
Comparative Table of Ad Formats and Creative Requirements ........................ 142
Summary ................................................................................ 143

### Chapter 17: Understanding Ad Accounts and Their Structures ........ 145

What Are Ad Accounts ......................................................... 145
    Common Structures of Ad Accounts on Major Platforms ......................... 146
    Google Ads ....................................................................... 146
    Facebook Ads .................................................................. 147
    The Trade Desk and Other Programmatic Platforms ...... 147
Ad Account Integrations and Extensions ........................... 148
Summary and Key Takeaways ............................................. 148

## TABLE OF CONTENTS

### Chapter 18: Understanding Conversions and Conversion Tracking .... 149
What Are Conversions, and What Is Conversion Tracking? ............................... 149
How Conversion Tracking Works ............................................................... 150
Major Conversion Tracking Tools and Their Uses ........................................ 150
    Google Ads Conversion Tracking ......................................................... 150
    Google Analytics ................................................................................ 151
    Facebook Pixel ................................................................................... 151
Using Tracking Parameters: UTM Codes ..................................................... 152
Key Takeaways ........................................................................................... 152

### Chapter 19: Competitor Analysis in Digital Marketing: Understanding Your Market Position ................................................. 155
What Is Competitor Research, and Why Is It Important? ................................ 155
Understanding the Competitive Landscape .................................................. 156
Tools and Techniques for Competitor Research ............................................ 156
Competitor Landing Pages: A Window into Their Marketing Strategy ............... 158
Integrating Tools for Comprehensive Analysis .............................................. 159
Comparative Table of Tools for Keyword Analysis ......................................... 160
Summary .................................................................................................. 161

### Chapter 20: Digital Marketing vs. Traditional Marketing: A Comparison ..................................................................................... 163
The Core Differences Between Digital and Traditional Marketing ................... 163
Comparative Table: Digital vs. Traditional Marketing .................................... 164
Practical Considerations for Marketers and Service Partners ........................ 166
Summary .................................................................................................. 166

xiii

TABLE OF CONTENTS

## Chapter 21: Digital Marketing Channels Overview: From Core to Specialized ..................................................167

Introduction to Core Digital Marketing Channels ............................................168
    Display Ads ..................................................................................................168
    Search Ads (SEM Ads) ................................................................................170
    Native Ads....................................................................................................172
    Social Media Ads .........................................................................................173
    Email Marketing ..........................................................................................176
    Mobile and In-App Ads ................................................................................178

Emerging Digital Marketing Channels.............................................................179
    Connected TV (CTV) ....................................................................................179
    Addressable TV (ATV) .................................................................................181
    Digital Out-of-Home (DOOH) ......................................................................182
    Cinema Ads with Programmatic Buying ....................................................184
    Print Ads with Programmatic Buying.........................................................185

Specialized Digital Marketing Channels.........................................................187
    Voice Search Ads .......................................................................................187
    Augmented Reality (AR) Ads ......................................................................188
    Podcast Ads ...............................................................................................190
    Interactive Content ....................................................................................191
    Blockchain and Crypto Ads........................................................................193

Visualization of All the Channels ....................................................................194
Comparative Table..........................................................................................195
Summary.........................................................................................................200

## Chapter 22: Advertising Formats and Their Creatives......................201

Overview of Advertising Formats ....................................................................201
    HTML Banners ............................................................................................203
    AMP Banners ..............................................................................................205

## TABLE OF CONTENTS

    Text Ads ................................................................................................. 207

    Responsive Search Ads ...................................................................... 210

    Responsive Display Ads ...................................................................... 213

    Audio Ads ............................................................................................ 216

    Video Ads ............................................................................................ 220

    Lead Ads ............................................................................................. 223

    Inventory Ads ...................................................................................... 226

    Shopping Ads ...................................................................................... 228

    Carousel Ads ....................................................................................... 231

    Interstitial Ads ...................................................................................... 234

    Native Ads ........................................................................................... 237

    Dynamic Ads ....................................................................................... 239

    App Install Ads .................................................................................... 242

    Sponsored Content ............................................................................. 245

    Pop-Up Ads ......................................................................................... 248

Advertising Formats Comparison Table ..................................................... 251

Summary ........................................................................................................ 255

### Chapter 23: Understanding Landing Pages ............................................ 257

Why Landing Pages Are Important ............................................................. 257

    The Pitfalls of Using a Homepage As a Landing Page ................... 258

    Significance in Advertising Algorithms ............................................ 259

    Correlation with Ads .......................................................................... 259

    Importance of Specificity and Context ............................................. 260

Optimizing Landing Page Information Structure ....................................... 260

    Visual Hierarchy ................................................................................. 260

What Is a Call-to-Action (CTA)? .................................................................. 262

xv

## TABLE OF CONTENTS

Utilizing Conversion Campaigns with Your Landing Page .................263
    Setting Up Conversion Tracking ..................................................263
    Tracking Visitors Without Conversion Goals ...............................264

Understanding SEO (Search Engine Optimization) and SEF (Search Engine Friendly) ..................................................................................264
    What Are SEO and SEF? ..............................................................265
    Continuous SEO and SEF Practices .............................................265

What Is SEA (Search Engine Advertising)? ....................................266
    Bridging SEO, SEF, and SEA ......................................................266

How HTML Structure Affects LLM (Large Language Models) and Other Artificial Intelligence Systems Comprehension of Web Pages .................266
    Introduction to HTML's Role in LLM Comprehension .................267
    Critical Elements of HTML for LLM Optimization .......................269
    Example of Implementing Effective HTML Structure ..................270
    Transitioning to Advanced HTML Practices ................................270

Summary and Key Takeaways ........................................................270

### Chapter 24: What Is Analytics? .................................................273

What Are and What Is the Role of First-Party and Third-Party Data .................273

Tracking and Data Privacy .............................................................274

Tracking Parameters Simplified .....................................................274

Main Analytics Platforms ..............................................................274

Key Metrics and Concepts .............................................................277
    Real-Time Visitors .......................................................................277
    Unique Visitors ...........................................................................278
    Acquisition .................................................................................279
    User IDs .....................................................................................280
    Visit Duration .............................................................................281

Unique Page Views .................................................................................. 282
Page Views .............................................................................................. 283
Entry Links .............................................................................................. 284
Exit Links ................................................................................................ 285
Events ..................................................................................................... 286
Page Fold ................................................................................................ 287
User Flow/User Journey ......................................................................... 287
Goals ....................................................................................................... 288
Campaigns .............................................................................................. 289
Comparison Table ................................................................................... 290

Why Analytics Matters in Marketing .......................................................... 293
Summary .................................................................................................... 293

## Chapter 25: Understanding Digital Marketing Specialists and Their Types ............................................................................................ 295

What Is a Digital Marketing Specialist and Which Types Are There .................. 295
Digital Marketing Specialists According to Working Place ................................ 296
Digital Marketing Specialists According to Knowledge and Experience ............ 296
Choosing the Right Specialist .......................................................................... 297
Summary ........................................................................................................... 297

## Chapter 26: The Landscape of Legal, Taxes, and Brand Protection in Digital Marketing ..................................................................... 299

What You Should Know Regarding Taxes, Legal Issues, Policies, and
Brand Protection ............................................................................................... 299
    Understanding Data Privacy Legislation and Its Importance ...................... 300
    The Impact of Data Privacy Legislation on Digital Marketing ..................... 303
    Why Country-Specific Taxes Are Important for Digital Marketing ............... 303
    What Is Advertiser Verification? ................................................................... 305

TABLE OF CONTENTS

What Are Network Policies? ............................................................. 306
How to Protect Your Brand in Digital Marketing ................................. 306
Summary ........................................................................................ 309

## Part II: CREATION | Pre-campaign Preparation | ...................... 311

## Chapter 27: Setting Marketing Goals: Crafting Strategic Objectives for Digital Campaigns ........................................................ 315

Clarifying Your Marketing Objectives ................................................ 315
Marketing Goals, Channels, and Ad Formats Recommendations/Guidelines .... 316
Categories of Marketing Goals ......................................................... 316
    Main Categories for Marketing Goals ............................................. 317
    Exploring Additional Categories of Marketing Goals ....................... 318
Brand Loyalty ................................................................................. 319
Advocacy ....................................................................................... 320
Lead Generation ............................................................................. 320
Comparison of Digital Marketing Campaign Categories ..................... 322
Understanding Risk and Choosing the Right Campaign Type ............. 325
Summary ........................................................................................ 326

## Chapter 28: Advertiser Channel Provider (Network) Selection ........ 327

Strategic Network Selection Based on Marketing Goals .................... 327
    Awareness Goals ......................................................................... 328
    Traffic Goals ................................................................................ 328
    Conversion Goals ........................................................................ 329
Evaluating Network Risk Profiles ...................................................... 329
    Evaluating Risks .......................................................................... 330
Summary ........................................................................................ 330

## Chapter 29: Integrating Traditional and Digital Media for Marketing Campaigns .................................................................333

Expanding Network and Media Recommendations .........................................333

    Detailed Recommendations Across Media for Each Goal ...........................334

    Awareness ................................................................................................334

    Traffic .......................................................................................................334

    Conversions .............................................................................................335

    Engagement .............................................................................................335

    Brand Loyalty ...........................................................................................336

    Advocacy ..................................................................................................336

    Lead Generation ......................................................................................337

Understanding Campaign Types and Their Risks Across Media ......................337

Summary ..........................................................................................................338

## Chapter 30: Format Recommendations for Digital Marketing Campaigns .................................................................................339

Introduction to Ad Format Characteristics .......................................................339

Understanding Various Ad Formats and Their Characteristics ........................340

    Awareness ................................................................................................340

    Traffic .......................................................................................................340

    Conversions .............................................................................................341

    Engagement .............................................................................................341

    Brand Loyalty ...........................................................................................342

    Advocacy ..................................................................................................342

    Lead Generation ......................................................................................343

Choosing the Right Mix of Formats ..................................................................343

Summary ..........................................................................................................344

TABLE OF CONTENTS

**Chapter 31: Digital Marketing Brief ........................................................ 345**

    Crafting a Comprehensive Digital Marketing Brief ............................................ 345

        Structuring Your Digital Marketing Briefings ................................................. 346

        Details of the Four Digital Marketing Briefings ............................................ 354

    What Your Providers Need to Know ................................................................ 364

        Understanding Your Campaign Goals and Expected Outcomes ............... 364

        Level of Involvement and Strategic Input ...................................................... 364

        Building or Setting Up ....................................................................................... 364

        Providing Suggestions ...................................................................................... 365

        Periodic Meetings and Status Updates ......................................................... 365

        Collaboration with Other Providers ................................................................. 365

        Important Dates for Projects ............................................................................ 365

        Deliverables for Team, Boss, and Stakeholders .......................................... 365

    Real-Life Scenarios of Misunderstandings ..................................................... 366

        Scenario A: Mismatched Campaign Goals .................................................... 366

        Scenario B: Lack of Strategic Input ................................................................. 366

        Scenario C: Unclear Deadlines ....................................................................... 367

        Expected Outcomes from a Digital Marketing Brief .................................... 367

    Summary .................................................................................................................. 368

**Part III: EXECUTION | During-Campaign Management | ............ 371**

**Chapter 32: Verification Bots from Advertising Channel Providers: Navigating Campaign Approvals and Pauses ................... 375**

    The Approval and Learning Phase ..................................................................... 375

        Creative Approval .............................................................................................. 376

        Learning Phase .................................................................................................. 376

    Common Reasons for Campaign Pauses ........................................................ 377

        Issues with Creative Approval ......................................................................... 377

        Landing Page Errors ......................................................................................... 377

TABLE OF CONTENTS

    Malware on the Landing Page ................................................................. 377

    Target-URL Modifications ....................................................................... 377

Handling False Positives ................................................................................. 378

Moving Forward ............................................................................................... 378

## Chapter 33: Understanding the Learning Phase in Digital Marketing Campaigns .............................................................................. 379

What Is a Learning Phase? ............................................................................. 379

Events Triggering a Learning Phase ............................................................. 380

    Budget Adjustments ................................................................................ 381

    Asset Changes ......................................................................................... 381

Navigating Changes During the Learning Phase ......................................... 381

Summary .......................................................................................................... 382

## Chapter 34: Understanding How Budgets Work in Digital Marketing Campaigns .............................................................................. 383

Introduction to Digital Marketing Budgets .................................................. 383

How Different Advertising Providers Handle Budgets ............................... 384

    Google Ads Budgeting ........................................................................... 385

Summary .......................................................................................................... 386

## Chapter 35: Understanding and Implementing Campaign Optimizations ........................................................................................... 387

Introduction to Campaign Optimizations ..................................................... 387

Why Optimize a Campaign ............................................................................. 388

Common Optimizations and Their Applications ......................................... 389

    Budget Adjustments ................................................................................ 389

    Keywords Management ......................................................................... 390

    Creative Adjustments ............................................................................. 391

    Targeting Adjustments ........................................................................... 391

Summary .......................................................................................................... 392

TABLE OF CONTENTS

### Chapter 36: Campaign Settings Adjustments: Timing and Access ..... 393
Understanding When You Can Change Campaign Settings ............................... 393
Where to Change the Settings of Your Campaign? .......................................... 395
Which Changes Impact Campaign Timing? ..................................................... 396
Summary .......................................................................................................... 396

## Part IV: Campaign Analysis ............................................................. 397

### Chapter 37: Navigating Digital Marketing Reports at Campaign Completion .............................................................................. 399
What Should a Report Look Like ..................................................................... 399
    Key Elements of an Effective Digital Marketing Report ............................. 400
    What Data Should My Provider Make Available .......................................... 402
    Frequency and Timing of Reporting ............................................................ 403
Understanding Pitfalls, Misinterpretations, and Vanity Metrics ....................... 403
Summary .......................................................................................................... 404

## Part V: Recommendations ............................................................... 407

### Chapter 38: Structuring Digital Marketing Efforts: Multiple Campaigns vs. Multiple Ad Groups vs. Multiple Ads ....................... 409
Introduction to Campaign Structuring .............................................................. 409
    Why Structure Matters ................................................................................. 410
Campaign Structure Overview .......................................................................... 410
    Multiple Campaigns ..................................................................................... 411
    Multiple Ad Groups in a Single Campaign .................................................. 412
    Which One to Choose .................................................................................. 413
    Multiple Ads ................................................................................................. 413
    When to Use Multiple Ads ........................................................................... 414
    Recommendations for Structuring Your Digital Marketing Efforts .............. 414

# TABLE OF CONTENTS

Planning Your Campaign Structure ................................................................. 416

Summary ............................................................................................................ 416

## Chapter 39: Evaluating Provider Recommendations in Digital Marketing Campaigns .................................................................. 417

Should I Implement All the Recommendations from My Provider .................... 417

    Understanding Provider Recommendations .............................................. 418

Weighing the Benefits and Risks of Advertiser Channel Provider Recommendations ............................................................................................. 418

    Alignment with Campaign Goals ................................................................ 418

    Technical Feasibility and Expertise ............................................................ 418

    Cost Implications ........................................................................................ 419

Practical Example ............................................................................................. 419

    Example: Google Ads Conversion Recommendations .............................. 420

Summary ............................................................................................................ 420

## Chapter 40: Digital Marketing Strategies for Small Companies ....... 421

Key Considerations for Small Companies in Digital Marketing ....................... 421

    Budget Allocation ....................................................................................... 422

    Choice of Campaign Types ........................................................................ 422

    Selection of Advertiser Channel Providers ............................................... 422

    Structure and Functionality of the Company Website .............................. 423

    Availability and Quality of Landing Pages ................................................. 423

Practical Example ............................................................................................. 424

Choosing Between Agency, Freelancer, or Self-Learning ................................ 424

    Agency or Freelancer ................................................................................. 424

Working with an Agency ................................................................................... 425

Hiring a Freelancer ........................................................................................... 425

## TABLE OF CONTENTS

Practical Example ................................................................. 426
    Courses, Self-Learning, and Experimentation ........................................... 426
Digital Marketing Courses ................................................................ 427
    Benefits of Digital Marketing Courses ..................................................... 427
    Practical Example ................................................................. 428
Self-experimentation ................................................................... 428
    Benefits of Self-experimentation ........................................................ 428
    Practical Example ................................................................. 428
Combining Learning and Practice ........................................................... 429
About Creatives and Settings ............................................................. 429
Default vs. Custom Settings .............................................................. 429
    Understanding Default Settings ......................................................... 430
    The Value of Custom Settings .......................................................... 430
    Practical Example ................................................................. 430
Quality of Creatives ................................................................... 430
    Importance of High-Quality Creatives .................................................... 431
    Practical Example ................................................................. 431
Leveraging Consultancy Services from Advertiser Channel Providers .............. 432
Summary ........................................................................... 432

## Chapter 41: Digital Marketing for Companies with Multiple Locations They Own ............................................................... 433

Tailoring Your Approach ................................................................ 433
Key Considerations for Multi-location Marketing ............................................. 434
    Options for Structuring Campaigns ...................................................... 434
Detailed Campaign Structuring ............................................................ 435
Adapting Campaign Criteria for Each Location ............................................... 436
Summary ........................................................................... 438

xxiv

TABLE OF CONTENTS

## Chapter 42: Digital Marketing for a Company with Many Independently Owned Locations and Partners .................................441

Key Considerations for Independently Owned Locations ..............................442

Understanding Local Context.............................................................442

Geotargeting: Adjustments Based on Location .........................................443

Customizing Campaign Elements: Adapting Campaign Criteria for Each Location ...................................................................................443

Location/Partner-Specific Keywords .......................................................443

Location/Partner-Specific Creatives ........................................................444

Location/Partner-Specific Landing Pages ................................................444

Demographics .................................................................................445

Supporting Partners and Privately Owned Locations ...................................445

Customizing Marketing Elements to Local Needs .......................................446

Summary..........................................................................................448

## Part VI: Overview of Social Media .........................................451

## Chapter 43: Social Media Overview: What Is Social Media and Social Media Activity? .................................................................453

The Decision to Have a Specific Social Media Account ..................................454

Owning Brand Handles .......................................................................454

Selective Presence ............................................................................454

Control Over Digital Assets......................................................................455

Overview of Social Media Networks .........................................................455

Facebook .......................................................................................456

X/Twitter .......................................................................................456

Instagram ......................................................................................456

LinkedIn ........................................................................................457

TikTok ..........................................................................................457

xxv

TABLE OF CONTENTS

    Pinterest ..................................................................................................457

    Less Known But Niche, Regional, and Decentralized-Alternative
    Social Media Networks............................................................................458

    Decentralized Social Networks...............................................................460

Differences Between Social Media, Social Ads, and Digital Marketing............460

Other Aspects of Social Media You Should Consider .....................................462

    Influencer Partnerships ..........................................................................462

    Social Listening and Reputation Management......................................464

    Content Strategies..................................................................................465

    Social Media Analytics...........................................................................467

    Social Media and SEO............................................................................468

    Crisis Management on Social Media .....................................................470

    Emerging Trends and Future Outlook ...................................................471

Key Points to Consider for Your Social Media Strategy ..................................473

    General Social Media.............................................................................473

    Influencer Partnerships ..........................................................................474

    Social Listening and Reputation Management......................................474

    Content Strategies..................................................................................475

    Social Media Analytics...........................................................................475

    Crisis Management on Social Media .....................................................475

    Emerging Trends and Future Outlook ...................................................476

## Part VII: Artificial Intelligence in Digital Marketing.................477

### Chapter 44: Enhancing Targeting with AI .........................................479

Understanding AI-Driven Targeting ................................................................479

Why AI Targeting Matters to Marketers..........................................................480

Evaluating the Implications of AI Targeting ....................................................481

Expectations Regarding Digital Marketing Service Providers.........................482

Summary and Key Takeaways ........................................................................482

## Chapter 45: Content Optimization with AI .......................................... 485

Enhancing, Not Replacing, Professional Creativity ........................................... 485

Challenges in Maintaining Brand Voice ........................................................... 486

Recognizing and Penalizing AI-Generated Content ......................................... 486

The Need for Expert Configuration .................................................................. 487

Understanding AI to Utilize It Effectively ......................................................... 487

Summary and Key Takeaways ......................................................................... 487

## Chapter 46: Managing Expectations: When AI Is Not the Answer .... 489

Understanding AI's Applicability and Limitations ............................................. 489

Evaluating AI's Role in Marketing .................................................................... 490

    Benefits of AI in Marketing .......................................................................... 490

    Drawbacks of AI in Marketing ..................................................................... 491

    Navigating AI's Challenges ......................................................................... 491

Practical Examples ............................................................................................ 491

Business Challenges of Implementing AI ........................................................ 492

Additional Considerations ................................................................................ 494

Summary ........................................................................................................... 495

## Chapter 47: Closing Words .............................................................. 497

## Annex 1: Digital Marketing Brief for Campaign Settings ................... 501

## Annex 2: Digital Marketing Brief for Campaign Creatives ................ 503

## Annex 3: Digital Marketing Brief for Campaign Monitoring ............. 505

## Annex 4: Digital Marketing Brief for Campaign Landing Page ......... 507

## Index .................................................................................................. 509

# About the Author

**Diego Adolfo Carrasco Gubernatis** is a versatile professional who combines expertise in marketing, software development, and entrepreneurship. His career, starting in Chile with business and marketing, led him to Germany where he refined his software development skills, focusing on PHP and Python while deepening his digital marketing knowledge.

Diego's diverse background, including early entrepreneurial ventures, has shaped his unique approach to technology solutions. He integrates insights from various fields, particularly digital marketing, to create innovative approaches.

Currently, as Product Lead for Digital and Data at MEHRKANAL, Diego merges his expertise in software development, data science, digital marketing, and artificial intelligence. He develops solutions that enhance automation, standardization, and simplicity in digital marketing.

Diego's passion for continuous learning drives him to explore new horizons. This allows him to approach challenges from multiple perspectives, drawing on his broad knowledge base to create effective, multifaceted solutions.

You can follow him on LinkedIn or on his website: `https://diegocarrasco.com`.

# Acknowledgments

I want to express my heartfelt gratitude to everyone who has supported me throughout this journey:

- To my wife and daughters, who inspire me to show that overcoming challenges and seizing opportunities, even when they seem daunting, are essential for growth and whose unwavering support and encouragement have been my greatest source of strength. Thank you for always being there for me.

- To my colleagues at MEHRKANAL, whose collaboration, insights, and questions have enriched my work and this book. Special thanks to Mario and Miri for their patience enduring all my endless monologues about the book and its contents.

- To the many companies and agencies I've had the privilege to work with; your challenges and successes have inspired me to share my knowledge and experiences.

- To Victor and Eva, who gave me their feedback on the early version of the book idea.

- To all marketers, who continuously strive to improve, stay up to date, and adapt to trends and technological developments. I know it's hard work, and this book is my grain of rice in helping you keep moving forward.

Thank you all for being part of this journey.

# Introduction

## What Is This Book About

You are working in marketing or handling tasks related to digital marketing, and you need to get things done. You have a lot to do, and you don't have the time to become a digital marketing expert, with all that that implies. You know what needs to be achieved. Figuring out what to use and how to achieve that is something for a third party to solve, research, and do.

Among the things **you may have to** do are **defining campaigns, launching new products and services, managing partners** and distribution channels, working with third parties to **develop creatives**, and **dealing with providers**, creatives, agencies, and freelancers.

Note that I use the concept "to deal" here because, quite often, it's not a straightforward task. You have to deal with third parties because the understanding of the same task or goal is different or because they don't understand what you are saying. You might be using different jargon or concepts specific to your industry, or you might be trying to apply a concept from print to digital, and they just don't get it. And the worst part is there are good reasons for this to be this way!

On one side, you're trying to balance and manage multiple tasks while attempting to translate and explain everything to your stakeholders—team, boss, investors, coworkers, etc. For example, imagine you're responsible for launching a new advertising campaign, and you need to explain the goals and objectives to your team, who might have different interpretations of what success looks like. In that case, you may try to use specific concepts, such as lead campaigns or conversion tracking, just to provide examples, without knowing if you can really implement them in your campaign. You just want to highlight that you care about sales and not just vanity metrics such as impressions.

---

**Note** Beware that impressions and other vanity metrics might be important for some kinds of campaigns, such as awareness campaigns, to position your brand.

---

On the other side, you're trying to convey your needs to the third parties who should be helping you, such as graphic designers, ad agencies, or marketing experts. However, as a busy professional, you don't have the time to become an expert in every aspect of marketing or read several books just to use the same jargon they use. You know that the jargon changes between providers, so it doesn't make much sense to do so. You might not have the expertise to edit an image for an ad or know the exact settings for one of the ten campaigns you have to launch this month, but you have a general idea of what you expect from the campaign. You might be able to specify it further if the right questions are asked, but you just don't know what the right questions are.

The thing is, you try to convey your needs as well as you can, but you realize there is no one-size-fits-all approach. There are hundreds of books on marketing theory, but not many practical guides for real-world marketing issues. You need a solution because your providers might suffer from "expert-blindness." For example, when working with a digital marketing agency, they might overlook crucial details because they're too focused on their expertise. You mention a campaign you read about that could be interesting for your brand, but you're not sure it works. The expert should tell you that. The problem is, they often take your word as final and invest resources to make it work, even when other solutions could achieve your goals faster.

## INTRODUCTION

In the best scenarios, they ask a hundred questions to understand you better. For example, they might ask about your target audience, messaging, or campaign objectives to align with your goals. But this can take several meetings and emails, wasting time and energy. In the worst case, they don't ask any questions and move forward assuming they understood you. Both scenarios are dangerous and time-consuming, leading to wasted resources and missed opportunities.

I've been there as an agency, freelancer, partner, and client, working with small and big companies. One thing I have seen in all cases is that each party uses different vocabulary and terms, works under different contexts, and has different priorities. This leads to misunderstandings that often result in unsuccessful marketing efforts and wasted resources.

A lot of time is lost because the right questions were not asked at the right time, or because one party did not know what the other needed or meant.

I know there are many books that explain marketing and digital marketing theory in great detail, but I haven't found any practical ones to follow or suggest to others for agreeing on one process and one set of concepts. That's why I'm writing this book. I aim to provide a framework or playbook for working with third parties in digital marketing, not tied to specific settings, advertising channels, formats, or trends, as they change quickly within a few years.

That is why I will focus on the concepts you should know, as these are almost the same for all providers, networks, and formats. Although the wording does change, the concepts stay the same. I will cover how to plan a digital marketing campaign, how to ask the right questions to control and monitor a campaign, and how to ask for the right data to evaluate it, while keeping in mind the goals you set for this area in your organization.

All this will be provided with templates, easy-to-follow steps, and examples you can use to create your brief, write emails asking the right questions, and get the right data to answer your stakeholder's questions, whoever that might be.

INTRODUCTION

If you're looking for step-by-step guides on setting up specific campaigns or detailed explanations of platforms like Google Ads or Facebook Ads, this book may not be what you need. But if you're focused on getting the job done and need just enough know-how to work effectively with experts, partners, and providers, then this book is for you.

Keep reading to learn how to do just that. You have been warned.

## How to Read This Book

This book aims to serve as a practical FAQ handbook. You can simply refer to the table of contents to find the section you need and get your questions answered. While I've structured the book to flow logically from one topic to the next, feel free to read it in any order that suits your needs.

This book is structured into seven parts. If you check the table of contents, you will quickly notice that it is really long. *This is on purpose.* Each part and chapter is as concise and minimal as possible, and each one tries to answer something specific regarding digital marketing.

The **first part** covers digital marketing and marketing **fundamentals**. These are concepts I have found important when dealing with digital marketing and which make it easier to communicate ideas and requirements and ask for information in the industry. It also informs you of some not-so-exciting but important topics such as legal issues, taxes, and brand protection. This part is for you to use as a reference, but I suggest you read Chapter 1 as this book introduces a new definition of digital marketing that I found more practical for day-to-day use.

The **second part** covers everything related to the **creation of a campaign**, such as marketing goals, network and format recommendations, and **the brief**, and introduces some templates you can use to make your life easier.

The **third part** covers everything you should know regarding the **execution of the campaign**, such as optimizations, targeting settings, and some of their implications.

The **fourth part** covers the **analysis of the campaign**, what you should ask for, and what you should receive in a report.

The **fifth part** contains some **personal recommendations** regarding settings and different use cases. These might be a bit off the theory but are practical.

The **sixth part** covers the **basics of social media**, including organic and paid content.

The **seventh part** covers my personal take on **artificial intelligence** in digital marketing.

I hope you enjoy the book, and I sincerely hope it helps you in your day-to-day job and makes your life a bit easier.

# PART I

# Digital Marketing: Fundamentals, Concepts, and Actors

Digital marketing is a vast and intricate field, filled with specific terms and concepts that vary widely across different advertising channels and formats. As you dive into this world, you'll encounter a unique jargon that can be both platform-specific and universally applicable, often with terms that overlap or differ slightly in meaning depending on the context. Without the right understanding, navigating this landscape can be daunting.

In this first part, I'll demystify the core concepts and key actors in digital marketing. I'll break down the essential terminology, explain the various roles of advertising channel providers, and explore how different components like targeting, bidding, and ad quality interact within the digital ecosystem. This section serves as your foundational guide, helping you to not only understand the language of digital marketing but also to apply it effectively as you progress through the book. By grasping these fundamentals, you'll be better equipped to navigate the complex and ever-evolving world of digital marketing with confidence.

# CHAPTER 1

# Defining Digital Marketing

According to *A Dictionary of Marketing* by Charles Doyle, digital marketing is

> digital marketing (online marketing, web marketing) The use of digital technology, including web and multimedia and processes in the development, distribution and promotion of products and services.
>
> —Charles Doyle, *A Dictionary of Marketing*
> (page 144; ISBN 9780199590230)

This definition is good for an academic environment but helps us little in the practice. It refers specifically to the use of digital technology but ignores the fact that, in practice, digital marketing is a process with several stages, the definition of the target and its context.

Given that I understand digital marketing as a process, here is a more practical definition that explicitly lists the three stages I use through the book as well as its main goal.

CHAPTER 1   DEFINING DIGITAL MARKETING

# Digital Marketing As Defined for This Book

For this book, digital marketing is defined as follows:

> Digital marketing is the **process** of creating, executing and analyzing marketing campaigns using multiple digital channels and formats to deliver a message to a set of target groups in specific contexts. This doesn't end when the campaign starts.
>
> —Diego A. Carrasco Gubernatis, 2024

Let's quickly analyze this definition and why it is important for us.

- By saying **process**, I am recognizing that digital marketing it is not something that ends when creating (or commissioning) a campaign, but something that requires your attention until you decide what to do with its results. This also means you have to understand how the process works if you want to improve it and get better results.

- I recognize that there are at least three parts in a digital marketing campaign: **creation**, **execution**, and **analysis**, which is also how this book is structured. This is important because each part requires another mindset and other information.

- With **multiple digital channels and formats**, I highlight that one campaign can make use of more than one channel and more than one format. For example, a Google Ads Campaign can use Responsive Display Ads and AMP Banners. If you take a campaign as a specific marketing initiative within your organization (e.g., a product launch), then a campaign can also

# CHAPTER 1  DEFINING DIGITAL MARKETING

spread across advertising channel providers, channels, and formats, making it quite complex to follow and analyze. For instance, you may use Google Video Ads and Facebook Carousel Ads for the same marketing initiative.

- A **message** is that which you want to communicate, be it a new product, service, brand, or something else, and usually matches what your audience is looking for. For example, *"buy a book about marketing."* The message is also related to several assets, such as images and videos. Once you define a message for your campaign, you have to adapt it to each individual advertiser channel provider, its channels, and its formats. (Check Chapter 3 on the digital marketing ecosystem to get more details in this regard.)

- A **set of target groups** means a set of *marketing personas*, which are (or find themselves) in **specific contexts**. For example, *people with certain characteristics who are now searching on Google for an electric car in France* or *people who live in Germany and are reading websites about insurance.*

With this definition, we are now able to understand that digital marketing is more than a concept and that there are many steps and actors involved.

If you don't understand this process, its actors, requirements, and possibilities, you will waste precious time and resources. But if you understand digital marketing as a process, with defined stages, then you will be able to successfully delegate, commission, and even implement campaigns. Once you understand the main parts of this process along with the main concepts, you will also find it a lot easier to use the platforms from almost all the advertising channel providers out there (e.g., Google Ads, Facebook Marketing, or The Trade Desk). All of them use the same concepts (some of them with different terms) because they also have to implicitly follow these steps.

Let me elaborate here a bit to clarify that point.

## A Closer Look at the Three Major Stages

The definition above states that there are three major stages in any digital marketing campaign: *Creation*, *Execution*, and *Analysis*.

These stages are better visualized in Figure 1-1.

CHAPTER 1  DEFINING DIGITAL MARKETING

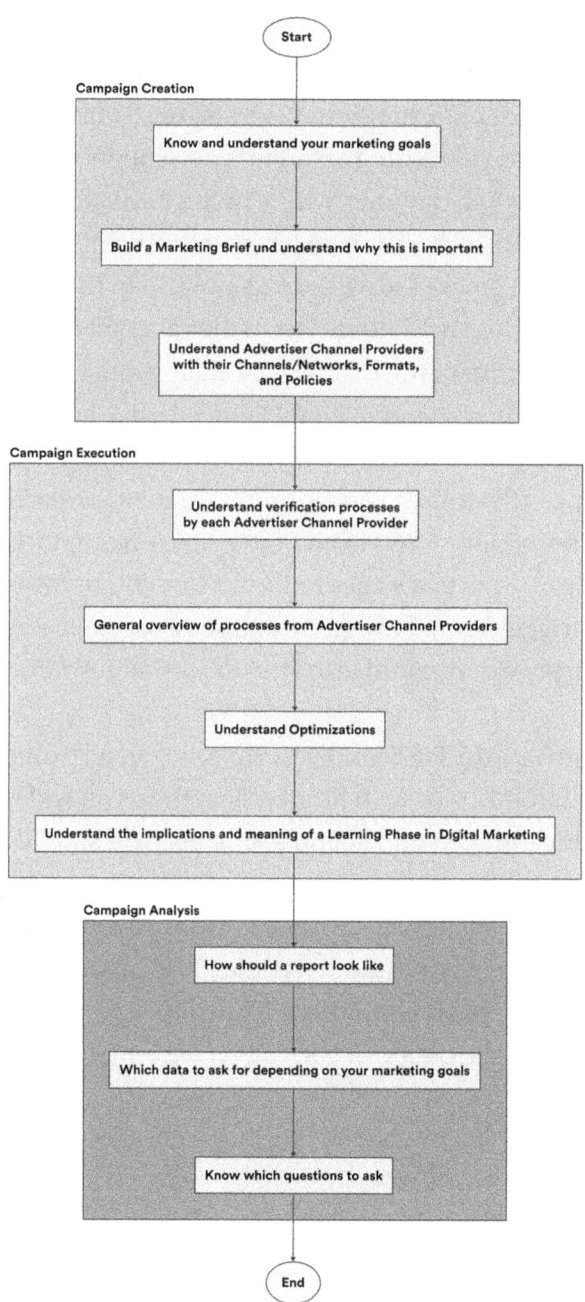

***Figure 1-1.*** *Stages of a digital marketing campaign*

## CHAPTER 1   DEFINING DIGITAL MARKETING

If you use an advertising channel provider that doesn't provide insights as to how and where your potential customers use the placements[1] they offer, then you cannot be sure where your message will be shown. This would be the same as publishing an ad in a newspaper without defining which newspaper, which day, and where in the newspaper the ad should be shown at. And it's not the same to have a prominent full-color ad on the front page or a small black-and-white text-only ad in the lower corner of the last page, so why would you do that in digital marketing if you don't do that in print? That's part of the CREATION stage: understand the context of your potential customers, your available placements, and *their ways*.

If we move to EXECUTION, and if you know that one of the benefits[2] of digital marketing is flexibility, you wouldn't want an advertising channel provider that doesn't allow you to change your campaign when you need to or that a change takes ages to be implemented. Not knowing that some changes trigger some background processes (like a new learning phase) by some providers could also lead to wasted resources and missed opportunities.

If we move to ANALYTICS, and you chose an advertising channel provider without reports, or with limited data then you will not be able to evaluate your campaign and act on its results. You should also keep in mind that, depending on the advertising channel provider, the KPIs they use might differ because they need to show values that suggest that you should keep using them (otherwise they lose business). If you don't understand the concepts behind those KPIs, you won't be able to correctly evaluate or interpret the data you get.

---

[1] Check Chapter 8 on Placements and Inventory.
[2] Check Chapter 20 on Digital Marketing vs. Traditional Digital Marketing.

# Why Digital Marketing Is Important

Your marketing efforts should evolve according to your customer's lifestyles and to the (ever-changing) contact points they have with your brand and organization. Nowadays, your customers are increasingly using digital channels and consuming digital products, and new ways to interact with them are *popping out of nowhere.*

**As marketers, we are in a position where we need to understand trends, tools, and ways to make our product and services known, *within budget,* and as fast as possible.** This means using new channels and formats as soon as they are available without making our brand look bad because we didn't know better.

Digital marketing allows companies of all sizes to compete for the same audiences without many limits. A startup can target the same customers as big companies, and sometimes they *win* because they knew how to use the new channels better or because they could react faster.

For big companies, reaction times are sometimes slower because there are more pieces (parties) involved, but with the right methodology, you can plan better and act faster.

The best reason to involve yourself in digital marketing is because your customers are using digital channels to research, make buying decisions, and finally make the buy. If you are not present there, they will buy from your competitors who are using those channels.

There may be companies for which digital channels are not important, but chances are that, if you got this book, this is not your case.

# Advantages and Disadvantages of Digital Marketing

Almost each advertising channel provider has its own learning platforms, certifications, and badges, but the general advantages or benefits they list are mostly the same:

- **Flexibility**: You can create a campaign anytime, with low entry cost and with semi-automated processes. You can follow its result in near real time, and you can act on its data and results to improve the campaign by making real-time adjustments or launching new campaigns.

- **Low Entry Cost for Advertisers**: The size of the advertiser doesn't really matter if you know how digital marketing works. You can set up a campaign to directly compete with big brands, or you can target specific audiences that you otherwise wouldn't reach.

- **Instant Results**: Once your campaign runs, you can check results and monitor them instantly (in most platforms). You can know how many clicks and impressions did each ad get, which placements did they appear on and analyze them by keyword, audiences, and many other variables.

- **Powered by Artificial Intelligence**: This is one of the advantages many platforms list, and it's both an advantage and a disadvantage at the same time. On one side, it makes everything easier by suggesting settings and ads for your campaigns based on a couple of questions and a landing page. The disadvantage is that

CHAPTER 1   DEFINING DIGITAL MARKETING

you don't really know who this digital brain is working for. The artificial intelligence takes data as input and processes it in a way that generates an output. If the input is of low quality, then the output will also be of low quality. And sometimes we tend to forget that.

Alongside the benefits, there are also some disadvantages that are not communicated as loudly or frequently as the advantages. The most important ones include

- **It's easy to overspend!** Once you grasp how digital campaigns operate, you'll realize the potential risks. Without setting any limits and adding a credit card without a campaign end date, it can continue indefinitely. Without a solid understanding of each advertising channel provider's workings, you might overlook details like Google Ads, which can exceed your daily budget by up to two times in a day and up to 30.4 times[3] in a month.[4] And those costs can accumulate quickly.

- **It's easy to misconfigure crucial elements** or to rely entirely on the platform or on the artificial intelligence behind it to handle everything correctly. It's important to remember that the platform also aims to profit from your usage. This means nothing comes truly free. If an advertising channel provider recommends

---

[3] https://support.google.com/google-ads/answer/1704443?hl=en&sjid=14049928104630598314-EU, accessed on 2024-02-14
[4] https://support.google.com/google-ads/answer/2375454?hl=en and https://support.google.com/google-ads/answer/6385083?hl=en

a specific bidding type or campaign strategy, it's essential to question whether it aligns with your situation, budget, and resources. Take conversion campaigns, for instance. While they offer compelling benefits, they're not suitable for everyone. You need a clear understanding of what constitutes a conversion, whether you can implement them on your website or platform, how you'll track them, how much you're willing to pay for each conversion, and if you're tracking the right conversions for your marketing goals. Simply acquiring contacts isn't sufficient if you can't effectively follow up with them, and selling products you no longer have in inventory is counterproductive. Given the intangible nature of the digital realm, it's easy to forget about a campaign until you receive the invoice. Depending on your settings, that invoice could amount to a substantial sum of money.

- **It's easy to be swayed by vanity metrics**: Achieving 2 million impressions or 10,000 clicks on your ad may feel gratifying, but do they truly impact your business? Ultimately, advertising serves to achieve marketing and organizational goals, typically falling into two categories: raising brand awareness or acquiring more clients (increasing sales). If your results don't help your marketing and organization's goals, but you feel you are somehow getting results, you might be a victim of vanity metrics.

## Summary

In this chapter, I defined digital marketing for this book and how I understand it as a process with three stages: creation, execution, and analysis. I also listed its main advantages and disadvantages, such as its flexibility and low entry barriers and the risk of misconfigurations and overspending. I also briefly touched the subject of vanity metrics.

In the next chapter, I will explain digital assets, why are they important, and how can you ask your service partner for enough data to at least get access to them.

# CHAPTER 2

# Digital Assets and Why They Are Important

Our digital assets are worth more than the price of the domain or the price of the website development.

Generally, we can categorize digital assets into two groups:

1. Tangible assets
2. Intangible assets

In tangible assets, we may include servers, computers, website code, etc.

The problem starts with intangible assets as they are, well, intangible. It's like calculating our brand equity: the way parts like perception, loyalty, and overall brand image are calculated is a subjective process. Sometimes these digital assets are not even in our control (such as our social profiles).

Within intangible digital assets, we may include

- Design
- User interaction and user behavior
- Content

- Social profiles
- Organic positioning
- Reach
- Brand equity
- Ad accounts

## Brand Equity

Brand equity is the value that a brand adds to a product or service, originating mainly from consumer perceptions rather than the actual product or service itself. This value shows how customers see the brand, such as luxurious, trustworthy, or innovative. If a person sees a brand as high quality, for example, this can result in a brand's market success, allowing for higher prices or a loyal customer base. This concept highlights the significance of brand perception (intangible) over tangible product features.

But why did I say that some of our intangible digital assets are not in our control?

Because they are not. They are not even our property; they are property of each social network or ad channel provider.

Let's take, for example, a Facebook page. You may create a Facebook page complying with all their policies, under a proper user profile, linked with a proper business account and get millions of followers. But if Facebook decides that you "broke" a policy, they are in their right to block, close, and even remove your page and account. If that happens, then you lose all your investments in the network.

You may think this does not happen, and that may be true for big brands that can actually get in contact with Facebook because they are "important" from a they-make-me-money point of view. This is not so

CHAPTER 2   DIGITAL ASSETS AND WHY THEY ARE IMPORTANT

possible for medium and small companies. Just check their developer forums or try to get in contact with a real person in support.

You can also take the example of @x handle in X (ex-Twitter), where the company forcibly took control of the handle, giving the original owner a new one.[1]

Do you believe that these rigorous verification processes only apply to social networks? Think again. Your advertising account is also subject to numerous verification procedures, both manual and automated. For instance, you must verify your business, and all creatives and copy must adhere to advertiser-channel-provider policies. Failure to comply can result in your ad account being temporarily blocked or permanently deactivated if corrective actions are not taken within specified timeframes. And all these policies and processes change regularly.

Taking all these issues into account, I've come up with a rule of thumb.

## Rule of Thumb for Handling Digital Assets

Focus your efforts and resources on digital assets you control the most. For those you don't, make sure to back them up regularly and secure access whenever possible.

Implementing this rule of thumb can be broken down into an easy-to-follow five-step process:

1. **Inventory of Your Digital Assets**: Make a list of all your digital assets, including websites, social media accounts, advertising accounts, content files, and other digital materials.

---

[1] The case was covered by several news sites. Here is one: https://techcrunch.com/2023/07/26/twitter-now-x-took-over-the-x-handle-without-warning-or-compensating-its-owner/

2. **Assess Control Levels**: Determine the level of control you have over each asset. Make sure assets you fully own and manage are under your complete control. Assets on third-party platforms may have varying degrees of control. Make sure you understand them.

3. **Prioritize Resources**: Allocate resources based on the level of control. Invest the majority of your time, effort, and resources into assets you fully control. These may include your website, email list, and proprietary content.

4. **Backup and Secure Access**: For assets that you don't have full control over, such as social media accounts or advertising accounts, prioritize regular backups and secure access. Set up two-factor authentication and ensure multiple team members have access credentials.

5. **Regular Review and Updates**: Periodically review your digital asset inventory and reassess control levels. Update your prioritization and resource allocation accordingly to ensure ongoing protection and management of your digital assets.

There are cases in which having access is not possible, such as when ad accounts are owned by your service provider. There are cases in which your provider will offer an all-inclusive service, where you pay by results or something similar, and they may not provide you with access to the account. In those cases, just make sure you have access to reports and that the creatives and copy used comply with your requirements. The important point here is that you should know in advance.

## Digital Assets and How to Save Them

You may think that discussing digital assets in a digital marketing book doesn't make much sense. All the contrary. If you don't realize that your website, social network accounts, passwords, creatives, advertising accounts, and so on are real assets, then you will ignore (or forget) to document them and implement some way to control them. Or even worse, you may leave everything to your provider without caring if they secured their access.

Let's take Facebook as an example. To create Facebook Ads, you need a Facebook page, an advertising account, and a business account. If you don't treat those as assets, you may tell your agency (or a friend) to create and manage those for you. After some time, you stop working with the agency and find another partner, just to realize that you no longer have access to your Facebook page and all the insights and results are no longer available. Why? You didn't own the page, your agency did. And you didn't ask for access nor negotiate the conditions.

Now that you know that these things are assets, you can ask for access and save them somewhere safe. Password Managers are a good way to save those credentials. I compiled a list of the most used ones on my website, as those are not directly related to this book.

Depending on the relation you have with your provider, you may use different approaches. It is important to make it in a nonaggressive way, as many providers are not so keen on giving such accesses because they lose control.

Here is an email you can use right now to ask for more details regarding your assets:

**Formal Email Template:**

Subject: Request for Details Regarding Our Digital Assets

Dear [Agency Name or Contact person],

I hope this email finds you well.

## CHAPTER 2   DIGITAL ASSETS AND WHY THEY ARE IMPORTANT

We are currently in the process of documenting our digital assets, and as part of this endeavor, we require access to our various accounts and platforms managed by your agency. Specifically, we need to compile a comprehensive list of our Facebook pages, Google Ads accounts, and any other relevant assets.

Could you please provide us with a detailed list of the pages and accounts you are managing on our behalf? Additionally, we would appreciate information on who from our team currently has access to these assets. In cases where none of our team members have access, we kindly request guidance on how we can obtain access or an explanation as to why access is restricted.

Thank you in advance for your assistance and cooperation in this matter.

Best regards,

[Your Name]
[Your Position]
[Your Company]
[Your Contact Information]

### Informal Email Template:

Subject: Quick Request Regarding Our Digital Assets

Hey [Agency/Freelancer's Name],

I hope you're doing well!

We're currently in the process of organizing our digital assets and could use your assistance. We need to compile a list of all the platforms and accounts you manage for us, such as our Facebook page, Google Ads account, and any other relevant assets.

Could you please provide us with a list of these assets along with details on who on our team has access to each one? If there are any assets that our team doesn't have access to, we'd appreciate guidance on how to obtain access or an explanation for the restriction.

Thanks so much for your help with this!

Best regards,

[Your Name]

Now you can ask your partners, experts, and providers and start building your digital asset inventory.

## Summary

In this chapter, I discussed why understanding digital assets is so relevant in the digital world. Differentiating between tangible and intangible assets, as well as identifying and documenting which assets are yours and which are not, helps you when making decisions on where to focus resources and time. I also provided two short email templates to ask your service partners for that information.

In the next chapter, I will introduce the concepts of advertising channel provider, channels, and formats.

# CHAPTER 3

# Structure of the Digital Advertising Ecosystem

In the rapidly evolving world of digital marketing, understanding the intricate relationships between advertising platforms, channels, and formats is crucial for the effective development and planning of your strategy and its execution. To better capture the complexity and organizational hierarchy of these elements, I introduce a hierarchical structure to explain this ecosystem.

Within this ecosystem, advertising channel providers such as Google Ads and Facebook serve a role analogous to TV networks. They own or manage multiple advertising channels. Channels represent the various platforms or environments where ads can be placed, similar to TV channels, and formats refer to the specific types of advertising, like display ads or search ads, akin to TV programs such as reality shows, news, and so on.

CHAPTER 3   STRUCTURE OF THE DIGITAL ADVERTISING ECOSYSTEM

# Understanding the Structure

Under this structure, I call an **advertising channel provider** any company which provides one or more channels or networks where you can place your ads. Such a channel or network can be one or more of the following:

- Websites
- Platforms
- Networks
- Social networks
- Apps

You can find a list of updated advertising channel providers on my website, but the most important ones as of 2024 are

- Google Ads (incl. YouTube, Google Play, Google Search, and Google Display Ads)
- Facebook/Instagram Ads
- Microsoft Ads
- X (Twitter) Ads
- Twitch Ads
- Amazon Ads
- TikTok Ads
- Outbrain
- LinkedIn Ads

CHAPTER 3   STRUCTURE OF THE DIGITAL ADVERTISING ECOSYSTEM

There are also some advertising channel providers that work only in specific geographical areas, such as

- Xing Ads
- Ströer (in Germany)
- Framen (in EU)

There are also companies that seek to consolidate those advertising channel providers under one platform. Those are usually called DSPs, or demand-side platforms. A DSP provides technology that allows advertisers, agencies, and digital marketing experts to buy digital advertising inventory across various advertiser channel providers and their channels, including display, video, audio, mobile, and connected TV, through programmatic advertising.

Each advertising channel provider provides a set of channels or networks where you can use one of the many formats available.

Figure 3-1 illustrates the relation of each concept.

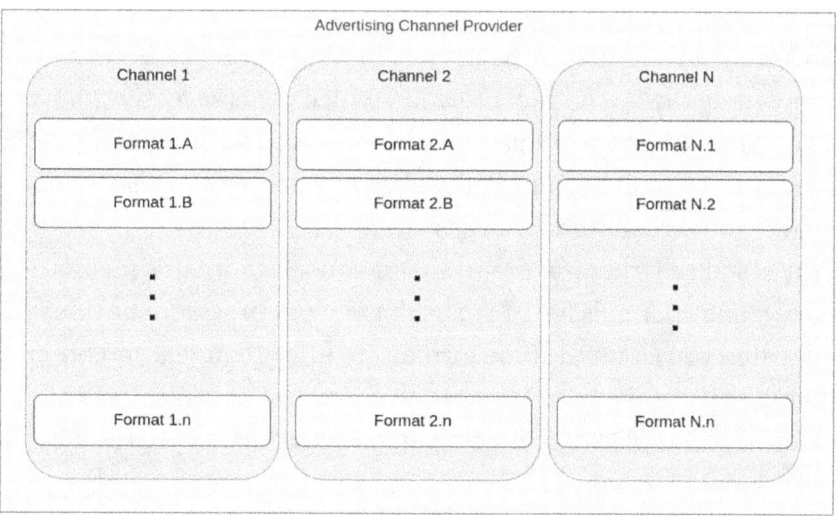

*Figure 3-1.* Diagram of a generic advertising channel provider

CHAPTER 3　STRUCTURE OF THE DIGITAL ADVERTISING ECOSYSTEM

The same graphic applied to Google Ads would be as shown in Figure 3-2.

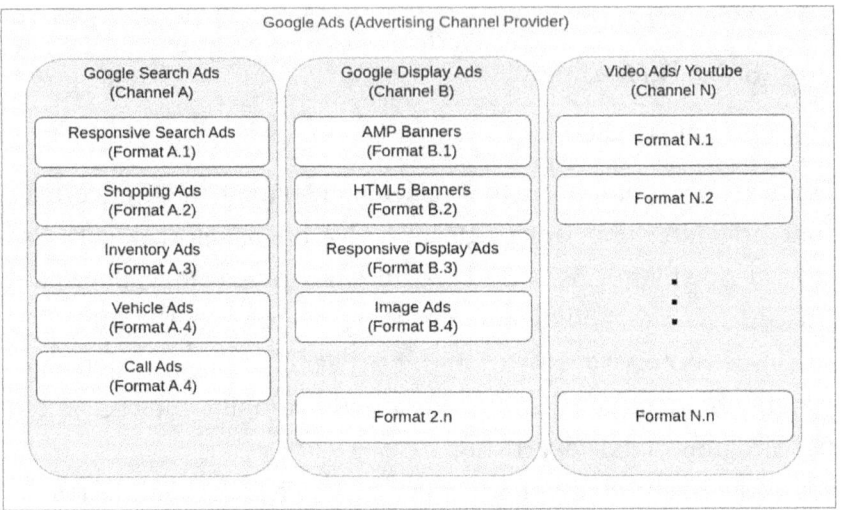

***Figure 3-2.*** *Diagram of Google Ads as an advertising channel provider*

This is a similar structure as the one in TV (television). You have a company (*advertising channel provider*) which owns several *channels* which in turn have many programs (formats). And sometimes, the same program (format) can be found on different channels and also in different companies (advertising channel providers).

Why is such a structure important for you? Because this means that there are some channels and formats that are not provider-specific, meaning that you can find some formats in other channels and other providers. This is great because you can share creatives (assets) and concepts, for example, for a display campaign by Google Ads and by Microsoft Ads.

## Four Pillars

In other words, such a structure allows you to understand the ecosystem in four pillars: **flexibility and reach, resource efficiency, strategic advantage,** and **innovation and engagement.**

Flexibility and reach are enhanced as advertisers realize that many formats transcend specific providers, allowing the design of universal campaigns deployable across multiple platforms. For instance, a display ad intended for Google Ads can also be utilized on Microsoft Ads seamlessly.

Resource efficiency is achieved by recognizing which formats and channels are interchangeable among providers, which allows the creation of adaptable marketing materials that are effective across various platforms. This efficiency saves significant time and resources.

The strategic advantage emerges from the ability to optimize ad placement and targeting strategies, knowing which formats can bridge various providers and channels. This insight facilitates more precise and effective marketing interventions.

Lastly, the ecosystem's structure encourages innovation and engagement. The use of diverse formats across different channels promotes both creative and technical innovation, leading to more captivating and impactful advertising campaigns tailored to varied audience needs.

## Summary

In this chapter, I introduce a structure to understand the digital advertising ecosystem. For this, I made an analogy to the structure found in television, where each TV company owns several channels and programs, but a program can be shown on many channels from several companies. This allows you to understand that there are cross-provider channels

CHAPTER 3   STRUCTURE OF THE DIGITAL ADVERTISING ECOSYSTEM

and formats. Given that, I define four pillars for this structure and why it is important, flexibility, resource efficiency, strategic advantage, and innovation, and how understanding this can allow you to make optimal use of your resources and prevent duplicated efforts and costs.

In the next chapter, I will explain what are awareness levels, which ones are there, and why you should understand them and use them in your digital marketing strategy.

# CHAPTER 4

# Understanding Customer Awareness Levels in Digital Marketing

Before we dive into the specific aspects of digital marketing, it's essential to understand the concept of customer awareness levels. Each potential customer you encounter is at a different stage of awareness about your products or services. These stages range from being completely unaware of a need, to recognizing the need and actively seeking your specific solution.

Identifying and understanding these levels allows us to tailor our marketing efforts effectively. By ensuring that we communicate the right message at the right time and in the right context, we increase our chances of reaching the most receptive audience.

## Comparing Awareness Levels: A Practical Example

Consider two potential customers in the market for a new family car. While you might be tempted to push your family-friendly SUV, it's vital to first assess the customer's awareness level. Here are some common oversights:

- Not all customers are aware of the SUV category or that your brand offers SUVs.

- Customers might be considering other types of vehicles, like sedans or vans.

- Your brand might be known for luxury rather than family vehicles, which could misalign with the customer's search intentions.

- The entire customer journey, from the initial search to the landing page experience, should be tailored based on their awareness level. For instance, someone unaware of SUVs as a potential solution will need basic information about why SUVs might meet their needs, whereas someone aware of your specific model might just be looking for price offers or detailed specifications.

It is perfectly valid to choose not to target customers at certain awareness levels, as long as these decisions are informed and deliberate.

## Visualizing Awareness Levels

These levels can be better visualized in a diagram. Starting from the top, where someone is completely aware of its needs and of you as a solution to that need, down to someone who doesn't even know he has a need (Figure 4-1).

CHAPTER 4   UNDERSTANDING CUSTOMER AWARENESS LEVELS IN DIGITAL MARKETING

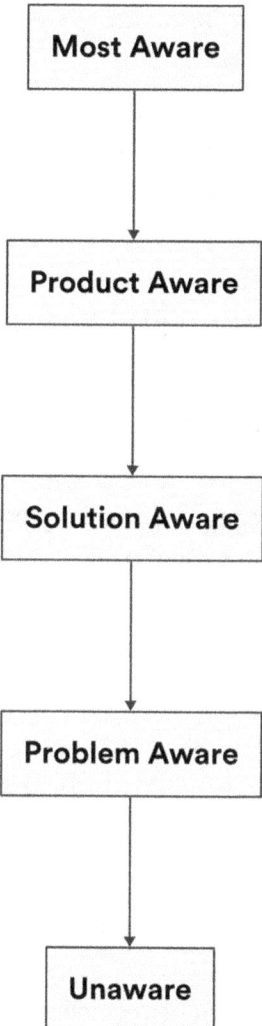

*Figure 4-1. Basic awareness levels diagram*

Let's break down these levels further with Table 4-1, which includes typical keywords associated with each stage.

*Table 4-1.* Basic awareness levels table with keyword examples

| Level | Description | Keywords, Interests |
|---|---|---|
| Most Aware | Customers know what you sell, understand how it works, and are ready to buy | Brand name, product names |
| Product Aware | Customers are aware of your products but have not decided to purchase yet | Competitors, product descriptions |
| Solution Aware | Customers seek solutions and might benefit from your product, but aren't aware of it | Features, results, scenarios |
| Pain/Problem Aware | Customers recognize they have a problem but don't know solutions exist. | Desires, goals, problems |
| Completely Unaware | Customers have no knowledge or awareness of the needs your products meet | Not typically targeted in paid search ads, unless awareness ads are used to make your customers aware of their need |

These awareness levels help us segment our marketing efforts more effectively.

Understanding the various stages of customer awareness can significantly enhance your digital marketing campaigns by aligning each campaign's strategy with the audience's familiarity with your product. Let's break down the stages of awareness, from most aware to completely unaware, and discuss how your approach to advertising can be tailored accordingly.

## Most Aware Customers

The "Most Aware" customers know your product well and are highly likely to purchase again. These are your brand advocates—the ones who follow every update you post, engage with your content, and remain loyal to your brand. The strategy for targeting them should be defensive, aimed at protecting and reinforcing brand loyalty. Here you would use targeted advertising that focuses on new features, member-exclusive offers, or upcoming products that keep the brand top of mind and renew their enthusiasm.

## Product Aware Customers

Moving to "Product Aware," these customers are aware that your product exists, yet they haven't made the decision to buy. This group is crucial because their purchase decision can swing based on how you position your product against competitors. They might be comparing various options, so your advertising costs could be higher here due to the need for broader targeting to outshine competitors. Highlighting product benefits, showcasing customer testimonials, and emphasizing unique selling propositions are effective tactics to convert their awareness into a purchase.

## Solution Aware Customers

Next are the "Solution Aware" customers. They are actively seeking solutions but might not be aware that your product can fulfill their needs. For such an audience, your marketing should focus on educating them about how your product serves as a solution. This involves detailed content that addresses specific problems, demonstrates product use cases, and provides clear, compelling reasons why your product is the better choice. Educational webinars, tutorial videos, and case studies can be effective in this stage.

## Pain or Problem Aware Customers

The "Pain/Problem Aware" ones recognize they have a problem, but aren't aware of the solutions available. They are looking for answers but haven't started considering specific products yet. This stage is your opportunity to introduce them to the solutions you offer. Content marketing that focuses on problem-solving, such as blogs addressing common issues, FAQs, and informative posts, can help bridge the gap between their pain and your solution.

## Completely Unaware Customers

Lastly, the "Completely Unaware" group doesn't know your product exists, or that a solution to their unidentified problem exists. Targeting this audience with product-specific ads is generally not cost-effective unless your goal is broad brand awareness. When the objective is to tap into this segment, you should deploy creative, broad-reaching campaigns that aim to educate the market about the existence of the problem and the solutions your brand provides. This could be executed through storytelling that resonates with the audience's everyday experiences, stirring up recognition of problems they hadn't previously articulated.

## Implementing Awareness in Strategy

Understanding how different customer awareness levels interact with your digital assets is key to aligning your marketing strategies effectively. Tailoring your approach based on the customer's stage in their journey can significantly enhance engagement and conversion rates.

CHAPTER 4  UNDERSTANDING CUSTOMER AWARENESS LEVELS IN DIGITAL MARKETING

# Incorporating Awareness Diagram with Customer Interactions

Let's visualize how varying levels of customer awareness influence their interaction with your marketing efforts. Figure 4-2 helps to clarify the type of content and strategies that are most effective at each awareness level.

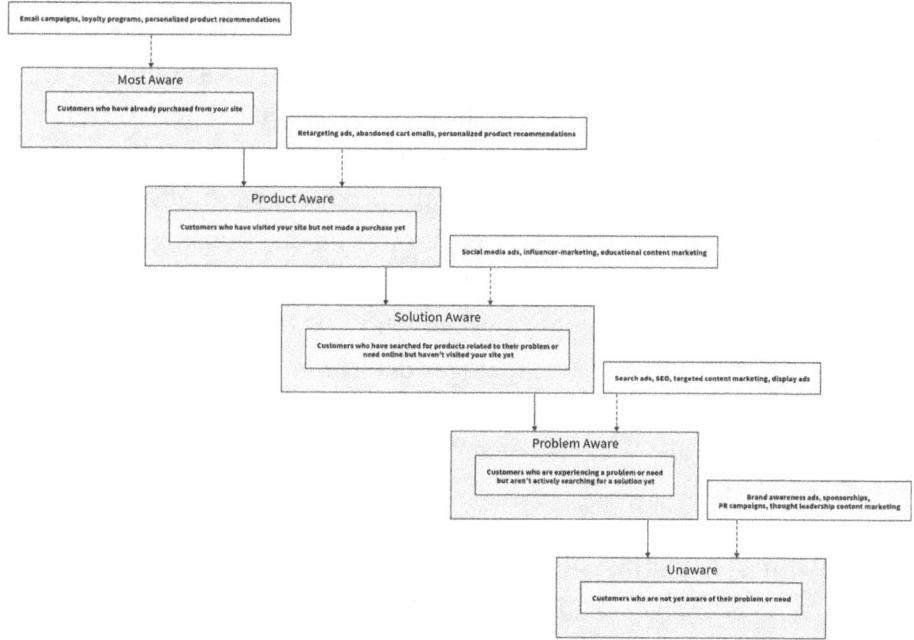

*Figure 4-2.* Awareness levels diagram with example customer interactions

# Example Strategy Details for Each Awareness Level

For customers who are "Most Aware," strategies such as email campaigns, loyalty programs, and personalized product recommendations help maintain and strengthen the existing relationship. These tactics encourage repeat purchases and elevate customer loyalty.

Moving on to "Product Aware" customers, they have already visited your site but haven't made a purchase. Here, retargeting ads and abandoned cart emails can nudge them closer to purchase, effectively utilizing their existing interest in your products.

"Solution Aware" customers are actively seeking solutions but may not be directly looking at your offerings. Utilizing search ads, targeted content marketing, and SEO can direct them to your site, providing the solutions they seek.

For those who are "Problem Aware," introducing your product as a solution through targeted social media ads, educational content, and influencer marketing can have a positive impact, moving them from recognizing a problem to considering your product as a solution.

Lastly, targeting the "Unaware" customers involves raising awareness about the problem first, before introducing your solution. Strategies like brand awareness campaigns, sponsorships, and thought leadership content are relevant in these early stages of customer engagement.

# Summary

In this chapter, I explained on the concept of customer awareness levels and their significance in shaping digital marketing strategies. Starting with the basics, we outlined the five key stages of awareness: Unaware, Pain/Problem Aware, Solution Aware, Product Aware, and Most Aware. I examined common mistakes marketers make when assuming customer awareness and emphasized the importance of tailoring content and campaigns to suit different levels.

I then visualized these levels through diagrams and tables, which not only aid in understanding but also serve as tools for planning and implementing marketing strategies. By segmenting audiences based on their awareness, marketers can more effectively target their messages, resulting in higher engagement and conversion rates.

CHAPTER 4   UNDERSTANDING CUSTOMER AWARENESS LEVELS IN DIGITAL MARKETING

Lastly, I discussed the practical application of these concepts through examples of how customers interact with digital assets, providing actionable strategies for each stage of awareness. Understanding and utilizing these insights can dramatically improve the precision and effectiveness of your marketing efforts, ensuring that the right message reaches the right customer at the right time.

In the next chapter, I will briefly discuss what Walled Gardens and the Open Web are and explore why they may (or may not) be relevant and important to you.

# CHAPTER 5

# Understanding Walled Gardens and Open Internet

If you've been exploring the realm of digital marketing or attending industry events, you may have encountered the terms "Walled Gardens" and "Open Web." But what exactly do these terms mean? In this chapter, I review both.

## Walled Gardens in Digital Marketing

A "walled garden" in the context of advertising refers to a platform that provides a comprehensive range of advertising services. These services include managing ad placements, audiences, inventory, and data collection all under one roof. These platforms are often described as "black boxes" because the internal workings—such as bid decision-making processes and the actual costs of platform use, support, placements, and data collection—are not transparent to the user. This lack of transparency can make it challenging to compare the effectiveness of campaigns across different channels and providers. However, walled gardens tend to simplify digital marketing, making it more accessible for most businesses. Examples of walled gardens include Google Ads, Facebook Marketing, and Amazon Ads.

## The Open Web

In contrast, the "Open Web" refers to parts of the Internet characterized by greater transparency compared to walled gardens. This segment includes major publishers and all other sites not encapsulated within platforms like Google Ads. Unlike Walled Gardens, the Open Web involves multiple platforms and providers, each with its own set of costs and responsibilities. Advertisers may need to separately manage audience data, media buying, and campaign analysis. This approach offers more granularity in managing campaigns but requires a deeper understanding and more hands-on involvement.

## Closing Thoughts

It's essential to keep your marketing objectives at the forefront of your decisions. Whether the platform is a walled garden or part of the open web, what matters most is reaching your audience effectively. However, it's also important to consider whether your company's values align with those of your advertising providers. For instance, if your brand champions transparency and an open Internet, you might prefer avoiding walled gardens. Conversely, if your priority is to maximize visibility where your customers are most active, the type of platform may be less significant.

## Summary

Choosing between walled gardens and the open web involves balancing ease of use, transparency, cost considerations, and alignment with your brand's values and goals. Understanding the nuances of each will help you make informed decisions that enhance your digital marketing strategy.

In the next chapter, I'll briefly explain what targeting is and introduce two types: general (broad) targeting and specific targeting.

# CHAPTER 6

# The Essence of Targeting in Digital Marketing

Targeting is a crucial component in digital marketing, allowing advertisers to direct their messages to specific groups of consumers based on various criteria. By tailoring ad exposure according to detailed settings such as demographics, interests, and behaviors, businesses can increase the relevance and effectiveness of their marketing efforts. Let's unpack what targeting entails in the realm of digital marketing and how different approaches can dramatically influence campaign outcomes.

At its core, targeting involves a series of settings and parameters used by advertising channel providers to determine who sees your ads and when they see them. This process not only varies from one platform to another but also depends on the specific objectives of each campaign and the preferred practices of marketing professionals.

**Important Considerations**
Note that not every targeting setting is universally applicable; effective targeting in one context may not yield the same results in another due to differences in audience behavior and platform algorithms.

CHAPTER 6   THE ESSENCE OF TARGETING IN DIGITAL MARKETING

# Delving Deeper: An In-Depth Look at Targeting

To better understand targeting, let's define it explicitly:

Targeting is the collection of settings and criteria used by advertising channel providers to decide the appropriate timing (when) and demographics (to whom) for displaying advertisers' messages and creatives. This can be broad, covering multiple channels and campaigns, or specific, customized to individual campaigns and channels.

—Diego Adolfo Carrasco Gubernatis

This definition includes several critical components of targeting, each of which contributes to its overall impact:

## Collection of Settings and Criteria

Targeting involves a variety of adjustable parameters available on advertising platforms. These can include user demographics like age and location, user interests such as technology or sports, and device types, and even user intent. These options enable marketers to sharpen the focus of their campaigns, enhancing both relevance and engagement.

## Messages and Creatives

Targeting not only determines who sees the ads but also influences when and in what format they are presented. This means that different creatives might be used for the same campaign depending on the target audience, such as varying the ad design and messaging for Android versus iOS users.

## Types of Targeting: Broad vs. Specific

I like to classify targeting depending on its use. For example, for targeting that will be used as defaults or as base for several marketing initiatives, I use the term "general targeting." If, on the other side, a marketing initiative requires specific settings and differs from the other initiatives I run, I consider that a "specific targeting." I generally define a "general targeting" for a client, a group of campaigns, or a set of marketing goals and then improve it by setting the specifics for each initiative. For instance, for a specific brand, the general targeting will consider its main target group, the positive or negative keywords, and placement lists and the costs. Then, for a specific product, I will improve it by limiting the placements, improving the keywords for that one product and for the awareness level of that one marketing initiative.

Let's explain both:

**General targeting** uses broad criteria to reach extensive audiences across various platforms and campaigns. This approach, while less precise, provides a foundation for building brand awareness and capturing a wide demographic.

In contrast, **specific targeting** hones in on detailed characteristics of a target audience and the unique goals of a campaign. This method allows for more precise alignment with potential customers' needs and interests, leading to greater campaign relevance and effectiveness.

## Example Application

Imagine a company selling winter sports equipment. For broad targeting, the strategy might involve reaching a general audience interested in outdoor winter activities. However, for their premium products designed for professional athletes, specific targeting would focus on those consumers' unique needs and preferences. This dual approach helps minimize campaign overlap and optimizes performance by ensuring that the marketing efforts match the audience's specific interests.

## Summary

In this chapter, we explored the intricacies of targeting in digital marketing—how it works, why it's used, and the differences between broad and specific targeting strategies. Understanding these concepts will help you craft effective digital marketing campaigns that resonate with your intended audience.

In the next chapter, I will explain what cannibalization in digital marketing is and how you can prevent it.

# CHAPTER 7

# Understanding Cannibalization in Digital Marketing

Cannibalization might sound like a drastic term, but in the context of digital marketing, it addresses a real and often costly issue. This concept is important for your initiatives as it affects the efficiency and effectiveness of your advertising budget. Let's delve into what cannibalization means in digital marketing and why it's critical to manage it carefully.

## The Concept of Cannibalization

Cannibalization occurs when multiple advertising campaigns target similar audiences on the same platform without clear differentiation in targeting criteria. This overlap causes the campaigns to compete against each other for the same ad placements. This not only drives up the costs due to increased bids but also reduces the overall effectiveness of your advertising efforts.

In this case, the concepts of general targeting and specific targeting will help you understand what I mean.

Let's say you have a general targeting and use it for three marketing initiatives. This means, in other words, that you will show three different ads to the same persons because your targeting for the three initiatives is the same. Let say now, that you define a specific targeting for each of your initiatives, which takes the general targeting as a basis. In this case, you will most likely add the name of each product to the negative keyword list of the other initiatives, so that Product A does not show its ad when someone searches for Product B, same with Product C. You may also have different competitors for each product, as each targets a different market. In that case, you will want to add the names of the competitors and their products to the Keyword Lists of each of these initiatives. Why? Because this will allow your ad from Product A to be shown when someone searches the product of your competitor, but not your other products.

## Bidding Wars and Budget Impacts

But, how does cannibalization work? Let's think you forgot to set a specific targeting for each of your initiatives, and analyze what would happen from a "Bid" perspective.

In digital marketing, advertisers set bids for ad placements. If several of your campaigns are bidding for the same audience (general targeting), this pushes up the cost per placement as each campaign tries to outbid the others. The result? Your campaigns "eat" into each other's budgets, which can be particularly damaging if the overlapping campaigns are not coordinated.

The advertising channel provider plays a role in determining how your ads are displayed based on the targeting criteria you set. If your targeting criteria for multiple campaigns are similar or overlapping, the system might pit these campaigns against each other in bidding wars, inadvertently driving up your costs and potentially causing some campaigns to underperform while others overspend.

## Addressing Cannibalization

To effectively address cannibalization, it's important to first recognize when it's happening. You can identify potential cannibalization by monitoring campaign performance and noting any unexpected inefficiencies or increased costs.

## Strategies to Mitigate Cannibalization

To minimize the risk of cannibalization, ensure that your campaigns have distinct and specific targeting preferences. This might involve

- Utilizing more granular targeting options to differentiate audiences (what I called specific targeting above and in the previous chapter)
- Scheduling campaigns at different times or in different geographic regions
- Tailoring messages and creatives to distinct audience segments

By implementing these strategies, you can prevent your campaigns from competing against each other, thereby optimizing your advertising spend and enhancing campaign performance.

# Summary

In this chapter, I've explored the concept of cannibalization in digital marketing, understanding how it can impact your advertising efforts and what strategies can be employed to mitigate its effects. Some key

CHAPTER 7   UNDERSTANDING CANNIBALIZATION IN DIGITAL MARKETING

terms here are general targeting and specific targeting. Key points to remember include

- Cannibalization results from overlapping targeting across multiple campaigns.
- It leads to increased costs and reduced effectiveness due to bidding wars.
- Proper campaign management and distinct targeting are essential to avoid cannibalization.

In the next chapter, I will explain the differences between placements and inventory (quick hint: it depends on the perspective), why lists with keywords to be excluded and list with keywords to be included are important, and why the concept of thumb-clicks is significant.

# CHAPTER 8

# Understanding Placements and Inventory

In the world of digital marketing, the placement of your ads is as important as understanding who sees them. In this chapter, I'll deepen your understanding of fundamental concepts such as placements and inventory. Additionally, I'll cover related concepts like blocklisting (formerly known as blacklisting), allowlisting (formerly known as whitelisting), and the strategic management of URLs, giving you comprehensive insights into effectively managing where your ads are displayed. I will also touch the case of thumb-clicks and why they are relevant for you to know.

## What Are Placements and Inventory?

First, let's clarify what I mean by placements and inventory, as these are basic concepts in determining where your ads appear.

**Placements** are specific locations within a medium—be it a website, a mobile app, or a video—where ads can be shown. The choice of placement significantly influences the effectiveness of an advertisement.

Placement is a concept mostly used by those who pay to place their ads.

**Inventory**, or ad inventory, refers to the total number of placements that a publisher offers. This includes all the potential spaces where ads can be displayed across a publisher's network.

Inventory is usually a concept used by those who sell spots for others to place their ads.

For you as a marketer who wants to place ads in specific spots, placement is the right concept. A placement can refer to several things, such as an app, an entire website, a specific page, a video, and so on. Essentially, a placement denotes a distinct "spot" that has the potential to capture someone's attention.

If you sell those "spots," then you use "inventory." If you buy them, then you use "placement."

# Advanced Concepts: Blocklisting, Allowlisting, and Managing URLs

To refine where your ads appear further and to boost their effectiveness, let's explore the concepts of blocklisting, allowlisting, and the role of URLs.

## Blocklisting and Allowlisting

Blocklisting (formerly known as blacklisting) means specifying certain websites or URLs where you do not want your ads to appear. This practice is essential for avoiding placements that may conflict with your brand values or fail to meet your campaign objectives.

Conversely, allowlisting (formerly known as whitelisting) involves specifying preferred websites where you want your ads displayed. This ensures your ads appear in environments relevant to your brand, reaching your target audience more effectively.

## Important Consideration

Understanding the nuances of allowlisting and blocklisting placements is crucial for your advertising strategy. Adding a placement to an allowlist doesn't guarantee that you'll win the bid for that specific spot; it simply means that the platform will prioritize it—and potentially similar placements—for your ads. Conversely, blocklisting a site ensures that your ads won't appear on that specific placement, but be mindful that they might still show up on similar ones.

## Role of URLs in Ad Placements

Effective URL management is important for both blocklisting and allowlisting strategies. It involves meticulous monitoring of where your ads are placed to ensure they only appear in desirable locations. This level of control maximizes the efficacy of your advertising spend by ensuring your ads resonate with your audience's preferences and behaviors.

## Practical Example of URL Management

Consider you are marketing a family-friendly product. You would likely allowlist URLs associated with family-oriented content and blocklist those related to adult content. This strategic placement ensures your ad aligns with the right audience in the right context.

CHAPTER 8   UNDERSTANDING PLACEMENTS AND INVENTORY

# The Importance of Monitoring Ad Placements

Monitoring where your ads are displayed plays a important role in the overall success of your campaigns. By keeping track of ad placements, you can

- Adjust strategies based on which placements perform best.
- Identify potential issues with non-performing ads.
- Ensure that your ads are seen by your target audience in a context that enhances the likelihood of engagement.

## Accurately Monitoring

Tools and analytics platforms are available to help track the performance of your ad placements. These tools can provide insights into viewer engagement and interaction, helping you understand what works and what doesn't.

# Blocklisting and Analyzing URLs

When it comes to blocklisting URLs, the key is to align your decisions with your company's values and the specifics of your brand. Typically, URLs that feature content or host communities that contravene your brand's values should be avoided. Here's how to analyze potential URLs for blocklisting:

CHAPTER 8   UNDERSTANDING PLACEMENTS AND INVENTORY

- Review the content of the website to ensure it matches your brand's ethos.
- Check for user-generated content that might conflict with your brand's standards.
- Consider the site's audience and whether it aligns with your target demographic.

Sometimes you will update your block list as you review your campaign's results and the placements on which your ad has been shown. Your service partner should help you decide on how to proceed here.

# Understanding Thumb-Clicks in Mobile Gaming Ads

In your journey through digital marketing, particularly in the mobile app ecosystem, you might encounter phenomena that initially seem beneficial but may actually signal underlying issues. One such phenomenon is "thumb-clicks" in smartphone games. This section will explore what thumb-clicks are, their implications, and how they are related to apps, especially games, on smartphones. Identifying thumb-clicks is possible when you monitor your placements and metrics such as CPC.

## Thumb-Clicks

Thumb-clicks refer to the accidental clicks users make while interacting with a mobile app, especially during gaming. These inadvertent interactions usually occur due to the placement of ads within the app's interface where users frequently touch. For example, an ad might be placed close to game control buttons, leading to accidental clicks.

CHAPTER 8   UNDERSTANDING PLACEMENTS AND INVENTORY

## Exploring the Impact

These clicks may initially seem like a boon due to high click-through rates (CTR), but they often result in a really low cost-per-click (CPC) because these interactions rarely convert into meaningful actions such as purchases or sign-ups. This is because the user did not intend to click the ad in the first place.

## Why Monitoring Thumb-Clicks Makes Sense

Identifying and understanding the impact of thumb-clicks is essential for advertisers, especially in the context of mobile games.

## Significance of Monitoring

Monitoring these clicks helps in distinguishing between genuine user interest and accidental clicks. This distinction helps when evaluating the true performance of an ad campaign. A high number of thumb-clicks may inflate your data, giving a misleading impression of an ad's effectiveness.

## Identifying Thumb-Clicks

Anomalies such as a sudden spike in clicks coupled with unusually low CPC can indicate the prevalence of thumb-clicks. Observing user behavior post-click—such as rapid departure from the landing page—can also provide insights into whether the clicks were intentional.

CHAPTER 8   UNDERSTANDING PLACEMENTS AND INVENTORY

# Evaluating Mobile Advertisement Strategy for Apps and Smartphone Games

If you're a marketer considering where to place your ads, there's an important decision to be made regarding mobile apps and smartphone games. This potentially requires a thorough understanding of whether these platforms align with your campaign goals and how to optimize the user experience to maximize returns from these advertisements.

## Ad Placement Strategy

Deciding to advertise on apps and games involves a strategic evaluation of whether these platforms reach your target audience effectively. It also involves choosing the right categories within these platforms that align with your branding and audience interests. For example, if you're marketing educational products, placing ads in educational or productivity apps could be more effective than in gaming apps.

## User Experience Considerations

When your ads successfully attract users, the next critical step is ensuring they land on a page that is optimized for their device. This means your landing page or designated action page should be mobile-friendly, with fast loading times and easy navigation. Even the most interested user will turn away if they encounter functional issues on your landing page.

# Summary

This chapter has equipped you with foundational knowledge on ad placements and inventory and introduced advanced tactics such as blocklisting, allowlisting, and URL management. It has also shed

CHAPTER 8   UNDERSTANDING PLACEMENTS AND INVENTORY

some light on the concept of thumb-clicks, especially in the context of mobile games, and why it might be detrimental for your campaign. By understanding and addressing thumb-clicks, you can ensure that your digital marketing efforts yield more reliable and actionable insights.

Some key takeaways are

- Strategic placement of ads enhances visibility and engagement.

- Careful management of URLs ensures your ads align with appropriate and effective contexts.

- Monitoring placements and analyzing URLs are crucial for optimizing ad performance and protecting brand integrity.

- Thumb-clicks are accidental interactions that can inflate campaign metrics.

- Thoroughly assess if advertising on apps and smartphone games fits your campaign objectives.

- Choose app categories that align well with your target audience.

- Ensure your landing pages are optimized for mobile devices to retain user interest and convert clicks into actions.

In the next chapter, I will explain target groups, audiences, and personas, highlighting their differences and how understanding them can impact your campaign planning and its likely performance. Quick hint: If your targeting is off, your campaign won't yield any results.

# CHAPTER 9

# Target Groups, Audiences, and Personas

Understanding the distinctions between target groups and audiences is important in digital marketing, specially when dealing with third parties. These concepts guide how you shape your marketing strategies to effectively reach the right people with the right message at the right moment.

## Introduction to Target Groups and Audiences

Understanding the distinctions between target groups and audiences helps you communicate with other parties and discuss the same "thing." It guides you in crafting marketing strategies that effectively reach the intended individuals.

CHAPTER 9  TARGET GROUPS, AUDIENCES, AND PERSONAS

A **target group** denotes a specific segment of the population identified for targeted marketing efforts. This group is defined based on various characteristics:

- **Demographics**: Includes age, gender, income, and education.
- **Psychographics**: Encompasses personality traits, lifestyles, and values.
- **Behavioral Data**: Considers interests, past purchases, and website visits.
- **Geographical Location**: Specifies the region where the individuals are located.

## Identify and Engage

By accurately identifying your target group, you can tailor your marketing messages and creative efforts to resonate deeply with potential customers, thus enhancing the relevance of your ads and increasing the likelihood of engagement.

## Example of Target Group Utilization

Imagine you run an online bookstore. Your target group might include young adults aged 18–24, who are university students, enjoy reading sci-fi novels, and frequently shop online. By defining these parameters, you create ads that speak directly to their interests and behaviors, thereby increasing the effectiveness of your marketing campaigns.

CHAPTER 9  TARGET GROUPS, AUDIENCES, AND PERSONAS

## Ad Platforms and Targeting Options

Different advertising platforms offer various tools to effectively reach your identified target groups. For instance:

- **Google Ads** enables the use of Audiences, Custom Audiences, and Demographic Targeting.
- **Facebook** offers targeting based on Interests and Behaviors, as well as geographic location.

## Understanding Who Sees Your Ads

It is essential to understand the complete profile of who should see and interact with your advertisements. This detailed knowledge allows marketing specialists to craft precise targeting strategies tailored to your campaign's needs.

## Understanding Audiences

The term **audience** describes the actual individuals who end up seeing and interacting with your ads. This group may not always perfectly align with your defined target group due to several factors:

- **Reach Extensions**: Sometimes, ad platforms expand the reach of your campaigns to include individuals who might be interested in your products or similar to your target group. In some cases, this is a setting that can be activated or deactivated.
- **Engagement Variability**: Your audience includes those who genuinely engage with your content, which can provide valuable insights into the effectiveness of your targeting strategies.

CHAPTER 9   TARGET GROUPS, AUDIENCES, AND PERSONAS

## Audience Analysis

Analyzing who your ads reach and how they interact with them can offer actionable insights, enabling you to refine future campaigns. For example, if you notice that individuals from an unexpected demographic are engaging with your ads, you might consider including this group in your future marketing plans.

# Understanding the Difference: Target Group, Audience, and Persona

In digital marketing, the concepts of target group, audience, and persona are concepts that help you sharpen your advertising focus but are also confused. While these terms are interrelated, they each play a unique role in how you approach your marketing strategy. Table 9-1 breaks down the differences between these terms and provides further clarifications.

*Table 9-1.* Comparing target group, audience, and persona

| Term | Definition | Example |
|---|---|---|
| Target group | A specific segment of people or customers that a brand or advertiser wants to reach with their marketing messages | Females aged 25–34 who live in urban areas and have an interest in fitness |
| Audience | The actual people who are exposed to and engage with a brand's marketing messages, often defined by real interaction data | Individuals who have visited a brand's website in the past 30 days |
| Persona | A detailed, fictional representation of a specific type of customer that a brand is targeting, created based on research and data analysis | Sarah, a 30-year-old marketing manager from Chicago who enjoys outdoor activities and travels frequently |

Now let's explore the nuances of each term:

**Target Group.** It's a broader category aimed at encapsulating a substantial segment of potential customers sharing common characteristics. Since the target group is quite broad, this category aids in setting the general direction for your marketing efforts but needs further refinement to maximize effectiveness.

**Audience.** This term refers to those within your target group who actually engage with your marketing—it's a subset of your target group. By analyzing interaction data, such as website visits or engagement with past advertising, you pinpoint your audience. This data-driven approach ensures that your marketing resources are focused on people who have already shown interest in what you offer.

**Persona.** A persona refines your audience further by creating a detailed, fictional character that embodies the traits of an ideal customer. This technique allows marketers like yourself to visualize the motivations, behaviors, and preferences of your target audience, leading to highly tailored marketing strategies. Personas enable you to craft messages that resonate deeply on a personal level, making them an essential tool for engaging effectively with your audience.

## Summary

Understanding the distinctions and interconnections between target groups, audiences, and personas can significantly enhance your marketing strategies, ensuring they are deeply aligned with the needs and behaviors of your potential customers.

CHAPTER 9  TARGET GROUPS, AUDIENCES, AND PERSONAS

Remember

- **Target Groups:** Set the broad scope of your marketing efforts.
- **Audiences**: Are those within your target group who actually engage with your marketing.
- **Personas**: Add depth to audience understanding and shape communication and marketing.

In the next chapter, I will explain what bids are in digital marketing, outline the most popular bidding strategies, discuss the risks associated with these strategies, and identify who bears these risks. I will also provide a quick overview of the main bidding strategies.

# CHAPTER 10

# Understanding Bids, Bid Strategies, and Their Impacts

In the Chapter 6 on Targeting, I used a concept called "Bids." In this chapter, I delve into the concept of bids in digital marketing. Understanding how bids work is akin to mastering the art of setting the right price at an auction to display your advertisement. It's not just about how much you're willing to pay, but also about choosing the appropriate strategy to make your investment count. Let's decode the terminology and strategies surrounding bids and explore how they influence the visibility and cost of your advertisements.

## Bids in Digital Marketing

A bid in digital marketing is essentially an offer you make in an auction setting to show your advertisement—it's the price you're willing to pay for someone to see or click on your ad. The higher your bid, the more likely it is that your ad will be displayed to your target audience.

CHAPTER 10   UNDERSTANDING BIDS, BID STRATEGIES, AND THEIR IMPACTS

Bids significantly influence ad display, but they are only one of several factors that determine if you win an auction. Other factors include ad quality and relevance to the audience, for example.[1]

Table 10-1 breaks down the difference between Bid Strategy and Bid Costs.

*Table 10-1.* *Bid strategy explained*

| Term | Definition | Example |
|---|---|---|
| Bid strategy | The method by which advertisers decide how much they are willing to pay for an ad | Using a cost-per-action (CPA) strategy to optimize ad delivery and aim for maximum conversions |
| Bid costs | The actual expenditure incurred by an advertiser for each ad impression or click | A campaign where the advertiser bids $1.50 per click and spends a total of $150 for 100 clicks |

## Popular Bid Strategies

Understanding various bid strategies helps in selecting the most suitable one based on your campaign goals and possibilities.[2]

- **Cost per Click (CPC):** You pay only when someone clicks on your ad.

- **Cost per Impression (CPM):** Payment is based on the number of impressions or views of your ad.

- **Cost per Action (CPA):** This focuses on paying only when specific actions are taken, such as a sale or signup.

---

[1] Check Chapter 11 on Ad Quality for more details.
[2] I speak here about possibilities because it's not easy for everyone to implement all bidding strategies. For example, to use a CPA strategy, you need to implement tracking codes in your website. If you don't have the access or knowledge to do this, you are better off using another bidding strategy.

CHAPTER 10   UNDERSTANDING BIDS, BID STRATEGIES, AND THEIR IMPACTS

There are several different strategies and the ones above are just an example. Next I will compare in a table the most common ones based on who's taking the risk, when do I as advertiser pay, their requirements to implement, and example use cases. But first, let's define what is risk for this book, and let me explain why this is important for you.

## Defining Risk in the Context of Bidding Strategies

In digital marketing, "risk" generally refers to the potential for not achieving the desired outcome from your ad spend. This could manifest, for example, as spending money without obtaining sufficient returns, such as not getting enough clicks, conversions, or engagement from the target audience or as getting results for a price that's too high for your goals.

Risk in bidding strategies can be seen as the level of certainty you have in achieving your marketing goals with a specific amount of budget at stake. The type of bidding strategy you choose directly influences this risk level. We can classify the risk based on the bidding type:

- **Fixed Bidding (CPC, CPM):** The advertiser bears most of the risk as payment is made regardless of conversion success.

- **Performance-Based Bidding (CPA, CPI):** The risk is shared, leaning more on the provider, as payment is made only when specific actions, like a sale or installation, are completed.

CHAPTER 10   UNDERSTANDING BIDS, BID STRATEGIES, AND THEIR IMPACTS

> **Note**   In the context of bidding strategies for digital marketing, a conversion is defined as a measurable action that a user takes as a result of interacting with your ad. This could be making a purchase, filling out a form, signing up for a newsletter, or any other action that aligns with your campaign goals. In bidding strategies, you often pay based on predicted or achieved conversions, making it crucial to **define** and **track** them accurately to evaluate the ROI[3] of your campaigns.

# Practical Definition of Risk

In the simplest terms, risk in the realm of digital marketing bids refers to the probability and potential extent of failing to achieve the expected results from paid advertisements. Every campaign will inherently carry some degree of risk due to variables beyond complete control, such as audience behavior, market competition, and market trends.

# Managing Risk

Understanding and managing risk in your bidding strategy involves selecting the right type of bid based on how much uncertainty you can accept in your campaign outcomes.

---

[3] Return of investment

CHAPTER 10  UNDERSTANDING BIDS, BID STRATEGIES, AND THEIR IMPACTS

## Choosing the Right Strategy

Analyzing past data, understanding your market, and clearly defining campaign goals are essential steps in mitigating risk. For instance, if direct outcomes like conversions are more uncertain, a CPA model might be safer. Conversely, if your goal is broad exposure or branding, a CPC or CPM model, despite its higher inherent risk, might be appropriate.

Here comes again the concept of "Awareness Levels" that I wrote of in Chapter 4. Some bidding strategies are better for some specific targets.

Now that you understand the concept of risks and you have a general understanding of what bids and bidding strategies are, let's compare them in Table 10-2.

CHAPTER 10  UNDERSTANDING BIDS, BID STRATEGIES, AND THEIR IMPACTS

Table 10-2. Detailed comparison of bidding strategies

| Strategy Name | Description | When You Pay | Use Case | Requirements | Other Names | Risk Bearer | Bidding Strategy Type |
|---|---|---|---|---|---|---|---|
| CPC (Cost per Click) | You pay for each click on your ads | Only when someone clicks on your ad | Driving website traffic | No specific requirements | PPC (Pay per Click) in Google Ads; CPC in Facebook Ads; CPC in The Trade Desk | Advertiser | Fixed bidding |
| CPM (Cost per Mille) | You pay for every 1,000 impressions of your ad | Each time your ad reaches 1,000 impressions | Building brand awareness | No specific requirements | CPM in most platforms; impression bidding | Advertiser | Fixed bidding |
| CPA (Cost per Action) | You pay only when a specific action (purchase, sign-up) is completed | When the defined action (purchase, sign-up) is completed by the user | Boosting conversions, like sign-ups or sales | Conversion tracking code | CPA in Google Ads; CPA in Facebook Ads; action bidding in The Trade Desk | Provider | Performance-based bidding |

68

## CHAPTER 10   UNDERSTANDING BIDS, BID STRATEGIES, AND THEIR IMPACTS

| Strategy name | Description | Use case | Requirements | Other names | Risk bearer | Bidding strategy type |
|---|---|---|---|---|---|---|
| CPV (Cost per View) | You pay when someone views your video ad | When your video is watched for a specified duration | Increasing video engagement | No specific requirements | CPV in Google Ads; CPV in Facebook Ads | Advertiser | Fixed bidding |
| CPI (Cost per Install) | You pay each time your app is installed | After the app is downloaded and app installed | Promoting app installations | App tracking code | CPI on most platforms | Advertiser | Performance-based bidding |
| eCPC (Enhanced Cost per Click) | A variation of CPC that adjusts your bid automatically to maximize conversions | Only when someone clicks on your ad, but bids are adjusted for better performance | Optimizing for conversions while still paying per click | Conversion tracking | eCPC in Google Ads | Advertiser | Fixed bidding |
| ROAS (Return on Ad Spend) | You set a target return from your ad spend | When the targeted return is achieved | Maximizing return from ad expenditure | Conversion tracking | ROAS in Google Ads; ROAS targeting | A balance between advertiser and provider | Performance-based bidding |

## Choosing the Right Strategy

Selecting a bid strategy should align with your marketing objectives. For instance, if your goal is brand awareness, CPM might be suitable. Conversely, if you want to drive sales, CPA could provide better returns.

# Detailed Analysis of Bidding Strategies and Risk Allocation

Each bidding strategy carries its unique approach, utility, and associated risk. Let's break down each strategy, understand who bears the risk, and identify the best scenarios for their use.

## Cost per Click (CPC)

CPC is ideal when you aim to drive traffic to a website. It's often used when direct user interaction with your online content is desired, such as reading a blog, exploring products, or filling out a survey. In these cases, you will want to pay special attention to your landing page, so that the user experience allows you to reach the goal you set after getting the visit. It won't help you in any way to get paid visitors to your landing page and then have them wait 10 seconds for it to load, for example.

## CPC Risk Bearing

In the CPC model, the risk is borne by the **advertiser**. You pay each time someone clicks on your ad, regardless of whether these clicks result in a conversion (such as a sale or sign-up).

## Use Case Example

A new blog seeking to build an audience could use CPC to drive interested readers to their latest posts. Since the goal is to increase visibility and engagement, paying for clicks aligns with their immediate objectives.

## Cost per Mille (CPM)

This strategy is best for building brand awareness. It ensures that your ad is seen by a large number of people, which is beneficial in campaigns aimed at gaining visibility rather than immediate conversions. Here, understanding the differences between Page Views and Unique Page Views is relevant. (Check Chapter 24 for more information)

## CPM Risk Bearing

The risk is also on the **advertiser** in the CPM model because you pay per thousand impressions irrespective of user engagement with the ad.

## Use Case Example

A company launching a new product might employ CPM to ensure that a wide audience sees their ads, helping to establish a market presence and inform potential customers about the new product.

## Cost per Action (CPA)

CPA is excellent for campaigns focused on specific conversion goals like sign-ups, downloads, or purchases because it ensures that you only pay when the ad achieves its intended effect.

## CPA Risk Bearing

In a CPA model, the risk shifts toward the **provider**. Payment is dependent on the user completing a specific action, which means the cost is directly linked to the success of the ad in driving conversions. Whether this action helps you achieve your marketing goals depends on how you define and track this action. This also means that the cost of one conversion can be many times more than the cost of a click. A reason for that is that the provider has to pay for the clicks and impressions that did not convert.

## Use Case Example

An e-commerce site wanting to increase sales could use CPA for a campaign promoting a new line of clothing, paying only when purchases are made from their ads.

## Cost per View (CPV)

CPV is suitable for campaigns aiming to increase engagement through video content, such as tutorials, product reviews, or brand storytelling.

## CPV Risk Bearing

The advertiser bears the risk in CPV campaigns because you pay based on video views, regardless of further engagement or action from the viewer.

## Use Case Example

A tech company releasing a new device might use CPV to show a product demonstration video that explains the unique features of the device to potential customers.

CHAPTER 10    UNDERSTANDING BIDS, BID STRATEGIES, AND THEIR IMPACTS

## Cost per Install (CPI)

CPI is ideal for mobile app campaigns where the primary goal is to increase the number of installations.

## CPI Risk Bearing

Risk is borne by the **advertiser** since payment occurs upon installation of an app, not guaranteeing the user's continued engagement or monetization from the app.

## Use Case Example

A mobile gaming company might use CPI to encourage downloads of their new game, aiming to build an initial user base on which to expand further marketing efforts.

## Enhanced Cost per Click (eCPC)

eCPC is beneficial when you want to maintain the simplicity of paying per click while also seeking to improve conversion through automated optimizations.

## eCPC Risk Bearing

Like traditional CPC, the risk is on the **advertiser**. Although this model uses algorithmic adjustments to aim for better conversion rates, payment is still made per click.

## Use Case Example

An online retailer could use eCPC to promote a special sale, with the system optimizing clicks that are more likely to convert into purchases.

## Return on Ad Spend (ROAS)

ROAS measures the amount of revenue your business earns for each dollar spent on advertising. It is a simple metric that helps you understand whether your advertising efforts are effective in generating sales. ROAS is effective when you are focused on maximizing the financial returns from your ad campaigns, ensuring that every dollar spent contributes to a definable revenue goal.

## ROAS Risk Bearing

In ROAS, risk is more balanced between the **advertiser and the provider**, as payment aligns with achieving a specific return on ad spend.

## Use Case Example

A luxury watch brand could use ROAS bidding to ensure that their ads on social media and other platforms produce sufficient sales relative to the amount spent on advertising.

---

**CALCULATING ROAS IN A DIGITAL MARKETING CAMPAIGN**

Even though this book doesn't deep dive into marketing math, understanding how to calculate Return on Ad Spend (ROAS) can give you significant insight into the financial impact of your digital marketing campaigns. Here, I'll outline an easy way to compute ROAS that you can use to quickly assess your campaigns' effectiveness.

CHAPTER 10   UNDERSTANDING BIDS, BID STRATEGIES, AND THEIR IMPACTS

## How to Calculate ROAS

Calculating ROAS is straightforward:

$$ROAS = \left( \frac{Revenue\ from\ Ad\ Campaign}{Cost\ of\ Ad\ Campaign} \right)$$

1. **Determine Revenue:** Start by computing the total revenue generated from the specific ad campaign. This involves tracking all sales that resulted directly from the campaign.

2. **Determine Costs:** Calculate the total amount spent on the ad campaign. Include all related expenses such as ad spend, agency fees, and any other costs incurred in running the ad.

3. **Divide Revenue by Costs:** Divide the total revenue from the ad campaign by the total costs. The resulting figure is the ROAS.

## Example of ROAS Calculation

Imagine your business spent $1,000 on a digital advertising campaign and generated sales worth $5,000. Your ROAS would be:

$$ROAS = \left( \frac{\$5,000}{\$1,000} \right) = 5$$

This means you earned $5 for every $1 you spent on advertising.

## Importance of ROAS

Calculating ROAS provides you with a general picture of how well your advertising dollars are working. A higher ROAS indicates a more profitable campaign. It helps you decide where to allocate your budget and make informed decisions about future marketing strategies.

In summary, understanding and calculating ROAS allows you to measure the effectiveness of your ad campaigns directly related to their cost.

# Exploring Programmatic Buying

Programmatic buying is a significant advancement in digital advertising. It automates the buying and selling of ads and optimizes the bidding process in real time, leveraging data and technology for precision targeting.

## What Programmatic Buying Is Not

It's crucial to understand that while programmatic buying simplifies processes and potentially increases efficiency, it does not guarantee campaign success without strategic input and continuous optimization from the marketer's side.

This means that you, as a marketer, cannot expect a campaign to succeed or to optimize your costs just because it is using programmatic buying. As its name highlights, this is "just" another way to buy.

## Alternatives and Considerations

While programmatic offers many advantages, alternatives like direct buying exist where relationships and predetermined prices can benefit certain campaign strategies, especially where specific placements and target audiences are concerned. It is also important to note that there are many players still implementing or testing programmatic features and in some cases, such as in those where there are many fragmented players and traditional media.

## Cons of Programmatic Buying

Challenges include potential issues with transparency, ad fraud, and less control over where ads appear. Ensuring a robust strategy and using trusted platforms can mitigate these risks.

# Summary

This chapter has equipped you with an understanding of how bids work in digital marketing, the impact of different bid strategies, and an introduction to programmatic buying. Key points include

- **Bids Defined**: Bidding in digital marketing is like participating in an auction, where you set a price to display your advertisements. The amount you decide to bid directly affects whether your ad will be displayed to your target audience, but it does not determine if you win the auction nor that you reach your goals. The Bid is just one more variable to consider.

- **Understanding Bid Strategies**: The strategy you choose decides how you pay. Whether it's per click, per thousand impressions, or per action, each has its own benefits and fits different marketing goals. Knowing the differences helps in aligning your budget with your objectives effectively.

- **Risk Factors**: Each bidding strategy comes with its own risk. Fixed bidding strategies like CPC and CPM place most of the risk on you, the advertiser, as you pay regardless of conversion success. Performance-based strategies like CPA shift some of the risk to the provider, as you pay only when a specific action is completed.

- **Programmatic Buying**: This is an advanced way of purchasing ad placements using automated technology. While it increases efficiency, it requires careful management and understanding to truly benefit from its capabilities. It does not replace the need for strategic insight.

- **Practical Application**: In choosing the right bidding strategy, consider what you aim to achieve. For direct interactions like clicks or specific actions like sign-ups, strategies that allow you to pay for those specific outcomes might be more beneficial.

In the next chapter, I will explain the concept of ad quality, why it is important from both an advertiser channel provider's perspective and for you as an advertiser. I will discuss what influences ad quality and the consequences of having good or bad ad quality. Additionally, I will explain what the ad quality score and ad quality ranking entail, what ad relevance means, and how it relates to creatives, messages, and copy.

# CHAPTER 11

# Exploring Ad Quality from Multiple Perspectives

In this chapter, I will help you understand the ad quality and its impact on the success of your digital marketing campaigns. You will explore what constitutes ad quality, why it's so important, and how it directly affects user experience from the creativity of the ad to the structure of the landing page. I will also examine some practical examples and discuss the potential risks associated with low ad quality.

I will explore the many aspects of ad quality within digital marketing from three key perspectives: the potential customer, the ad provider, and the advertiser. Each viewpoint offers unique insights into how ad quality impacts the overall effectiveness of digital marketing campaigns. By understanding these perspectives, you can enhance your strategies for better engagement and results. I will explore what constitutes ad quality, why it's so important, and how it directly affects user experience from the creativity of the ad to the structure of the landing page point of view. I'll also examine some practical examples and discuss the potential risks associated with low ad quality.

CHAPTER 11   EXPLORING AD QUALITY FROM MULTIPLE PERSPECTIVES

# Defining Ad Quality

Ad quality refers to how effective and relevant your advertisement is in engaging and resonating with the intended audience. It includes several factors such as clarity of the message, visual appeal, alignment with the audience's preferences, and adherence to advertising guidelines.

## High-Quality Ads

These ads grab the audience's attention effectively, convey the message clearly, and drive the desired actions like clicks, conversions, or enhancing brand awareness. The quality continues even after the click; it ensures the landing page maintains the audience's engagement by being relevant and informative, providing a continuous user experience flow from the ad to the landing page. To do so, the message and content of the ad should be related to the content of the landing page the user reaches after clicking the ad. It should consider the context in which the ad was shown, taking into account who clicked it and why.

## Low-Quality Ads

On the other hand, if ads are irrelevant, misleading, or poorly designed, they lead to negative user experiences and diminish the campaign's performance. A poor-quality or irrelevant landing page further deteriorates user experience.

## Ad Quality Tracking

Ad quality is monitored by advertising channel providers using various metrics and is crucial in determining the ad's visibility and auction dynamics. Non-compliance with quality standards on landing pages can lead to ad rejection or even account suspension.

> **Note** Most of the advertising channel providers check the landing page when the ads are created, checking for accessibility, policy compliance, and other factors. If the landing page does not comply, the ad will be rejected, and in the worst cases, the ad account will be blocked.

## The Customer's View on Ad Quality

From a potential customer's perspective, the quality of an ad significantly affects their engagement and perception of the brand.

Experience factors influencing customers include

- **Relevance**: The ad should speak directly to the customer's desires or needs. If the user was looking for a new smartphone, he should not see an ad for a new car.

- **Clarity and Appeal**: Ads must be clear in their messaging and visually appealing to capture attention. You should clearly communicate what the user will get by clicking your ad, for example, a discount, more information on a new device, or something similar. A user does not want to click an ad expecting one thing and getting something entirely different.

- **Engagement**: High-quality ads prompt customers to engage further, leading them to a landing page that should ideally mirror the expectancy created by the ad.

**Practical Example for Customers:** Consider an online retailer promoting winter apparel. A high-quality ad would feature appealing images of winter scenes and clothing, clear information on discounts, and direct customers to a landing page with a seamless shopping experience. This cohesive journey significantly raises the chance of purchase.

## The Ad Provider's View on Ad Quality

Ad providers, such as Google or Facebook, use ad quality as a criterion to determine which ads get displayed and how they are ranked during auctions.

Ad provider's ad quality role includes

- **Auction Influence**: Ad quality affects the ad's position in auction systems by influencing its ad rank. Higher quality usually results in better ad positioning and potentially lower costs.

- **Quality Assessment**: Providers evaluate ads based on several dimensions including relevance to the search query, user engagement metrics, and the quality of the landing page. For example, the advertiser channel provider *saves* the interactions of the user and your landing page (when possible and correctly configured) and uses that data in future auctions.

## Provider's Practical Insights

For ad providers, maintaining a high standard of ad quality ensures user satisfaction and trust in the platform. For instance, Google assesses ads on factors ranging from landing page experience to *expected* click-through rates to maintain these standards.

## The Advertiser's View on Ad Quality

For advertisers, ad quality is critical in determining the success of their marketing efforts.

Advertiser's priorities include

- **Effective Message Delivery**: Ensuring the ad communicates the intended message in a clear and engaging manner. This way, the ad will engage the right potential customers who are willing to buy, engage, or take the action you need to reach your marketing goals.

- **Conversion Optimization**: High-quality ads with well-aligned landing pages increase the probability of conversions.

- **Cost Efficiency**: Better ad quality often leads to more cost-effective campaigns, as higher-quality scores can lower CPC rates.

## Advertiser's Example Scenario

A software company launches an ad campaign for a new product. The ad features engaging content and directs users to a user-friendly landing page, enhancing the likelihood of subscriptions. Effective alignment and high ad quality lead to increased conversions and reduced acquisition costs.

## Exploring Ad Quality Score and Ad Quality Ranking

In this section, you and I will dive deeper into the components of ad quality within digital marketing, specifically ad quality score and ad quality ranking. These concepts will help you understand how your ads perform within the ecosystem of digital advertising providers like Google Ads and Facebook Ads.

CHAPTER 11   EXPLORING AD QUALITY FROM MULTIPLE PERSPECTIVES

# Ad Quality Score: What It Is and Why It Matters

The ad quality score is a metric used by advertising platforms to assess the relevance and quality of your ad based on several factors. Here, I will explore what those factors are and how they influence your digital marketing efforts.

## Ad Quality Score Explanation

The ad quality score is primarily influenced by three main components, which include the *expected* click-through rate (CTR), ad relevance, and landing page experience. Each component is rated, typically on a scale from 1 to 10, with a higher score indicating better performance.

- **Expected Click-Through Rate (CTR)**: This predicts how likely it is that your ad will be clicked when shown.

- **Ad Relevance**: This measures how closely your ad matches the intent behind a user's search.

- **Landing Page Experience**: This assesses how relevant and useful your landing page is to people who click your ad.

## Practical Example

If you're advertising a new coffee shop, your ad quality would be high if your ad text clearly mentions "new coffee shop," the keyword matches these terms, and your landing page offers all the necessary information about the coffee shop's location, menu, and hours in an easily navigable format. Should you target mobile devices, then your landing page should also provide a mobile version or be responsive to allow the user to navigate it from its mobile device.

## Effects of Ad Quality Score

A higher-quality score generally leads to better ad placements and lower costs per click. This is because platforms like Google prioritize user experience; they want to ensure the ads displayed are useful and relevant.

The ad quality score is not always available in all platforms. Sometimes you should contact their support (as it's the case with Google Ads) to know if your score is high or low.

# Ad Quality Ranking: Determining Visibility and Auction Outcomes

Ad quality ranking plays an important role in determining where and how often your ads are shown in response to queries. It is closely tied to the ad auction process.

## Ad Quality Ranking Explained

When your ad competes in an auction to be shown, ad providers calculate its ad rank based on your bid amount and the quality score. The better your ad quality, the better its placement for a given bid. In the case of equal bids, the ad with a better ad quality ranking will win the auction.

- **Your Bid**: How much you're willing to pay per click.

- **Quality Score**: The combined value of your ad's expected CTR, relevance, and landing page experience.

- **Auction-Time Ad Quality**: Occasionally, other factors like the user's device, location, and time of day can affect ad quality assessments during the auction.

CHAPTER 11   EXPLORING AD QUALITY FROM MULTIPLE PERSPECTIVES

## Ad Rank and Its Consequences

This ranking affects not just whether your ad is shown, but also its positioning on the page, which directly impacts visibility and click-through rates.

## Breaking Down Ad Relevance

Ad relevance refers to how closely your ad aligns with the interests and intent of the target audience. This alignment directly affects how positively the audience perceives your ad, which in turn influences click-through rates and overall campaign effectiveness.

- **Copy Consistency**: The ad copy should accurately reflect the product or service being offered, without misleading the viewer.
- **Keyword Alignment**: The keywords chosen for the ad must match the terms your target audience is using in their searches.
- **Contextual Matching**: The ad should fit the context in which the user is operating. For example, an ad for sports equipment popping up in sports-related content is more relevant than the same ad appearing amid unrelated news articles.

## Enhancing Landing Page Quality

The landing page is where your potential customers arrive after clicking on your ad. The quality of this page profoundly influences the likelihood of conversion from visitor to customer.

CHAPTER 11   EXPLORING AD QUALITY FROM MULTIPLE PERSPECTIVES

- **Page Content and Ad Message Alignment**: Ensure that the landing page delivers what the ad promises. If your ad speaks about a discount offer, the landing page should immediately reflect this offer clearly.

- **User Experience Design**: The design of the page should facilitate an easy and enjoyable experience for users. This includes mobile responsiveness, fast loading times, and intuitive navigation.

- **Credibility and Transparency**: Elements such as customer testimonials, clear contact information, and easy access to policies like returns and privacy should be included to build trust.

## Practical Example

Imagine an ad campaign for a new series of cooking classes. The ad, featuring engaging images of a cooking session and an enticing call-to-action, directs users to a landing page. This page should then provide comprehensive class details (aligned with the ad), show testimonials from past participants, and offer an easy registration process. The harmony between the ad and the landing page enhances user experience and increases the likelihood of registration.

## Diagrammatic Representation of Factors Influencing Ad Quality and Ad Position

Figure 11-1 shows how all of these plays together.

# CHAPTER 11    EXPLORING AD QUALITY FROM MULTIPLE PERSPECTIVES

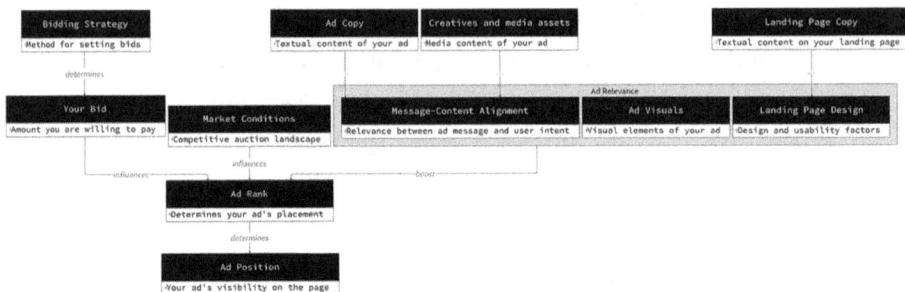

*Figure 11-1. Ad Rank and Quality Score Components in Digital Advertising*

This diagram outlines how each element influences the other ones and how all of them influence your ad position.

Let's simplify and connect how each part influences your ad's journey from creation to viewer interaction:

Firstly, the **Bidding Strategy** you choose directly determines how much you are prepared to spend on your campaign and how your budget should be spend. It's like setting a budget for an auction, where your strategy dictates the ceiling amount you're willing to reach.

Moving down the chain, your **Bid** along with the **Market Conditions and the Ad Relevance** play critical roles. Your bid is what you agree to pay, but the market conditions, which include the competitive landscape, influence how far your money will go. These factors come together to affect your **Ad Rank**, which is essentially a measure of where your ad gets placed. Higher ranks generally mean better visibility.

Now, diving into the creation of the ad itself, the **Ad Copy** and **Media Assets** are crucial. These need to not only grab attention, but also be relevant to the specific context of your target audience's interests or search intents. This relevance helps in crafting the **Ad Message** and **Ad Visuals**, ensuring that what the audience sees is both engaging and aligned with their expectations or needs.

Additionally, after the viewer clicks on your ad, the **Landing Page** comes into play. This page needs to be a seamless continuation of the persuasion and engagement journey. It should not only match the ad in terms of message and style but also be user-friendly, encouraging further interaction, such as making a purchase, signing up for more information, or another marketing goal.

All these elements—how much you bid, the appeal and relevance of your ad copy and visuals, and the user-friendliness of your landing page—combine to enhance your **Ad Rank**. A better rank improves your ad's chances of being seen and acted upon by the right people at the right time.

In essence, each component from your bidding strategy to your landing page quality works in concert to ensure your ad not only appears before eyes but engages minds and encourages actions. By understanding and optimizing each element, you enhance your campaign's potential for success.

# Summary

In this chapter, I covered the different layers of ad quality:

- **Ad quality score** is a diagnostic tool provided by some platforms to help you optimize ad relevance and user experience.

- **Ad quality ranking** impacts the visibility of your ads and depends both on your ad's quality and your bid.

- Understanding both is key to managing an effective and cost-efficient digital marketing campaign, but understanding **ad quality** in general helps you craft a great campaign that reaches your marketing goals.

CHAPTER 12

# Understanding Digital Marketing Metrics

This chapter focuses on the most commonly used digital marketing metrics such as CPC, CPV, CPM, clicks, and CTR. I explore these metrics to give you an understanding of their role in digital campaigns and draw comparisons with traditional print advertising to highlight their unique benefits.

## Understanding Key Digital Marketing Metrics

Before diving into comparisons with traditional media, let's clarify these fundamental digital metrics that I've used in previous chapters and that you might have previously encountered in reports and campaign results.

What are CPC, CPV, CPM, Clicks, and CTR? We can divide these metrics in two categories: cost definitions and click metrics.

### Cost per Click (CPC)

CPC indicates the price you pay each time someone clicks on your ad. CPC is fundamental in managing your digital advertising campaign's budget efficiently.

## Importance of CPC

I highlight CPC's importance as it directly affects how effectively you can control your advertising spend. Monitoring CPC is a way to assess financial efficiency and to optimize the overall impact of your campaigns.

If you're overseeing a campaign, knowing the CPC will help you determine how much you're spending to engage potential customers, which is fundamental in measuring the return on your investment. Monitoring it also helps you discover unusual situations, such as Thumb-Clicks or Seasonal Trends.

## CPC Mechanics

In CPC bidding, typically available on platforms like Google Ads, you set a maximum price you are willing to pay for each click. The actual CPC may vary based on the level of competition for ad space and the relevance and quality of your ad (check Chapter 11 on Ad Quality for more details). Well-crafted, highly relevant ads can attract more clicks at a lower cost.

## Relevance to Bidding Strategies

CPC helps for managing budgets in cost-focused bidding strategies. Whether you are manually setting bid limits or using automated systems to adjust bids, CPC provides a measurable value that influences decision-making.

## Other Relevant Concepts

CPC is closely linked to the effectiveness of your ads and how well you target your intended audience. A more precise target that resonates well with your audience can lead to lower CPC costs due to higher click-through rates.

## Impact of High-Competition Keywords

Dealing with high CPC due to competitive keywords involves strategic choices. You must decide whether the high cost is justified by the potential to reach a valuable audience. If essential for reaching your marketing goals, such targeting should be considered a strategic investment. In these cases, you, as the campaign manager or campaign overseer, must make a strategic decision. You can either choose to avoid these high-cost keywords to keep your overall expenses down, or continue to target them because they are crucial for your campaign's success. As long as this decision is made consciously, understanding the potential impact on your budget and campaign outcomes, it is a valid approach.

A good partner should offer to analyze keywords when they are working on the targeting, and you should also get a report stating the costs of the most important keywords at the time of the analysis. Some partners also include a brief trend analysis for you to understand seasonal situations. With that information, you can discuss with your partner if a specific keyword is important or not and if it should be included regardless of costs.

## CPC Practical Example

Imagine you're running an ad for a book release. If your CPC is $0.50 and you receive 200 clicks, your total expenditure would be $100. This helps you when evaluating how much you are investing to attract readers and for you to decide if it is worth it to pay that much per click.

Now, let's say you're advertising a new coffee shop. If your CPC is $0.20 and you receive 100 clicks, your total cost would be $20. But let's say you are running your campaign on the International Coffee Day (October 1) or on Mother's Day when users usually look for coffee shops. In those cases, specific keywords will have a higher-than-normal costs.

## Improving Your CPC

To reduce your CPC, enhance your ad's relevance and appeal to increase your click-through rate, thereby potentially lowering costs. Improving targeting to focus on an audience more likely to engage can also reduce wasted clicks and making sure the keywords you are including or excluding match your expected results. Discussing optimization strategies with a digital marketing expert or your service partner can lead to more cost-effective ad placements.

## Cost per View (CPV)

CPV measures the price you pay when someone views your video ad. In video advertising, CPV is essential for managing and understanding campaign costs effectively.

### Importance of CPV

I emphasize CPV's importance as it directly impacts the cost-effectiveness of video campaigns. Monitoring CPV helps control expenses while gauging audience engagement through video views. The CPV also depends on the platform and video ad type, as there are some formats where the user can ignore the ad and others where the user has to see the complete video before continuing with what they were doing.

### CPV Mechanics

In CPV bidding, typical on platforms like YouTube, you can specify the maximum price you're willing to pay per view. A view generally counts when a viewer watches your video for at least 30 seconds or interacts with it.[1] Factors like quality score and ad rank competition influence CPV.

---

[1] https://support.google.com/google-ads/answer/2472735?hl=en

## CPV in Bidding Strategies

CPV suits video campaigns prioritizing viewer engagement, useful for boosting brand awareness or showcasing new products. It aligns well with strategies valuing visual impact over immediate sales conversions (awareness driven instead of conversion driven).

## Connections to Other Concepts

Viewer engagement and video content quality are closely linked to CPV. Platforms often lower CPV for engaging videos that retain viewers longer, enhancing user experience on their sites.

## Handling High CPV Rates

High CPV rates often result from targeting competitive keywords or sought-after audience segments. Deciding whether to target these despite higher costs involves weighing potential engagement against the expense. If crucial for your campaign, such targeting should be seen as an investment in your brand. This is similar to what I wrote about CPC above.

## Practical CPV Example

Consider a video ad for a new smartphone with a CPV of $0.10. If the ad receives 1,000 views, the cost totals $100.

## Reducing CPV

Enhancing video quality can increase engagement, potentially reducing CPV. Refer to the Chapter 11 on Ad Quality for more details on how to improve it. Consult a digital marketing expert or your service partner for strategies tailored to optimize your video ads.

CHAPTER 12   UNDERSTANDING DIGITAL MARKETING METRICS

# Clicks

Clicks in digital marketing represent the act of a user pressing a mouse button on a digital ad. Each click measures user interaction with online advertising content.

## Importance of Clicks

I emphasize the importance of clicks as they directly indicate interest and engagement from potential customers. Tracking clicks helps assess the effectiveness of your digital ads and guides optimization efforts.

## Mechanics of Clicks

When you run digital ads, platforms like Google Ads or social media sites record each click. This data provides insights into how compelling your ad is to your target audience. Effective ads encourage more clicks, suggesting higher engagement and interest. If your ad is not generating any clicks, it could mean that your ad is not interesting or engaging enough or that you are targeting the wrong target group. If your ad is neither getting any clicks nor so many impressions, then it means you are not winning enough auctions, and you should review your biding strategy, targeting, and ad quality.

## Connection to Other Metrics

Clicks are closely linked to other key performance indicators such as click-through rate (CTR) and conversion rate. CTR compares clicks to impressions, showing the percentage of viewers who click on your ad. Conversion rate measures how many clicks lead to desired actions, like purchases or sign-ups. Refer to Chapter 10 on Bidding Strategies for more details on conversions.

## Impact of User Interaction

User interaction through clicks can significantly affect the perceived success of an ad campaign. High numbers of clicks often correlate with effective ad placement and targeting, while low clicks might suggest a need for ad revision or better targeting.

## Practical Example of Click Analysis

Suppose your campaign for a new coffee maker generates 1,000 clicks from an ad viewed 10,000 times. Analyzing these clicks, particularly looking at subsequent conversions, helps you understand how effectively the ad attracts and engages potential buyers. It is important to note that clicks alone won't help you analyze results. Once the user clicks your ad, they will land on your website. Even if your ad is great and gets many clicks, it won't help you if your landing page is not engaging with the users. Refer to the Chapter 23 on Landing Pages for more details on this.

## Enhancing Click Performance

To improve the performance of your ads in terms of clicks, focus on crafting compelling ad copy and visually appealing designs. Also, refine targeting to ensure your ads reach individuals more likely to be interested in what you are offering. Using what I discussed in Chapter 4 on Awareness Levels will help you here. Collaborating with a digital marketing expert can provide additional strategies to increase clicks and overall ad effectiveness.

# Click-Through Rate (CTR)

CTR quantifies the percentage of people who click on your ad after seeing it. It serves as a key metric in digital marketing to measure the immediate response of your audience to your ads and helps you understand if the persons seeing your ad are truly interested in it enough to click for more information.

> **Note** If you are not measuring success by user interaction, then this metric is irrelevant for you. Such is the case for awareness campaigns in most of the cases.

## Importance of CTR

I emphasize CTR's importance as it directly reflects the effectiveness of your ad copy and design in capturing the audience's attention. A higher CTR indicates that your ad is relevant and appealing to viewers (meaning your creative is appealing, your copy is engaging, and your targeting is most likely correct), which is crucial for driving traffic and achieving campaign goals.

## How CTR Works

CTR is calculated by dividing the number of clicks your ad receives by the number of times your ad is shown (impressions), multiplied by 100 to express the result as a percentage. This formula makes CTR a straightforward indicator of how well your ad engages users.

$$\text{CTR Calculation}$$
$$\text{CTR} = \frac{\text{clicks}}{\text{impressions}} \times 100\%$$

## CTR in Campaign Optimization

CTR helps in evaluating which ads resonate best with your target audience and which ones may need improvement. A higher CTR means usually that an ad is more relevant than an ad with a lower CTR, when all the other settings remain the same.

## Relation to Other Marketing Metrics

CTR is often analyzed with other metrics such as conversion rate and cost-per-click (CPC). While CTR measures initial engagement, conversion rate assesses the effectiveness of the ad in prompting users to complete a desired action, such as making a purchase or signing up for a newsletter. Remember that conversion metrics require tracking of conversion actions.

## Impact of CTR on Digital Marketing

High CTR can enhance campaign performance by increasing the likelihood of more conversions and achieving better ad placements without increasing ad spend. Advertiser channel providers such as Google Ads will prioritize ads with high CTR as it usually means good user experience. Conversely, a low CTR might indicate that your ads are not effectively tailored to the audience or that the ad placement is not optimal.

## Practical Example of CTR

Imagine you run two ads for a new book release. Ad 1 is shown 20,000 times and receives 200 clicks. Your CTR would be 1%, calculated as (200 clicks / 20,000 impressions) * 100. Ad 2 is shown 10,000 times and receives 400 clicks. Your CTR would be 4%, calculated as (400 clicks / 10,000 impressions) * 100. From this, you can say that Ad 2 is a better ad for your campaign, as it is getting more users to click your ad (ceteris paribus).

Figure 12-1 shows the thought process on how to understand this simplified example. You will note that you have to consider all the relevant metrics, in this case the relation of clicks and impressions. More impressions are not always better.

CHAPTER 12   UNDERSTANDING DIGITAL MARKETING METRICS

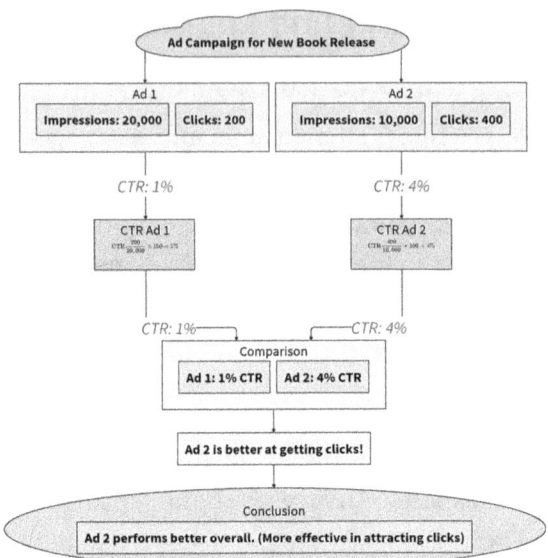

*Figure 12-1.* *Comparative analysis of CTR for two book release ads*

## Improving Your CTR

To enhance your CTR, focus on refining ad relevance through good targeting and compelling ad creatives. Testing different versions of your ads (A/B testing) can also help identify the most effective elements. Consulting with a digital marketing expert can provide insights into advanced strategies to further boost your CTR and overall ad performance.

## Impressions

Impressions measure the number of times an ad is displayed, regardless of whether it was clicked or not. This metric helps you understand the reach of your digital advertising campaigns and if you are winning enough auctions.

## Importance of Impressions

Impressions indicate how often your ad is visible to users. This visibility is fundamental for building brand awareness and ensuring your message reaches a wide audience. Depending on your campaign goal, its importance might vary. For awareness campaigns, impressions are an important metric, as they explain the reach of your campaign. For a conversion campaign, conversion rate, CTR, and clicks are more important.

## How Impressions Work

Impressions are counted each time your ad appears on a user's screen. This count includes multiple appearances to the same user, which is useful for assessing the frequency of ad exposure within your target market. This frequency, on platforms such as Facebook Ads, tells you whether your target groups are appropriate or too small.

## Connection to Other Metrics

Impressions are often analyzed alongside click-through rate (CTR) and reach. While impressions count how often an ad is displayed, reach indicates the number of unique users who see your ad. Comparing impressions with CTR provides insights into ad effectiveness in engaging viewers.

## Impact of Impressions on Campaigns

High numbers of impressions can increase brand awareness and contribute to a campaign's success by saturating the market with your message. However, focusing solely on impressions without considering engagement and conversion may lead to inefficient spending, depending on your campaign goal. Refer to Chapter 27 for Marketing Goals.

## Practical Example of Tracking Impressions

Suppose your campaign for an upcoming event generates 500,000 impressions. This number reflects the extensive visibility of your ad, crucial for driving interest and attendance, but not enough to know if the viewers have a real interest. If I compare impressions with Print Brochure Delivery, impressions are how many persons had the brochure in their hands, but not how many read it.

## Optimizing Impressions

To optimize impressions, ensure your ads are well-placed within high-traffic channels and are targeted effectively to match audience preferences. Enhancing ad quality can also improve visibility and performance. Regularly reviewing ad placement and audience targeting strategies with a digital marketing expert can lead to more effective use of impressions in your campaigns.

# Conversion Rate

Conversion rate measures the percentage of users who take a desired action after interacting with your ad. This could be making a purchase, signing up for a newsletter, or completing a registration form.

## Importance of Conversion Rate

I emphasize the importance of conversion rate as it directly reflects the success of your advertisements in converting viewers into customers or leads. A high conversion rate indicates that your marketing efforts are effective and aligned with user expectations and needs. It is important to remember that a big part of the conversion depends on the user experience and user journey on your landing page. Refer to Chapter 13 on User Journey for more information.

## How Conversion Rate Works

The conversion rate is calculated by dividing the number of conversions by the total number of interactions, such as clicks, and then multiplying by 100 to get a percentage. This calculation helps you understand how well your ad is performing in terms of prompting user actions.

Conversion Rate Calculation

$$\text{Conversion Rate} = \frac{\text{conversions}}{\text{clicks}} \times 100\%$$

## Connection to Other Metrics

Conversion rate is closely tied to other performance metrics like clicks, impressions, and CTR. While clicks and impressions measure user interaction and exposure, conversion rate focuses on the outcome of those interactions.

## Impact of Conversion Rate on Digital Campaigns

A high conversion rate enhances the overall return on investment for campaigns, as it means more users are completing the desired actions. Conversely, a low conversion rate might indicate issues with ad relevance, targeting accuracy, or the user experience on the landing page.

If your desired action is not correctly defined, then it does not really matter how good your conversion rate is.

## Practical Example of Conversion Rate

Imagine your online ad campaign for a new product received 1,000 clicks, and 50 users ended up making a purchase. The conversion rate would be 5%, calculated as (50 conversions / 1,000 clicks) * 100.

## Improving Your Conversion Rate

To improve your conversion rate, focus on optimizing the landing page to ensure it is persuasive and user-friendly. Additionally, refining ad copy and visuals to increase relevance and appeal can lead to better user engagement and higher conversions. Discussing these strategies with a digital marketing expert can provide more in-depth insights into effectively boosting your conversion rate. Refer to Chapter 23 for more details on Landing Pages and Chapter 11 for more information on Ad Quality.

# Reach

Reach refers to the **total number of unique users** who see your advertisement. It measures the extent of audience exposure to your message, playing an important role in increasing brand awareness and campaign visibility. If differs from Impressions in that it measures unique users and not just impressions.

## Importance of Reach

Knowing the reach of your campaigns helps you understand how widely your message is being seen, which is an important metric for brand penetration and awareness.

## How Reach Works

Reach is calculated by counting the unique viewers of an ad over a specified period. Unlike impressions, which can count multiple views by the same user, reach only counts each user once, providing a clear picture of how many **distinct people** your campaign has touched.

## Connection to Other Metrics

Reach is often analyzed alongside frequency, which measures how many times, on average, a single user sees your ad. Together, these metrics can tell you not only how many people you are reaching, but also how often they are seeing your message and if your target group's size is big enough.

## Practical Example of Measuring Reach

Suppose your campaign for a new fitness app is displayed on various social media platforms and is seen by 100,000 unique users. This number signifies your campaign's reach, reflecting its potential to attract a large audience.

## Enhancing Your Reach

To enhance your reach, consider diversifying your ad placements across multiple platforms and using specific targeting to include broader demographics. Also, in the case of social media, engaging content that encourages shares can organically expand your reach. Regularly consulting a digital marketing expert can provide you with strategies to further extend your reach and optimize your advertising efforts. Check Chapter 43 for an Overview of Social Media.

# Frequency

Frequency in digital marketing refers to the average number of times a single user views your advertisement during a specific period. It quantifies how often your ads are shown to individuals, highlighting the intensity of your campaign's exposure.

## Importance of Frequency

The importance of frequency falls in establishing brand recall and reinforcing your message. A higher frequency ensures that your advertisement stays top of mind with your audience, which can be critical for campaigns aiming to influence behavior or decision-making, but a value that is too high might tell you that your target group (and your campaign reach) is too small. This is usually an important metric when using specific targeting criteria together with geographic restrictions.

## How Frequency Works

Frequency is calculated by dividing the total number of ad impressions by the reach of the campaign. This metric provides insight into how repeatedly a viewer is exposed to the same advertisement, which is relevant for measuring the potential impact of the ad on viewer behavior. The frequency is calculated by dividing the impressions by the reach.

$$\text{Frequency Calculation}$$
$$\text{Frequency} = \frac{\text{impressions}}{\text{reach}}$$

## Frequency in Marketing Strategies

Optimal frequency can vary based on campaign goals. For awareness campaigns, a higher frequency might be beneficial to ensure the message stays in the audience's memory. For conversion-driven campaigns, however, too high a frequency might lead to ad fatigue, reducing its effectiveness.

## Connection to Other Metrics

Frequency closely interacts with reach to determine an ad's overall effectiveness. While reach measures the breadth of an audience, frequency measures depth of exposure among that audience.

## Impact of Frequency on Campaigns

Managing frequency carefully is vital as it can affect both engagement and audience perception. Appropriate frequency can enhance engagement and recall, while excessive frequency can annoy users and potentially harm brand perception.

## Practical Example of Frequency

Imagine a scenario where your video ad campaign received 1,000,000 impressions and reached 200,000 unique users. The frequency of your campaign would be 5, indicating that, *on average*, each user saw your ad five times.

## Managing Your Frequency

To manage your frequency effectively, you can use *frequency capping*, a feature available in some advertiser channel providers that limits the number of times your ads are shown to the same person, to prevent overexposure. Also, varying your ad creatives can keep the content fresh and maintain user interest. Regular review and adjustments based on performance data and user feedback are recommended to find the ideal frequency for your campaigns.

# Share of Impressions

Share of impressions, also known as impression share, is a metric that indicates the percentage of impressions your ads receive compared to the total number of impressions that your ads could potentially receive. This metric helps assess the visibility and presence of your ads within the eligible market.

## Importance of Share of Impressions

Share of impressions directly reflects the competitiveness and effectiveness of your ad campaigns. Understanding this metric allows you to gauge how well your ads are performing against potential market opportunities and competitor activities.

## How Share of Impressions Works

Share of impressions is calculated by dividing the number of impressions your ad receives by the total number of impressions it was eligible to receive, then multiplying by 100 to get a percentage. This eligibility is determined by your current ad settings, including targeting and bid strategies.

$$\text{Impression Share Calculation}$$
$$\text{Impression Share} = \frac{\text{impressions}}{\text{eligible impressions}} \times 100\%$$

## Role of Share of Impressions in Marketing Campaigns

This metric helps you evaluate the adequacy of your ad exposure and identify potential missed opportunities. If your share of impressions is low, it may indicate that your ads could reach more people if adjustments were made to bids, budgets, or targeting.

## Connection to Other Metrics

Share of impressions is often analyzed with other performance metrics such as click-through rate (CTR) and conversion rate.

## Impact of Share of Impressions on Campaign Effectiveness

A high share of impressions suggests that your ads are capturing a large portion of the available market, which can lead to increased brand awareness and higher campaign effectiveness. Conversely, a low share might signal the need for strategic adjustments to enhance visibility and competitiveness.

## Practical Example of Share of Impressions

Suppose your digital ad campaign for a new product launch receives 500,000 impressions, and the total number of impressions available in the market is 1,000,000. The share of impressions for your campaign would be 50%, calculated as (500,000 / 1,000,000) * 100.

Thus, your campaign has captured 50% of the available impressions in the market for this product category. This indicates that half of the total potential audience saw your ad, which can be a significant metric in evaluating the reach and effectiveness of your campaign.

## Optimizing Your Share of Impressions

To optimize your share of impressions, consider increasing your ad budget or adjusting your bid strategies to compete more effectively for available impressions. Additionally, refining your targeting criteria can help ensure your ads are reaching the most relevant audience, potentially increasing your share. Regular monitoring and strategic adjustments based on campaign data and market conditions are essential for maintaining an optimal share of impressions.

## Cost per Mille (CPM)

CPM measures the cost of 1,000 ad impressions. It is a standard metric used to price advertising space within digital marketing, emphasizing the cost-efficiency of ad reach.

## Importance of CPM

CPM allows you to evaluate how much you are paying to expose your ad to a thousand viewers. Understanding CPM is important for budgeting in advertising campaigns, particularly when brand awareness is a primary goal, and it is also a metric used in traditional media, allowing you to compare results and costs.

### How CPM Works

CPM is calculated by dividing the total cost of an advertising campaign by the number of impressions generated, then multiplying by 1,000. This metric provides a clear indication of the cost-effectiveness of reaching a broad audience.

$$\text{CPM Calculation}$$
$$\text{CPM} = \frac{\text{Total Costs}}{\text{Impressions}} \times 1000$$

## CPM in Advertising Strategies

CPM is commonly used in campaigns aimed at boosting brand visibility rather than immediate conversions. It is especially relevant when you need to ensure widespread exposure of your advertising message across various platforms, and you need one metric to compare their results.

## Connection to Other Metrics

CPM interacts with other key performance indicators such as impressions and reach. While CPM focuses on the cost of impressions, understanding both the total number of impressions and the unique reach are essential for assessing the overall impact and efficiency of your advertising spend.

## Impact of CPM on Campaigns

A lower CPM means you are paying less for a thousand impressions, which can help maximize the reach of a limited advertising budget. Conversely, a higher CPM might indicate more targeted or competitive ad placements, necessitating careful planning to balance costs with the potential for greater engagement.

## Practical Example of CPM

Imagine you launch an ad campaign with a budget of $500, and it generates 100,000 impressions. The calculation for this CPM is shown in Figure 12-2.

$$\text{CPM Calculation}$$
$$\frac{\$500}{100{,}000} \times 1{,}000 = \$5$$

*Figure 12-2. CPM calculation for a practical example*

Thus, the CPM for your campaign is $5. This means that you are spending $5 for every 1,000 impressions your ad receives.

CHAPTER 12   UNDERSTANDING DIGITAL MARKETING METRICS

## Managing Your CPM

To manage your CPM effectively, consider optimizing your ad targeting to reduce wasted impressions and focus more precisely on your intended audience. Additionally, experimenting with different ad formats and placements can also influence your CPM and improve the cost-effectiveness of your campaigns. Regular analysis and adjustments based on performance data are recommended to ensure you are achieving the desired balance between cost and exposure.

# Comparing Digital and Traditional Marketing

While digital marketing metrics provide immediate and actionable data, traditional print advertising presents challenges in measuring direct impact.

**Print Advertising:** The effectiveness of print ads is often measured through indirect methods such as changes in sales following a campaign or through surveys, which lack the immediacy and precision of digital metrics.

## Integrating Digital Tracking in Print

To bridge the gap between digital and print advertising, consider integrating digital tracking elements within your print ads:

> **UTM Parameters:** Include URLs with UTM parameters to track how much traffic is driven to your website from the print ad. For this, consider the use of URL Shorteners.

**QR Codes:** Adding a QR code to your print ads can provide a direct link to digital content or offers, making it easy for readers to engage further online.

## Summary

In this chapter, I explained some of the most important metrics in digital marketing, such as CPC, CPV, CPM, clicks, and CTR. These metrics revolutionize how marketing success is measured and optimized, offering advantages that are not typically available with traditional print advertising:

- **Detailed Metrics:** Digital marketing provides a granular view of campaign performance.

- **Immediate Adjustments:** The real-time data allows for quick modifications to enhance campaign results.

- **Comprehensive Understanding:** Integrating digital tracking into traditional methods can enrich overall marketing strategies.

In the next chapter, I will explain what a customer journey is, why it is important, and how understanding it can help you with your digital marketing campaigns.

# CHAPTER 13

# Understanding the Customer/Buyer Journey

In this chapter, I will explore the concept of Customer/Buyer Journey in digital marketing. This journey outlines the stages a customer goes through when interacting with a business, from the initial awareness all the way through to the purchase, and potentially post-purchase interactions. It is essential for marketers, like you and me, to understand this process as it helps in crafting targeted marketing strategies that lead to successful conversions.

## Defining Customer Journey

The customer journey is the process a user undergoes when deciding to purchase a product or service. It encompasses all interactions, from discovering your brand to becoming a loyal customer.

In digital marketing context, this journey can be visualized through various stages, where each step can serve a specific marketing purpose and has a potential targeted digital ad placement.

CHAPTER 13   UNDERSTANDING THE CUSTOMER/BUYER JOURNEY

# Detailed View of the Customer Journey with a Diagram

To help you understand the dynamics of the customer journey better, let's examine Figure 13-1 that depicts a simplified example of how digital marketing ads play a role at each stage of the process.

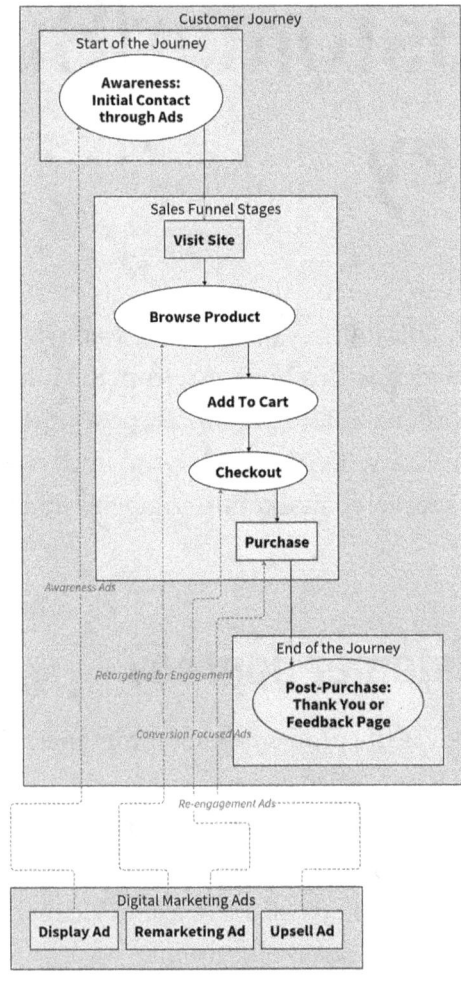

*Figure 13-1. Example of how digital marketing ads play a role in the customer journey*

But what does this diagram means in real life?

Imagine we start at the very beginning, the "**Start**" stage. Here, customers first bump into your branding through digital ads cleverly placed to grab their attention. This is akin to shaking hands at a networking event. You want to make a good impression because this sets the tone for the interactions to come.

Now, let's step forward to where the "**Visit Site**" node lights up. The potential customers, intrigued by your initial handshake, have decided to visit your virtual storefront—your website. Here, your goal is to keep them engaged. You've invited them in, and now it's time to captivate them further.

Moving along, we find ourselves at "**Browse Product**." It's like guiding the customer through the aisles of your store. They're interested, looking around, and considering what you have to offer. It's important to make sure that everything is well-organized and easy to find, as this consideration phase is critical for nudging them toward making a decision.

We arrive now at "**Add To Cart**," a promising milestone. They're no longer just browsing; they're starting to make selections. However, our journey isn't over yet. Just like a friendly shop assistant, we need to ensure that they don't walk away before completing their purchase.

As we approach "**Checkout**," it's like guiding them to the cashier. This process should be as smooth and hassle-free as possible to prevent any last-minute change of minds. It's the final hurdle before achieving our goal, which is the "**Purchase**."

Finally, we reach "**End**," which isn't really an end but a new beginning. Here, you thank them perhaps at a beautiful exit or a follow-up feedback page, with hopes of welcoming them back soon. This last touchpoint is essential for building lasting relationships and turning one-time buyers into repeat customers.

CHAPTER 13   UNDERSTANDING THE CUSTOMER/BUYER JOURNEY

**Note**   To fully leverage the customer journey, consider creating a similar diagram tailored to your specific customers. You may find that their journey is more intricate than you initially thought. This detailed mapping can reveal valuable insights and opportunities for you and your team to enhance their experience.

## Summary

The customer journey is not just a linear pathway but often involves multiple cycles and revisit stages, especially in the digital age where retargeting and re-engagement strategies play significant roles. Understanding this journey allows you to tailor your marketing strategies more effectively, targeting customers with the right message at the right time and understand why targeting, creatives, messages, and landing pages are all related.

In the next chapter, I will delve into what keywords are, how to use them, and what impact they have on your campaign.

CHAPTER 14

# Keywords in Digital Marketing: What They Are and Why They Matter

I've already written about targeting, placements, bids, and ad quality. One concept that is closely related is Keyword. Keywords are important for digital marketing, as they serve as the connectors between user searches, their context, and your digital content. In this chapter, you will understand what keywords are, differentiate between positive and negative keywords, and explore their significance in advertising campaigns, helping you understand how to use them effectively in your marketing strategies.

CHAPTER 14  KEYWORDS IN DIGITAL MARKETING: WHAT THEY ARE AND WHY THEY MATTER

# Keywords and How They're Used

Keywords are phrases or terms that users enter into search engines or that characterize the content on a website. They play a crucial role in targeting advertisements based on user intent (in search engines) and context (on websites in the cookieless world[1]).

A **positive keyword** is a term you target to activate your ads; when this keyword aligns with a user's search query or appears on a website they are visiting, your ad is likely to be displayed.[2] Conversely, a **negative keyword** is a term you specify to prevent your ad from appearing, refining targeting and enhancing ad relevance.

# The Role of Keywords in Digital Advertising

Understanding this dual nature of keywords helps you optimize the use of your campaign budget and prevents underperforming campaigns. Let's explore this in more detail.

## Positive and Negative Keywords

Positive keywords target users actively searching for related products or services to those phrases, increasing the likelihood of engaging interested audiences. For example, a keyword like "summer hiking shoes" can direct potential buyers to a relevant product page.

---

[1] I've written this before: the digital marketing landscape changes quickly. The last announcement from Google suggest that the cookies might not disappear after all. The concept is nonetheless relevant and I will explain it. Here is the latest update: https://privacysandbox.com/news/privacy-sandbox-update/.

[2] Of course, a lot has to happen for your ad to be shown. Check Chapters 10 on Bids and Chapter 11 on Ad Quality to understand more.

Negative keywords, on the other hand, filter out unwanted traffic. If you sell new books, using "used books" as a negative keyword prevents your ads from appearing in such search queries.

You can mix both positive and negative keywords in the same campaign to further specify the target you want to reach. For instance, you can target "new laptops" as a positive keyword together with "cheap" as a negative keyword.

## Keywords and Contextual Advertising

Contextual advertising leverages keywords to match ad content with relevant site content, enhancing the relevance of ads based on the environment in which they appear. This form of advertising uses keywords to assess the theme of a webpage and then serves ads that are relevant to that theme.

For instance, if you targeted the keyword "Product A features" and there is a blog post where the details of such product are discussed, your ad may appear there, but not in a blog post where the details of Product B are discussed.

## How Contextual Targeting Works

Contextual targeting involves placing ads on web pages based on the keywords those pages contain.[3] This method shows your ads in an environment relevant to the advertising content, which can significantly increase user engagement and ad performance. For instance, an ad for baking supplies appearing on a recipes site that frequently discusses baking techniques is more likely to resonate with the site's visitors.

---

[3] The keywords may or may not be explicitly defined. Using machine learning and natural language processing, the advertiser channel providers can extract keywords from content.

The process begins with the advertising channel provider scanning the content of a page for keywords and then matching these to the keywords selected in your ad campaign. This alignment means that your ads are not just targeted based on user profiles or past behavior, but are specifically related to the content the user is currently viewing, thereby enhancing the likelihood of clicks and conversions.

## Integrating Keywords with Ad Copy and Landing Pages

Keywords should trigger ads and resonate through the ad copy and the content of the landing page. This ensures that when users click through, they find exactly what they were searching for, greatly enhancing user satisfaction and conversion rates. This emphasizes the importance and impact of Landing Pages specific for each campaign in your digital marketing efforts. Check Chapter 23 on Landing Pages if you want more details.

For example, if your ad campaign targets "organic coffee beans," your landing page should prominently feature organic coffee products, and the copy should reinforce the benefits of organic coffee, echoing the user's search intent.

## Understanding Keyword Match Types

When you define keywords in the platform of the advertiser channel provider you chose, depending on their platform, you may add more details on how you want to target them. This is called keyword match type. Keyword match types determine how closely a keyword needs to match with a user's search query to trigger an ad. Each match type offers different levels of control over ad triggers, affecting how broadly or narrowly your ads are targeted.

## Types of Keyword Matches

Keyword matches are categorized to control how closely a user's search query must align with your selected keyword to trigger an ad.

**Broad Match** is the default setting in most advertiser channel providers that provides the widest reach. When you set your keyword to broad match, your ad may appear on searches that include not only the exact keyword but also a wide range of related terms including misspellings, synonyms, and other variations related to the keyword. For example, using "hiking boots" as a broad match keyword could result in your ad appearing for searches like "walking shoes," thereby capturing a broader audience potentially interested in similar products.

**Phrase Match** offers a more controlled targeting approach, ensuring that your ad appears only for searches that include a specific phrase or close variations of that phrase in the same order. This match type strikes a balance between reach and relevance. If your keyword is set to phrase match, such as "women's hiking boots," your ad might be displayed in response to "buy women's hiking boots," but it would not trigger for "boots for hiking women." This ensures more precise targeting by aligning ad displays with the exact search phrases used by potential customers.

**Exact Match** is the most restrictive type of keyword match, targeting the narrowest audience by showing your ad only to those who search for the exact keyword or very close variations of that keyword. This match type is ideal for targeting specific demographics or for products and services with very specific search behaviors. For instance, if "men's leather boots" is set as an exact match keyword, the ad would only appear for searches like "men's leather boots" or slight variations such as "leather boots for men," but not for broader searches like "boots for men." This precision helps in minimizing irrelevant impressions and focusing your advertising efforts on users with the highest intent to purchase or engage.

*Table 14-1. Comparison of keyword matches types*

| Match Type | Description | Example Keyword | Triggered by Search Query |
|---|---|---|---|
| Broad match | Shows on searches related to your keyword, including synonyms and related terms | Hiking boots | Walking shoes, trail boots, buy boots for hiking |
| Phrase match | Shows on searches that include your keyword in the same order, allowing for slight variations | Women's hiking boots | Buy women's hiking boots, women's boots for hiking |
| Exact match | Shows on searches that match your keyword exactly or are close variations of that keyword only | Men's leather boots | Men's leather boots, leather boots men |

These match types help you control how broadly, or narrowly, you wish to cast your net. Choosing the right match type can greatly influence the effectiveness of your campaigns by ensuring your ads appear in the most relevant searches, thus improving both click-through and conversion rates.

## Strategic Use of Keyword Match Types

Incorporating a mix of keyword match types in your campaigns can optimize your reach and effectiveness. For instance, you might use broad match to capture a wide audience early in a campaign to gather data on how people are searching. As you refine your strategy, incorporating more phrases and exact matches can help you target the most promising prospects more precisely, thereby increasing relevance and reducing wasted ad spend.

CHAPTER 14   KEYWORDS IN DIGITAL MARKETING: WHAT THEY ARE AND WHY THEY MATTER

# Keyword Selection, Costs, and Budgeting

Selecting the right keywords and effectively understanding their associated costs have an impact on the success of any digital marketing campaign. This section delves into the pricing of keywords, the mechanics of CPC (Cost per Click) and Max CPC, and how these pricing strategies relate to managing your daily or overall campaign budget. For more details on Bidding Strategies, check Chapter 10.

## Understanding Keyword Costs and CPC

Keywords vary in cost; each keyword has an associated average and maximum cost influenced by factors such as demand, competition, and seasonal trends. The cost for each keyword often results from a bidding process within the advertising platform, similar to an auction, where the highest bidder gains the most visibility. Cost per Click (CPC) is the price you pay each time a user clicks on your ad. The CPC is influenced by the quality of your ad and its relevance to the search query,[4] along with your bidding strategy. For instance, if you choose a keyword with an average cost of $2 but set your Max CPC at $1.5, you may not win the bid if competing bids exceed $1.5, thus preventing your ad from being displayed.

## Max CPC and Its Implications

Max CPC is the highest amount you are willing to pay for a click on your ad, which is crucial for controlling your advertising spend while aiming to maximize ad visibility. It is essential to find a balance in your Max CPC setting that reflects the potential return on investment (ROI) from each click. Setting it too high may deplete your budget quickly without

---

[4] Check Chapter 10 on Bids and Chapter 11 on Ad Quality.

improving conversion rates proportionally, while setting it too low might prevent your ads from showing at all. Properly researching and setting your Max CPC is thus important to campaign performance.

## Budgeting for Keywords

Your campaign budget should accurately reflect the costs of your chosen keywords. A well-considered budget ensures you can maintain your ad placements throughout the campaign without prematurely exhausting funds before reaching your goals. Keep in mind that keyword costs may fluctuate due to external factors such as competitive campaigns or changes in search trends (which I explain later in this chapter). Regularly monitor and adjust your keyword strategy and budget allocations, especially for long-term campaigns, to stay competitive and cost-effective.

## Keyword Research Tools and Techniques

I just discussed the impact of keywords in your digital marketing efforts. But how do you research them? To aid in this process, various robust keyword research tools and effective techniques are available that can significantly enhance your keyword selection efforts.

Several popular tools are essential for anyone looking to optimize their keyword strategy. Google Keyword Planner[5] is a Tool from Google, particularly useful for those managing Google Ads. It helps in identifying keywords relevant to your business and provides estimates on search volumes and the associated costs of targeting these keywords. SEMrush[6] expands on these capabilities, offering a comprehensive suite of tools that includes competitor analysis and tracking positions in Google's

---

[5] https://ads.google.com/home/tools/keyword-planner/
[6] www.semrush.com/

search engine results pages (SERPs). Ahrefs[7] is another valuable resource, known for its detailed keyword reports, content explorer, and competitive analysis features. Moz Keyword Explorer[8] offers insights with its keyword suggestions, SERP analysis, and evaluations of keyword difficulty. Similarly, SERanking[9] provides tools akin to SEMrush and Ahrefs, supporting extensive keyword analysis and strategic planning.

Your service provider is usually in charge of researching the keywords. In case you want to dive into doing it yourself, you can use any of the tools above. They all do the job.

When identifying high-value keywords, it's important to **start by understanding the search volume** of each keyword, which reflects how often it is entered into a search engine over a specific period. This will give you an idea of the potential traffic a keyword could generate. Additionally, analyzing the **competition for each keyword** is important; more competitive keywords will generally require greater effort and higher costs to rank effectively. You should also assess the relevance of these keywords to your target audience to ensure they align with the interests and needs of your potential customers. Finally, consider using keyword tools to gain insights into trends and seasonality. These tools can help you adjust your strategy to capitalize on periods when certain keywords gain popularity, thereby optimizing your campaign's impact and reach.

## Keyword Optimization Strategies

Optimizing your keywords in time can significantly improve your search engine rankings and drive more targeted traffic. This section outlines strategies to enhance your keyword optimization efforts, ensuring that your online presence is both effective and efficient.

---

[7] https://ahrefs.com
[8] https://moz.com/explorer
[9] https://seranking.com

Effective keyword optimization involves strategic placement of keywords throughout your website to enhance SEO and user understanding. Keywords should be incorporated naturally into high-impact areas such as title tags, meta descriptions, headers, and throughout the content where relevant. Including keywords in the URL structure also helps both search engines and users understand the topic of the page (this is also known as friendly URLs), enhancing the clarity and SEO potential of your site.

Maintaining an appropriate keyword density is also important to signal the topic of your content to search engines effectively without resorting to keyword stuffing, which can negatively impact your SEO efforts. Keywords should be used sufficiently throughout the content to maintain a natural flow, integrating them as part of valuable and informative text that serves the reader's interests and needs. Those keywords should also be those that your users and clients are using. For instance, if all your users refer to your product's category as "Category A," it does not make any sense to name it "Category B" in your Landing Page, even if that is the correct category. If you do that, your content will not be found, and you want it to be found and your ad quality to be adequate to participate and win auctions.

## Long-Tail Keywords

I have discussed the main-stream keywords, those with high and medium competition. But there is another category of keywords, the so-called long-tail keywords.

Long-tail keywords are typically longer and more specific phrases than more commonly searched keywords. They are less competitive but highly targeted to specific user intents, making them attractive for attracting a specific niche audience.

The specificity of long-tail keywords means that the traffic they attract is often more likely to convert because these users are looking for exactly what you offer. For example, a user searching for "best price on organic green tea bags in New York" demonstrates a clear intent to purchase, making this long-tail keyword potentially more valuable than a more generic "green tea." These keywords also will most likely generate less, although more targeted, traffic.

## Keyword Trends and Seasonality

Understanding the trends in your market and industry allows you to understand the fluctuations in keyword effectiveness and costs due to seasonal trends, specific events, or changing market conditions.

Keywords can exhibit significant variations in search volume, costs, and competition depending on the time of year, major events, or even changes in consumer behavior. For instance, retail keywords like "Christmas gifts" spike during the holiday season, while travel-related terms might peak during the summer months. This means that "Christmas gifts" will cost more near the end of the year and a lot less after Christmas.

Events, whether they are global, such as the Olympics, or local, like a regional festival, can also influence keyword effectiveness. You need to anticipate these changes to align your strategies with user interests and plan your digital marketing campaigns accordingly.

But how to proactively plan for these situations? You can analyze historical data to predict when certain keywords are likely to become popular. Tools like Google Trends can help identify these patterns by showing the search volume changes for specific queries in specific regions over time.

By monitoring keyword trends and seasonality, you can make informed decisions about when and how to adjust your keyword strategies and thus your digital marketing efforts.

## Local SEO and Local Keyword Targeting

For businesses targeting specific geographic areas, local SEO and local keyword targeting are specific approaches you can take to improve the likelihood of reaching your target group.

Local keywords refer to using phrases that explicitly include geographical locations and are used by potential customers searching for services or products in their area. These keywords are crucial for businesses like restaurants, retail stores, service providers, and more, as they help to attract traffic from users who are most likely to visit in person or make a local inquiry.

## Keyword Intent and User Behavior

Understanding keyword intent and aligning it with user behavior are also relevant for your digital marketing efforts, although a little more specific.

What is this intent and user behavior, and where does that come from? The main source is *"The Theory of Planned Behavior"* by Icek Ajzen. Although not specific for digital marketing, I find interesting how you can use the intent to improve your targeting efforts.

There are different **Types of Keyword Intent**. The first one is the **Informational Intent**, where keywords are used by users who are seeking information. Typically, these queries are questions or broad topic searches without any commercial intent behind them. For instance, "how to tie a tie" or "what is blockchain technology" are examples of informational intent.

Next come **Navigational Intent**, where users have a specific website or destination in mind and their queries reflect navigational intent. These keywords often include brand names or specific service names, such as "Facebook login" or "Nike store locator." Users using these keywords are usually trying to reach a particular website or place.

Finally, you have the **Transactional Intent**. This intent is displayed by users ready to make a purchase or perform another specific action. Keywords reflecting transactional intent often include terms like "buy," "deal," "discount," or very specific product names, e.g., "buy iPhone 12" or "best deals on yoga mats today."

Understanding these intents allows you to **align Keyword Strategies with User Intent**, thus tailoring your content and ads to meet their expectations, thereby increasing the relevance and effectiveness of your campaigns.

For informational keywords, you can focus on creating rich, informative content that addresses the queries comprehensively. Blogs, FAQs, and tutorial videos are suitable formats that can help address these needs.

When targeting navigational intent, ensure that your SEO and SEM strategies make it as easy as possible for users to find your brand or specific services. Optimize your site structure and metadata to improve visibility for these types of searches.

For transactional keywords, optimize your landing pages to drive conversions. Ensure that these pages are straightforward, with clear calls to action and streamlined purchase processes. Your content here should reinforce the benefits of the product or service and include reviews or testimonials when appropriate, as well as use the right HTML elements to help the search engines understand your page.

# Summary

In this chapter, I've delved into the role that keywords play in digital marketing. Here are the main points to remember:

- **Keywords bridge user intent with your content**, which is relevant for targeting in both search and display advertising.

- **Effective use of positive and negative keywords** ensures your ads appear in relevant searches and contexts, improving campaign effectiveness.
- **Contextual targeting uses keywords to align ads with relevant site content**, allowing you to show your ads in a context relevant for you and the user.
- **Consistent alignment of keywords with ad copy and landing pages** is vital for fulfilling user expectations and achieving high conversion rates.

In the next chapter, I will explain the different types of digital marketing campaigns.

## CHAPTER 15

# Exploring Types of Digital Marketing Campaigns

In this chapter, I will explore the various types of digital marketing campaigns and the differences between them. Understanding these distinctions will help you choose the right type of campaign based on your marketing goals, target audience, and the channels that are most likely to engage them effectively. Table 15-1 lists some of the more popular ones.

## Additional Campaign Types to Consider

I've covered a wide range of digital marketing campaign types in Table 15-1, as those are the main types that are used, from display advertising to influencer marketing. However, as the digital marketing landscape is constantly evolving, there are always new strategies and technologies emerging that can enhance your marketing efforts. Here, I will explore additional campaign types that might be beneficial for your marketing strategy, ensuring you're not missing out on any innovative opportunities.

CHAPTER 15  EXPLORING TYPES OF DIGITAL MARKETING CAMPAIGNS

*Table 15-1.* *Prominent campaign types*

| Campaign Type | Description | Use Cases and Examples |
|---|---|---|
| Display advertising | Utilizes banner ads, images, and videos to promote products or services across websites and apps | Ideal for brand awareness and retargeting campaigns. *Example*: A clothing retailer uses display ads on fashion blogs to promote a new line of summer wear |
| Search engine marketing (SEM) | Uses paid search engine results to drive traffic to a website, often through PPC (pay per click) or CPC (cost per click) campaigns | Effective for driving sales and lead generation. *Example*: A local bakery uses Google Ads to appear in search results when potential customers search for "birthday cakes near me" |
| Social media advertising | Employs social media platforms to engage with and promote to targeted audiences | Great for building community engagement and direct consumer interaction. *Example*: A fitness brand launches an Instagram campaign promoting healthy lifestyle tips and their new workout gear |
| Mobile advertising | Specifically designed for mobile devices, this includes in-app ads, mobile search ads, and mobile video ads | Suits campaigns aiming to reach users on mobile devices with high engagement. *Example*: A game developer uses in-app ads within mobile games to drive downloads of their latest game |

(*continued*)

***Table 15-1.*** (*continued*)

| Campaign Type | Description | Use Cases and Examples |
|---|---|---|
| Native advertising | Matches the look and feel of the medium where it appears, making it less intrusive and providing a smoother user experience | Useful for subtly integrating promotional content. *Example*: A travel company uses articles on popular travel blogs to subtly promote tour packages |
| Video advertising | Leverages video content to engage users on websites, social media, and other digital channels | Excellent for storytelling or demonstrating products. *Example*: A home improvement store creates DIY project videos that show how to use their tools and materials |
| Influencer marketing | Involves partnerships with social media influencers to promote products or services to their followers | Best for reaching niche markets with authentic voices. *Example*: A beauty brand collaborates with well-known beauty influencers on YouTube to review their skincare products |
| Email marketing | Uses email communications to promote products or services, enhance brand recognition, and build customer loyalty | Ideal for personalized promotions and updates. *Example*: An online bookstore sends monthly newsletters with book recommendations and exclusive discounts |
| Affiliate marketing | Performance-based marketing where affiliates are paid to promote the advertiser's products on their channels | Useful for extending market reach through various affiliate networks. *Example*: A tech company uses a network of tech bloggers and vloggers to promote software tools through affiliate links |

## Content Marketing

Content marketing focuses on creating and distributing valuable, relevant, and consistent content to attract and retain a clearly defined audience—ultimately, to drive profitable customer action.

**Example**
Publishing informative blog posts or white papers that address common customer pain points.

## Retargeting Campaigns

Retargeting aims to re-engage users who have previously interacted with your brand but did not convert. By targeting these users with specific ads, the chances of conversion increase.

**Example**
Displaying ads for products that a visitor viewed on your website but did not purchase.

## Referral Marketing

Referral marketing encourages existing customers to refer new customers to your business, typically incentivized with rewards for both the referrer and the referee.

**Example**
Offering a discount to both parties when a referred friend makes their first purchase.

## Account-Based Marketing (ABM)

Account-based marketing is a targeted approach that treats individual accounts as markets in their own right, designing highly personalized campaigns.

**Example**
Creating customized marketing campaigns aimed at key decision-makers within a specific company.

# Summary

In this chapter, we've covered an array of digital marketing campaigns, each with distinctive characteristics and ideal use cases:

- **Understand the Specifics**: Each type of campaign offers unique benefits and is suitable for different marketing objectives.

- **Choose Wisely**: Select the campaign type that aligns most closely with your marketing goals, target audience's preferences, and the type of message you wish to convey.

- **Integration Is Key**: Consider integrating multiple types of campaigns for a comprehensive strategy. For example, combining social media advertising with influencer marketing can amplify your reach and authenticity.

In the next chapter, I will explain what creatives are; the differences between creatives, messages, and copy; and their main types.

## CHAPTER 16

# Crafting Creatives, Messages, and Copy for Effective Digital Marketing Campaigns

In this chapter, I'll briefly review the elements that make your digital ads not just visible, but engaging and effective and then look at them more closely in Chapters 22 and 27–30. Understanding the nuances of creatives, messages, and copy is essential for crafting ads that resonate with your audience. I will explore the various types of creatives used across different ad formats, what you should expect from your service partners, and how a well-prepared brief can facilitate the creation of impactful advertising content.

In Chapter 22, I will go into the details of the most used formats. In chapter 27, I will explain the different goals a digital marketing campaign can have and recommend some formats that match well with them. Finally, in Chapter 30, I will discuss the types of ads and formats and how their characteristics match specific criteria of your campaign.

CHAPTER 16 CRAFTING CREATIVES, MESSAGES, AND COPY FOR EFFECTIVE DIGITAL MARKETING CAMPAIGNS

# Understanding Creatives, Messages, and Copy

In the context of digital marketing, *"creatives"* refers to the visual and textual elements that constitute an advertisement. This includes everything from the images and videos to the text and interactive elements that appear in your ads.

Creatives encompass various components such as banners, images, videos, and copy (text). Each format has its own set of requirements, which can vary by platform and ad type.

The term "messages" refers to the core idea or theme that you want to communicate through your ad. It's the main takeaway you want your audience to understand. Essentially, it's the central concept that you aim to imprint in the minds of your audience, making it important to the overall impact of the ad. The message should be consistent across the campaign and also consistent across campaigns with the brand. The message should also align with the brand promise and your brand's product personality. This ensures that your audience receives a coherent and unified communication, reinforcing the brand identity and values at every touchpoint. A well-aligned message helps in building trust and recognition, making it easier for the audience to connect with your brand and understand what it stands for.

"Copy" is the text part of your ads. It complements the visuals and helps to convey your message effectively. Copy includes headlines, descriptions, and call-to-actions (CTAs), all of which are relevant in engaging your audience and driving the desired response.

# Types of Creatives and Their Usage

Different marketing goals and platforms require different types of creatives. Here's a rundown of the three most common creatives and practical examples of their usage.

**Display ads** often use AMP or HTML banners that are rich in media and designed to catch the eye quickly. **Image ads** utilize compelling images combined with minimal text to convey a message instantly. **Search ads** focus on text, including headers and descriptions, that are directly tied to search keywords.

For example, a clothing brand might use an image ad featuring their latest collection for a social media campaign aimed at driving brand awareness. Meanwhile, the same brand's search ads for a specific product like "men's winter jackets" will focus more on descriptive copy that includes price and product details.

I won't go into more detail here because later in the book I will cover each format and their use for different campaign types and goals in detail. However, I find it's important to explain early in the book why creatives, messages, and copy are essential, what the differences are, and how they vary depending on the campaign type and goal. Additionally, it's important to understand the link between your campaigns, ads, brand promise, and brand personality. This connection will become more relevant as we delve deeper into digital marketing.

You've already read about awareness levels, target groups and audiences, targeting, and keywords. All these elements are interconnected, and if your creatives, message, and copy are not relevant and aligned, all your other preparations will not matter.

## Collaboration with Service Partners

When developing creatives, you will often collaborate with various service partners such as digital agencies, freelance designers, and copywriters. Here's a brief overview of what to expect from them and how a detailed brief can help.

CHAPTER 16   CRAFTING CREATIVES, MESSAGES, AND COPY FOR EFFECTIVE DIGITAL MARKETING CAMPAIGNS

Digital agencies handle comprehensive campaign creation, including creatives, and you can expect them to provide professional, market-aligned advertisements based on your brief. Freelance designers are often tasked with creating specific visual elements and require clear guidelines on style and branding. Copywriters focus on crafting the copy that communicates your message effectively and persuasively.

Providing a clear and detailed brief[1] that includes your campaign goals, target audience details, desired message, and aesthetic preferences ensures that all creative elements are aligned with your overall marketing strategy. I cover "Briefs" later in the book (Chapter 31) and include practical examples and templates. This approach helps to streamline the collaboration process and ensures that the output from your service partners meets your expectations and enhances your campaign's effectiveness.

# Comparative Table of Ad Formats and Creative Requirements

Let's break down the main ad formats and their specific requirements in terms of creatives, copy, and messages Table 16-1 shows the three formats with their creative, copy, and message requirements for you to understand the key differences.

---

[1] Check Chapter 31 for more details and examples of a digital marketing brief. You also have the templates in the annexes.

CHAPTER 16   CRAFTING CREATIVES, MESSAGES, AND COPY FOR EFFECTIVE DIGITAL MARKETING CAMPAIGNS

***Table 16-1.*** *Overview of the three most used formats in a comparison table*

| Ad Format | Creative Requirements | Copy Requirements | Message Alignment by Awareness Level |
|---|---|---|---|
| Display ads | High-resolution images or videos; AMP specifications if applicable | Short, engaging text that complements the visual | Broad message for general awareness; less direct call-to-action |
| Image ads | High-quality, visually appealing images that reflect the brand | Minimal text; often a powerful headline or tagline | Direct and appealing for both awareness and consideration stages |
| Search ads | Engaging copy | Focused, keyword-rich descriptions and headers | Highly targeted messages intended for conversion or deep consideration |

# Summary

In this chapter, I've detailed the components that make up creatives, messages, and copy for digital ads. We've explored the three main types of creatives suited for various ad formats, how to work effectively with service partners, and provided a comparative table that outlines the requirements for those three ad formats. You can refer to Chapter 22 for an exhaustive list of formats and their details. The main takeaways I need you to take home are

- Creatives make your ads visually engaging and are tailored to fit the format and platform of your campaign. These include images, videos, and copy.

## CHAPTER 16  CRAFTING CREATIVES, MESSAGES, AND COPY FOR EFFECTIVE DIGITAL MARKETING CAMPAIGNS

- Messages should be clear and resonate with the intended audience, varying depending on their awareness level and should match your branding.

- Copy needs to support your visuals and message and should be crafted to attract, inform, or persuade.

In the next chapter, I will explain what ad accounts are and describe their most common structures on major platforms.

CHAPTER 17

# Understanding Ad Accounts and Their Structures

In this chapter, I'll explore the world of ad accounts across various digital platforms. Understanding how ad accounts are structured will help you effectively manage your digital marketing campaigns and prevent misunderstandings with your partners and providers. Each advertising channel provider offers different account structures and has different requirements.

## What Are Ad Accounts

Ad accounts are specialized accounts provided by advertising channel providers which allow businesses to create, manage, pause, and pay for their advertising campaigns. These accounts are often tied to a specific payment method or profile and are essential for hosting the campaign's settings, creatives, and for tracking results and analytics.

Ad accounts serve multiple functions, including campaign management, financial control, and performance tracking.

Campaign management involves creating and modifying ad campaigns. Financial control includes managing budget allocations and expenditures. Performance tracking focuses on monitoring and analyzing the effectiveness of campaigns.

## Common Structures of Ad Accounts on Major Platforms

Different advertising platforms have distinct structures for their ad accounts, accommodating various features and functionalities as per the needs of marketers. Knowing these structures is important in order to understand why some partners work the way they do and will also help you manage account ownership in a better way.

## Google Ads

Google Ads utilizes a hierarchy that begins with the **Manager Account** (formerly known as My Client Center or MCC), which can manage multiple Google Ads accounts.

Under the MCC, individual **Google Ads accounts** are created, each linked to a specific payment profile.

Among its features, a MCC account allows centralized management of multiple accounts, including consolidated billing and easy performance comparison.

**Example**
If you operate an agency that handles advertising for several clients, an MCC account allows you to manage all these accounts under one umbrella, simplifying operations and billing processes.

## Facebook Ads

For Facebook Ads, the structure includes **a Business Manager** which centralizes all ad management and asset control. Within this, you need to verify your business.

Connected to Business Manager are **Ad Accounts**, along with assets like Facebook pages, Instagram accounts, and Pixels.

**User and Partner Management**: Facebook allows you to link and verify partners and users to various assets, enhancing security and collaboration.

**Example**
A retail brand can manage its advertising across Facebook and Instagram, analyze performance using a Facebook Pixel, and grant access to a marketing agency to co-manage campaigns, all within the Business Manager.

## The Trade Desk and Other Programmatic Platforms

These platforms may have unique structures tailored to their services, like Real-Time Bidding (RTB).

Account types can vary based on the capabilities given to manage ads across different publishers and inventory sources.

**Example**
On The Trade Desk platform, your account setup might allow integration with third-party data providers to enhance targeting accuracy.

CHAPTER 17  UNDERSTANDING AD ACCOUNTS AND THEIR STRUCTURES

## Ad Account Integrations and Extensions

Many platforms offer integrations with other services to enhance ad features. For instance:

- **Google RSA Extensions**: Require access to Google My Business for location extensions.
- **Facebook Campaigns**: Might need access to WhatsApp to run ads that engage users on WhatsApp.

**Example**
A restaurant using Google Ads might integrate with Google My Business so that their ads also display the restaurant's location, hours, and real-time updates, improving local search ad effectiveness.

## Summary and Key Takeaways

This chapter has provided a general look at how ad accounts are structured across various platforms and how understanding these structures can help you better manage your digital marketing efforts:

- Different ad platforms have distinct structures and features, all designed to help you manage and optimize your campaigns more effectively.
- Knowing how to navigate these account structures and utilize available integrations can significantly enhance your work with partners.

In the next chapter, I will explain conversions, conversion tracking, tracking parameters, and the impact of data privacy policies on tracking.

# CHAPTER 18

# Understanding Conversions and Conversion Tracking

In this chapter, I'll guide you through the world of conversions and conversion tracking in digital marketing. Understanding what a conversion is and how to effectively track them can significantly influence the success of your digital marketing efforts and will also help you understand what your service providers are doing (or not doing). I'll explain what conversion tracking is and how it works with specific codes and tools and explore the implications of using such technologies, including key considerations around data privacy.

## What Are Conversions, and What Is Conversion Tracking?

In digital marketing, a "conversion" refers to **any significant action that a user takes as a result of interacting with your ad**. This might be clicking on a link, completing a form, making a purchase, or even a sign-up. Tracking these conversions helps you understand how effectively your ads are leading to user actions.

**Conversion tracking** involves using specific codes, known as tracking tags, codes, or pixels, that you integrate into your website or landing pages. These codes allow advertising platforms to monitor how users interact with your site after clicking on your ad.

## How Conversion Tracking Works

Tracking codes are added to your webpage, which communicate with the ad platform whenever a conversion action is completed by a user. This setup enables ad platforms to record these actions, helping you measure the effectiveness of your advertising efforts in real time.

**Example**
Suppose you run a Google Ads campaign to promote a new product. By integrating a Google Ads conversion tracking code on the purchase confirmation page, you can track how many purchases were made by users who clicked on your ad.

## Major Conversion Tracking Tools and Their Uses

Different ad platforms provide their specific tools for conversion tracking, each designed to integrate seamlessly with their advertising services. Here are three examples:

## Google Ads Conversion Tracking

This tool is used to track actions like purchases or sign-ups after a user interacts with ads within the Google network, and it's part of Google Ads.

CHAPTER 18   UNDERSTANDING CONVERSIONS AND CONVERSION TRACKING

## Google Analytics

Google analytics offers comprehensive tracking capabilities that not only measure conversions but also provide detailed insights about user behavior on your website across all sources.

## Facebook Pixel

A Facebook Pixel is a computer code (usually JavaScript code) that is added to your website to track events and interactions. The Pixel allows you to measure the effectiveness of your advertising by understanding the actions people take on your website (for example, if a person clicked a link, or submitted a form) and it's part of Meta's platform.

Table 18-1 compares the three tracking tools above.

*Table 18-1. Comparison between Google Ads Conversion Tracking, Google Analytics and Facebook Pixel*

| Tracking Tool | Description | Integration Example |
| --- | --- | --- |
| Google Ads Conversion Tracking | Tracks user actions specifically from Google Ads | Placed on a "Thank You" page to track purchases |
| Google Analytics | Provides detailed user behavior insights and conversion tracking from all sources | Integrated site-wide for holistic performance metrics |
| Facebook Pixel | Specifically tracks conversions from Facebook ads and provides analytics | Implemented on key website pages to track actions like form submissions or product additions to cart |

151

CHAPTER 18   UNDERSTANDING CONVERSIONS AND CONVERSION TRACKING

# Using Tracking Parameters: UTM Codes

UTM (Urchin Tracking Module) codes are URL parameters used to track the effectiveness of online marketing campaigns. They help marketers understand the source of traffic and which campaign directs it.

**Example**
Adding `?utm_source=facebook&utm_medium=cpc&utm_campaign=product_launch` to your URL can tell you that the click came from a Facebook ad campaign specifically designed for a product launch.

**Understanding Data Privacy in Conversion Tracking**
With the use of tracking codes and detailed user analytics comes the responsibility of managing data privacy. This is especially crucial given regulations like GDPR in Europe and similar laws worldwide that govern user data protection.[1]

There are two rules of thumb when dealing with data privacy:

It's important to ensure that your use of tracking technologies complies with all relevant data privacy laws.

Always inform users about the data you collect and how it will be used, ensuring transparency and building trust.

# Key Takeaways

In this chapter, I gave you an overview of what conversions are and how to track them, as well as some examples of the tools to do that and their implications in data privacy. You should at least remember that:

- Conversions represent significant user actions that digital marketing campaigns aim to achieve.

---

[1] Check Chapter 26 on the Legal Landscape in Digital Marketing for more on this.

CHAPTER 18   UNDERSTANDING CONVERSIONS AND CONVERSION TRACKING

- Conversion tracking involves integrating specific codes provided by ad platforms into your website to monitor these actions.

- Different tools like Google Analytics, Google Ads Conversion Tracking, and Facebook Pixel cater to specific platforms but are crucial for comprehensive performance measurement.

- Understanding and properly implementing UTM codes can enhance tracking precision, which may also be used cross-platform.

- Navigating data privacy responsibly is crucial in the use of tracking technologies.

In the next chapter, I will delve into competitor analysis, why it is important, and some tools for that purpose.

CHAPTER 19

# Competitor Analysis in Digital Marketing: Understanding Your Market Position

In this chapter, I delve into the significance of conducting a thorough competitor analysis in digital marketing. Understanding what your competitors are doing not only informs your strategy but also highlights potential areas where you can differentiate yourself. I'll explore how to analyze competitor keywords, ads, and landing pages and provide practical tools and methods for conducting this analysis effectively.

## What Is Competitor Research, and Why Is It Important?

Competitor research in digital marketing extends beyond simply knowing who your competitors are. It involves a deep dive into the specifics of their marketing strategies, particularly the keywords and concepts they use to attract your potential customers.

Remember, understanding the awareness level of your target audience is crucial when analyzing competitor strategies. If customers are finding your competitors while searching for terms unfamiliar to you, it's a sign you need to align your messaging and keywords more closely with customer expectations.

## Understanding the Competitive Landscape

Your competitors aren't just those offering similar products or services. They include any business appearing in search results where potential customers might expect to find you. This broadens the scope of who you consider a competitor, making thorough analysis all the more important.

**Example**
If you're selling lightweight laptops but only advertise using the term "ultrabooks," whereas your competitors use both "lightweight laptops" and "ultrabooks," they may capture traffic from potential customers unfamiliar with the term "ultrabook."

## Tools and Techniques for Competitor Research

To conduct effective competitor research, you can utilize various tools[1] and techniques that offer insights into their strategies.

1. **Tools for Competitor Keyword Research**
   - **SEMrush:** Provides detailed analytics on what keywords your competitors are using, how much traffic these keywords garner, and how you might incorporate them into your strategy.

---

[1] I am not endorsing nor selling these tools. I just name them here for your reference.

- **Ahrefs**: Offers tools to see the organic and paid keywords your competitors target, giving you insights into their search marketing tactics.

- **SE Ranking**: Offers comprehensive SEO and competitor analysis features that help you identify the keywords your competitors are ranking for and the ones driving their traffic.

- **Google Ads Keyword Suggestion Tool**: Google's own tool provides suggestions based on actual Google search data, helping you find relevant keywords that are in line with what users are currently searching for.

- **Google Search Suggestions**: Also from Google, this feature gives you real-time keywords suggestions when you start typing in the search box. It's a quick way to see common searches related to your principal keyword.

- **Google Search Console**: For those who have it implemented, Google Search Console can show you which keywords bring users to your site and how your pages are performing in the search results.

- **Matomo**: An open-source analytics platform, Matomo provides insights similar to Google Search Console and has strengths in privacy and data ownership that some prefer.

2. **Tools for Analyzing Competitor Ads**
   - **SpyFu**: Allows you to view the types of ads your competitors are running and their performance in terms of engagement and conversion.

- **Adbeat:** Focuses on display advertising, offering insights into where and how competitors are running display campaigns.

- **SE Ranking:** Offers comprehensive SEO and competitor analysis features that help you identify the keywords your competitors are ranking for and the ones driving their traffic.

3. **Manual Alternatives**

    - Regularly browsing competitors' websites and noting any changes in their marketing campaigns.

    - Using incognito mode to search for keywords and see which competitors appear in search results and what ads they display.

**Example**

Imagine you're tweaking the keyword strategy for your online fitness equipment store. By using SE Ranking, you could discover that your competitors are focusing heavily on "affordable home gym equipment," a keyword phrase you hadn't considered closely, allowing you to adjust your content and ad strategies accordingly.

# Competitor Landing Pages: A Window into Their Marketing Strategy

Analyzing your competitors' landing pages can provide more profound insights into their sales funnel and customer journey. These pages reveal how competitors position their products, the kind of messaging they use, and the overall user experience they offer.

**Example**

A competitor's landing page for a high-end camera might highlight features like resolution and durability, using technical language and comparison charts, indicating a target audience that values in-depth product details and comparative analysis.

# Integrating Tools for Comprehensive Analysis

Using multiple tools can provide a more rounded view of the competitive landscape. Here's how you could integrate these tools for a holistic keyword strategy:

1. **Start with Broad Searches**: Use Google's Keyword Suggestion Tool to generate a wide list of potential keywords.

2. **Refine and Expand**: Apply SE Ranking or similar tools to dig deeper into specific competitors and identify their top-performing keywords.

3. **Monitor Performance**: Utilize Google Search Console and Matomo to track how changes to your keyword strategy affect your site's traffic and search performance.

While leveraging these tools, always be mindful of the data privacy laws applicable in your region, especially when using analytics tools that track user data.

CHAPTER 19    COMPETITOR ANALYSISIN DIGITAL MARKETING: UNDERSTANDING YOUR MARKET POSITION

# Comparative Table of Tools for Keyword Analysis

Table 19-1 shows an overview of the tools I mentioned, helping you decide which ones might suit your needs best.

*Table 19-1. Comparative table of tools for keyword analysis*

| Tool | Use Case | Features | Example Integration |
|---|---|---|---|
| SE Ranking | Comprehensive SEO and competitor analysis | Keyword ranking, competitor analysis, backlink checking | Combine with Google Ads suggestions for broad strategy planning |
| Google Ads Keyword Suggestion Tool | Keyword discovery based on Google's extensive data | Generates keyword ideas and traffic estimates | Start here for initial keyword brainstorming |
| Google Search Suggestions | Real-time user search term generation | Provides autocomplete suggestions based on user input | Use for augmenting keyword lists with real-time data |
| Google Search Console | Website performance tracking via Google search | Tracks search performance, keywords, and user behavior | Monitor after implementing new keywords |
| Matomo | Privacy-focused web analytics | Site analytics, keyword analysis without third-party data sharing | Ideal for GDPR-compliant user data handling |

**Tracking Codes and Privacy** Data privacy is a crucial aspect when analyzing digital marketing metrics. Always ensure compliance with global data protection regulations like GDPR or CCPA when using tracking technologies.

# Summary

In this chapter, I gave you an overview of what is a competitor analysis for digital marketing and which tools you can use. You should at least remember the following:

- Competitor analysis helps refine your digital marketing strategy by understanding what strategies your competitors are employing.

- Utilizing advanced tools like SEMrush, Ahrefs, or manual methods provides strategic insights into competitor keywords, ads, and landing pages.

- Choose tools that offer both comprehensive data and integration options to streamline your marketing analysis efforts.

In the next chapter, I will make a comparison between digital and traditional marketing campaigns, highlight their core differences, and include a comparison table for an overview.

# CHAPTER 20

# Digital Marketing vs. Traditional Marketing: A Comparison

In this chapter, I'm going to dissect some of the key differences between digital and traditional marketing. This topic is interesting if you're transitioning from a traditional marketing background or if you're trying to understand why digital marketing is becoming increasingly dominant in today's business landscape. I will explore aspects such as speed, costs, flexibility, and measurability and provide a comparative table to visually summarize these differences.

## The Core Differences Between Digital and Traditional Marketing

Digital and traditional marketing differ greatly in several core aspects—each with its own advantages and limitations. The main differences are speed, costs and flexibility, reactions times, and result analysis. Let's walk through these differences:

CHAPTER 20   DIGITAL MARKETING VS. TRADITIONAL MARKETING: A COMPARISON

The **speed** in digital marketing is completely different from that of traditional marketing. If you know what you are doing, launching a campaign can be quick and efficient and take a couple of hours. You can create and deploy multiple campaigns across different networks rapidly, often with the ability to utilize automated tools like AI-generated content or shopping feeds. In contrast, traditional marketing methods such as print require significant lead times for design, testing, production, and distribution.

Digital marketing offers **flexibility in costs** thanks to budget management and campaign adjustments. You can start with any budget, adjust spend in real time, and pause or stop campaigns at will. Traditional marketing often requires a substantial initial investment in print and distribution, with little flexibility once the campaign is launched.

Your **reaction times** in digital marketing allows for immediate adjustments based on campaign performance. If an error is spotted or if a particular aspect of the campaign is underperforming, changes can be made almost instantly. In traditional marketing, adjustments are cumbersome and costly once the material is printed and distributed.

The ability to **analyze the results** and measure the impact of a digital marketing campaign is significantly advanced, with tools to track clicks, impressions, conversions, and detailed audience behavior. Traditional marketing relies more on indirect result measurements like sales variations post-campaign or tracking mechanisms such as QR codes or special offer codes.

# Comparative Table: Digital vs. Traditional Marketing

To provide a clearer understanding, Table 20-1 compares digital marketing with traditional marketing across several key variables.

## CHAPTER 20  DIGITAL MARKETING VS. TRADITIONAL MARKETING: A COMPARISON

*Table 20-1.* Digital vs. traditional marketing

| Aspect | Digital Marketing | Traditional Marketing | Notes |
| --- | --- | --- | --- |
| Initial setup cost | Generally low | Typically high | Digital channels offer scalable options suitable for all budgets |
| Flexibility | High | Low | Digital campaigns can be adjusted or halted at any moment |
| Reach | Global | Usually local or regional | Digital marketing isn't limited by geographical boundaries |
| Reaction times | Immediate | Slow | Changes in digital campaigns can be made quickly and efficiently |
| Results tracking | Detailed and real time | Indirect and delayed | Digital tools offer precise tracking and analytics |
| Asset reusability | High | Low | Assets like ad creatives can be easily modified and reused in digital formats |

While the digital marketing landscape offers numerous benefits such as precise targeting, real-time data analytics, and broad geographical reach, traditional marketing methods still hold significant relevance today. The value of traditional marketing primarily hinges on your target group. If your audience includes a demographic more attuned to traditional media—such as print newspapers, television, or direct mail—these channels can be incredibly effective. Consequently, balancing digital and traditional marketing approaches can be essential, depending on the behaviors and preferences of your target audience. Understanding and integrating both approaches based on your specific market needs will provide a comprehensive marketing strategy that captures all potential engagement opportunities.

## Practical Considerations for Marketers and Service Partners

When managing or transitioning to digital marketing campaigns, it's important to work closely with service partners who understand both the potential and the limitations of digital channels.

Service partners should provide clear guidance on optimizing digital campaigns across various platforms. They should be adept at using tracking tools and interpreting data to refine marketing strategies.

A well-prepared brief helps ensure all parties understand the campaign objectives, desired outcomes, and available resources. It guides the creation of creatives and the choice of platforms, ensuring coherence in marketing messages.

## Summary

In this chapter, I have outlined the key differences between digital and traditional marketing:

- Digital marketing offers speed, cost-effectiveness, flexibility, and precise measurability.

- Traditional marketing, while sometimes offering richer tactile experiences, lacks the immediacy and adaptability of digital methods.

- Understanding these differences is crucial for effectively allocating your marketing budget and resources.

In the next chapter, I will delve into the available channels, providing an in-depth overview of their characteristics for you to understand their pros, cons, and use cases.

# CHAPTER 21

# Digital Marketing Channels Overview: From Core to Specialized

In this chapter, I will give you a general overview of digital marketing channels. I've classified them into three categories: core, emerging, and specialized channels in an effort to make them easier to understand. I will cover core channels, expand into the less traditional and emergent sectors like DOOH (digital out-of-home) and cinema advertising, and give you an overview of specialized channels such as voice search ads. This will help you understand the wide array of available channels, including their specific use cases, advantages, disadvantages, and their main ad formats.

Please remember that digital marketing is a dynamic world, and there could be new emergent channels not covered in this book. Most of this book's jargon and processes are directly related to core and emergent channels. Specific channels, such as augmented reality ads, may use specific concepts not covered in this book.

CHAPTER 21   DIGITAL MARKETING CHANNELS OVERVIEW: FROM CORE TO SPECIALIZED

I classify display ads, search ads, native ads, social media ads, email marketing ads, and mobile and in-app ads as core channels. Connected TV, addressable TV, digital out-of-home, cinema ads, and print ads with programmatic buying get into the emerging channels, and voice search, augmented reality, podcasts, interactive content, and blockchain and crypto ads are specialized channels.

I will start with the core channels.

# Introduction to Core Digital Marketing Channels

Core channels represent the most utilized and well-known channels in digital advertising. They are used by most agencies, freelancers, and other service partners, and its formats, details, and targeting options are well known. You can expect your service partner to have experience on how to use core channels and get similar results over and over again.

## Display Ads

Display advertising represents one of the core channels of online marketing, encompassing various graphical advertisements placed around web content, within apps, or on social media platforms. This form of advertising is known for capturing attention through visual appeal.

***Advantages***
Display ads offer high visibility and a broad reach, making them an excellent choice for getting your message out across a wide array of digital landscapes. Their prominent placement can significantly increase brand awareness and draw traffic to your website. For Display Ads to return the expected results, Ad Quality and Targeting should be appropriate for your

target group, and their visuals and message should resonate with your audience.[1]

### *Disadvantages*
The main challenge with display ads lies in their potential to be ignored, especially if not targeted or designed appropriately. **Ad blindness** is a common issue where users subconsciously ignore banner-like information, which can diminish the effectiveness of your campaigns. You can prevent part of this blindness by creating creatives and copy that resonate with your target audience.

### *Examples*
A typical example of display advertising is banner ads on news websites, where they are strategically placed to attract the reader's attention without interrupting article reading.

### *Use Cases*
These ads are particularly effective for brand awareness campaigns where the goal is to capture as many eyes as possible across varying demographics and placements and for getting visitors for your landing page (for instance, in the case of click campaigns).

### *Main Ad Formats*
The most common formats for display ads include video ads, image ads, and banner ads, each offering different levels of engagement depending on the content and context of their placement.

### *Key Requirements*
One of the crucial requirements for successful display advertising is the need for creativity in visual design. Ads must be visually appealing to stand out amidst a sea of content and capture user interest.

---

[1] Check Chapter 6 on targeting and Chapter 11 on ad quality for more details.

### Targeting

Effective targeting is essential for the success of display ads. Advertisers need to target their ads based on demographics, interests, and behaviors to ensure they reach the appropriate audience, making the ads more relevant and less likely to be ignored. You should also consider the context your audience is in (by using, e.g., keywords present in the content[2]) to make sure your creatives resonate with them.

## Search Ads (SEM Ads)

Search Engine Marketing, commonly known as SEM, features advertisements that are shown in search engine results. This method can be tremendously effective as you're catching potential customers in the act of seeking out products or services like yours. This is called by some the user intent, and some platforms also allow you to target specific intents, such as buying intent.[3]

### Advantages

The main strength of SEM lies in its ability to target users with a specific intent in a context in which they are already looking for something. When users search for specific terms, they have a clear intention, and presenting them with your ad at that moment maximizes visibility and increases the likelihood of conversion. As you read in Chapter 11 on Ad Quality, advertiser channel providers decide whom, when, and where to show your ad based on a multitude of variables, which seek to make sure that your ad resonates with the user that will see it.

### Disadvantages

However, the high effectiveness of SEM means it's a popular strategy, which can drive up costs significantly. Especially in competitive markets,

---

[2] Check Chapter 14 on keywords for a quick overview.
[3] Check the section "Keyword Intent and User Behavior" in Chapter 14 for more on intents.

you might find yourself in a bidding war over popular keywords and even in cannibalization situations[4] if you are not careful with your targeting settings. A good keyword research, target group definition, and competition research will help you minimize these risks.

### *Examples*

For instance, if you're retailing athletic footwear, placing ads for "buy sports shoes online" can attract buyers who are ready to purchase, providing immediate visibility to your store. If your footwear is specific for, say, running, then adding that keyword will prevent showing your ad to people looking for biking footwear that will most likely not be interested in your product.

### *Use Cases*

This strategy is particularly potent for driving immediate sales. By targeting users who are actively searching to buy, you can significantly shorten the buyer's journey.

### *Main Ad Formats*

The primary format used in SEM is text ads. These are straightforward, focusing on delivering a concise message based on the user's search terms. These ads should match the copy on your landing page and should deliver on their promise. If your copy mentions a promotion, you should have that promotion available on your website.

### *Key Requirements*

To succeed with SEM, you must invest time in keyword research and continually optimize your campaigns based on performance data if you run a long-term campaign. This ongoing refinement helps maintain cost-efficiency and effectiveness.

---

[4] Check Chapter 7 on cannibalization for more information.

### Targeting

At its core, SEM is all about keyword-based and intent-based targeting. You select keywords related to your products or services, and your ads appear when those keywords are searched. The precision of your keyword strategy directly influences the success of your campaigns. The keywords you select are directly related to the awareness level[5] of your target group. Of course, other criteria such as demographics and geo targeting also play a role in SEM.

## Native Ads

Native advertising represents a seamless integration of ads into the content of the placement, ensuring that the user experience remains uninterrupted. These ads mimic the form and function of natural content (thus the name native ads) within the environment they appear in, making them less obtrusive and more engaging for users.

### Advantages

Native ads are known for their subtlety, which often results in higher engagement rates compared to more overt advertising formats. By blending in with the platform's content, they maintain the user's flow and can improve the receptivity of your message when the targeting is right.

### Disadvantages

The very subtlety that makes native ads appealing can also be a drawback. Because they blend in so well, it's possible that users might not recognize them as ads, which can sometimes reduce the direct impact you might expect from more straightforward advertising approaches.

---

[5] Check Chapter 4 on awareness levels for more on this.

## Examples
A common example of native advertising can be seen in sponsored articles on news portals. These articles are designed to look like standard news items, but they promote specific products or brands subtly within the content.

## Use Cases
Native ads are particularly effective for campaigns aimed at enhancing the user experience without a disruptive sales pitch. They are excellent for storytelling, thought leadership, or softly introducing a new product or service in line with the content the user is already consuming.

## Main Ad Formats
The typical formats for native advertising include sponsored content and in-feed ads. These formats are designed to flow naturally with the site's regular content, providing a smooth visual and contextual user experience.

## Key Requirements
For native ads to be effective, the content must closely match the native content of the platform on which it's displayed. This matching involves not just the visual design but also the tone and style of the writing.

## Targeting
Effective native ads use contextual and interest-based targeting to make sure that the ads meet the likely interests of the viewers based on the content they are engaging with, thereby enhancing relevance and engagement.

# Social Media Ads

Social media platforms[6] like Facebook, X (ex-Twitter), and Instagram have become ubiquitous in the digital advertising space, offering a dynamic environment where targeted content can reach a broad or highly specific audience.

---

[6] Check Chapter 43 for an overview on social media.

## CHAPTER 21   DIGITAL MARKETING CHANNELS OVERVIEW: FROM CORE TO SPECIALIZED

How specific the audience can be depends on the information the user gives the social media platform and its use and activity on it. It also depends on the data privacy policies for each geographic location. For example, in Europe the platforms can use less tracking than in other areas where data privacy is not that important. The reach is also dependent on the number of users in a specific region. For instance, if you are aware that your target group does not use Facebook, then a campaign on that platform won't give you good results.

### *Advantages*
The power of social media ads lies in their detailed targeting capabilities which allow you to segment audiences by demographics, interests, behaviors, and more, ensuring your messages reach the right people. These channels also boast high user engagement, making them ideal for interactive campaigns.

### *Disadvantages*
However, the very features that make social media platforms so attractive also demand a high level of commitment. Constant content creation and optimization are necessary to keep up with the fast-paced nature of these platforms and to remain relevant to your audience. If you are hoping for broad reach using organic content, then you have to invest on the platform creating content and interacting with your followers. If you use paid ads, then you still have to have a social media strategy, as the users will most likely visit your profile to know more about your brand and your products. If your profile is deserted, you will leave a bad first impression.

### *Examples*
Consider a scenario where a fashion brand launches an Instagram ad campaign for its new summer collection. By using vibrant image ads, engaging video content, and interactive carousel ads, the brand can showcase various styles, drawing users into its colorful world of fashion.

### Use Cases

Social media ads are particularly effective for building brand engagement and fostering customer loyalty. They provide a platform for brands to not only advertise but also interact directly with their customers, answer their queries in real time, and quickly gauge feedback on new products or campaigns.

### Main Ad Formats

The main formats employed in social media advertising include image ads, which capture attention with compelling visuals; video ads, which can tell a deeper story or demonstrate a product in action; and carousel ads, which allow multiple images or videos in a single ad, giving users a richer experience.

### Key Requirements

Creating content that resonates and engages is crucial. The content needs to be not only visually appealing, but also aligned with the interests and preferences of the target audience to encourage interaction and engagement.

### Targeting

Effective social media advertising employs detailed demographic, psychographic, and behavioral targeting to tailor content that is likely to interest and engage the specified segment of users. Because of data privacy policies,[7] this is not so easy in some regions, and some advertiser channel providers tend to suggest using automated targeting options instead of detailed targeting. Their documentation not always details why, but it is understandable if they can track each time less detailed data about their users and use more artificial intelligence models to try to understand user behavior.

---

[7] Check Chapter 26 for an overview of the legal landscape in digital marketing.

# Email Marketing

Email marketing utilizes the direct and personal nature of email to promote products and services while fostering relationships with potential and existing customers. This channel is a staple in digital marketing strategies due to its precision and customization capabilities and is usually undervalued in comparison to other channels.

### *Advantages*
One of the most significant advantages of email marketing is the level of direct communication it enables. You can reach your audience right in their inboxes, which allows for highly personalized interactions. This personal touch can significantly enhance the effectiveness of your campaigns (if done right), especially when it comes to customer retention and loyalty.

### *Disadvantages*
However, a major challenge with email marketing is the potential for emails to be marked as spam. This not only prevents your messages from reaching your audience but can also hurt your brand's reputation. Ensuring your email content is relevant and welcomed is crucial to avoid falling into the spam folder. By working with service providers with experience in email marketing, you will be able to prevent most of its disadvantages, but not all of them.

### *Examples*
A classic example of email marketing is sending out a monthly newsletter that keeps your subscribers informed about the latest news, tips, or offers related to your industry. Another common practice is sending promotional emails that provide exclusive offers or discounts to your email list.

In email marketing, one important point is how you get the emails in your list. Nowadays, there are many best-practices that, on one side, help you prevent your emails to be classified as spam, but on the other side, make it more difficult for you to grow your email list. One example is double-opt-ins, where the user can subscribe to your email list in a form and then has to confirm that subscription by clicking a link on an email.

### Use Cases

Email marketing is particularly effective for loyalty programs and lead nurturing. For instance, you can send targeted offers to repeat customers or provide valuable content that moves leads further along the buying process. This is usually related to email funnels, where you set up a series of emails depending on the interactions the user has with them and your brand.

### Main Ad Formats

The predominant formats used in email marketing are email newsletters, promotional emails, and transactional emails. Each format serves different purposes, from educating your audience to driving sales. Depending on how you got the email address and the term and conditions your users agreed on, you may or may not send promotional content. Each case is unique, and I suggest asking your service partner for more information if you have any doubts.

### Key Requirements

To execute effective email marketing campaigns, you need a robust email list built with proper consent from the recipients. Engaging content that adds value to your subscribers is critical to keep open rates high and maintain a healthy sender reputation.

### Targeting

Effective targeting in email marketing relies on detailed segmentation of your subscriber list. This might include demographic segmentation, past purchase behavior, or engagement level, allowing you to tailor your messages according to the specific needs and interests of different audience segments.

CHAPTER 21   DIGITAL MARKETING CHANNELS OVERVIEW: FROM CORE TO SPECIALIZED

# Mobile and In-App Ads

Mobile and in-app advertising involves placing ads within mobile applications, which allows you to capture user´s attention directly within the app environment, where they are already engaged.

*Advantages*
The primary strength of mobile and in-app ads lies in their ability to hold users' attention, where they already spend a lot of their digital time. These ads can yield high engagement rates, especially if they are well-integrated into the app experience without being too intrusive.

*Disadvantages*
However, the major limitation comes from the device itself—the small screen size of most mobile devices can restrict the amount of content you can effectively display. This requires more creativity and precision in ad design. Another disadvantage is the so-called thumb-click. I explained this in more detail in Chapter 8.

*Examples*
A classic example is in-game ads within mobile games, which can range from banner ads displayed during game pauses to full-screen interstitial ads between levels. These ads can even be interactive, like rewarded video ads that offer in-game rewards for watching a full advertisement.

*Use Cases*
These ads are particularly useful for promoting app-specific products or services, such as new app features or premium content upgrades. They are also effective for campaigns meant to increase user engagement and retention within the app.

*Main Ad Formats*
The primary formats for mobile and in-app advertising include banner ads, which usually appear at the top or bottom of the app; interstitial ads,

which are full-screen ads shown at natural transition points in the app; and rewarded video ads, which users choose to watch in exchange for in-app rewards.

*Key Requirements*
Creating successful mobile and in-app ads demands mobile-optimized creative content that is visually appealing and quick to load. The ads must be designed to provide value without disrupting the user experience. If your ad leads to a landing page outside an app, then this has to be optimized for mobile devices.

*Targeting*
Effective targeting for mobile and in-app ads often utilizes app usage data and demographic information. This ensures that the ads are shown to users who are most likely to find the ad relevant and engaging based on their previous interactions within the app.

# Emerging Digital Marketing Channels

Emerging channels incorporate digital advancements into traditional advertising, offering new ways to reach audiences as technology evolves.

## Connected TV (CTV)

Connected TV (CTV) brings together the world of traditional television and digital streaming, allowing advertisements to be displayed on Internet-connected televisions via streaming apps such as Hulu or Netflix.

*Advantages*
The primary advantage of using CTV for advertising is its ability to merge the extensive reach of traditional television with the precision of digital targeting. This combination allows you to present your ads to a broad audience while still tailoring your message to specific viewer preferences.

### Disadvantages

However, CTV comes with challenges, notably the fragmentation of platforms and the generally higher costs associated with producing and distributing high-quality video content. Navigating through various platform requirements and ensuring content compatibility can also complicate campaign execution.

### Examples

Imagine deploying targeted ads for a new home decor line during a popular home renovation show streamed on Hulu. This method ensures your ads are seen by viewers interested in home improvement, maximizing relevance and engagement.

### Use Cases

CTV is especially effective for targeted brand advertising, where the goal is to combine the impact of visual media with tailored ad delivery. It's ideal for reaching audiences watching specific types of content, where the non-intrusive format of the ads can complement their viewing experience without disruption.

### Main Ad Formats

Video ads are predominant in CTV, capitalizing on the high-definition display capabilities of modern televisions to capture viewer attention with visually engaging content. Image ads are also available on some platforms.

### Key Requirements

Producing high-quality video content is a must, as poor-quality ads can detract from viewer experience and reduce campaign effectiveness. Ensuring that your content meets the technical specifications of various CTV platforms is also crucial.

*Targeting*
Targeting on CTV is driven by viewer behavior and preferences. This can include factors such as previous viewing habits, program preferences, and even time-of-day viewing patterns, allowing for highly specific audience targeting.

## Addressable TV (ATV)

Addressable TV (ATV) is a new approach in television advertising, where different ads are displayed to different households even though they might be watching the same program. This innovation allows for a more individualized advertising experience.

ATV leverages technology to segment TV audiences based on specific data collected through set-top boxes or features available in Smart TVs, enabling advertisers to tailor their messages to different demographics within the same viewer base.

*Advantages*
The major advantage of ATV is its high level of targeting precision, which ensures that your advertising budget is utilized more efficiently. By focusing on households that match your target demographic, ATV minimizes waste and enhances the effectiveness of ad spend.

*Disadvantages*
However, one significant challenge with ATV is the need for detailed consumer data, which raises important privacy concerns. Advertisers must navigate these sensitively and comply with relevant data protection regulations to avoid backlash and legal complications.

**Examples**
An example of ATV in action would include targeting pet owners with specific pet food commercials during family-oriented television shows, ensuring that the ads shown are relevant to the household's interests.

### Use Cases
ATV allows companies to focus their television advertising efforts on the segment of the audience most likely to be interested in their products or services, rather than broadcasting the same ad to all viewers.

### Main Ad Formats
The primary format used in ATV is video ads, which are customized to appeal to different viewer segments based on the collected set-top box data. Image ads in L format are also widely supported.

### Key Requirements
To implement ATV effectively, you need to establish partnerships with cable providers or other platforms that support addressable TV technology. These partnerships are necessary to access viewer data and to distribute the ads appropriately.

### Targeting
Targeting in ATV is household-specific and show-specific. This data might include viewing habits, demographic information, or other relevant details that help define each household's consumer profile.

## Digital Out-of-Home (DOOH)

Digital out-of-home advertising represents modern outdoor advertising technologies such as digital billboards and electronic signs that enrich public spaces. Unlike static billboards, DOOH can show animated or changing content that grabs attention in real time.

### Advantages
The dynamic nature of DOOH allows for frequent content changes, allowing advertisers the flexibility to update their messaging in real time. This adaptability, combined with the broad and instant reach of DOOH, makes it an effective channel for catching the attention of large audiences as they commute or go about their daily activities.

# CHAPTER 21 DIGITAL MARKETING CHANNELS OVERVIEW: FROM CORE TO SPECIALIZED

**Disadvantages**

However, the advanced technology involved in DOOH comes with high initial setup and ongoing maintenance costs. The investment required to establish and sustain a DOOH campaign can be significant, often making it more suited to larger brands or those dedicated to long-term outdoor campaigns. By working with partners that are already integrated with DOOH Inventory, you will have lower entry costs. The use of programmatic buying for those providers that support this buying method also allows for more opportunities.

**Examples**

One common application of DOOH is digital billboards in high-traffic areas, such as city centers or busy highways, which display varying content like news updates, weather, or targeted ads based on the time of day or current events.

**Use Cases**

DOOH is particularly valuable for campaigns that require broad reach and the ability to react to real-time information. For instance, a retail brand can use DOOH to promote flash sales during specific times of the day to drive foot traffic to nearby stores.

**Main Ad Formats**

The primary format used in DOOH advertising includes dynamic digital displays that can present video or animated content, enhancing the visual appeal and engagement potential of the ads.

**Key Requirements**

To implement a successful DOOH campaign, advertisers need access to high-traffic public locations where digital displays are permissible and visible. Ensuring optimal placement is crucial to maximize audience exposure.

### Targeting

DOOH allows for targeting based on specific times or locations, catering to audiences when and where engagement is most likely to occur. This level of targeting helps optimize the impact of each displayed ad, ensuring it reaches relevant viewers.

## Cinema Ads with Programmatic Buying

Cinema advertising with programmatic buying represents an innovative approach where traditional cinema ads are purchased and placed through automated, real-time bidding systems. This method combines the precision of digital targeting with the immersive, high-impact environment of movie theaters.

These ads allow advertisers to leverage data to target specific audiences attending a movie screening, adjusting ad placements based on factors like movie genre and session times.

### *Advantages*

The primary benefit of cinema advertising is the captive audience it secures. Ads displayed before movie start times reach an audience that is already engaged and receptive, providing an unmatched visual and audio impact due to the cinematic environment.

### *Disadvantages*

A limitation of this medium is the restricted number of sessions, which can limit the ad's reach. Unlike continuous online platforms, the opportunity for ad placement is bound to the cinema's schedule and the specific movie's popularity.

### *Examples*

Imagine targeting ads for a new luxury car before screenings of a highly anticipated action film known to attract a demographic likely to be interested in high-end vehicles. This precise targeting ensures your ad spend is directed toward a relevant audience.

### Use Cases

This format is particularly valuable for high-impact promotional campaigns that aim to create substantial brand impressions. Brands looking to launch new products or generate buzz around special events might find this advertising method especially beneficial.

### Main Ad Formats

The primary format in cinema advertising is video ads, which allow for dynamic, compelling storytelling that takes full advantage of the theater's audio and visual capabilities.

### Key Requirements

Creating cinema ads requires producing high-quality video content that is compliant with cinema specifications, ensuring it looks and sounds great on the big screen.

### Targeting

Targeting for cinema ads is typically based on the genre of the movies and the specific session times, aiming to match the ad content with the interests of the audience attending.

## Print Ads with Programmatic Buying

Print ads with programmatic buying involve the strategic placement of printed advertisements, which are bought and managed using digital programmatic technologies. This approach allows advertisements in print media to be as targeted and data-driven as online ads.

### Advantages

One of the key benefits of integrating programmatic techniques with print advertising is the ability to target specific demographics effectively, utilizing the existing trust and credibility associated with traditional print media. This hybrid approach combines the accountability and specificity of digital targeting with the tangible, reputable presence of print.

### Disadvantages
Despite its novel approach, one downside to this method is that it lacks the immediacy and interactivity of entirely digital channels. The lifecycle from ad design to publication can be longer compared to digital ads, and audience engagement is less easily measured and cannot be optimized in real time.

### Examples
Consider a scenario where a luxury watch brand targets affluent readers by placing ads in the lifestyle section of nationally circulated newspapers. These ads are programmatically bought to appear in editions distributed in high-income zip codes.

### Use Cases
This method is particularly useful for campaigns that aim to leverage the authoritative voice of traditional print, augmented by digital precision. It's ideal for brands that want to maintain a strong physical presence while benefiting from targeted advertisement placements.

### Main Ad Formats
The primary formats used in this type of advertising are printed display ads, which can range from small placements to full-page spreads.

### Key Requirements
Successful execution of print ads with programmatic buying requires close coordination between digital ad platforms and traditional print publishers. Ensuring that the targeting data translates effectively into the print layout and distribution logistics is crucial.

### Targeting
Targeting for these ads is typically focused on reader demographics and regional distribution, aligning ad placements with audience characteristics that are most likely to respond to the specific content of the ad.

CHAPTER 21   DIGITAL MARKETING CHANNELS OVERVIEW: FROM CORE TO SPECIALIZED

# Specialized Digital Marketing Channels

These channels, while not as widespread, provide targeted solutions and leverage cutting-edge technology to engage niche audiences effectively.

## Voice Search Ads

Voice search advertising refers to reaching users via voice-activated devices such as Google Home and Amazon Alexa. It's a dynamic way to interact with your audience by integrating into their daily routines of seeking information through voice commands.

### *Advantages*

The key advantage here is the direct integration into the rapidly expanding use of voice-activated devices. It provides a unique opportunity to engage with users in a highly personal and unobtrusive manner, often during activities that require hands-free assistance.

### *Disadvantages*

However, this channel is still in its early stages concerning advertising metrics and success measurement. Tracking the effectiveness of these ads can be challenging due to the nascent analytics available for voice interactions.

### *Examples*

Imagine a food company that creates voice search ads offering quick cooking tips or recipes when a user asks how to make a certain dish. These ads provide immediate and useful content directly related to the user's query.

### *Use Cases*

Voice search ads are particularly effective for engaging users during hands-free activities, like cooking or driving. They provide timely and useful information or aid, enhancing the user's experience with valuable interaction.

## Main Ad Formats

The predominant format for this type of advertising is audio ads, designed to be clear and engaging to listen to, without the visual support present in other advertising formats.

## Key Requirements

To achieve effective voice search advertising, your content must be optimized for voice search. This involves understanding the nuances of natural language queries and creating content that smart devices can select as the best answer. Clear, concise, and engaging audio content is crucial.

## Targeting

Targeting for voice search ads tends to focus on user queries and interactions with their voice assistants. This requires a deep understanding of common queries related to your product or service and how users might phrase them during a voice search.

# Augmented Reality (AR) Ads

Augmented reality (AR) advertising is transforming the way brands interact with their audiences by offering immersive experiences directly through users' devices. This cutting-edge technology superimposes digital information onto the real world, enhancing the way products and services are presented and experienced.

## Advantages

The primary benefit of AR ads is their high level of engagement. By offering interactive and immersive experiences, AR ads significantly increase user retention and interaction, providing a memorable brand experience that's more likely to lead to conversion. They allow potential customers to visualize products in a realistic setting or interact with digital elements in innovative ways.

### Disadvantages

However, the implementation of AR ads requires access to advanced technology and the development of compatible apps or web platforms, which can be resource-intensive. The development process demands expertise in AR technology and might involve higher costs compared to more traditional ad formats.

### Examples

A notable example is a cosmetics brand using AR for virtual try-ons within their mobile app. Users can see what different makeup products look like on their own faces through their device's camera, enhancing the shopping experience and aiding in decision-making.

### Use Cases

AR ads are particularly effective for interactive product demonstrations and providing rich product experiences. They are invaluable for sectors where how a product looks or functions is crucial to the purchase decision, such as fashion, interior design, or technology.

### Main Ad Formats

The main formats for AR ads include interactive experiences that users can engage with within an AR-capable app or website. These might feature virtual product try-ons, interactive games, or educational experiences embedded into the real world.

### Key Requirements

To create effective AR ads, having an AR-capable app or platform is essential. This platform must be able to handle sophisticated AR content and provide a seamless user experience. Additionally, the creative content for AR ads needs to be meticulously designed to ensure that it is realistic and functional within the AR environment.

### Targeting

Effective targeting for AR ads often involves understanding user behavior and technological compatibility. Users who are more tech-savvy and frequently engage with innovative digital content are more likely to appreciate and interact with AR features.

## Podcast Ads

Podcast advertising provides a unique and intimate way to reach audiences through audio content. These ads are embedded within podcasts, either as part of the audio stream or inserted dynamically, creating opportunities for personal and direct engagement with listeners who are already engaged in the podcast's topic.

### Advantages

The principal advantage of podcast ads is the personal and direct connection they facilitate with listeners. Hosts often read these ads, leveraging their trusted relationship with the audience. This can increase the perceived authenticity and credibility of the advertised products or services.

### Disadvantages

However, the audio-only format of podcasts limits the types of messages that can be effectively communicated. Visual elements of products or complex demonstrations that require visual aid cannot be conveyed through this medium.

### Examples

An example of effective podcast advertising could be a tech company sponsoring a popular technology podcast. The host might mention the company's latest gadget in a segment, describe its features, and possibly share a personal testimonial about their experience with the product.

CHAPTER 21    DIGITAL MARKETING CHANNELS OVERVIEW: FROM CORE TO SPECIALIZED

*Use Cases*

Podcast ads are incredibly effective for building brand authenticity and for engaging niche audiences who are deeply interested in the podcast's subject. They are particularly beneficial for brands looking to establish a strong connection with dedicated communities.

*Main Ad Formats*

The main formats in podcast advertising include audio spots, which are pre-produced ads played during the podcast, and host-read ads, where the host integrates the ad content naturally into their dialogue.

*Key Requirements*

For effective podcast advertising, it's crucial that the ads align well with the podcast's content and audience expectations. Ads should resonate with the podcast's theme to avoid disrupting the listener experience. High-quality audio production is also essential to maintain the professionalism of both the ad and the podcast.

*Targeting*

Targeting for podcast ads typically revolves around the podcast's theme and the demographics of its listeners. Understanding the listener base's interests and preferences is key to creating ads that are relevant and engaging.

## Interactive Content

Interactive content require users to actively engage with web-based interactions. This type of content ranges from quizzes and games to interactive infographics and assessments, providing a hands-on experience that can significantly deepen the user's connection to the brand.

### Advantages

The main advantage of using interactive content is the potential to increase user engagement significantly. By involving users in an active manner, you encourage them to invest more time and thought into the interaction, which can heighten their interest in your brand and message.

### Disadvantages

However, the main challenge with implementing interactive content lies in its complexity. Creating effective interactive tools often requires advanced web development capabilities and strong UX/UI design skills to ensure that the interaction is both enjoyable and functioning smoothly.

### Examples

Consider an example where a health brand provides an online quiz that assesses a user's lifestyle habits to offer personalized health tips. This not only engages users by involving them directly but also provides personalized value, making the interaction beneficial and memorable.

### Use Cases

Interactive content is particularly useful in educational campaigns or customer engagement initiatives where the goal is to involve the audience deeply. It's excellent for promoting learning, changing behaviors, or encouraging exploration of your brand's offerings.

### Main Ad Formats

The most common formats for interactive content include web-based tools like quizzes, games, or interactive videos. These platforms allow users to engage directly with the content, providing immediate feedback or results based on their input.

### Key Requirements

Developing interactive content requires a robust understanding of web development and strong skills in UX/UI design. The content must be accessible, intuitive, and engaging to ensure users complete the interaction.

### Targeting
Effective targeting for interactive content often involves understanding user interests and engagement patterns. By tailoring content to fit user preferences or behaviors, you increase the likelihood of active participation.

## Blockchain and Crypto Ads

Blockchain and crypto advertising platforms utilize decentralized technology to record ad transactions, ensuring that data is immutable and transparent. This can significantly reduce fraud and increase trust among users and advertisers alike.

### Advantages
A major advantage of using blockchain for advertising is the enhanced security and transparency it provides. Transactions on these platforms are verifiable on the blockchain, making it nearly impossible to falsify records or misrepresent data.

### Disadvantages
However, the complexity of blockchain technology can be a barrier to entry for some marketers. Understanding and implementing blockchain solutions requires a specific set of skills and knowledge, which may not be readily available to all marketing teams.

### Examples
Consider crypto wallets that use blockchain ads to reach potential customers on digital platforms that support cryptocurrency transactions. These ads reassure users of the security and reliability of the wallet service.

### Use Cases
This type of advertising is particularly effective for reaching audiences that are tech-savvy and interested in topics related to security, technology, and finance. Campaigns might focus on promoting blockchain-based services or enhancing brand credibility within tech circles.

*Main Ad Format*

The predominant formats used in blockchain and crypto advertising are often display ads placed on websites or platforms that are themselves blockchain-aware or crypto-friendly.

*Key Requirements*

To effectively implement blockchain and crypto ads, marketers need a solid understanding of blockchain technology and access to networks that support blockchain advertising. This might include specialized knowledge of how the blockchain works and the ability to navigate its landscape.

*Targeting*

Targeting for these ads is often focused on users who have demonstrated interest in technology and cryptocurrencies. Marketers might use data on past behavior, such as visits to tech or finance websites, to refine their audience targeting.

Blockchain and crypto ads can be seen as targeting settings and as an advertising channel. Here is a quick clarification. As **targeting settings**, they help in defining the audience within traditional digital marketing channels based on their interest or involvement in crypto and blockchain. As an **advertising channel**, blockchain technologies offer novel platforms and methods for executing and managing advertisements, particularly in ensuring transparency and engaging directly with a tech-savvy audience.

# Visualization of All the Channels

Figure 21-1 shows all the channels with their categories in a simple diagram.

# CHAPTER 21  DIGITAL MARKETING CHANNELS OVERVIEW: FROM CORE TO SPECIALIZED

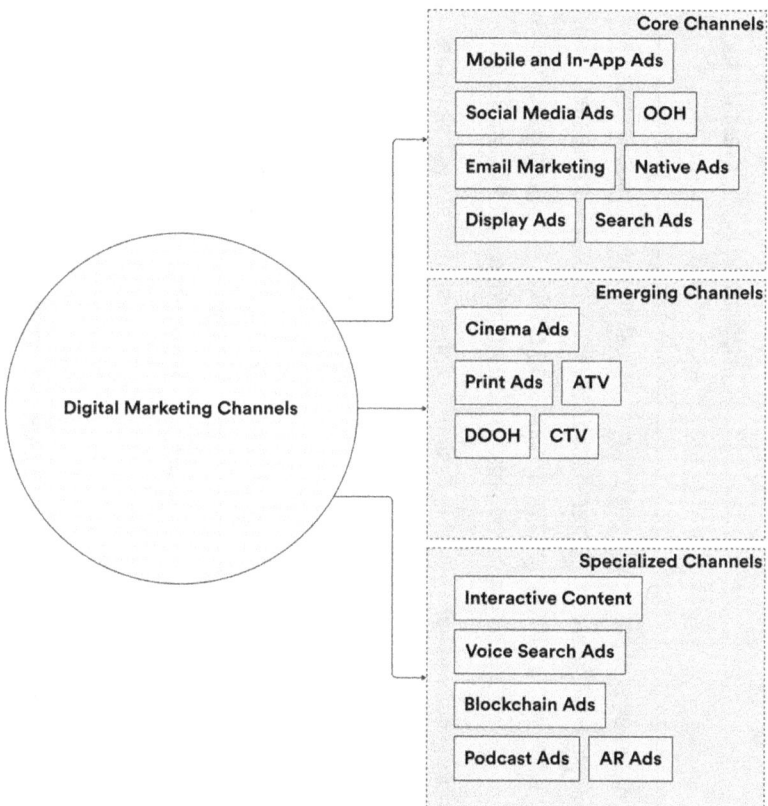

*Figure 21-1.* *Overview of Digital Marketing Channels*

## Comparative Table

To get a better overview of all the channels, here is a comparison table.

## CHAPTER 21  DIGITAL MARKETING CHANNELS OVERVIEW: FROM CORE TO SPECIALIZED

*Table 21-1. Summary and comparison table of digital marketing channels*

| Channel Name | Category | Description | Use Case | Key Benefits | Data Privacy Implications | Why It's Interesting for Marketers |
|---|---|---|---|---|---|---|
| OOH with programmatic buying | Core | Digital out-of-home ads bought programmatically | Brand awareness in high-traffic areas | High visibility; programmatically optimized placements | Must comply with public ad display regulations | High impact, automated buying increases efficiency |
| Display ads | Core | Visual ads on websites and apps | Brand awareness; retargeting | Flexible design options; broad reach | Adhere to data protection and privacy laws | Versatile across many sites, measurable impact |
| Search ads | Core | Ads displayed on search engine results pages | Driving traffic and conversions | High intent targeting; immediate results | Manage customer data responsibly | Directly captures active searchers, increasing conversion likelihood |
| Native ads | Core | Ads matching the media format of their environment | Seamless integration with user content | Non-disruptive; higher user engagement | Transparency in sponsored content needed | Blends with content, improving user acceptance |

# CHAPTER 21  DIGITAL MARKETING CHANNELS OVERVIEW: FROM CORE TO SPECIALIZED

| | | | | | |
|---|---|---|---|---|---|
| Social media ads | Core | Ads on social platforms like Facebook and Instagram | Engaging specific demographics | Advanced targeting; high engagement | Critical to handle data per platform policies | Deep audience insights, dynamic engagement tools |
| Email marketing | Core | Direct promotional messages via email | Targeted promotions; direct customer communication | Personalized messages; measurable responses | Compliance with anti-spam laws necessary | Direct line to customers, high personalization potential |
| Mobile and in-app ads | Core | Ads displayed within mobile applications | Engage mobile users; promote app-specific offers | High user engagement; targeted to mobile behavior | Must manage app data and permissions carefully | Captures the growing mobile user base effectively |
| CTV | Emerging | Ads delivered via connected TV devices | Broadening reach with targeted TV ads | Combines TV's visual impact with digital targeting | Respecting viewer privacy with data collection | Merges traditional TV reach with digital precision |

*(continued)*

## CHAPTER 21 DIGITAL MARKETING CHANNELS OVERVIEW: FROM CORE TO SPECIALIZED

*Table 21-1. (continued)*

| Channel Name | Category | Description | Use Case | Key Benefits | Data Privacy Implications | Why It's Interesting for Marketers |
|---|---|---|---|---|---|---|
| ATV | Emerging | Targeted ads via addressable TV technologies | Precision marketing in TV advertising | Household-level targeting; wastes less ad spend | Household data usage must be privacy compliant | Ultra-targeted TV ads enhancing ROI |
| DOOH | Emerging | Digital signage in public spaces | Dynamic public advertising | Real-time content updates; interactive options | Public display rules around data and content | Dynamic, often interactive, and highly visible |
| Cinema ads with programmatic buying | Emerging | Programmatic ads in cinema screens | Captive audience marketing | High impact; audience-specific content | Ad content and placements must align with venue rules | High engagement potential during leisure activity |
| Print ads with programmatic buying | Emerging | Targeted print ads bought programmatically | Reaching specific readership demographics | Integrates print's credibility with digital efficiency | Must respect data used for targeting | Brings precision targeting to traditional media |

## CHAPTER 21  DIGITAL MARKETING CHANNELS OVERVIEW: FROM CORE TO SPECIALIZED

| | | | | | |
|---|---|---|---|---|---|
| Voice search ads | Specialized | Audio ads triggered by voice search | Engaging users via voice-activated devices | Direct interaction; growing use of voice tech | Voice data handling needs rigorous privacy measures | Taps into the expanding use of voice technologies |
| Augmented reality ads | Specialized | Immersive ads using AR technology | Interactive brand experiences | Memorable, engaging user interactions | User data from AR interactions requires careful handling | Offers novel, engaging ways to experience a brand |
| Podcast ads | Specialized | Advertisements integrated into podcasts | Targeting podcast listeners | Personal and direct connection with listeners | Listener data usage and privacy must be considered | Appeals to dedicated audiences; personal touch |
| Interactive content | Specialized | Engaging ads that require user interaction | Educational and engaging campaigns | High user involvement; potential for virality | Interaction data must be managed transparently | Drives engagement through active participation |
| Blockchain and crypto ads | Specialized | Ads related to blockchain and cryptocurrencies | Targeting tech-savvy, finance-focused audiences | Enhanced security; niche market reach | Highly sensitive data requires robust security | Accesses niche markets with high investment potential |

199

CHAPTER 21   DIGITAL MARKETING CHANNELS OVERVIEW: FROM CORE TO SPECIALIZED

In Table 21-1, you find a comparative analysis of various digital marketing channels categorized by core, emerging, and specialized types, each described with their use cases, key benefits, data privacy implications, and relevance to marketers. This format helps you quickly grasp the nuances and strategic importance of each channel, informing better decision-making for campaign planning.

# Summary

In this chapter, I gave you an overview of the main digital marketing channels, and I classified them into three categories for easier understanding. You should at least remember the following:

- This chapter covered a broad spectrum of digital marketing channels, from the widely used core channels to specialized platforms that cater to specific needs.

- Understanding the unique characteristics and requirements of each channel allows you to tailor your marketing strategies effectively, maximizing reach and engagement.

- Emergent and specialized channels offer innovative opportunities for engagement, often involving the latest technologies, but you have to consider that these are harder to use.

In the next chapter, I'll list and explain the main formats used in these channels and highlight the most important aspects to consider.

CHAPTER 22

# Advertising Formats and Their Creatives

In this chapter, I explore various advertising formats and their specific creatives. Each format varies in its design, delivery, and impact, making it essential to understand their unique aspects to effectively plan and execute your advertising strategies.

## Overview of Advertising Formats

I will give you an overview of 17 formats, with their specifics. Here is the list of formats as an overview:

1. **AMP Banner and HTML Banners**: Banners designed using AMP for fast mobile loading; HTML 5 banners can also be interactive.

2. **Image Ads**: Graphical ads of varying sizes and formats.

3. **Text Ads**: Ads consisting of headline text, a URL, and a description, typically seen in search engine results.

4. **Responsive Text Ads**: Ads adjusting size, appearance, and format automatically to fit available spaces.

5. **Responsive Display Ads (RDA):** Ads adjusting automatically in size, appearance, and format, utilizing uploaded assets like images, videos, headlines, and descriptions.

6. **Audio Ads:** Ads delivered in audio format, used on platforms like podcasts and music streaming.

7. **Video Ads:** Ads using video content, appearing before, during, or after other video content and other placements.

8. **Lead Ads:** Ads designed for collecting user information such as email addresses directly within the ad.

9. **Inventory Ads:** Ads promoting multiple products from an inventory, often personalized dynamically based on a feed.

10. **Shopping Ads:** Ads showing products with images, prices, and business names, used in ecommerce.

11. **Carousel Ads:** Ads allowing multiple images or videos each with its own link, ideal for product showcasing or to tell a story.

12. **Interstitial Ads:** Full-screen ads covering the host app or site interface, used during transition points on mobile.

13. **Native Ads:** Ads blending in with surrounding content, designed to mimic the platform's look and feel.

14. **Dynamic Ads:** Ads personalizing content automatically based on a user's past behavior, such as viewed items.

15. **App Install Ads:** Ads designed specifically to drive app downloads, featured across various platforms.

16. **Sponsored Content**: Articles or posts resembling editorial content but paid for by advertisers.

17. **Pop-Up Ads**: Ads that appear in a new window over or under the website content, often used to grab attention or promote special offers.

Let's move into the details of each one.

## HTML Banners

HTML banners leverage a combination of HTML, CSS, and JavaScript, enabling advertisers to implement animations, videos, and other interactive elements. These creative features make HTML banners a powerful tool for captivating audiences and driving engagement.

*Figure 22-1. Example mockup of an HTML banner*

Figure 22-1 represents a standard 250x250 pixel HTML banner, with an image, a header, and the URL. An HTML banner can have as much or as little information as you want.

### Why HTML Banners Matter

HTML banners provide an enhanced user experience through interactivity that static banners can't offer. This makes them particularly effective at capturing the user's attention and encouraging more profound engagement with the ad's content. With animations you also display more information compared to a static banner.

### Usage Recommendations

For effective use, HTML banners should be designed responsively to ensure they look great across all devices. Additionally, keeping animations subtle and ensuring quick load times are essential practices to prevent user distraction or frustration.

### Related Concepts

Interactive content, animation, and responsive design are key concepts related to HTML banners. Understanding these areas can significantly boost the effectiveness of your ad creatives.

### Example Use Case

Imagine an automotive company launching a new model. They could use an HTML banner with interactive elements allowing users to change the car's color and view it from different angles directly within the ad, significantly enhancing interaction rates.

### Relevant Channels

HTML banners are suitable for

- Display ads
- Mobile and in-app ads
- Social media ads

This broad applicability makes them a versatile option in digital marketing campaigns.

**Important Requirements**
It is crucial that HTML banners adhere to web standards for accessibility and responsiveness. Ensuring compatibility across different browsers and devices is also essential.

**Advantages**
The interactive nature of HTML banners can lead to higher engagement rates. Additionally, their ability to include rich media like video and audio can provide a more immersive experience than static ads.

**Disadvantages**
HTML banners require more bandwidth and can lead to longer loading times if not optimized correctly. They might also require higher levels of skill and resources to create effectively compared to simpler ad formats.

# AMP Banners

In today's fast-paced, mobile-first world, it's crucial for your advertisements to load quickly and effectively engage users on all of their devices. This is where AMP (Accelerated Mobile Pages) banners come into play.

AMP banners are streamlined HTML ads designed specifically for fast loading on mobile devices. Utilizing the AMP framework, these banners ensure that your content reaches your audience without the frustrating wait times.

**Usage Recommendations**
It's best to use AMP banners when targeting users who primarily access content via mobile devices, especially in regions with slower Internet connections. Keep the design simple but compelling to capture attention quickly without overwhelming the user.

**Related Concepts**
Efficiency and mobile optimization are key concepts associated with AMP banners. These reflect the core purpose of the AMP framework—to streamline content for swift mobile performance.

**Example Use Case**

Imagine a sports apparel company launching a limited-time sale. They could deploy AMP banners to promote the sale across various mobile platforms, ensuring that the ads load instantly even during high-traffic periods, which enhances user engagement and potentially increases conversion rates.

**Relevant Channels**

AMP banners are particularly effective in

- Mobile and in-app ads
- Display ads targeting mobile users

These channels benefit from AMP banners' quick-loading capabilities.

**Important Requirements**

Ensure that your AMP banners are compliant with the AMP specification and regularly update them to align with the latest standards and best practices in mobile advertising.

Some advertiser channel providers may not support AMP banners or only support a subset of their features, such as Google Ads.

**Advantages**

The main advantage of AMP banners is their speed, which significantly reduces load time and improves the overall user experience on mobile devices.

**Disadvantages**

One limitation of AMP banners is their restrictive nature, as they sometimes require compromises in creative design and functionality to maintain high performance.

### Key Points of AMP Banners

- AMP banners significantly reduce mobile ad load times, enhancing user engagement.
- They are best used in mobile-focused advertising channels, such as in-app and display ads.
- While offering speed, AMP banners may require simplified designs, which could limit creative execution.

## Text Ads

Text ads are one of the simplest yet most effective forms of digital advertising. They are primarily composed of a headline, description, and often a display URL. They are designed to convey a clear, direct message to the user, prompting immediate action such as a click.

The number of text fields varies from one advertiser channel provider to another, as well as the maximum number of characters per field.

Text ads are a quick way to connect your offerings with those actively seeking similar solutions, and mainly make use of keywords and intents in your targeting.

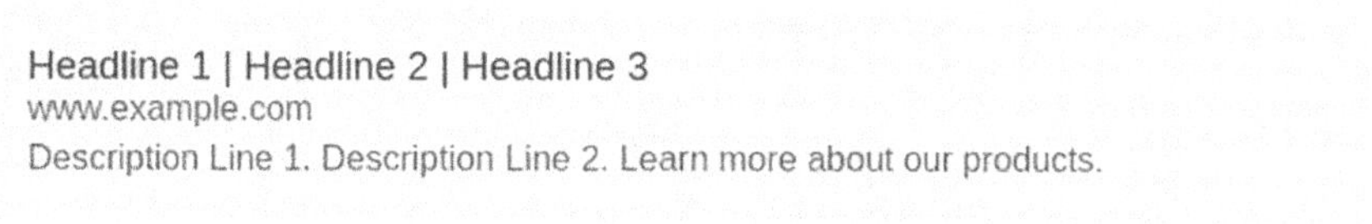

> Headline 1 | Headline 2 | Headline 3
> www.example.com
> Description Line 1. Description Line 2. Learn more about our products.

*Figure 22-2.* Example mockup of a search ad

### How to Create Effective Text Ads

When creating text ads, focus on clear, actionable language and relevance to the keywords or audience you aim to target. It's essential that your ads address the user's intent and offer a compelling reason to click.

# CHAPTER 22　ADVERTISING FORMATS AND THEIR CREATIVES

You need to be aware of the Awareness Level of your target group and adapt your message to it.[1]

**Why Text Ads Matter**
Text ads are important because of their simplicity and effectiveness in reaching target audiences directly through search results and web content. These ads are straightforward, making them easily comprehensible and quick to load, which enhances the user experience (when they are correctly crafted).

**Usage Recommendations**
For text ads to be effective, it's crucial that they be clear, concise, and contain a call to action. Ensure your ads are targeted correctly using appropriate keywords that resonate with your potential customers.

**Related Concepts**
Search engine marketing (SEM), keyword optimization, and click-through rates (CTR) are fundamental concepts related to text ads. Understanding these can greatly improve the effectiveness of your text ads campaign.

**Example Use Case**
Imagine a local bakery that uses text ads to promote their weekend sale on pastries. By targeting keywords like "fresh bakery items" and "weekend pastry sale," they attract customers who are already looking for such products, directly leading to increased foot traffic and sales.

**Related Channels**
Text ads are primarily effective in

- Search ads
- Display ads (as contextual text ads)
- Native ads

---

[1] Check Chapter 4 on Awareness Levels for more details on this.

# CHAPTER 22   ADVERTISING FORMATS AND THEIR CREATIVES

These channels utilize text ads to blend seamlessly with the content, ensuring higher engagement and relevance. The most known example is Google Search Ads, which appear above the search results.

**Important Requirements**

Text ads should have precisely targeted keywords and comply with the advertising standards of the platforms they're hosted on, such as character limits and prohibited content guidelines.

**Advantages**

Text ads are cost-effective and simple to create. They provide immediate results and are easy to modify, making them ideal for testing different marketing strategies.

Nowadays, you can use artificial intelligence tools to craft great search ads, when you understand the limitations of those tools.[2]

**Disadvantages**

Despite their simplicity, text ads have limitations in engagement due to the lack of visual elements. They might also face high competition, especially for popular keywords, which can drive up the cost.

**Key Points for Text Ads**

Text ads offer an approach to reach specific audiences directly through their simple yet powerful format. They are especially effective in search-driven marketing strategies, providing direct responses to user queries. However, their impact might be less than more visual ad formats, requiring strategic keyword usage and clear calls to action.

- Text ads consist of a headline, description, and a display URL, crafted to elicit direct user actions.

---

[2] Check Part 7 on Digital Marketing and Artificial Intelligence for more details on this.

- They are effective for reaching users who are actively searching for specific information or services.

- Best practices include using clear, actionable language and maintaining relevance to the target audience.

## Responsive Search Ads

Responsive Search Ads differ from traditional text (search) ads by allowing advertisers to provide multiple headlines and descriptions. The advertiser channel provider's machine learning algorithms then test different combinations and learn which performs best based on search queries.

Responsive Search Ads (RSAs) represent a dynamic approach in search advertising that allows marketers to enter multiple headlines and descriptions. Responsive Search Ads then automatically adjust their content based on user search terms, displaying the most relevant combination of provided headlines and descriptions. This flexibility increases the chance of your ads meeting user needs and intentions.

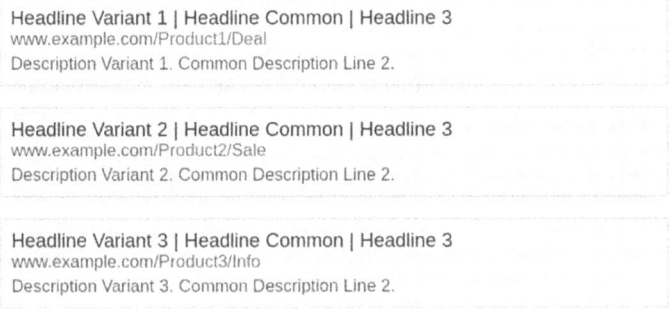

*Figure 22-3. Example mockup of responsive search ads*

Figure 22-3 represents three variants of a Responsive Search Ad. You can see that there are many elements:

CHAPTER 22   ADVERTISING FORMATS AND THEIR CREATIVES

- Headlines
- Descriptions
- Paths
- Urls

**Why Responsive Search Ads Are Important**
Responsive Search Ads provide a more flexible and effective way to capture user attention. They allow for greater customization and are tailored in real time to align with user search intent, potentially increasing both click-through and conversion rates. They leverage machine learning to optimize ad performance without continuous manual testing. This efficiency enables you to reach a broader audience with messages that resonate more precisely with their search queries.

**How to Best Utilize Responsive Search Ads**
When setting up RSAs, provide a diverse set of headlines and descriptions that capture different aspects of your offer. This variety gives the algorithm more options to test and optimize, leading to more effective ads. Always keep in mind that the message and copy should resonate with your user and match its context and the landing page.

**Example of Effective Responsive Search Ads in Action**
Consider a travel agency that utilizes RSAs to promote vacation packages. By providing several headlines and descriptions focusing on different destinations, amenities, or promotions, the RSA selects the most relevant ad content for each search query, improving click-through rates and conversions.

**Related Channels**
Responsive Search Ads are primarily effective in

- Search ads

211

Their direct link to user search intent makes them particularly valuable for search engine platforms where users are actively looking for specific information or products, such as Google or Bing.

**Key Considerations and Requirements**
Maintaining a clear and concise message across all variations is paramount. Additionally, regularly review the performance metrics provided by platforms like Google Ads to adjust and refine your RSA assets for better results.

**Advantages**
The primary advantage of RSAs lies in their ability to adapt: they can dynamically match various user intents, potentially leading to higher engagement and better conversion rates than static ads.

**Disadvantages**
One challenge with RSAs is the lack of control over exactly which combinations are shown, which can make testing specific messages difficult. Additionally, the initial setup requires creating more content, which might increase the workload.

Some platforms allow you to pin some fields to specific positions, which allows a greater control.

**Key Points of RSAs**

- Responsive Search Ads optimize themselves to show the most pertinent message (from the texts you created) to users, increasing the likelihood of campaign success.

- They require diverse sets of headlines and descriptions to function effectively, capitalizing on machine learning for optimal performance.

- While they offer high adaptability and potential for increased engagement, they also demand more initial content creation and offer less control over exact ad presentations.

CHAPTER 22   ADVERTISING FORMATS AND THEIR CREATIVES

# Responsive Display Ads

Responsive Display Ads are a dynamic advertising format designed to automatically adjust its content and format to suit different ad spaces and devices. Similar to Responsive Search Ads, which we discussed earlier, these ads utilize machine learning to optimize their performance across display networks.

Responsive Display Ads allow you to provide multiple assets (like images, videos, headlines, descriptions, and logos), which are then automatically arranged to fit available ad spaces on the display network. This technology simplifies ad creation and increases ad effectiveness by adapting to various environments.

The main difference with RSAs is the additional assets such as images, logos, and videos.

**The Significance of Responsive Display Ads**

Responsive Display Ads are crucial for marketers aiming to achieve broad coverage and engagement across diverse digital environments. These ads optimize themselves based on the performance data, ensuring that the best combination of assets is displayed to your audience.

For optimal usage, you have to ensure that all assets provided are high quality and aligned with your branding. It's also advised to update your asset pool regularly to keep your ads fresh and engaging.

**Application Example: Real Estate Agency**

Consider a real estate agency that uses Responsive Display Ads to promote new listings. By submitting multiple images of properties, along with various call-to-action (CTA) phrases, the ads can automatically adjust to display optimally on different websites within the display network, attracting potential clients looking for new homes.

CHAPTER 22   ADVERTISING FORMATS AND THEIR CREATIVES

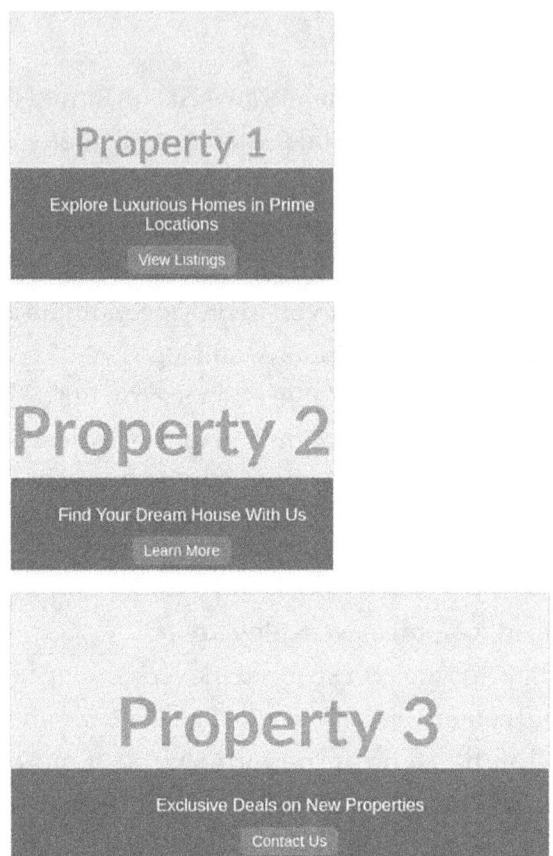

*Figure 22-4.* *Example Mockup of Responsive Display Ads*

In Figure 22-4, these are the key features:

**Dynamic Property Images**: Each ad features a different property image to demonstrate the variety of listings available.

## CHAPTER 22   ADVERTISING FORMATS AND THEIR CREATIVES

**Adjustable CTAs**: Different CTAs like "View Listings," "Learn More," and "Contact Us" cater to various stages of customer intent and engagement.

**Visual Design**: The design includes a semi-transparent overlay at the bottom for text, ensuring legibility against the potentially complex background of a property photo. (again, this is just an example).

## Suitable Channels for Responsive Display Ads

Responsive Display Ads work well within

- Display ads
- Social media ads (when linked to ad display networks)

Their ability to adjust makes them suitable for campaigns targeting a wide range of devices and screen sizes.

## The Positives of Using Responsive Display Ads

A significant advantage of using Responsive Display Ads includes their flexibility and the efficiency of ad management. They eliminate the need to create multiple static ads for different specifications, saving time and resources.

## Challenges with Responsive Display Ads

However, one difficulty might arise from the lack of control over exactly how these ads appear in every instance, potentially leading to inconsistent presentations of your brand.

## Key Points for Responsive Display Ads

- Responsive Display Ads offer an adaptive solution to display advertising, ensuring your ads perform well regardless of device or ad space size.

- They require less manual intervention while potentially providing better engagement and conversion rates due to their optimized content delivery, but pose a challenge in controlling what they show in each case.

# Audio Ads

In the world of digital marketing, engaging your audience through multiple senses can significantly enhance message retention. This is where audio ads come into play. Audio Ads are an addition to the powerful tools for capturing attention and fostering memorable brand experiences.

Audio ads are commercials designed to convey information through auditory means, usually presented during podcasts, streaming music services, and other audio platforms.

They typically integrate within audio content, reaching listeners engaged in music or podcast sessions. This format leverages sound, including voice, effects, and music, to communicate marketing messages.

**Why Audio Ads Are Important**

Audio ads offer unique advantages by connecting with listeners in moments when their eyes might be busy, but their ears are available. They fill the gaps with visual digital marketing strategies by reaching audiences during screen-free activities like driving, exercising, or cooking.

**Crafting Effective Audio Ads**

For optimal impact, keep your audio ads concise and engaging. Use a clear and compelling call to action, and make sure your brand's key message is delivered effectively. Voice tone, quality, and background sounds play significant roles in the listener's reception and sentiment towards the ad.

## Example of Effective Audio Ads Execution

Consider a fitness app that uses audio ads on popular workout music playlists. The ads encourage listeners to download the app with high-energy, motivating language that aligns with the listeners' workout goals and playlist vibe, potentially increasing app downloads among a target fitness-conscious audience.

Let's analyze what an audio ad for this example could be like:

Ad Audio Content Description

- **Opening Music**: Energetic, upbeat music that resonates with the workout theme to grab attention immediately.

- **Voice Over**: Dynamic and motivating voice that encourages listeners to stay active and engaged with their fitness goals.

- **Main Message**: Promotes the features of the fitness app, emphasizing how it can enhance the listener's workout experience.

- **Call-to-Action (CTA)**: Directs listeners to download the app, with an easy-to-remember URL or through a direct link on the Spotify app interface.

- **Closing Jingle**: A catchy, memorable tune or tagline that reinforces the app's brand.

Script example

[Upbeat, high-energy background music starts]
Voice Actor: "Ready to take your workout to the next level? Get the ultimate fitness companion right on your phone!"
[Background music intensifies]

Voice Actor: "With [App Name], track your progress, get custom workouts, and join a community that keeps pushing forward, just like you!"
[Sound effect: Heartbeat or weights clanking]
Voice Actor: "Tap the banner now to download and start your journey to fitness today! Visit www.getfitapp.example on your mobile."
[Background music fades with a motivational jingle]
Voice Actor: "[App Name], where every workout counts!"

**Adding Visual Elements**

In some cases, such as in Spotify, you can also add visual elements to your Audio Ad, such as images and videos.

This would look as Figure 22-5.

- **Visuals**: While the audio plays, a compelling visual will be displayed in the Spotify app interface. This can include the app's logo, a motivational tagline, and a vibrant background that fits the energetic theme.

- **Interactive Element**: A clickable overlay or banner that says "Download Now" or "Learn More," which leads directly to the app's download page.

CHAPTER 22   ADVERTISING FORMATS AND THEIR CREATIVES

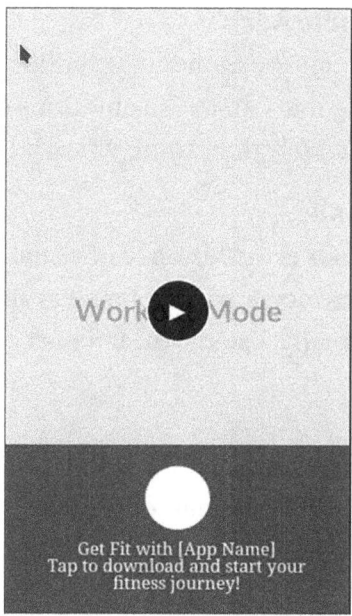

***Figure 22-5.*** *Example Mockup of an Audio Ad with Video*

Relevant Channels for Audio Ads

Audio Ads are effectively used in

- Podcast ads

- Streaming music services

These platforms are ideal as they already cater to users engaged primarily through auditory content.

**Key Considerations and Requirements**

Ensure that your audio ads are designed with high-quality sound production. Poor sound quality can diminish the credibility and professionalism of your ad and, by extension, your brand.

### Advantages of Using Audio Ads

Audio ads can uniquely capture audience attention with memorable, creative audio messaging that can evoke emotions or resonate on a personal level more effectively than some visual ads.

### Challenges with Audio Ads

One limitation of audio ads is the absence of visual elements, which can be a drawback if your product or service benefits significantly from visual demonstrations. Additionally, listener ad fatigue can occur if ads are too frequent or intrusive.

### Key Points for Audio Ads

- Audio ads use sound to market products or services, fitting seamlessly into listeners' daily routines without requiring visual attention.

- They are especially powerful on platforms where users engage with audio content, like podcasts and music streaming services.

- Effective audio ads require careful consideration of content quality, strategic placement, and audience targeting to avoid intrusion and improve engagement.

## Video Ads

Video ads are a dynamic and visually engaging advertising format. Video ads can capture attention, evoke emotion, and drive user engagement in ways that other formats may not.

These ads incorporate moving images and sound to tell a story or present a product, making them one of the most engaging forms of advertising available today. They can be found across various platforms, from social media to streaming services.

This format allows advertisers to communicate more complex messages that capture viewer attention more effectively.

**Why Video Ads Are Effective**

Video ads are effective because they combine sight and sound, which can significantly enhance message retention and emotional connection. They allow for creative **storytelling** that can make a brand or product memorable.

**Producing Compelling Video Ads**

To create compelling video ads, focus on clear, engaging storytelling and high-quality production. Your video should have a clear message and call to action, whether it's to educate about a product or to provoke an emotional response.

**Example of Effective Video Ads**

Consider a tech company launching a new smartphone. They could use a video ad that highlights the phone's innovative features through a day-in-the-life scenario that resonates with tech-savvy consumers, thereby increasing interest and potential sales.

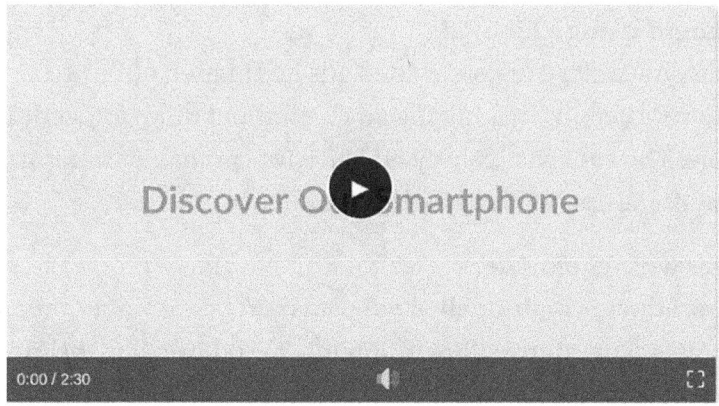

*Figure 22-6.* Example Mockup of Video Ad

CHAPTER 22   ADVERTISING FORMATS AND THEIR CREATIVES

**Relevant Channels for Video Ads**

Video ads are versatile and can be effectively used across multiple channels:

- Social media ads
- Streaming services (CTV, ATV)
- Mobile and in-app ads
- Video sharing platforms like YouTube
- Audio platforms with video support like Spotify

These platforms are ideal for video ads due to their high engagement and broad reach.

**Key Considerations and Requirements**

Ensure that your video ads are optimized for each platform in terms of length, format, and quality. Also, consider the viewing habits of your target audience, such as whether they are likely to view the video with sound on or off.

**Advantages of Using Video Ads**

The primary advantage of using video ads lies in their ability to engage viewers deeply, making the advertisement more impactful and memorable. They are particularly effective for campaigns aiming to create strong emotional connections with the audience.

**Challenges with Video Ads**

However, producing high-quality video ads can be resource-intensive, involving significant time, effort, and budget. Additionally, the increasing prevalence of ad blockers can affect the visibility of video ads, as well as the availability of paid plans without ads in many video platforms.

**Key Points for Video Ads**

- Video ads engage audiences through powerful storytelling and visual appeal.
- They can be used effectively across various digital platforms.
- Successful video ads require thoughtful planning, creative design, and careful execution.

# Lead Ads

Lead ads are specialized ad formats that allow potential customers to submit their information through a form integrated directly within the ad. This makes the process quicker and more user-friendly, as users do not need to navigate away from their current engagement.

**Why Lead Ads Are Important**
Lead ads reduce the friction typically associated with lead generation processes. By providing a convenient and quick method to sign up or show interest, these ads can effectively increase conversion rates and grow a business's potential customer base.

**Crafting Effective Lead Ads**
To maximize the potential of lead ads, ensure your forms are as concise as possible. Only ask for essential information to reduce user burden and include clear, compelling calls to action. Transparently communicate what users gain by submitting their data, whether it's exclusive content, a product demo, or a consultation.

**Example of Effective Lead Ads: LinkedIn Campaign**
Consider a B2B software company that uses LinkedIn lead ads to drive sign-ups for a free trial of their product. The ad targets professionals within the industry by showcasing key benefits and features of the software.

CHAPTER 22   ADVERTISING FORMATS AND THEIR CREATIVES

Interested users can sign up through the LinkedIn ad interface, instantly providing their profile information, which is typically comprehensive and verified. This seamless integration helps the company build a high-quality lead database efficiently.

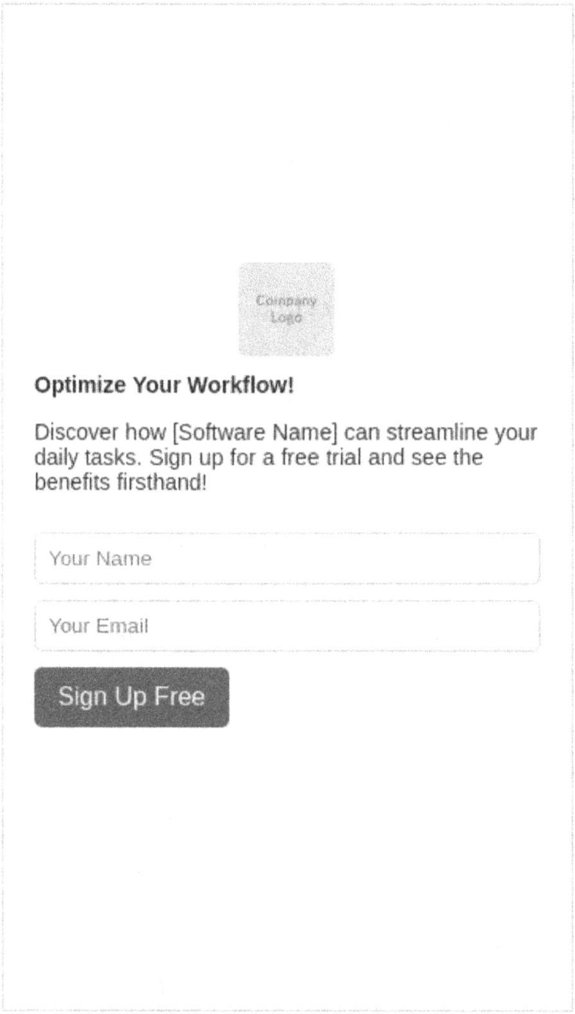

*Figure 22-7. Example Mockup of a Lead Ad*

## CHAPTER 22   ADVERTISING FORMATS AND THEIR CREATIVES

**Relevant Channels for Lead Ads**

Lead ads are particularly effective in

- Social media ads (like those on LinkedIn, Meta Ads, TikTok)
- Email marketing
- Google Ads lead form extensions

These platforms allow marketers to target specific demographics and directly engage with a focused audience.

**Key Considerations and Requirements**

It is important to ensure that privacy and data protection regulations are strictly followed when using lead ads. Clearly inform users how their information will be used and obtain consent wherever necessary. Also prepare and test any funnel that lead form will trigger before launching the ad.

**Advantages of Using Lead Ads**

Lead ads offer the distinct advantage of simplifying the data collection process and improving the user experience, leading to higher conversion rates and a more efficient sales cycle.

**Challenges with Lead Ads**

However, designing lead ads that yield high-quality data without demanding too much information from users can be a challenge. Additionally, maintaining compliance with data protection laws requires meticulous attention. From a cost perspective, leads that come from lead ads will most likely cost more. Check Chapter 10 on Bids and Chapter 15 on Campaign Types for more information.

**Key Takeaways**

- Lead ads are powerful tools for direct engagement and efficient lead collection.

- They are best used on platforms like LinkedIn, where detailed professional user profiles can directly feed into CRM systems.
- Effective lead ads balance the need for information with user convenience and legal compliance.

## Inventory Ads

Inventory ads are automated ads that use your product data feed to generate ad content directly related to your inventory. This powerful tool allows you to advertise specific products to customers based on their interests or your stock levels.

### Why Inventory Ads Are Effective

Inventory ads offer a seamless connection between your product catalog and potential customers. By automatically updating in near real time, these ads are particularly valuable for businesses with extensive or frequently changing inventories.

### How to Implement Inventory Ads

To effectively implement inventory ads, maintain an organized and regularly updated product data feed (such as a Spreadsheet). This feed should include detailed descriptions, availability status, pricing, and images for each item in your inventory.

> **Caution** Each platform may require different fields. Check those requirements before preparing your product data.

### Example of Effective Inventory Ads Usage: Online Retailer

Imagine an online retailer with a rapidly changing selection of clothing. By employing inventory ads, they can automatically promote items

# CHAPTER 22   ADVERTISING FORMATS AND THEIR CREATIVES

that are newly in stock or on sale, directly targeting ads to users who have previously shown interest in similar products. This leads to higher engagement rates and more efficient conversions.

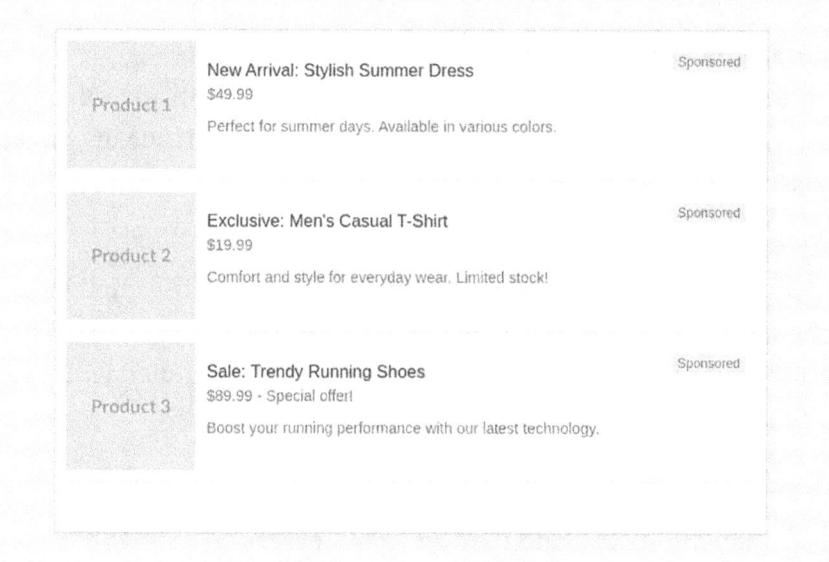

*Figure 22-8. Example Mockup of INventory Ads*

**Relevant Channels for Inventory Ads**

Inventory ads are suitably deployed across

- Display ads
- Social media ads
- Shopping platforms

Utilizing these channels enables businesses to reach a wide audience and direct potential customers back to their online store or physical locations.

## Key Considerations and Requirements
Ensure your inventory system can integrate seamlessly with advertising platforms to keep your ads accurate and current. Also, privacy concerning customer data must be correctly managed to build trust.

## Advantages of Using Inventory Ads
The primary advantage of inventory ads is their ability to advertise specific, in-stock products to interested customers, which can drastically increase purchase intent and satisfaction.

## Disadvantages of Inventory Ads
However, dependency on accurate inventory data can be a challenge; discrepancies in stock levels might lead to customer frustration if advertised products are not available. This has to be handled with care, as such situations can lead to issues in ad quality.[3]

## Key Points of Inventory Ads

- Inventory ads automate ad content creation based on near real-time inventory data, allowing for relevant and timely product advertising.

- They are particularly useful for businesses with large or fluctuating inventories.

- Maintaining precise inventory information is crucial to the effectiveness of these ads.

# Shopping Ads

Shopping ads allow businesses to visually promote their products through images, product details, and pricing directly within the search results or on dedicated shopping platforms. These ads are highly visual and utilize product data feeds to display relevant information automatically.

---

[3] Check Chapter 11 on Ad Quality for more details.

## Why Shopping Ads Are Important

Shopping ads provide a direct and simplified path for online shoppers to view products and make purchases straight from the ad. They use rich media, including images and prices, to entice customers, making them more likely than standard text ads to convert browsing into sales.

## Structuring Effective Shopping Ads

Ensure that your product feeds are comprehensive, with up-to-date images, accurate product descriptions, and competitive pricing. High-quality content in your feed directly impacts the performance of your shopping ads.

## Example of Effective Shopping Ads: Online Electronics Store

An online electronics store utilizes shopping ads to promote their newest line of smartphones. By including high-resolution images, short descriptions, quick comparisons with older models, and pricing information in their ads, they attract tech enthusiasts looking for the latest gadgets. The ads link directly to the product purchase page, facilitating an easy transaction.

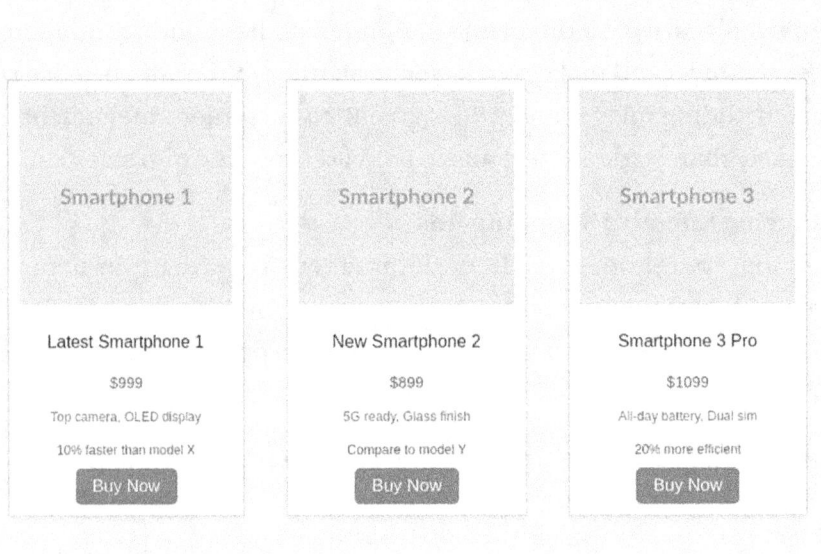

***Figure 22-9.*** *Example Mockup of Shopping Ads*

**How Shopping Ads Differ from Inventory Ads**

While both shopping ads and inventory ads (as previously discussed) rely on product data feeds, shopping ads focus more on individual products with specific information in each ad. In contrast, inventory ads dynamically adjust and display based on the overall data of available products and may change depending on inventory levels.

**Relevant Channels for Shopping Ads**

Shopping ads are effectively utilized on

- Search engines (like Google Shopping)
- Ecommerce platforms

These platforms cater specifically to users in a shopping mindset, making them ideal for direct product advertising.

CHAPTER 22   ADVERTISING FORMATS AND THEIR CREATIVES

**Key Considerations and Requirements**
It is crucial to comply with the shopping ad guidelines of each platform, which may include specifics about image resolution, text allowances, and pricing display. Maintaining an accurate and compliant product feed is basic for successful ad placements.

**Advantages of Using Shopping Ads**
Shopping ads directly drive higher engagement and conversions by showing detailed product information at the point of interest on shopping and search platforms.

**Challenges with Shopping Ads**
However, maintaining a competitive edge can be challenging due to the need for continual optimization of product listings and pricing strategies to stand out in a crowded market.

**Key Points on Shopping Ads**

- Shopping ads allow for direct promotion of products with detailed visuals and information, enhancing the possibility of conversion.

- They require meticulous product feed management and adaptation to platform-specific guidelines.

- Unlike inventory ads, shopping ads focus more narrowly on individual products for direct consumer interactions.

# Carousel Ads

Carousel Ads are a visually engaging advertising format that allows users to scroll through multiple images or videos. This dynamic format is particularly effective for showcasing various products or telling a brand story in segments.

Carousel ads consist of multiple content cards that users can interactively scroll through. These ads are used extensively on social media platforms to provide a richer, more engaging user experience.

### Why Carousel Ads Matter
Carousel Ads are relevant due to their ability to showcase multiple aspects of a product or brand within a single ad unit. They engage users by allowing them to interact with the content directly, increasing the time spent with the ad and, subsequently, the likelihood of conversion.

### Creating Engaging Carousel Ads
To maximize the effectiveness of Carousel Ads, ensure each panel or slide is compelling on its own yet cohesive when viewed as part of the whole sequence. Clear, high-quality images, consistent branding, and direct calls to action are essential.

### Comparing Carousel Ads with Other Formats
Unlike single image or video ads, such as those used in standard display and shopping ads, Carousel Ads provide a unique advantage by combining several interactive elements in one ad. This contrasts with lead ads or shopping ads, which typically focus on converting user interest directly into leads or sales with less interactive storytelling.

### Example of Effective Carousel Ads: Fashion Retailer
A fashion retailer uses Carousel Ads on social media to highlight its new seasonal collection. Each slide features a different outfit with direct links to shop the items. This approach showcases diversity in the collection and drives direct engagement from customers interested in specific pieces.

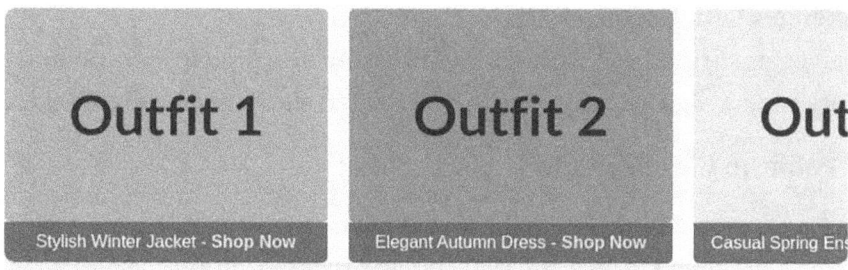

***Figure 22-10.*** *Example Mockup of a Carousel Ad*

**Relevant Channels for Carousel Ads**

Carousel ads are particularly effective in

- Social media ads (Facebook, Instagram)
- Mobile and in-app ads

These platforms support the interactive elements of Carousel Ads, making them ideal for engaging with a tech-savvy audience.

**Key Considerations and Requirements**

When designing Carousel Ads, it's crucial to optimize the load times of each image or video to prevent lag, which can diminish user experience and engagement.

Each slide should be useful for the user on its own, but at the same time make sense with all together slides as a whole.

**Advantages of Using Carousel Ads**

Carousel Ads provide the flexibility to highlight multiple products or aspects of a story within a single ad, offering engaging browsing experiences directly within the ad.

### Challenges with Carousel Ads
However, ensuring each element in the carousel is equally compelling and maintaining a high-quality standard across all slides can be challenging.

### Key Points to Carousel Ads

- Carousel Ads are highly interactive, allowing for detailed storytelling and showcasing of multiple products.

- They are best utilized on social media and mobile platforms, where users are more likely to engage with swappable content.

- Effective Carousel Ads combine visual appeal with clear, actionable calls to action across all slides.

## Interstitial Ads

Interstitial ads are a form of digital advertising format that covers the interface of their host application or website. These ads are particularly notable for their full-screen format that captures user attention by pausing the underlying content. This makes them highly effective for engaging users, but they must be used judiciously to avoid hindering the user experience.

Interstitial ads are full-page ads that appear at transition points in an app or website, such as between articles or game levels. They command attention by temporarily taking over a user's screen, providing advertisers a captive audience for their message.

### Why Interstitial Ads Are Impactful
Unlike other ad formats like carousel or video ads, interstitials **temporarily pause user interaction** with the primary content, commanding undivided attention. This unique placement can substantially increase visibility and engagement compared to ads that coexist with content.

CHAPTER 22    ADVERTISING FORMATS AND THEIR CREATIVES

**Creating Effective Interstitial Ads**

To maximize user engagement without disrupting user experience, ensure that interstitial ads are well-timed and easily dismissible. They should offer relevant and engaging content to make the interruption worthwhile. Clarity in the call to action and visually appealing design are specially important.

**Comparing Interstitial Ads with Other Formats**

Interstitial ads differ significantly from carousel or inventory ads in their execution. While carousel ads invite users to interact with multiple elements within a single ad unit and inventory ads dynamically showcase products based on availability, interstitial ads focus on capturing attention at key moments by fully occupying the screen space.

**Example of Effective Interstitial Ads: Mobile Gaming App**

Imagine a mobile gaming app that uses interstitial ads between game levels. An ad promoting a new game level pack appears just after a player completes a level. The timing leverages the player's current engagement and interest, potentially leading to higher conversion rates than a standard banner ad displayed during gameplay.

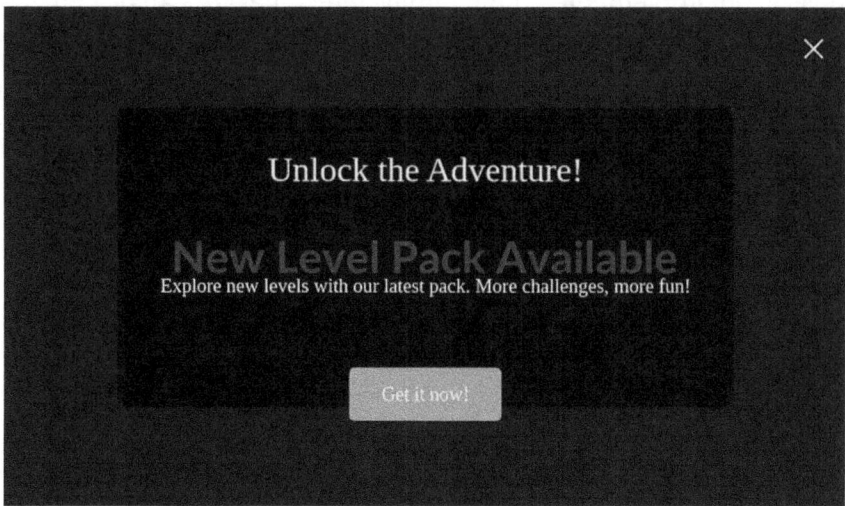

*Figure 22-11.* *Example Mockup of an Interstitial Ad*

235

CHAPTER 22    ADVERTISING FORMATS AND THEIR CREATIVES

**Relevant Channels for Interstitial Ads**

Interstitial ads are particularly effective in

- Mobile and in-app ads
- Gaming apps
- Display ads (while being careful about user experience)

Their ability to fill the screen makes them suitable for mobile environments where user focus can be captured momentarily.

**Key Considerations and Requirements**

It's crucial that interstitial ads respect user experience by not appearing too frequently or taking too long to dismiss. Compliance with platform guidelines, such as those of Google Ads for mobile apps, is essential to avoid penalties.

**Advantages of Using Interstitial Ads**

The primary advantage of interstitial ads is their high visibility and user engagement, attributed to their full-screen format and strategic placement.

**Challenges with Interstitial Ads**

However, if not implemented thoughtfully, interstitial ads can be perceived as intrusive and negatively impact the user experience, potentially leading to app uninstalls, high bounce rates, or detrimental perception of your brand.

**Key Points for Interstitial Ads**

- Interstitial ads provide a unique way to engage users by fully capturing screen space during natural transitions in app or website use.
- They require careful implementation to balance user engagement with user experience.
- These ads are most effective when used in mobile environments, where their full-screen advantage can be fully utilized.

# Native Ads

Native ads are a sophisticated (and less known) form of digital advertising designed to blend seamlessly with the content in which they are placed. Unlike traditional display or interstitial ads that distinctly appear as ads, native ads mimic the formatting and style of the surrounding content, making them less intrusive and more engaging for users.

Native ads are advertisements that are so well integrated into the page content, layout, and design that they appear as part of the editorial flow of the page. This integration enhances user experience by providing value through relevant and interesting content.

**Why Native Ads Are Effective**

Native ads are less likely to be perceived as annoying compared to more blatant advertising formats like interstitial ads. By matching the look and feel of the content, they respect the user's browsing experience and maintain the aesthetic integrity of the content platform.

**Crafting Effective Native Ads**

To create effective native ads, align them closely with the content's tone, style, and quality. They should offer relevant information or services that add to the user's interaction with the content platform, rather than diverting it.

**Comparing Native Ads with Other Formats**

Native ads differ significantly from formats like interstitial or shopping ads, which are designed to stand out and capture immediate attention. Unlike shopping ads that directly showcase products, native ads subtly integrate promotional messages within content, aiming to engage rather than interrupt.

**Example of Effective Native Ads: Lifestyle Blog**

Consider a lifestyle blog that features native ads for home decor. An article about modern home design might include native ads from furniture brands, styled as part of the blog's content. Readers interested in home design naturally engage with the ads, perceiving them as additional information rather than a hard sell.

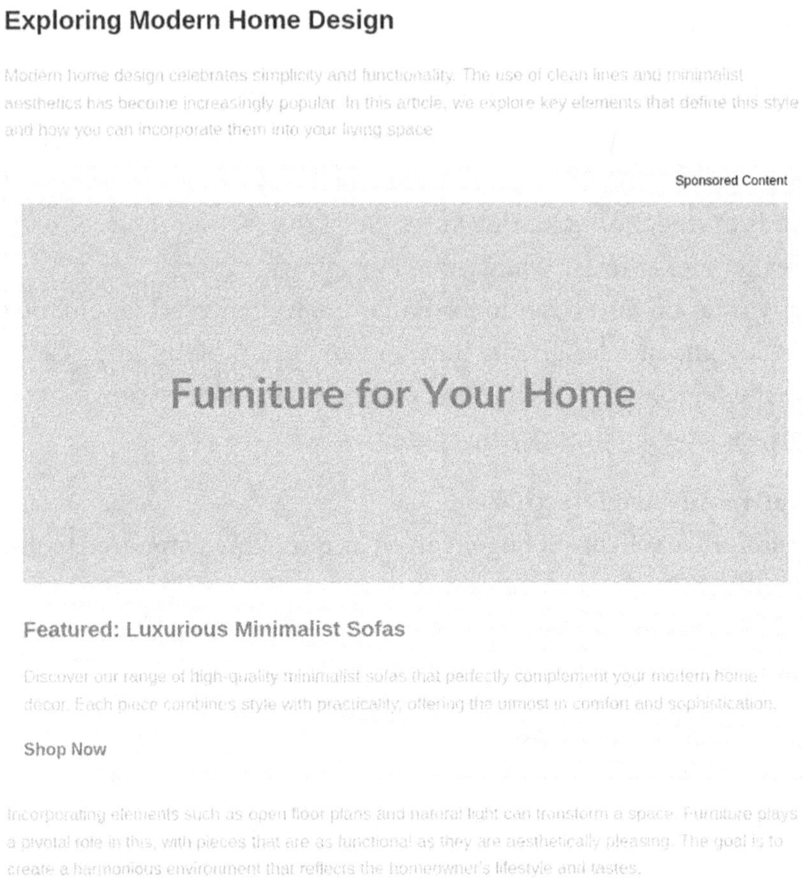

## CHAPTER 22  ADVERTISING FORMATS AND THEIR CREATIVES

**Exploring Modern Home Design**

Modern home design celebrates simplicity and functionality. The use of clean lines and minimalist aesthetics has become increasingly popular. In this article, we explore key elements that define this style and how you can incorporate them into your living space.

Sponsored Content

**Furniture for Your Home**

**Featured: Luxurious Minimalist Sofas**

Discover our range of high-quality minimalist sofas that perfectly complement your modern home decor. Each piece combines style with practicality, offering the utmost in comfort and sophistication.

Shop Now

Incorporating elements such as open floor plans and natural light can transform a space. Furniture plays a pivotal role in this, with pieces that are as functional as they are aesthetically pleasing. The goal is to create a harmonious environment that reflects the homeowner's lifestyle and tastes.

*Figure 22-12. Example Mockup of a Native Ad*

**Relevant Channels for Native Ads**

Native ads work well on

- Content platforms such as news sites and blogs
- Social media feeds

These channels support the content-driven approach of native ads, making them effective for audiences seeking to consume articles, posts, or videos.

## Key Considerations and Requirements

Maintain transparency by clearly marking native ads as sponsored content. This adheres to advertising standards and builds trust with your audience by ensuring honesty in advertising.

## Advantages of Using Native Ads

One significant advantage of native ads is that they are more engaging and less disruptive, which can lead to higher click-through rates and better user retention.

## Challenges with Native Ads

However, creating high-quality native ads can be resource-intensive, requiring careful alignment with both the platform's content and the intended audience's expectations.

## Key Points for Native Ads

- Native ads integrate seamlessly into the content environment, providing a non-disruptive user experience.

- They are most effective when aligned closely with the content's tone and user expectations.

- While native ads offer a more subtle approach to advertising, they require careful planning and execution to maintain authenticity and effectiveness.

# Dynamic Ads

Dynamic ads offer a highly customizable advertising experience tailored to individual user behavior and preferences. Unlike static ads, dynamic ads can change in real time based on data about the viewer. This adaptability makes them an interesting tool for marketers looking to optimize engagement and relevance.

Dynamic ads use algorithms to **adjust their content** based on user data such as past behavior, demographic information, or search patterns. This enables marketers to deliver highly personalized ad experiences across various digital platforms.

**Why Dynamic Ads Are Relevant**
Dynamic ads stand out because they respond to the user's immediate needs and interests, potentially increasing their effectiveness over static ads that remain the same for every viewer. By adapting content based on real-time data, dynamic ads deliver a more relevant and engaging experience, helping to drive conversions and brand loyalty.

**Comparing Dynamic Ads with Other Formats**
Unlike native ads or carousel ads, which blend in with content or provide a browsing experience within the ad, dynamic ads aim to capture attention by presenting the most relevant possible offer or message to each user. While carousel ads allow users to interact by scrolling through multiple elements, and native ads emphasize non-disruptive integration into content platforms, dynamic ads focus on personalization based on user data.

**Example of Effective Dynamic Ads: Ecommerce Platform**
Consider an ecommerce platform using dynamic ads to recommend products. Based on the browsing history of a user who recently viewed several sports shoes, the dynamic ad displayed could feature similar sports shoes or related sporting goods. This makes the ad more relevant and increases the chance of the user engaging with the ad and returning to the website.

CHAPTER 22   ADVERTISING FORMATS AND THEIR CREATIVES

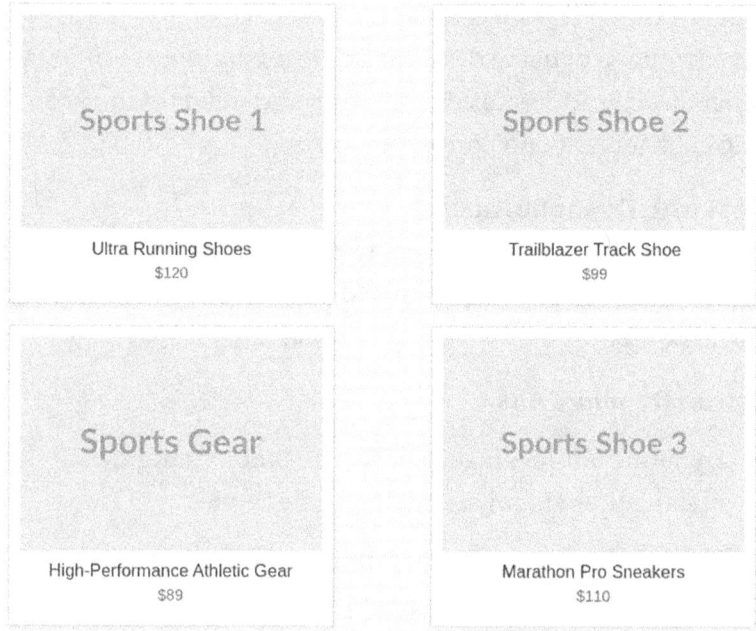

*Figure 22-13.* *Example Mockup of Dynamic Ads*

**Relevant Channels for Dynamic Ads**

Dynamic ads are particularly effective on

- Social media platforms
- Online retail websites
- Search engine advertising

These platforms allow for the integration of user data into ad serving systems, making them ideal for deploying dynamic ads.

**Key Considerations and Requirements**

It's important to ensure compliance with data protection regulations when using user data to personalize ads. Transparency with users about how their data is being used is also essential to maintain trust.

241

### Advantages of Using Dynamic Ads
The main advantage of using dynamic ads is their ability to offer tailored content that directly addresses the interests and needs of the user, thus enhancing engagement and conversion rates.

### Challenges with Dynamic Ads
Creating dynamic ads requires access to reliable and comprehensive user data, and missteps in personalization can lead to privacy concerns or irrelevant ad content.

### Key Points in Dynamic Ads

- Dynamic ads leverage user data to tailor content, making them highly engaging and effective.

- They are best used in environments where user data can be ethically and effectively leveraged to enhance relevance.

- Careful handling of data and persuasive ad design are key to maximizing the benefits of dynamic advertising.

## App Install Ads

App Install Ads are a specialized advertising format aimed at encouraging users to download and install mobile applications. Unlike dynamic ads that adjust content based on user data, or native ads that blend seamlessly with content, App Install Ads focus specifically on driving app installations through clear, direct calls to action.

App Install Ads are explicitly designed for mobile and tablet campaigns to boost the downloads of apps. They usually contain direct links to app download pages in mobile app stores, simplifying the process for potential users to acquire the app.

CHAPTER 22  ADVERTISING FORMATS AND THEIR CREATIVES

**Why App Install Ads Are Relevant**

These ads are important because they directly connect potential users with the means to install the app, bypassing additional information or distractions. This direct approach can significantly increase conversion rates from ad impressions to app installations.

**Creating Effective App Install Ads**

To develop effective App Install Ads

- Focus on concise, persuasive messages that highlight the unique features or benefits of the app.

- Use eye-catching visuals that immediately grab attention and communicate the application's purpose.

- Include a clear, compelling call to action like "Install Now" that drives the user toward downloading the app.

**Difference from Other Ad Formats**

App Install Ads differ from formats like carousel ads or video ads by not just engaging the user with creative content, but by being singularly focused on prompting an immediate app installation. They bypass the typical storytelling or exploratory interaction found in other ad types.

**Example of Effective App Install Ads: Fitness Mobile Application**

A fitness app might use App Install Ads to target health enthusiasts on social media platforms. The ad would feature a strong call to action, engaging visuals of the app in use, and a direct link to the app's page on the app store, making the download process as seamless as possible for the user.

# CHAPTER 22  ADVERTISING FORMATS AND THEIR CREATIVES

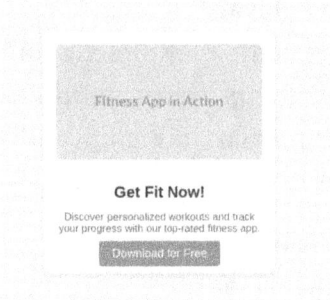

***Figure 22-14.*** *Example Mockup of an App Install Ad*

**Relevant Channels for App Install Ads**
These ads are particularly effective on

- Social media platforms
- Mobile advertising networks

Both channels allow targeting specific demographics likely to be interested in the app, based on user behavior and preferences.

**Key Considerations and Requirements**
The crucial considerations include targeting the ad appropriately to reach potential users likely interested in the app, and continuously testing and optimizing ad elements based on performance data to improve conversion rates.

**Advantages of Using App Install Ads**
The primary advantage of these ads lies in their ability to drive direct action (app installations) efficiently, making them a valuable asset in mobile app marketing campaigns.

**Challenges with App Install Ads**
Challenges include the high competition among apps, leading to potentially high costs per click, and the need for strong differentiation to capture user interest quickly.

**Key Points to App Install Ads**

- App Install Ads are optimized to streamline the journey from ad interaction to app installation.

- They are distinct from other ad formats by focusing on direct installation rather than broader engagement or information sharing.

- Effectively leveraging these ads involves clear messaging, proper targeting, and continuous optimization.

# Sponsored Content

Sponsored content focuses on creating and sharing content in collaboration with a publisher or creator that aligns with your brand's values. Unlike traditional ads or more disruptive formats like interstitial ads, sponsored content integrates with a platform's organic content, offering value through stories or articles that organically include your product or service.

Sponsored content is paid content that resembles the publication's editorial content but is paid for by an advertiser. It is designed to blend in naturally with the usual content found on the platform, providing a less intrusive user experience.

**Why Sponsored Content Is Effective**

Sponsored content is effective because it engages readers through content that they find interesting and relevant, thereby reducing the appearance of overt advertising. This format fosters trust and credibility by associating your brand with content that the audience already enjoys and trusts.

**Crafting Effective Sponsored Content**

To create impactful sponsored content, partner with platforms or creators who resonate with your target audience. The content should match

# CHAPTER 22  ADVERTISING FORMATS AND THEIR CREATIVES

the tone, style, and quality of the host's regular offerings, making it informative, engaging, and subtly aligned with your marketing objectives.

**Differences from Other Ad Formats**

Unlike display or video ads that clearly stand out as promotional, sponsored content is designed to feel less like an advertisement and more like a natural part of the platform's usual content. This approach contrasts sharply with formats like app install ads, which aim to direct users to take a specific action, such as downloading an app.

**Example of Effective Sponsored Content: Culinary Blog Collaboration**

Consider a kitchenware company that partners with a popular culinary blog to create sponsored posts featuring recipes that use the company's tools. The posts include links to purchase the tools directly, providing a seamless transition from content to commerce.

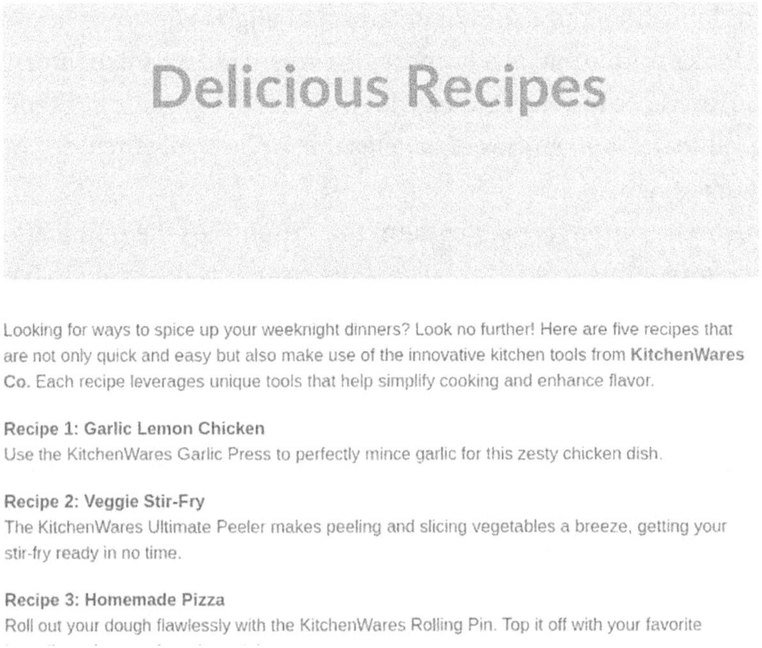

## Delicious Recipes

Looking for ways to spice up your weeknight dinners? Look no further! Here are five recipes that are not only quick and easy but also make use of the innovative kitchen tools from **KitchenWares Co.** Each recipe leverages unique tools that help simplify cooking and enhance flavor.

**Recipe 1: Garlic Lemon Chicken**
Use the KitchenWares Garlic Press to perfectly mince garlic for this zesty chicken dish.

**Recipe 2: Veggie Stir-Fry**
The KitchenWares Ultimate Peeler makes peeling and slicing vegetables a breeze, getting your stir-fry ready in no time.

**Recipe 3: Homemade Pizza**
Roll out your dough flawlessly with the KitchenWares Rolling Pin. Top it off with your favorite

*Figure 22-15. Example Mockup of Sponsored Content*

## Relevant Channels for Sponsored Content

Sponsored content is particularly effective on

- Blogs
- News websites
- Social media platforms

These channels allow for deeper storytelling and are often trusted sources of information for users.

## Key Considerations and Requirements

Ensure transparency by clearly labeling the content as sponsored to comply with advertising standards and maintain audience trust. Moreover, maintaining the quality and relevance of the content is crucial to its effectiveness.

## Advantages of Using Sponsored Content

Sponsored content can enhance brand perception by delivering useful or entertaining information in a format that readers already favor, potentially leading to better engagement and brand loyalty.

## Challenges with Sponsored Content

However, creating content that balances promotional messages with genuine value can be challenging. It also requires careful selection of partners whose audience aligns with your target market.

## Key Points for Sponsored Content

- Sponsored content integrates advertising into editorial content, enhancing credibility and audience engagement.
- It differs from other ads by its non-disruptive nature and alignment with the host's content.
- Effective sponsored content is informative, engaging, and subtly incorporates marketing objectives.

CHAPTER 22   ADVERTISING FORMATS AND THEIR CREATIVES

# Pop-Up Ads

Pop-Up Ads are a form of digital advertising known for its direct and prominent placement. Unlike the subtler, integrated approach of native ads or the dynamic personalization of dynamic ads, pop-up ads focus on capturing immediate attention by appearing directly over or beneath the content a user is viewing.

Pop-Up Ads are advertisements that appear in new browser windows or layers over the content the user is currently engaging with. There are several types:

- **Pop-Under**: Open a new ad window behind the current browser window.

- **Pop-Overs**: Overlay an ad on top of the current page content.

- **Pop-Ups**: Open a new window displaying the ad.

---

**Note**   Pop-up ads are not explicitly listed as a distinct advertising format offered by major ad platforms like Google Ads or Meta Ads. However, they can be considered a variation or subcategory of certain ad formats, as they depend on the inventory of each platform.

---

**Pop-Up Ads in Digital Marketing**

Pop-Up Ads are designed to capture immediate attention, making them effective for promotions or crucial messages that advertisers want to emphasize strongly. However, their intrusive nature means they must be used judiciously to avoid negative user experiences.

## Crafting Effective Pop-Up Ads

To mitigate potential backlash, ensure that pop-up ads

- Are easy to dismiss
- Offer significant value, such as exclusive discounts or critical information
- Are used sparingly to avoid overwhelming the user

## Differences from Other Ad Formats

Pop-Up Ads contrast distinctly with formats like sponsored content or carousel ads, which either blend with the content or invite user interaction in a less disruptive manner. While interstitial ads share some similarities with pop-ups in terms of screen domination, pop-up ads are often more abrupt because they can trigger at any point, not just during natural content transitions.

## Example of Contextually Appropriate Pop-Up Ads: Ecommerce Website

Imagine an ecommerce site where a pop-up ad offers a 10% discount code for first-time visitors. The ad appears when a user first lands on the site, providing immediate, actionable value that can enhance their shopping experience without significant disruption.

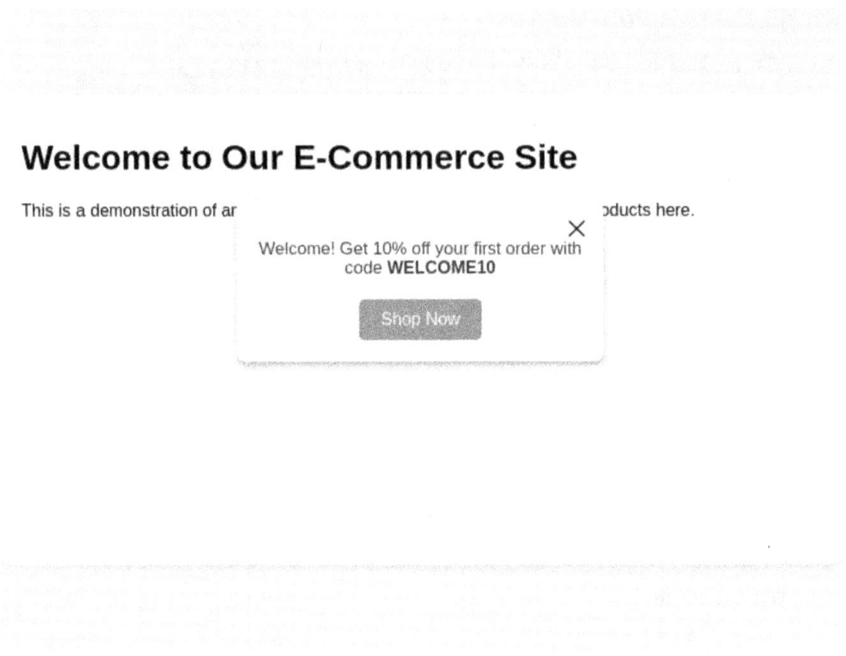

*Figure 22-16. Example Mockup of a Pop-Up Ad*

**Relevant Channels for Pop-Up Ads**
Pop-Up Ads can be effectively used in

- Websites that control their ad environments
- Ecommerce platforms looking to boost conversions with timely offers.

**Key Considerations and Requirements**
Pop-Up Ads must adhere to web standards and best practices to avoid being blocked by browsers and to ensure a positive user experience. They should also comply with legal requirements concerning digital advertising and user privacy.

**Advantages of Using Pop-Up Ads**
The primary advantage is their ability to grab attention quickly, making them useful for critical or timely messages.

## Challenges with Pop-Up Ads

However, their intrusive nature can frustrate users, potentially leading to negative perceptions of the brand or increased user bounce rates.

## Key Points to Pop-Up Ads

- Pop-Up Ads are a direct but intrusive advertising format that can be effective if used appropriately.

- They require strategic placement and valuable content to be effective without alienating users.

- Compared to other ad types, pop-ups are more aggressive in capturing user attention and demand careful consideration of user experience.

# Advertising Formats Comparison Table

This section provides a concise comparison of the various digital advertising formats we've discussed. Each format is distinct in its approach and applicability, depending on the advertising goals and the channels used. Understanding the nuances of each advertising format is crucial for effectively deploying digital marketing strategies. Table 22-1 will help you grasp the key characteristics of each format, their most effective channels, and examples of advertising channel providers that support these formats.

**Table 22-1.** *Comparison table of digital marketing formats*

| Name | Description | Related Channels | Example Advertising Channel Providers |
|---|---|---|---|
| AMP banner | Fast-loading ads designed for mobile devices, improving user experience by reducing load time | Mobile and in-app ads, display ads | Google Ads |
| HTML banners | Interactive banners made using HTML5, allowing animations and dynamic content for engaging users | Display ads, social media ads | Google Ads, Facebook Ads |
| Text ads | Simple, direct ad format using text only, typically seen in search results | Search ads, display ads | Google Ads, Microsoft Ads |
| Responsive search ads | Ads that automatically adjust their content based on user search terms using AI | Search ads | Google Ads, Microsoft Ads |
| Responsive display ads | Visually adaptive ads that automatically adjust size, appearance, and format to fit available ad spaces | Display ads | Google Ads, Microsoft Ads |
| Audio ads | Ads delivered in audio format, often used in podcasts and music streaming services | Podcast ads, Music streaming platforms | Spotify, Apple Music |

(*continued*)

## CHAPTER 22 ADVERTISING FORMATS AND THEIR CREATIVES

*Table 22-1.* (*continued*)

| Name | Description | Related Channels | Example Advertising Channel Providers |
|---|---|---|---|
| Video ads | Dynamic ads using video content to engage users, often used on social media and video platforms | Social media ads, streaming services | YouTube, Facebook |
| Lead ads | Ads designed specifically for collecting lead information through integrated forms | Social media ads, mobile ads | Facebook Ads, LinkedIn Ads |
| Inventory ads | Dynamic ads linked directly to the advertiser's inventory to show real-time availability and info | Shopping platforms, display ads | Google Shopping, Amazon Advertising |
| Shopping ads | Product-focused ads that include images, prices, and a link directly to purchase | Search engines, ecommerce platforms | Google Shopping, Amazon |
| Carousel ads | Multi-image or video ads allowing users to swipe through different content pieces | Social media ads, mobile ads | Facebook, Instagram |
| Interstitial ads | Full-screen ads displayed at transition points in apps or websites, covering the interface | Mobile and in-app ads | AdMob, Facebook |

(*continued*)

*Table 22-1.* (*continued*)

| Name | Description | Related Channels | Example Advertising Channel Providers |
|---|---|---|---|
| Native ads | Ads that match the look, feel, and function of the media format where they appear | Blogs, news websites | Taboola, Outbrain |
| Dynamic ads | Ads that automatically adjust their content to the viewer's interests and behaviors | Social media platforms, online retail websites | Facebook, Amazon |
| App install ads | Ads aimed at encouraging users to download an application | Mobile advertising networks, social media platforms | Google Ads, Facebook Ads |
| Sponsored content | Content that mimics the style and tone of a platform's regular content but is paid for | Blogs, news websites | BuzzFeed, Forbes |
| Pop-up ads | Types of disruptive ads that appear over the top of or beneath webpage content | Websites | Not specifically supported by major ad networks due to user experience concerns |

This table serves as a quick overview to compare the various advertising formats I have explained this far, helping you choose the right one based on your specific marketing needs and the channels you intend to use.

# Summary

In this chapter, I have explored a wide array of digital advertising formats, each tailored to meet specific marketing objectives and suit different audience interactions. From the immediate impact of pop-up ads to the subtler approach of native advertising, and from the dynamic personalization of dynamic ads to the focused conversion drive of app install ads, I've covered a spectrum designed to equip you with the knowledge to select the right advertising format for your campaigns.

Here are the key points to remember:

- **AMP and HTML banners** enhance user engagement with fast-loading and interactive content, suitable for mobile and web platforms.

- **Text ads and responsive search ads** provide straightforward and effective ways to reach audiences directly in search environments.

- **Video and audio ads** engage users deeply, leveraging sound and visual elements to grab attention and evoke emotional responses.

- **Dynamic ads** offer personalization at scale, adapting in real time to fit individual user profiles for increased relevance.

- **Native ads and sponsored content** blend seamlessly with editorial content, enhancing credibility and user experience without being overly disruptive.

- **Interstitial and pop-up ads** capture immediate attention by filling the screen, useful for making a significant impact at key interaction points.

- **Carousel ads** allow users to interact with multiple elements of content, providing a richer browsing experience within the ad itself.

- **Shopping and inventory ads** connect users directly with products, integrating real-time inventory data to reflect current availability and options.

These ad formats provide diverse tools that can be strategically deployed to achieve specific marketing objectives, from building brand awareness to driving sales, depending on your target audience and desired outcomes.

In the next chapter, I will discuss landing pages, why they are so important, and the main aspects you should know about them.

# CHAPTER 23

# Understanding Landing Pages

Landing pages stand at the heart of successful digital marketing campaigns. They are where potential customers land after clicking on an ad and where they make critical decisions about proceeding with your brand. This chapter will explore the strategic role of landing pages, their essential elements, and best practices to optimize them for higher conversions and enhanced user experience.

## Why Landing Pages Are Important

A landing page is where your potential customers make crucial decisions on how to proceed with the offers or information presented. The design and content of your landing page significantly influence user actions and, consequently, the success of your advertising campaigns.

Landing pages should be tailored to a specific campaign or audience, unlike general homepages. They focus on a single objective, which could range from signing up for a newsletter or buying a product, to downloading a white paper. Here, the link between the ad that brought the user here and the page itself must be seamless.

CHAPTER 23   UNDERSTANDING LANDING PAGES

A well-designed landing page can significantly decrease the cost per lead and increase the ROI of your digital marketing campaigns. They're designed to provide exactly what the ad promised, removing any potential friction from the user conversion process.

Imagine you click an Ad that advertises the new car of a known brand, expecting to find more information regarding the car, only to get to the homepage of the brand. The usual behavior of that user in this situation is to close the page and keep browsing. At that moment you lost the cost of the click, the opportunity to convert a visitor into a customer and your "ranking" in the algorithm of the advertising channel provider.

What was that last thing? Which algorithm?

To make it simple, there is a sort of formula which the advertising channel provider uses to show your Ad to a specific user. That formula considers the content of your ad and your landing page, the settings of your campaign, and the "experience" of the user with your campaign (this is also called **landing-page experience**). If the user gets away as fast as they found it, it means that your campaign does not fulfill the requirements of that user for its context. In other words, the advertising channel provider will stop showing your campaign to that kind of user. (For more on this, check Chapter 11 on ad quality for more details.)

The landing page is important, isn't it?

# The Pitfalls of Using a Homepage As a Landing Page

Using a homepage as a landing page is generally a poor practice because homepages are typically designed to serve multiple purposes and cater to the entirety of a visitor's journey. This can confuse users who arrive with a specific intention. A dedicated landing page ensures that the messaging is precise and aligned with the expectations set by your ads.

A user who is looking for something specific has an "intent" and hopes that he finds what he is looking for. The job of the advertising channel provider is to show the right ad (from a pool of too many ads) to the right user in the right context.

This means that if your ad promises the last car model at a discounted price, the landing page should show something related to that promise. Why? Because the user expects to find that information on your page; otherwise he would have not clicked the ad in the first place.

Secondly, if you know that you have a user coming which clicked an ad with a specific content, you have the possibility to prepare a landing page which "speaks" to this user directly, increasing the possibility of conversion (or getting a new customer).

Not having a well-enough landing page means you are throwing the resources you invested in the campaign in a black box and hoping that your campaign works (mostly by luck). It may also get you a blocked Google Ads account, for example, because of breaking their policies.

## Significance in Advertising Algorithms

Landing pages also play a critical role in the algorithms used by advertising providers like Google Ads. These algorithms assess the relevance and user experience of your landing page to determine the quality score of your ads. A poor landing page experience, indicated by users quickly leaving the page, could result in your ads being shown less often or to less-qualified audiences.

## Correlation with Ads

It's imperative that there is a strong correlation between the ad content, its targeting, and the content of the landing page. This alignment ensures that the expectations set by your ad are met when a user clicks through, improving user satisfaction and the likelihood of conversion.

## Importance of Specificity and Context

A user clicking on a specific ad has a particular intent, which your landing page should fulfill directly. For instance, if your ad is about a discount offer, your landing page should detail this offer clearly. Sending users to your homepage can dilute this intent, reducing the effectiveness of your campaign.

# Optimizing Landing Page Information Structure

A landing webpage's design and content should guide users toward taking specific actions. This requires understanding the principles of visual and information hierarchy.

# Visual Hierarchy

Defines how elements are organized and presented on your page. Here's a basic guideline:

- Utilize a single primary header (h1 tag) to denote the main subject or offer on the page.
- Employ secondary (h2) and tertiary (h3) headers for subtopics or details.
- Ensure content is displayed using appropriate HTML tags, such as p for paragraphs and img for images, with alt descriptions for accessibility and SEO.
- Keep your landing page responsive, especially if a significant portion of your audience visits through mobile devices.
- Incorporate at least one call-to-action (CTA) to guide users toward conversion actions like form submissions or purchases.

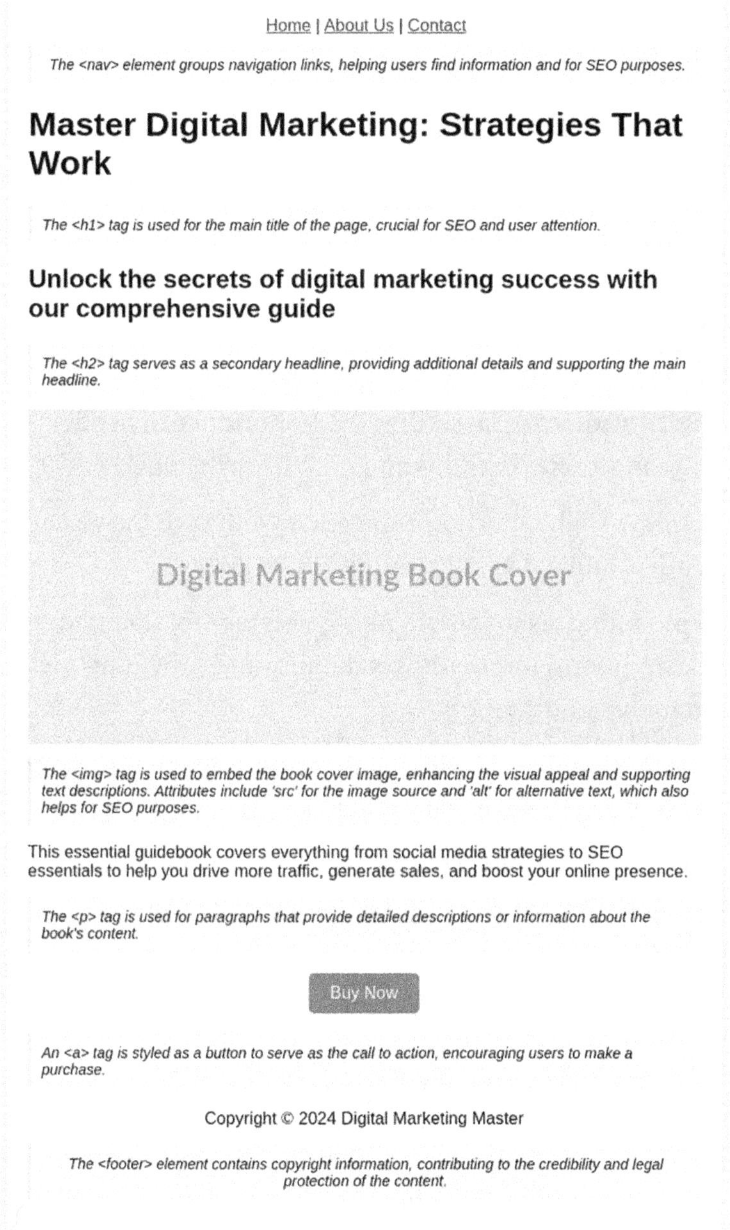

# CHAPTER 23   UNDERSTANDING LANDING PAGES

*Figure 23-1.  Example of the structure of a landing page*

Figure 23-1 illustrates an example of an efficient layout for a landing page selling a book, emphasizing hierarchy and user flow, leading naturally to a call-to-action. This is, of course, an example and can be improved in many ways, such as adding testimonials, a section highlighting what the reader will learn from the book, and additional CTAs with other copy, but let's analyze this basic example.

Explanation of the Annotated Elements:

- **<nav>**: Explains the role of navigation links in user orientation and SEO.

- **<h1> and <h2>**: Describes the importance of header tags in structuring content and improving SEO.

- **<img>**: Highlights how images can enhance the visual appeal and aid in storytelling.

- **<p>**: Indicates the use of paragraph tags for detailed descriptions, improving readability and providing valuable information.

- **<a> with button styling**: Shows how links can be styled as buttons to drive actions, such as making a purchase.

- **<footer>**: Discusses the footer's role in providing essential information and enhancing the website's credibility.

# What Is a Call-to-Action (CTA)?

A call-to-action is a design element, usually in the form of a button or link, that prompts users to take a specific action. The clarity and visibility of the CTA are vital—it must stand out and communicate the desired action succinctly, like "Sign Up," "Learn More," or "Buy Now." In the example above is "Buy Now." We can improve it with something more specific, like "Order your copy now!"

CHAPTER 23   UNDERSTANDING LANDING PAGES

# Utilizing Conversion Campaigns with Your Landing Page

Conversion campaigns are an important type of digital marketing campaigns, and they track the conversions by tracking user interactions on your landing page. The interactions that culminate in a valuable action, such as filling out a contact form or making a purchase, are called conversions. Understanding how to effectively set up and track conversions can significantly enhance your ability to optimize campaigns and improve ROI.

## Setting Up Conversion Tracking

To effectively track conversions, you'll need to integrate a tracking code provided by your advertising channel provider into your landing page. These codes enable the tracking of user actions and are essential for measuring the success of your campaigns. Here are some examples:

- **Google Ads Campaigns**: Utilize tracking codes from Google Analytics or Google Ads to monitor conversions directly tied to your ads.

- **Facebook Ads**: Implement the Facebook Pixel to track user activities and optimize ad delivery based on collected data.

- **Other Providers**: Many other advertising platforms offer their own proprietary tracking solutions. Ensure that you use the correct tracking setup for the platform you are using.

Additionally, some website platforms support Tag Managers, such as Google Tag Manager and Matomo Tag Manager, which simplify the management of multiple tracking codes on a single page.

For more on conversion tracking, check Chapter 18 on Understanding Conversions and Conversion Metrics.

**What Is a Tracking Code?**
A tracking code is a snippet of code that records interactions on your page—such as clicks or form submissions—to gauge the performance of your digital campaigns.1

## Tracking Visitors Without Conversion Goals

In some instances, like running brand awareness campaigns, you may not have specific conversion goals. However, tracking overall visitor behavior is still crucial:

- Deploy general website analytics tools, such as Google Analytics or Matomo, to gain insights into visitor behavior patterns across your site.

- Analyze metrics such as page views, session duration, and bounce rates to understand engagement and identify areas for improvement[1].

## Understanding SEO (Search Engine Optimization) and SEF (Search Engine Friendly)

In this section, I'll delve into SEO and SEF, two concepts in digital marketing that help you enhance your website's visibility and accessibility via search engines like Google, Bing, and Yandex.

---

[1] For more on metrics in digital marketing, check Chapter 12.

## What Are SEO and SEF?

SEO (Search Engine Optimization) involves optimizing your website so that search engines can easily understand, crawl, and index its content effectively. SEF (Search Engine Friendly), on the other hand, refers to the design and development aspects of your website that make it easier for search engines to navigate and index.

Optimizing your website involves several key practices:

- Utilizing the correct HTML tags (such as h1, h2, p, and meta tags) to structure your content logically.

- Enhancing the website's loading speed, as faster websites are favored by search engines.

- Using appropriate metadata that helps describe and differentiate your content.

- Creating and submitting a sitemap to search engines, which helps them discover all the pages on your site.

**What Is Metadata?**
Metadata refers to data about data. In the context of a website, metadata includes elements like descriptions for search engines, links to social media accounts, and images specifically designed to be shared on social networks. This meta-information, while not always directly visible to site visitors, is critical for search engines and sharing on social media platforms.

## Continuous SEO and SEF Practices

Ensuring your website remains optimized for SEO and SEF is an ongoing process. Regularly updating your content, reassessing your website's load speed, and updating your sitemap are crucial to maintaining and improving your search engine rankings.

CHAPTER 23   UNDERSTANDING LANDING PAGES

## What Is SEA (Search Engine Advertising)?

Moving from SEO and SEF, it's important to understand SEA, or Search Engine Advertising, which complements organic search strategies by placing paid ads within search engine results.

This is what you may typically know as Search Ads.

## Bridging SEO, SEF, and SEA

While SEO and SEF focus on improving organic search performance, SEA allows for direct advertisement within search engine results. Combining these strategies effectively can lead to a comprehensive search engine presence, maximizing both visibility and engagement.

## How HTML Structure Affects LLM (Large Language Models) and Other Artificial Intelligence Systems Comprehension of Web Pages

Understanding how HTML structure influences the ability of large language models (LLMs) such as Perplexity, ChatGPT, and others to understand your landing page or website is more relevant than ever. As LLMs increasingly mediate our interactions online, whether through search, customer support, or content interaction, optimizing your HTML becomes imperative for ensuring these models can accurately interpret and interact with your content.

## CHAPTER 23   UNDERSTANDING LANDING PAGES

# Introduction to HTML's Role in LLM Comprehension

The structure and semantics of your HTML code play an important role in how effectively LLMs can understand, process, and serve content from your website to users. By adhering to best practices in HTML structure, you can enhance the LLM's ability to extract and comprehend the relevant information, thereby improving user interactions and accessibility.

To better understand how an LLM understands your website, I will use a story.

# The Tale of Two Websites: The Power of HTML Structure in LLM Comprehension

In today's digital marketplace, your website is the gateway to your products and services. Imagine a potential customer, let's call her Emily, who is searching for the latest eco-friendly skincare products. At the same time, envision two companies, EcoGlow and NatureCare, both selling what Emily is looking for. However, their websites tell very different stories to search engines and, more critically, to sophisticated tools like Large Language Models (LLMs) employed by search engines.

**Emily's Journey and the Role of an LLM**
When Emily types her query into the search engine, the LLM springs into action. It begins by scrutinizing available web content to find the best match for her needs. Here, the structure of the web pages it scans is crucial. A well-structured website uses HTML effectively to guide the LLM through its content, much like clear signage helps a visitor navigate a large store effortlessly.

**EcoGlow: A Beacon of Clarity**
EcoGlow's website is a paragon of good HTML practice. It uses semantic HTML tags that clearly distinguish between headings, main content, navigation, and footers. Its pages are adorned with appropriate titles, meta

descriptions, and structured data that make it a breeze for the LLM to understand what each page is about. When Emily's search terms match the content flagged by these HTML signals on EcoGlow's site, the LLM quickly establishes relevance and fetches the information, placing EcoGlow high in Emily's search results.

Emily clicks on the link; finds exactly what she needs thanks to the clear, engaging, and informative layout; and feels confident in making a purchase.

**NatureCare: Lost in the Digital Shuffle**
Conversely, NatureCare's website suffers from poor HTML structure. Lack of proper headings, inconsistent use of tags, and sparse metadata create a confusing landscape for the LLM. When it visits NatureCare's site in response to Emily's query, it struggles to parse the page's content effectively. The signals it relies on to gauge relevance and content quality are weak or missing, causing the site to rank poorly in the search results.

Despite having products similar to EcoGlow's, NatureCare misses the opportunity to connect with Emily because it failed to communicate effectively with the LLM. Emily never sees NatureCare's offerings; thus, a potential sale is lost.

**The Tale's Moral**
This story of EcoGlow and NatureCare illustrates the profound impact of HTML structure on a website's visibility and usability:

- **Effective HTML structure facilitates better understanding and interaction** by LLMs, thereby improving search engine rankings and user experience.

- **Poor HTML structure obscures content**, making it difficult for LLMs to assess and serve your pages to potential customers like Emily.

# Critical Elements of HTML for LLM Optimization

**Structural Semantics**

- Using semantic HTML elements (`<header>`, `<footer>`, `<main>`, etc.) helps LLMs discern the role and relevance of different parts of your website, ensuring they recognize main content versus supplementary material.

**Headings and Hierarchy**

- Properly structured headings (`<h1>` through `<h6>`) guide LLMs in understanding the hierarchical organization of content, which is crucial for parsing the primary topics and subtopics on your page. Check the section above on hierarchy of a landing page for more details.

**Accessibility Features**

- Implementing accessible HTML, such as labels for form inputs and alt text for images, provides contextual clues that help LLMs better understand the non-text elements of your site.

**Metadata and Structured Data**

- Enhancing your page with metadata tags (`<title>`, `<meta>` descriptions) and structured data (JSON-LD, Microdata) allows LLMs to get detailed and organized information about the contents and purpose of your page.

CHAPTER 23   UNDERSTANDING LANDING PAGES

## Example of Implementing Effective HTML Structure

Suppose you are developing a website for an ecommerce platform. By structuring your product pages with clear semantic tags, descriptive headings for each section, and rich metadata describing each product, LLMs can more effectively understand and interact with the page. This setup improves SEO and enhances the performance of AI-driven tools like chatbots or recommendation systems that rely on this structured comprehension to assist users.

## Transitioning to Advanced HTML Practices

Understanding the more intricate elements of HTML structure and their impact on LLM interactions is just the first step. As technology and user interfaces evolve, the way LLMs interpret web content will also advance. By continuously updating and refining your HTML practices, you can ensure that your site remains comprehensible and accessible to both human users and sophisticated AI models.

# Summary and Key Takeaways

**Regarding the Structure of Landing Pages**

- Landing pages are essential for converting ad-driven traffic into customers.
- They must be directly relevant to the ads and designed to facilitate user decisions.
- Proper landing page optimization involves strategic use of visual hierarchy, specific CTAs, and ensuring content alignment with user intent.

## CHAPTER 23   UNDERSTANDING LANDING PAGES

**Regarding Conversions and Landing Pages**

- Conversion tracking is essential for understanding the impact of your digital marketing efforts and optimizing future campaigns.

- Proper setup of tracking codes and compliance with data privacy laws are crucial for accurately measuring conversions and maintaining user trust.

- Even without direct conversion goals, monitoring overall visitor behavior can provide valuable insights into campaign performance and website efficacy.

**Regarding SEO and SEF**

- SEO and SEF are crucial for making your website more accessible and comprehensible to search engines.

- Proper use of metadata, HTML tags, site speed optimization, and sitemaps are essential for good SEO and SEF.

- SEA offers a direct advertising approach that complements organic strategies, providing increased visibility in search engine results.

**Regarding Artificial Intelligence**

- A well-structured HTML is crucial for LLMs to understand and interact effectively with your website.

- Key elements such as semantic markup, proper use of headings, accessibility, and rich metadata play significant roles.

- Optimizing these elements can lead to better content delivery, enhanced user interaction, and improved overall site performance for AI-driven applications.

CHAPTER 23   UNDERSTANDING LANDING PAGES

In the next chapter, I will give you an overview of what is meant by analytics in digital marketing, the roles of first and third-party data, key metrics and concepts, and why analytics matter in digital marketing.

**Note**   Ensure compliance with local data privacy laws when implementing tracking. For instance, countries such as Germany, France, and Holland require explicit user consent for tracking activities.

# CHAPTER 24

# What Is Analytics?

Analytics enables us to understand and improve our business strategies and digital marketing initiatives by examining data. Whether you're engaged in marketing, business, or technology, analytics aids in making informed decisions and optimizing performance. But data and analytics only help if you have at least a general idea of what they mean and what their main metrics are.

In this chapter, I'll explore basic analytics metrics, first- and third-party data, tracking, data privacy, and specific tracking parameters.

## What Are and What Is the Role of First-Party and Third-Party Data

First-party data is collected directly from your interactions with customers, such as data from your website, CRM, or social media interactions. Third-party data is sourced from outside providers and consist of information that you didn't collect yourself. Both data types provide insights that assist in targeting and personalization.

I elaborate on data privacy in Chapter 26.

## Tracking and Data Privacy

Tracking involves the monitoring of user interactions on digital platforms, analyzing where traffic originates, how users interact, and what actions they take. Aligning these practices with data privacy regulations is important for protecting user information and building trust.

## Tracking Parameters Simplified

Tracking parameters, like MTM (Matomo Tag Manager) and UTM (Urchin Tracking Module), are snippets added to URLs that help identify the source of traffic, aiding in the assessment of different marketing strategies.

Here is an easy example, where the text after the *?* are the tracking parameters:

https://diegocarrasco.com/?*mtm_campaign=offline&mtm_source=qr-code*

Here are two tools to help you create these URLs:

- Matomo's URL Builder
- Google Ads URL Builder

## Main Analytics Platforms

Choosing the right analytics platform involves comparing features, ease of use, and compliance with data privacy standards. Table 24-1 shows a comparative table of popular and alternative analytics platforms.

*Table 24-1. Comparative table of analytics platforms*

| No | Name | Description | Website | Company | Use Requirements | GDPR Compliance | Data Privacy Compliance |
|---|---|---|---|---|---|---|---|
| 1 | Google Analytics | In-depth analytics for web and mobile | https://analytics.google.com | Google | Easy to integrate | Depending on region[1] | Depending on region |
| 2 | Matomo | Privacy-focused analytics platform | https://matomo.org | Matomo | Server installation required | Yes. Cookie Banner optional depending on configuration | Yes. Cookie Banner optional depending on configuration |
| 3 | Adobe Analytics | Advanced analytics solution | https://adobe.com/analytics | Adobe | Subscription based | Depending on region and configuration[2] | Depending on region and configuration |

(*continued*)

[1] https://piwikpro.de/blog/ist-google-analytics-dsgvo-konform/
[2] https://business.adobe.com/products/analytics/general-data-protection-regulation.html

*Table 24-1.* (continued)

| No | Name | Description | Website | Company | Use Requirements | GDPR Compliance | Data Privacy Compliance |
|---|---|---|---|---|---|---|---|
| 4 | Piwik Pro | Privacy-centered analytics tool | https://piwik.pro | Piwik LLC | Server installation required | Yes[3] | Yes |
| 5 | GoatCounter | Simple web analytics emphasizing privacy | www.goatcounter.com | GoatCounter | Account needed or self-hosting | Yes[4] | Limited |

---

[3] https://piwik.pro/privacy-compliance/
[4] www.goatcounter.com/help/gdpr

CHAPTER 24   WHAT IS ANALYTICS?

# Key Metrics and Concepts

Analyzing digital marketing campaigns involves understanding various metrics. I will explain the main metrics and then compare them in Table 24-2.

# Real-Time Visitors

This metric displays the number of visitors currently active on your site. It provides immediate insight into the effects of promotional activities or content changes.

**Why Is Real-Time Visitors Important for Digital Marketing**
The Real-Time Visitors metric gives a snapshot of the current level of engagement on your website. For marketers, this is a crucial indicator to measure instant reactions to campaigns, social media posts, or blog updates, allowing for timely adjustments.

**When Are Real-Time Visitors Important for a Campaign**
This metric is most valuable during the execution phase of a campaign, especially when fresh content goes live or a new product is launched. It's also incredibly useful during high-traffic events or promotions to monitor performance in real time and discover opportunities (such as visitor sources) or problems (e.g., unexpected exists).

**Related Digital Marketing Metrics**
Real-Time Visitors is closely associated with metrics like Page Views. It is also related with clicks on a digital marketing campaign. You would expect that each click on the ad translates to a page view and real-time visitor (depending on when you see this metric). Page views coming from digital ads with a low duration might mean that you are either reaching the wrong audience, you have an issue with your landing pages which makes your visitor to exist early in his journey, or something similar.

### Example Situation or Use Case
Imagine launching a flash sale announced via an email campaign. By monitoring Real-Time Visitors, you can observe a spike in traffic immediately after the email is sent. This real-time data helps assess the initial reaction and engagement level of your audience, providing guidance on whether to intensify promotional efforts or make quick content adjustments to better capture visitor interest.

## Unique Visitors

Unique Visitors tracks the number of **distinct individuals** who visit your website over a specific time period.

### Why You Should Track Unique Visitors
Tracking Unique Visitors helps you measure the scope of your website's reach. This metric shows how many **different** people are engaging with your content, which is important for understanding the appeal of your marketing efforts.

### When to Focus on Unique Visitors
Monitor Unique Visitor metrics throughout your campaign, especially during the evaluation phase. This metric is crucial when launching new products or entering new markets, as it provides insights into how many new potential customers are being attracted. If there is a huge difference between Visitors and Unique Visitors for the same campaign (check tracking parameter), you might want to check the ad frequency (check Chapter 12).

### Related Metrics
Unique Visitors is related to Reach, which tells you about the potential audience size, and Impressions, which count how many times your content is displayed. Understanding these relationships helps in defining and assessing the overall impact of your campaigns.

### Example Use Case

Imagine you've launched a new blog series intended to draw in a new segment of customers. By tracking Unique Visitors, you find out if new individuals are exploring your content, or if your current audience is just viewing it more frequently. This helps you adjust your content strategy to ensure it truly resonates with the intended new audience.

## Acquisition

Acquisition details the channels that bring visitors to your website.

### Why You Should Track Acquisition

Knowing where your site's traffic comes from helps you judge which marketing channels work best, which ones you should focus on, which ones you can improve and maybe which ones you should drop. This understanding allows you to better allocate your marketing efforts and budget. It's relevant for optimizing both current and future campaigns, ensuring that you invest in channels that yield the best returns.

### When to Focus on Acquisition Metrics

Keep track of acquisition data throughout all campaign phases. This metric is especially useful when you're experimenting with new channels or refining current ones. It's also important when reviewing the performance after a campaign, helping you make more informed decisions about where to focus future efforts.

### Related Metrics

Acquisition ties together with Traffic Sources, CPC (Cost per Click), CTR (Click-Through Rate), and Impressions. These metrics collectively help assess the performance of your marketing activities and gauge how each channel contributes to your overall traffic.

**Example Use Case**
Consider a scenario where you implement campaigns across social media, search engines, and email. By examining your acquisition data, you find that the majority of traffic is driven by your email efforts rather than social media. This insight might lead you to allocate more budget to your email marketing while tweaking your social media strategy to improve performance.

# User IDs

User IDs provide a way to track the activities of a logged-in user across multiple sessions and visits, creating a consistent and comprehensive view of their interactions with your website.

Depending on the region your visitor is in, and the analytics platform you are using, you have to be aware of data privacy policies. Check Chapter 26 for an overview on data privacy.

**Why You Should Track User IDs**
Tracking User IDs allows you to connect multiple sessions and interactions of the same user as a coherent journey. This is beneficial for recognizing patterns in user behavior, improving customer satisfaction through personalized content, and optimizing the overall user experience.

**When to Focus on User IDs**
This metric is particularly important when you are trying to understand long-term user behavior or engagement. It is crucial during and after marketing campaigns to track individual user response over multiple interactions, helping you refine your strategies based on user behavior insights.

**Related Metrics**
User IDs interact with metrics like Visit Duration, Page Views, and Events. These connections help you understand not just when users visit, but how they engage with content over time, providing a full picture of their journey on your site.

**Example Use Case**

Suppose you manage a subscription-based educational platform. By tracking User IDs, you determine which sections of your site subscribers frequently return to, and which sections are rarely revisited. This insight enables you to enhance underperforming areas and tailor recommendations, thereby increasing value and engagement for the users.

## Visit Duration

Visit Duration measures the **average** amount of time visitors spend on your website during a single session.

**Why You Should Track Visit Duration**

Understanding how long visitors stay on your site provides insights into the effectiveness of your content and usability of your website. If visitors spend a long time on your site, it often indicates that they find your content valuable and engaging.

**When to Focus on Visit Duration**

This metric is relevant both during and after a marketing campaign. It is particularly useful when evaluating the impact of changes to content, layout, or navigation on your site. Knowing when and why to check this metric helps you make informed decisions about design and content strategies. If the visit duration is too short, it might mean there is a poor match of the page content and the user interest. This is particularly important for digital marketing campaigns where you pay for clicks or conversions, and you expect the user to do something on your page.

**Related Metrics**

Visit Duration is linked with metrics such as Page Views and Bounce Rate. It may also be linked to Ad Quality, depending on the advertising channel provider you are using. These metrics together help paint a detailed picture of user engagement. High page views and longer visit durations typically suggest positive engagement, while a high bounce rate might indicate issues with the site that need addressing.

**Example Use Case**
Consider you've recently revamped a section of your website and introduced some new tutorials. By monitoring Visit Duration, you discover that users are spending significantly more time on these pages compared to others. This indicates the new content is engaging and valuable to your audience, and thus you might consider expanding similar content to other sections.

# Unique Page Views

Unique Page Views measure the number of sessions during which a specific page was viewed at least once. This metric helps you understand how frequently unique content on your site is accessed during different sessions.

### Why You Should Track Unique Page Views
Tracking Unique Page Views lets you see how many distinct sessions include visits to specific pages on your site. It is effective for measuring the reach of particular content and determining what drives interest among your visitors.

### When to Focus on Unique Page Views
This metric is useful throughout the life cycle of a campaign but is particularly vital after you've launched new content or made significant updates. Monitoring during these times helps you understand how these changes influence visitor behavior.

### Related Metrics
Unique Page Views are closely related to Total Page Views and Bounce Rate. While Total Page Views count all views, Unique Page Views filter these by sessions, providing clearer insight into actual engagement without repeated views by the same user in the same session.

### Example Use Case
Imagine you've posted a new article on your website. By tracking Unique Page Views, you find that 200 unique sessions have included the article page within the first week. This number, compared to other content pieces, helps you gauge interest and decide on promoting the article further or creating similar content.

## Page Views

Page Views count all views of a page by any visitor, including multiple views by the same visitor. This metric gives a total overview of how often content on your site is accessed.

### Why You Should Track Page Views
Tracking Page Views provides an aggregate number of how often your pages are viewed. This data helps you to identify which areas of your site attract the most attention and which may require enhancement.

### When to Focus on Page Views
Concentrate on Page Views during the execution and after the campaign phases. This metric is particularly useful for A/B testing different page layouts or content types to see which one engages your audience more effectively.

### Related Metrics
Page Views are typically analyzed alongside Unique Page Views and Bounce Rate. While Unique Page Views indicate distinct visits to a page, the total Page Views count can highlight if certain content is repeatedly viewed within a single visit, suggesting engaging or valuable information.

### Example Use Case
Suppose your website introduces a new interactive feature that you expect will keep visitors engaged. By tracking the Page Views for the pages containing this feature, you notice a significant rise in views. This increase could indicate that the feature is popular and keeping visitors on your site longer, prompting further investments in similar innovations.

# Entry Links

Entry Links identify the first page a visitor lands on when they arrive at your website. This metric helps determine which external or internal sources are effectively directing traffic to your site.

**Why You Should Track Entry Links**
Understanding which pages serve as entry points helps you evaluate the effectiveness of your marketing efforts across different channels. It points to which campaigns or external links are successfully drawing visitors, providing valuable insights for optimizing your funnel.

**When to Focus on Entry Links**
Focus on Entry Links throughout your campaign, especially during the launch of new marketing initiatives or after making significant changes to your digital presence. Monitoring this metric helps assess the response to these changes.

**Related Metrics**
Entry Links are linked with Acquisition, as both metrics provide insights into where your visitors come from. These metrics combined can offer a comprehensive view of how external sources contribute to your incoming traffic.

**Example Use Case**
Suppose you are running a promotional campaign via various platforms such as social media and email. By analyzing the Entry Links, you discover that the majority of traffic comes from your email links rather than social media. This insight could lead you to focus more on optimizing your email campaign strategy to maximize traffic and conversion rates.

# Exit Links

Exit Links track the last page visited before a viewer leaves your website. This metric helps you identify potential problem areas that may cause visitor drop-off.

**Why You Should Track Exit Links**
Monitoring Exit Links lets you pinpoint pages or steps in the conversion process where visitors tend to leave your site. Once identified, you can optimize those pages to prevent drop-offs and improve the overall effectiveness of your website (unless you want them to exit your website on those pages).

**When to Focus on Exit Links**
You should particularly focus on Exit Links during website revisions or after implementing changes in your content or structure. It's also important to monitor these links regularly to continually improve your site's user experience.

**Related Metrics**
Exit Links relate closely to Bounce Rate and Page Views. While Bounce Rate indicates visitors leaving after viewing only one page, Exit Links provide a deeper dive into specific pages from which users exit, helping to understand their last interaction.

**Example Use Case**
Suppose you notice a high number of exits from a particular page on your checkout process. By investigating the Exit Links data, you identify that many users are leaving at the shipping options page. This might suggest that shipping costs or options are unsatisfactory, prompting you to reassess and improve your shipping policies or presentation.

## Events

Events track specific interactions on your website that go beyond page views, like downloads, video plays, or forms submissions. These user actions offer a look into how visitors engage with your content.

**Why You Should Track Events**
Tracking Events is essential for pinpointing which elements of your site effectively engage users and lead them toward important conversion actions. This understanding aids in refining your content and marketing strategies.

**When to Focus on Events**
While it's useful to monitor Events throughout a campaign, they become particularly important during user engagement evaluations and when testing new interactive features or content. It's during these phases that insights into specific behaviors can inform significant improvements.

**Related Metrics**
Events are often evaluated alongside Page Views and Conversion Rates. The interaction among these metrics offers insights into not just how many times a page was visited, but also what actions were taken during those visits, and how these actions contribute to overall campaign goals.

**Example Use Case**
Consider a situation where you've added a new demo video on your product page. By tracking the Event of video plays, you discover a strong correlation between video views and purchases. This insight suggests that the video effectively convinces visitors of the product's value, encouraging more such content to facilitate user decision-making. You might also find out that users are stopping the video after just a couple of seconds, which may mean the content is not resonating with your users.

# Page Fold

The Page Fold is the portion of your webpage that is visible without scrolling.

### Why You Should Monitor Page Fold
The content above the Page Fold is the first thing visitors encounter. Ensuring that critical information and engaging content are visible without scrolling can significantly increase user engagement and conversion rates.

### When to Focus on Page Fold
This metric is particularly important when you are designing or redesigning your website. It's valuable during the testing phase of website layouts to see how changes affect visitor interactions.

### Related Metrics
Page Fold engagement is closely related to Bounce Rate and Time on Page. Together, these metrics can tell you a lot about initial user engagement and whether the content placed at the top of the page is effective.

### Example Use Case
Imagine you redesign your homepage to include a new promotional banner within the Page Fold. By observing changes in the Bounce Rate and Time on Page, you determine whether this new element catches attention and encourages visitors to stay longer, thereby enhancing their overall engagement with your site.

# User Flow/User Journey

User Flow or User Journey maps out the path a visitor takes through your website from the entry point to the exit. Understanding this journey is key to optimizing the user experience.

### Why You Should Monitor User Flow/User Journey
Following the User Flow helps you understand your visitors' behavior patterns and preferences, which guides improvements in site design and content arrangement. It helps pinpoint where users encounter problems or lose interest.

### When to Focus on User Flow/User Journey
This metric becomes specially important when assessing user engagement throughout various stages of their interaction with your website. It is particularly valuable after changes to your site's structure or when introducing new content.

### Related Metrics
User Flow is related to metrics like *Entry Links*, *Exit Links*, and *Page Views*. These metrics combined give a good picture of how users interact with your site—from where they enter, how they move, and where they eventually leave.

### Example Use Case
Suppose you've recently redesigned your online store. By analyzing the User Flow, you notice that many visitors drop off from the product details page to the checkout. This suggests a need for a smoother transition or clearer calls to action on the product pages.

## Goals

Goals are specific interactions or behaviors you track that quantify success, such as form submissions, product purchases, or reaching a certain page.

### Why You Should Monitor Goals
Setting and tracking Goals allow you to measure how well your website converts visitor actions into desired outcomes. This is crucial for understanding the efficacy of your marketing tactics and making data-driven decisions to optimize performance.

### When to Focus on Goals

You will want to establish Goals at the planning stage of any campaign and to monitor them throughout the campaign lifecycle. They are especially important for evaluating the success of specific marketing initiatives post-launch.

### Related Metrics

Goals are inherently connected to other metrics like Conversion Rate, which measures the percentage of visitors who complete a Goal, and User Flow, which can show the path visitors take before completing a Goal.

### Example Use Case

Assume you have launched an ecommerce site and set a Goal for the number of checkouts completed. By tracking this Goal, you find that while many users add items to their cart, few complete the checkout process. This insight leads you to streamline the checkout process, perhaps by reducing the number of steps and improving form design, to increase conversion rates.

## Campaigns

Campaigns refer to coordinated marketing efforts that aim to achieve specific business objectives, such as increasing brand awareness or boosting sales. In digital marketing, campaigns utilize various channels and tactics to reach and engage target audiences effectively.

### Why You Should Track Campaigns

Monitoring your campaigns is essential as it allows you to see which elements are performing well and which are not. This insight helps you make informed decisions about budget allocation, channel selection, and creative approaches. You can track campaigns using tracking parameters in the landing page urls of your ads. Refer to tracking parameters in the section above.

### When to Focus on Campaigns

From the planning phase to the post-execution analysis, campaigns need continuous attention. It is especially critical to evaluate them during and after their run to understand their effectiveness and to derive lessons for future campaigns.

### Related Metrics

Campaigns interact closely with metrics like Conversion Rates, Reach, and Impressions.

### Example Use Case

Let's say you've launched a multichannel campaign using social media, email, and pay-per-click advertising to promote a new product. By analyzing the performance, you find that while your social media ads have the highest engagement, email contributes most to actual conversions. This information can guide your future strategy to prioritize email marketing while refining your social media tactics.

## Comparison Table

*Table 24-2. Comparison table of the most popular metrics*

| No | Metric | Description | Use Case Example |
| --- | --- | --- | --- |
| 1 | Real-Time Visitors | Shows the number of visitors currently active on your site. | Use this metric during a live campaign to make immediate adjustments based on visitor response. |
| 2 | Unique Visitors | Counts each visitor once within a specified time period, regardless of how many times they visit. | Track the reach of a new promotional campaign over a month to gauge its ability to attract new visitors. |

*(continued)*

*Table 24-2.* (*continued*)

| No | Metric | Description | Use Case Example |
|---|---|---|---|
| 3 | Acquisition | Details the origin of your traffic—how visitors find you. | Analyze which marketing channel (social media, email, search engines) is most effective at driving traffic. |
| 4 | User IDs | Tracks signed in visitors to understand interaction across multiple visits. | By analyzing behavior, tailor a personalized marketing strategy to increase user engagement. |
| 5 | Visit Duration | Measures the average time spent by a visitor per session. | Evaluate the engagement level with content. Longer durations indicate content is engaging or too complex. |
| 6 | Unique Page Views | Tracks repeat views by the same visitor during the same session for a more accurate count | Measure the effectiveness of a landing page design in capturing interest |
| 7 | Page Views | Total views of a page, including repeat views by the same visitor in the same session | Utilize to gauge overall interest in specific content or pages on your site |
| 8 | Entry Links | Shows the first page visited by the user in a session | Identify which external links or pages are successfully attracting visitors |
| 9 | Exit Links | Indicates the last page visited before a user leaves | Highlight potential problem areas where you're losing visitor interest |

(*continued*)

*Table 24-2. (continued)*

| No | Metric | Description | Use Case Example |
|---|---|---|---|
| 10 | Events | Interactions with content that can be tracked separately from a page view, such as downloads or video plays | Measure the interaction levels with call-to-action features to adjust them for better performance |
| 11 | Page Fold | The portion of the webpage visible without scrolling. Important for understanding what captures immediate attention | Use to test different elements above the fold to see which result in longer visit durations or more conversions |
| 12 | User Flow/Journey | The path a user travels through your website starting from the entry point to the exit | Analyze the common pathways to optimize user experience and conversion paths |
| 13 | Goals | Specific interactions or behaviors you track that signify success, such as form submissions or product purchases | Track conversion rates for specific campaigns to see if they meet predefined objectives |
| 14 | Campaigns | Tracking specific marketing efforts through UTM parameters to analyze effectiveness | Assess the performance of different marketing campaigns in terms of traffic generation and conversion rates |

## Why Analytics Matters in Marketing

For marketers, understanding analytics allows for better strategy adjustments and decisions based on actual data. This knowledge ensures resources are allocated effectively, and campaigns are targeted to meet specific objectives.

## Summary

I have explored the fundamental aspects of analytics in digital marketing. This included the most used platforms, tracking parameters, and key metrics to monitor your campaigns and website.

In the next chapter, I will explain what constitutes a digital marketing specialist for the purposes of this book, what they do, and the different types that exist. This information will help you decide whom to choose to assist with your digital marketing campaign initiatives.

# CHAPTER 25

# Understanding Digital Marketing Specialists and Their Types

In this chapter, I will explore the role of a digital marketing specialist. The focus will be on discussing their responsibilities and the variety of roles available within the industry. This insight will help you identify the right type of digital marketing specialist for your needs, ensuring that you choose a service provider capable of effectively conveying your message to the right audience.

## What Is a Digital Marketing Specialist and Which Types Are There

A digital marketing specialist is a professional skilled in utilizing various advertising channel providers and their capabilities to effectively deliver your marketing messages. These specialists ensure that your content reaches the appropriate audience, in the right context and at the optimal time, all while staying within budget.

CHAPTER 25    UNDERSTANDING DIGITAL MARKETING SPECIALISTS AND THEIR TYPES

In this field, specialists can vary widely based on their workplace environment and their specific knowledge and experience. Understanding these distinctions is crucial for selecting the appropriate specialist for your marketing efforts.

## Digital Marketing Specialists According to Working Place

The working environment of digital marketing specialists can vary, and this often influences their approach and availability. Here's a breakdown.

**Freelancer**
A freelancer is an individual who offers their services on a project-by-project basis. They might specialize in particular sectors or possess a broad range of digital marketing skills. Evaluating a freelancer's certifications, track record, and references can provide reassurance of their expertise.

**Agency**
An agency employs a team of specialists and typically offers a wider range of digital marketing services. The reputation of the agency itself lends credibility, supported by the collective experience of its team.

**Employee in Your Company**
These are specialists who work as part of your internal team, commonly referred to as colleagues. They are integrated into the company's culture and have a vested interest in the company's long-term marketing success.

## Digital Marketing Specialists According to Knowledge and Experience

The depth of knowledge and the focus area also distinguish digital marketing specialists.

**Advertiser Channel Provider Specialist**

This specialist boasts in-depth knowledge of one or more advertising platforms. They understand the nuanced settings and formats specific to each platform, which can maximize campaign efficacy.

**Consultant**

Consultants strategize which channels, formats, and settings best align with your marketing objectives. While some consultants implement strategies themselves, others may coordinate with advertiser channel provider specialists to ensure best practices are followed across various platforms.

## Choosing the Right Specialist

When selecting a digital marketing specialist, consider your specific needs, budget, and the complexity of your campaigns. Freelancers or agency specialists might suit project-based work, while hiring an internal employee could be beneficial for ongoing marketing strategies.

## Summary

In this chapter, I provided an overview of digital marketing professionals and what to expect of them classified according to expertise and working place.

The main things you should remember are

- Digital marketing specialists are crucial for navigating the complex landscape of online advertising, ensuring your messages reach the intended audience effectively.

## CHAPTER 25  UNDERSTANDING DIGITAL MARKETING SPECIALISTS AND THEIR TYPES

- They vary by workplace environment—freelancer, agency, or internal company employees—and each offers distinct advantages.

- Specialists also differ in their depth of knowledge, from platform-specific experts to consultants who design overarching marketing strategies.

In the next chapter, I will give you an overview of the legal and tax aspects of digital marketing. While you will still need to consult your legal and tax advisor on these issues, this information will at least prepare you with the right questions to ask.

CHAPTER 26

# The Landscape of Legal, Taxes, and Brand Protection in Digital Marketing

In this chapter, I will introduce you to essential aspects of legal considerations, tax implications, and brand protection strategies within the realm of digital marketing. These topics are intricate and can significantly influence the implementation of your digital marketing initiatives. Understanding the basics will equip you to ask informed questions when consulting your legal and tax advisors.

## What You Should Know Regarding Taxes, Legal Issues, Policies, and Brand Protection

Navigating the digital marketing landscape entails more than just crafting compelling content and engaging with your audience; it also involves understanding and adhering to various regulations and protecting your brand.

CHAPTER 26   THE LANDSCAPE OF LEGAL, TAXES, AND BRAND PROTECTION IN
                 DIGITAL MARKETING

# Understanding Data Privacy Legislation and Its Importance

*This overview does not constitute legal advice.* Please consult a lawyer for any legal concerns. **You have been warned.**

> [...] Of equal concern is the collection, use, and sharing of personal information to third parties without notice or consent of consumers. 137 out of 194 countries had put in place legislation to secure the protection of data and privacy.
>
> —United Nations (https://unctad.org/page/data-protection-and-privacy-legislation-worldwide)

The necessity of complying with data privacy laws cannot be overstated, especially when your digital marketing efforts span multiple countries. Below are key regulations categorized by continent.

## Regulations in Europe

- **General Data Protection Regulation (GDPR):** Governs data protection across all EU member states.[1]

- **ePrivacy Regulation:** Set to replace the ePrivacy Directive, focusing on electronic communications.

- **ePrivacy Directive:** Currently governs privacy in electronic communications within the EU.[2]

---

[1] https://gdpr-info.eu/
[2] https://eur-lex.europa.eu/LexUriServ/LexUriServ.do?uri=CELEX:32002L0058:en:HTML

## Regulations in North America

- **California Consumer Privacy Act (CCPA)**: Grants California residents significant control over their personal information.[3]

- **Personal Information Protection and Electronic Documents Act (PIPEDA)**: Canada's federal privacy law for private sector organizations.[4]

## Regulations in South America

- **Lei Geral de Proteção de Dados Pessoais (LGPD)**: Brazil's comprehensive data protection law.[5]

## Regulations in South Africa

- **Protection of Personal Information Act (POPIA)**: South Africa's data protection statute.[6]

---

[3] https://leginfo.legislature.ca.gov/faces/codes_displayText.xhtml?division=3.&part=4.&lawCode=CIV&title=1.81.5

[4] www.priv.gc.ca/en/privacy-topics/privacy-laws-in-canada/the-personal-information-protection-and-electronic-documents-act-pipeda/pipeda_brief/

[5] In Portuguese: www.planalto.gov.br/ccivil_03/_ato2015-2018/2018/lei/L13709compilado.htm

[6] https://popia.co.za/

CHAPTER 26  THE LANDSCAPE OF LEGAL, TAXES, AND BRAND PROTECTION IN
           DIGITAL MARKETING

## Regulations in Asia

- **Personal Data Protection Act (PDPA)**: The PDPA is Singapore's data protection law that regulates the collection, use, and disclosure of personal data by organizations in Singapore. It also grants individuals certain rights over their personal data.[7]

- **Information Technology (Reasonable Security Practices and Procedures and Sensitive Personal Data or Information) Rules**: These are data protection rules issued by the **Indian government** under the Information Technology Act, 2000. They set out requirements for the collection, use, and disclosure of sensitive personal data or information by companies in India.[8]

- **Personal Information Protection Act (PIPA)**: PIPA is Japan's data protection law that regulates the handling of personal data by businesses and grants individuals certain rights over their personal data.[9]

- **Personal Data Protection Law (PDPL)**: The PDPL is a data protection law that was introduced in Thailand in 2020. It sets out rules for the collection, use, and disclosure of personal data by organizations and grants individuals certain rights over their personal data.[10]

---

[7] www.pdpc.gov.sg/overview-of-pdpa/the-legislation/personal-data-protection-act
[8] www.meity.gov.in/content/information-technology-act-2000-0
[9] www.cas.go.jp/jp/seisaku/hourei/data/APPI.pdf
[10] https://pdpathailand.com/en/

Understanding these laws helps ensure that your digital marketing practices are compliant and respect user privacy, which is critical for maintaining trust and authority.

## The Impact of Data Privacy Legislation on Digital Marketing

Effective digital marketing relies on data to target and retarget potential customers; however, data privacy laws can impose restrictions that might complicate these efforts. For instance, data collected in Europe under GDPR must be handled with strict protocols—potentially necessitating significant operational adjustments for compliance.

## Why Country-Specific Taxes Are Important for Digital Marketing

*This is not tax advice.* Consult a tax professional before making decisions. **You have been warned.**

Understanding the tax implications related to digital marketing is important. For example, several countries have implemented taxes specific to digital advertising services and digital platforms, which can affect your marketing budget and strategy.

Austria and other countries have digital-marketing-specific taxes. This means that if you are a German-based company, and you want to advertise your products in Austria (another German-speaking country), then you may have to additionally pay taxes on the costs of your marketing efforts in that country.

The following is an abstract of the main taxes. This is by no way a complete list.

Here is a list of the most important taxes related to digital marketing efforts.

## Digital Marketing-Related Taxes in Europe

- **Austria**: Digital advertising services are subject to value-added tax (VAT). Austria has also implemented a digital services tax (DST) on certain digital services, including online advertising.[11]

- **France**: France has implemented a digital services tax (DST) on certain digital services, including online advertising.

- **Italy**: Italy has implemented a digital services tax (DST) on certain digital services, including online advertising.

- **Spain**: Spain has implemented a digital services tax (DST) on certain digital services, including online advertising.

## Digital Marketing-Related Taxes in North America

- **United States**: Sales tax may apply to digital advertising services depending on the state and the specific type of advertising. Some states have adopted laws that specifically tax digital advertising services, while others apply sales tax to all services. For example, Maryland has implemented a tax on digital advertising, while Washington has implemented a tax on all digital services. Source: www.avalara.com/blog/en/north-america/2021/10/more-states-strive-to-tax-online-ads-despite-challenges.html

---

[11] www.bmf.gv.at/en/topics/taxation/digital-tax-act.html

CHAPTER 26   THE LANDSCAPE OF LEGAL, TAXES, AND BRAND PROTECTION IN DIGITAL MARKETING

## Digital Marketing-Related Taxes in South America

- **Argentina**: Argentina has implemented a tax on digital services, including online advertising.[12]

## Digital Marketing-Related Taxes in Asia

- **India**: India has implemented a tax on digital advertising services.[13]

# What Is Advertiser Verification?

Depending on your industry and the countries in which you implement digital marketing initiatives, you may need to verify your identity with advertiser channel providers to ensure credibility and adhere to platform standards. Major platforms like Google Ads and Facebook require advertiser verification to mitigate the risk of fraud and enhance the advertising ecosystem's integrity.

- **Google Ads**: Google Ads requires advertiser verification for some advertisers. Source: https://support.google.com/adspolicy/answer/9703665?hl=en

- **Facebook Ads**: Facebook Ads requires advertiser verification for some advertisers and for some types of ads. Source: www.facebook.com/business/help/2992964394067299?id=288762101909005

---

[12] https://servicioscf.afip.gob.ar/publico/abc/ABCpaso2.aspx?id_nivel1=563&id_nivel2=566&id_nivel3=2486 y https://www.argentina.gob.ar/normativa/nacional/decreto-354-2018-309281

[13] www.bloomberg.com/news/articles/2022-12-23/india-to-review-gst-rules-on-how-it-taxes-foreign-digital-services

- **Twitter Ads**: Twitter Ads requires advertiser verification for financial services advertisers. Source: `https://business.twitter.com/en/help/ads-policies/ads-content-policies/financial-services.html`

- **LinkedIn Ads**: LinkedIn Ads requires advertiser verification for some advertisers. Source: `www.linkedin.com/legal/ads-policy`

- **Pinterest Ads**: Pinterest Ads requires advertiser verification for some advertisers. Source: `https://help.pinterest.com/en/business/article/advertiser-verification`

## What Are Network Policies?

Network policies issued by ad providers govern the acceptable use of their services. These policies cover content standards, privacy, user interaction, and more to ensure that advertising practices do not harm users or the platform's reputation.

## How to Protect Your Brand in Digital Marketing

Protecting your brand extends beyond registering trademarks. It involves managing how your brand appears online, responding to both positive and negative interactions, and ensuring that your advertising does not inadvertently align your brand with undesirable content or contexts.

Some key points in protecting your brand in the digital world are

- Understanding the legal, tax, and regulatory environments is crucial for effective and compliant digital marketing.

## CHAPTER 26  THE LANDSCAPE OF LEGAL, TAXES, AND BRAND PROTECTION IN DIGITAL MARKETING

- Protecting your brand involves careful management of your digital presence and maintaining consistency and integrity in how it represents itself online.

- Data privacy is not merely a regulatory requirement but a cornerstone of building trust with your audience.

One thing that is important to understand is that you are already doing digital marketing, whether you like it or not. In fact, maybe it is not you who is doing it, but your customers and competitors. Not monitoring your brand, not owning your social media handles,[14] and so on means that you are not in charge of your brand on the Internet. You may do digital marketing but not care about what placements are used (and, e.g., show your brand Ad on a website where war is endorsed and this goes against your values).

Protecting your brand in digital marketing is important to maintain its reputation and ensure that it is not associated with any negative or harmful content. Here are some steps you can take to protect your brand in digital marketing.

- **Monitor Your Brand Mentions**: Regularly monitor social media, review sites, and other online channels to see what people are saying about your brand. This can help you identify any negative sentiment or potential brand threats.

- **Set Up Alerts**: Use tools to receive notifications whenever your brand is mentioned online. This can help you stay on top of brand mentions and respond to any negative feedback or comments.[15]

---

[14] @username, facebook.com/your-brand are examples of social media handles. Every social media platform has such things.

[15] Check `https://diegocarrasco.com/alter-tools` this page to get the most popular tools for this.

- **Claim Your Brand's Social Media Handles**: Claim your brand's name on all major social media platforms to prevent others from using it to misrepresent your brand. This will also help you maintain a consistent brand identity across different channels. If you are not planning on using them actively, you can also communicate that.[16]

- **Use Trademark Protection**: Register your brand name and logo as trademarks to protect them from unauthorized use. This can help prevent others from using your brand name or logo in a way that could damage your brand reputation.

- **Be Careful with Ad Placements and Targeting Settings**: When running digital ads, be sure to choose reputable ad networks and platforms that have strict ad policies and guidelines. This can help ensure that your ads are not placed next to harmful or offensive content. You should also at least be aware of what targeting settings are being used. Check out Chapter 6 for more information on this topic.

- **Monitor Your Digital Ads**: Regularly review your digital ads to ensure that they are compliant with ad policies and guidelines and that they align with your brand values and messaging. (Although most ad providers will send you a message if you ever break their policies.)

---

[16] Check `https://diegocarrasco.com/social-media-profiles-not-in-use-templates` this page for some useful message templates.

- **Respond to Negative Feedback**: If you receive negative feedback or comments about your brand online, respond to them promptly and professionally. This can help mitigate any potential damage to your brand reputation and show that you are committed to addressing customer concerns.

# Summary

In this chapter, I provided an overview of the legal and tax landscape related to digital marketing. Although you cannot take this as legal or tax advice, knowing that certain laws and taxes exist and have an impact on your business and digital marketing initiatives is a big step forward.

The key points you have to remember are

- Understanding the legal, tax, and regulatory environments is crucial for effective and compliant digital marketing.
- Protecting your brand involves careful management of your digital presence and maintaining consistency and integrity in how it represents itself online.
- Data privacy is not merely a regulatory requirement but a cornerstone of building trust with your audience.

In the next chapter, I will elaborate on setting digital marketing campaign goals, related recommended bidding strategies and formats, and their risks.

# PART II

# Creation | Pre-campaign Preparation |

## Laying the Foundation for a Successful Digital Marketing Campaign

Before moving into the dynamic world of digital ads, it's crucial to set the stage properly. Now that you already have the foundations on digital marketing and understand the jargon and the main concepts, I'll dive right into preparing a campaign.

This part is all about the essential groundwork you need to do before your ads ever see the light of day online. Remember, a well-planned beginning sets the tone for the entire campaign.

Just as in traditional marketing, every digital marketing campaign requires a solid foundation. You'll need to define clear goals, identify your target audience, and determine the key performance indicators (KPIs) you'll use to measure success. But there's a catch in the digital realm—the ease of getting started. Platforms like Google Ads and Facebook Ads are designed to lower the entry barriers, enticing you to dive in headfirst. However, this ease can often lead to skipping over these crucial foundational steps.

PART II  CREATION | PRE-CAMPAIGN PREPARATION |

This part aims to ensure you're fully prepared before you begin. Whether you're a seasoned marketer looking to refine your approach or you're new to the game and need to understand the basics, the insights here will guide you in making informed decisions. We'll cover how to set effective marketing goals, choose the right ad providers, navigate through different networks and formats, and craft a comprehensive digital marketing brief.

This part is here in the hopes that you at least know what you should take into account. If you don't, then at least you will do that consciously.

As I dive into pre-campaign preparation, each area I explore is designed to ensure your digital marketing efforts are built on solid ground. Here's a narrative walkthrough that explains the purpose of each chapter and provides practical examples to illustrate key concepts.

## Setting Marketing Goals

Understanding how to set realistic and measurable objectives is vital. It's important to recognize that the optimal approach might not always be feasible. You need to evaluate your strategy and resources to set achievable goals.

**Example**
Suppose you aim to implement conversion tracking, but being new to the market, you are unsure about your audience. It's wiser to begin by increasing visits to your website and analyzing visitor behavior.
This approach allows you to gather valuable data, which you can use to refine your strategy in subsequent campaigns. Remember, learning about your audience cost-effectively should precede more expensive goals like conversions, and paying for clicks is a lot cheaper than paying for conversions in digital marketing (remember you read about this in Chapter 10?)

# Choosing Ad Providers and Networks

Selecting the right platforms for your needs is crucial as different networks offer varied benefits. The key is to align your choice with your marketing objectives and the specific characteristics of your target audience.

**Example**

Imagine your brand values presence in a well-known newspaper, which, however, is not available on Google Ads but is accessible via The Trade Desk. You would then need to plan your campaign specifically for The Trade Desk, considering their requirements, like the minimum media budget and supported ad formats. This choice ensures your ads appear in the desired context, potentially enhancing campaign effectiveness.

# Understanding Advertising Formats

Grasping the different advertising formats available will allow you to choose the one that best conveys your message and makes the best use of your available resources. Consider how the medium can influence the message and the potential reuse of existing assets.

**Example**

If your campaign's success hinges on visual engagement, like images and videos, then opting for responsive search ads might not suit your needs. Conversely, if you have existing video or print ads, consider transforming these into digital formats like YouTube or Addressable TV Ads to cut costs and maintain message continuity. Always evaluate the recommendations from your consultants or agencies critically; they should align with your resources and goals, not just their expertise.

As a Rule of Thumb: A good consultant should also be able to dive into new areas or tell you that a specific requirement is not their area of expertise. In most cases, there will be many partners working together, and it's better to understand their strengths and weaknesses to make the right decisions.

PART II   CREATION | PRE-CAMPAIGN PREPARATION |

# Crafting a Digital Marketing Brief

Creating a digital marketing brief is central to the direction and success of your campaign. This document should clearly communicate your needs and expectations to all stakeholders involved. It's ok to make mistakes and improve it over time, but you need a first version to work from.

A well-crafted brief ensures that everyone from your freelance consultants to your digital agencies understands the campaign's objectives and strategies. This clarity helps in harmonizing efforts and achieving consensus, which is crucial for the campaign's success. I'll provide you with templates and guidance to streamline this process, ensuring you can communicate effectively with your partners.

Together, these chapters will equip you with the knowledge to start your digital marketing campaign on solid ground, ensuring you're not just another advertiser who skipped the homework. Staying mindful of these preliminary steps can dramatically enhance the effectiveness and efficiency of your digital marketing efforts.

CHAPTER 27

# Setting Marketing Goals: Crafting Strategic Objectives for Digital Campaigns

In this chapter, I'll guide you through the process of setting realistic and achievable marketing goals. This is the first critical step before diving into any digital marketing campaign. It's crucial to understand that while you may aim for the optimal outcomes, these may not always be feasible given your current resources and market standing. Understanding and setting the right goals will help you effectively utilize your resources and establish a strong foundation for your campaign's success.

## Clarifying Your Marketing Objectives

Let's begin by identifying what you're truly aiming to achieve with your digital marketing efforts. Your objectives should not only align with your business's overall strategies, but also be clear and measurable.

## Example

Imagine you're launching a new product and want to implement conversion tracking to measure its initial uptake. However, if you're relatively new to the market and still learning about your audience, it might be more cost-effective to first focus on increasing traffic to your website. This approach enables you to collect valuable data about user behaviors, preferences, and demographics. Analyzing this information will allow you to tailor your future strategies and gear up for conversion-focused campaigns with more precision. At the same time, with such an approach, you will have less learning-related costs as clicks are less expensive than conversions.

# Marketing Goals, Channels, and Ad Formats Recommendations/Guidelines

It's essential to understand your marketing goals clearly and choose the appropriate channels and ad formats that can yield better results for those specific goals. Here, I break down each goal category to help you strategize effectively.

# Categories of Marketing Goals

There are three main categories under which you can classify digital marketing goals. I will later introduce four additional categories that extend these three main ones:

**Main Categories**

1. Awareness
2. Traffic
3. Conversion

**Additional Categories**

4. Engagement
5. Brand loyalty
6. Advocacy
7. Lead generation

# Main Categories for Marketing Goals

As I wrote above, your marketing goals can be classified into one of the following categories: awareness, traffic, or conversion.

Remember to keep in mind that for all campaigns, the experience and preparation of the landing page is as (if not more) important than the ad itself. The ad is the invitation to come and visit your store, but the landing page is the entry to your store. Should it not work or not deliver as the user expected, then the visitor will quickly leave.

> **Note** Remember there are many metrics you can use. Refer to Chapter 12 on Metrics for more details on which metrics work with other (e.g., Impressions and CTR).

## 1. Awareness

The primary aim here is to increase visibility and awareness of your brand, product, or service. The main metric or Key Performance Indicator (KPI) to track is usually the number of times your ad was seen (impressions).

**Example**

If your goal is to build brand awareness, you might choose high-impact visual ads (display ads or video ads) displayed on platforms like Instagram, YouTube, or popular blogs, where visuals are compelling and likely to catch user attention. These ads can be less about clicks and more about leaving a memorable impression.

## 2. Traffic

The aim is to attract visitors to your website or another online destination, such as a social media profile or an app. The KPI for traffic-oriented campaigns is usually clicks.

**Example**
Suppose you want to draw attention to a newly published blog post. In this case, you might use Google Ads with a CPC model where you pay for each click, ensuring each dollar spent directs a potential reader to your website.

## 3. Conversions

This goal focuses on encouraging users to take a specific action, such as making a purchase, signing up for a newsletter, or filling out a contact form. The KPI here is the conversion rate, the percentage of visitors who complete the desired action.

**Example**
For a campaign designed to increase sign-ups for a webinar, you might use Facebook Ads optimized for conversions. You would only pay when a user signs up, aligning costs directly with your primary campaign objective.

# Exploring Additional Categories of Marketing Goals

As I've covered in the previous section, setting clear and actionable marketing goals is a must to the success of your digital marketing campaigns. You're already familiar with the three primary categories—Awareness, Traffic, and Conversion—which serve as the pillars for most digital marketing strategies. However, the landscape of digital marketing is vast and continually evolving, introducing other goal categories that might align with specific business needs or campaign objectives. Let's explore additional categories that could enhance your digital marketing initiatives beyond the conventional triad.

Remember that not all these marketing goals are available as a choice in all advertiser channel provider platforms.

## 4. Engagement

Moving beyond the initial click, **Engagement** refers to how actively users interact with your online content. This might involve time spent on your website, comments on a blog post, shares of a social media update, or views on a video.

**Example**
Imagine you've launched a series of educational videos about cooking. While your initial goal might be driving traffic (clicks) or conversions (sign-ups), fostering engagement—measured by video views, likes, and shares—can help establish your brand as a thought leader in this niche.

# Brand Loyalty

**Brand loyalty** focuses on deepening relationships with existing customers to encourage repeat business, often through loyalty programs, exclusive offers, or personalized content.

**Example**
Suppose you run an ecommerce store for pet supplies. By creating a loyalty program that offers members special discounts and early access to new products, you encourage repeat purchases, increasing customer lifetime value.

## Advocacy

**Advocacy** aims to turn satisfied customers into active promoters of your brand. Satisfied customers share their positive experiences through word-of-mouth, online reviews, or testimonials, which can be more convincing than traditional advertising.

**Example**
You've implemented a customer referral program where existing customers are encouraged to refer friends to your service, and in return, both parties receive a discount. This strategy increases conversions through new sign-ups and strengthens existing customer relationships and builds your brand's community.

## Lead Generation

While closely related to conversions, **lead generation** is about collecting information from potential customers (leads) who might purchase in the future. This involves nurturing leads through the sales funnel with targeted content and interactions until they are ready to buy.

**Example**
Let's say your business specializes in custom home renovations. By offering a free ebook on "Top Trends in Home Design" in exchange for email addresses, you collect valuable leads who have expressed interest in home improvement and whom you can nurture with tailored email campaigns until they're ready to initiate a project.

I wrote "funnels" up there. It's important to prepare this funnel **before** launching the campaign. Otherwise, you risk getting leads but not following up on them.

## Preparing Your Marketing Funnel Before Launch

Understanding and setting up your marketing funnel is important before launching any campaign that uses them. The **funnel** is a concept that helps you visualize the **customer journey** (remember I wrote about this in previous chapters?) from initial awareness to the final sale and beyond. It ensures you're ready to capture and nurture leads effectively throughout all stages of their journey.

### Why a Pre-launch Funnel Setup Is Critical

Setting up a pre-launch funnel is critical for several reasons. Firstly, lead capture is a significant step. Without a funnel in place, you might capture leads but lose them due to a lack of follow-up or engagement strategies. A well-structured funnel ensures that leads are nurtured and moved through the stages effectively.

Efficiency is another important factor. Preparing your funnel ensures that each part of the customer's journey is designed to systematically guide them to the next stage. This increases the chances of conversion by creating a seamless and logical progression for the customer.

Measurement is essential for continuous improvement. A well-defined funnel allows you to measure successes and identify bottlenecks at each stage. This enables continuous optimization, ensuring that you can refine your strategies and improve the overall effectiveness of your funnel.

### Steps to Prepare Your Funnel

Defining the stages of your funnel is necessary for a structured approach. Clearly outline each stage, starting from awareness and moving through consideration to decision. Each stage needs a distinct definition to ensure that both you and your team understand the journey a lead takes from the initial contact to the final decision.

Aligning content with these stages is the next step. Prepare content and tactics tailored specifically to each stage. This ensures that the material you provide effectively drives the lead to the next phase. Proper alignment of content is crucial for smooth progression through the funnel, as it addresses the needs and concerns of the lead at each stage, guiding them seamlessly from awareness to decision.

Setting up tracking is essential for measuring the effectiveness of your funnel. Implement tools and systems designed to track progress and interactions at each stage. These tools provide valuable insights into how leads move through the funnel and where they might be dropping off. Tracking allows you to measure effectiveness and make necessary adjustments to optimize the conversion process.

By preparing your funnel in advance, you set a structured path for your leads, enhancing their experience and your campaign's effectiveness. Remember also that a funnel does not have to be only in the digital world. You may send an email and follow up with a printed letter, and then make a quick call. You should always remember that a well-prepared funnel is your roadmap to successful conversions and efficient use of the leads you become

# Comparison of Digital Marketing Campaign Categories

Table 27-1 contains a detailed comparison table that outlines each campaign type, providing clear descriptions, examples, use cases, recommended bidding strategies, suitable ad formats, and typical KPIs.[1]

---

[1] This table is to be taken as an example and is not complete, meaning that there may be more KPIs, ad formats, use cases, and examples to each campaign type as those included in the table.

## CHAPTER 27 SETTING MARKETING GOALS: CRAFTING STRATEGIC OBJECTIVES FOR DIGITAL CAMPAIGNS

*Table 27-1. Comparison table of digital marketing categories*

| Campaign Type | Description | Example | Use Case | Bidding Strategy | Ad Format | Key Performance Indicators (KPIs) | Why These KPIs? |
|---|---|---|---|---|---|---|---|
| Awareness | You aim to increase brand visibility | An ad displaying a new soft drink logo | To make your brand known to the public | Cost per Mille (CPM) | Banner ads, video ads | Impressions; how many times was your ad seen? | Measuring impressions helps track the reach of your ad |
| Traffic | To drive users to a specific digital destination | An ad that leads users to a newly launched blog | To increase visitors to your new website | Cost per Click (CPC) | Display ads, PPC ads | Clicks; the count of users who click the ad | Clicks measure direct user action to visit your site |
| Conversions | Aim to encourage a specific user action | An ad promoting a sign-up for a free trial | To generate leads or sales from your ad | Cost per Action (CPA) | Conversion-optimized ads | Conversion rate; the percentage of visitors who convert | Focuses on the effectiveness of the ad in driving actions |

(*continued*)

# CHAPTER 27  SETTING MARKETING GOALS: CRAFTING STRATEGIC OBJECTIVES FOR DIGITAL CAMPAIGNS

Table 27-1. (continued)

| Campaign Type | Description | Example | Use Case | Bidding Strategy | Ad Format | Key Performance Indicators (KPIs) | Why These KPIs? |
|---|---|---|---|---|---|---|---|
| Engagement | Enhance user interaction with your content | An interactive ad game promoting a new app | To keep users engaged with your ad content | Cost per Engagement (CPE) | Interactive ads, social media ads | Engagement rate; measures interactions like shares, comments | Indicates how compelling and engaging the ad is |
| Brand loyalty | Deepen relationships with existing customers | Rewards program ad for frequent buyers | To retain customers and encourage repeat business | Cost per Acquisition (CPA) | Email marketing, loyalty program ads | Customer retention rate; the rate at which existing customers return | Shows effectiveness in building long-term customer relationships |
| Advocacy | Encourage customers to promote your brand | Referral program ad offering benefits for both referrer and referee | To leverage word-of-mouth promotion | Cost per Acquisition (CPA) | Referral program ads, testimonial ads | Advocacy rate; measures referrals and brand mentions | Assess the success of turning customers into advocates |

CHAPTER 27   SETTING MARKETING GOALS: CRAFTING STRATEGIC OBJECTIVES FOR DIGITAL CAMPAIGNS

# Understanding Risk and Choosing the Right Campaign Type

In digital marketing, the choice of campaign type—awareness, traffic, or conversions, as well the additional categories—also determines who bears the financial risk.

**Awareness Campaigns** often carry more risk for you as the advertiser since you pay per impression, regardless of user engagement.

**Traffic Campaigns** moderately distribute risk between you and the ad provider, as costs are incurred per click, depending on how well the ad compels users to visit your site.

**Conversion Campaigns** shift most of the risk to the ad provider. You pay only when a user completes a specific action, which generally comes at a higher cost per action but ensures that your spending directly corresponds to tangible results.

**Engagement Campaigns**: Moderate risk for both advertiser and provider; you pay for interactions that may not always result in direct conversions.

**Brand Loyalty Campaigns**: Lower risk for the advertiser, as you're investing in already engaged customers to foster retention.

**Advocacy Campaigns**: The risk leans toward the advertiser, relying on customers to act as brand promoters, which can be unpredictable.

**Lead Generation Campaigns**: Risk is more balanced but leans toward the advertiser; though you gather potential leads, conversion to actual sales can vary, and an important part of the process depends on your funnel.

CHAPTER 27   SETTING MARKETING GOALS: CRAFTING STRATEGIC OBJECTIVES FOR
              DIGITAL CAMPAIGNS

## Summary

In this chapter, I've explained the categories under which you can classify a digital marketing campaign. This is relevant for setting effective marketing goals and aligning them with suitable digital channels and ad formats. I also provided recommendations of channels, bidding strategies, and formats depending on the goals you set for your campaign.

In the next chapter, I will discuss the characteristics you should look for in advertiser channel providers depending on your campaign goals. This includes deciding whether to use platforms like Google Ads, LinkedIn Ads, or others.

# CHAPTER 28

# Advertiser Channel Provider (Network) Selection

In this chapter, I will explore how to systematically evaluate and select advertising networks that best serve your marketing goals. The choice of network requires understanding each platform's core capabilities, audience reach, and targeting infrastructure and how these features can serve your specific campaign goals and manage associated risks. I'll use current popular networks as examples, while equipping you with the knowledge to evaluate future platforms based on similar criteria.

## Strategic Network Selection Based on Marketing Goals

The landscape of digital advertising networks is vast, with each platform offering distinct characteristics like audience composition, targeting capabilities, and measurement tools. Let's explore how to match these networks with your goals.

## Awareness Goals

When evaluating networks for awareness campaigns, examine each platform's ability to reach your target audience at scale. Key network selection criteria include audience size, demographic coverage, and engagement metrics.

**Example**
Facebook, Instagram, YouTube, and Display Ads are ideal for these objectives. They provide extensive audience networks (in the locations that support it) with high engagement rates and adequate targeting tools for maximizing reach, making them perfect for grabbing attention and increasing brand visibility.

**Characteristics to Look For**
High user engagement and broad reach are key features of networks that are effective for awareness campaigns.

When evaluating Networks for Awareness, remember to research (or ask your partner to do so) whether a specific network is interesting for your Target Group in your geographical area of interest. Not all platforms have broad reach. For example, remote areas with low-speed Internet connection will not be able to use YouTube in the way you expect them to. There are also some geographical areas where it's harder to reach certain groups because of data privacy policies, which means that it's harder for the network to identify who will see the ads.

## Traffic Goals

For traffic objectives (for example, getting new visitors to your website), consider networks that offer robust targeting options to connect with audiences who have shown interest in similar products or services. Look for platforms whose core functionality helps identify users actively seeking content or solutions.

**Example**
Google Ads stands out for such campaigns due to its search network infrastructure and powerful search intent targeting, which allows you to capture users actively searching for related keywords (known as buying intent in their audience settings, check Chapter 14 for more details).

**Characteristic to Look For**
Search-based targeting capabilities are crucial for networks that can help achieve traffic goals efficiently.

## Conversion Goals

For conversion-oriented objectives, evaluate networks based on their conversion tracking capabilities, audience segmentation features and ability to optimize for specific actions. Detailed demographic and behavioral targeting can help you reach users most likely to convert. Always check each platform's conversion measurement features.

**Example**
LinkedIn's network infrastructure provides detailed professional targeting options, making it effective for B2B conversion goals, allowing ads to be shown based on professional details such as job functions or industry sectors.

**Characteristic to Look For**
Deep targeting options that match your audience's profile are essential for networks best suited to driving conversions.

## Evaluating Network Risk Profiles

Understanding how different networks handle campaign delivery and billing models will help you manage your marketing spend more effectively.

## Evaluating Risks

Evaluating risks involves understanding the nature of different networks. *Awareness networks* generally carry higher risk for you since you invest in impressions that are not guaranteed to convert. However, they are essential for broadening your brand reach, making them a crucial part of your marketing strategy.

*Traffic networks* offer a moderate risk level. You pay for clicks, which balances costs with the potential for direct interaction. This approach ensures that your spending is more closely tied to user engagement, making it a balanced option.

*Conversion networks* often entail lower risk from an advertiser's perspective. You pay for actual conversions, ensuring that your costs align with specific marketing results. This reduces the uncertainty associated with other types of networks and makes your investment more efficient.

**Example**
X (ex-Twitter) can serve well for awareness due to its viral nature, while Google Ads can be preferable for traffic and conversions due to its intent-driven approach.

## Summary

You've learned how to evaluate and select advertising networks by understanding their core capabilities, audience characteristics, and risk profiles. Here's what we covered:

- Select your networks based on platforms capabilities, reach and targeting features and confirm they work for your specific marketing goals.
- Understand network-specific risk profiles and billing models.

## CHAPTER 28 ADVERTISER CHANNEL PROVIDER (NETWORK) SELECTION

- Evaluate networks based on their core strengths for different marketing objectives.

In the next chapter, I will discuss network selection across media providers, such as digital ads, social media, TV, and billboards. I'll cover which ones you should consider for specific campaign goals and offer some insights on their associated risks.

CHAPTER 29

# Integrating Traditional and Digital Media for Marketing Campaigns

In this chapter, I will explore how to combine traditional and digital media in your marketing campaigns, focusing on media integration strategies and programmatic buying opportunities. I'll discuss how different media, from social platforms to traditional channels like TV and billboards, can be optimized for the seven primary marketing goals. Tailoring your strategy to include these varied media will maximize your campaign's effectiveness, especially as programmatic buying expands these options.

## Expanding Network and Media Recommendations

Different types of media can complement each other to amplify your campaign's impact. Understanding how to integrate traditional and digital channels and aligning your campaign's objectives with the right combination of channels, you ensure a more targeted and potentially more successful marketing approach.

# Detailed Recommendations Across Media for Each Goal

Let's detail the suitable networks and other media channels for each marketing goal, considering both digital and traditional platforms. I also expand on the previous chapter by adding four new goals: engagement, brand loyalty, advocacy and lead generation.

## Awareness

Awareness goals can benefit from combining the broad reach of traditional media with digital marketing. Social media platforms like Facebook and Instagram are effective for reaching a broad audience. Billboards, both traditional and digital, can be booked programmatically for wider reach. TV, especially with programmatic buying, allows for targeted ad spots during relevant programming.

For example, coordinating digital billboards in high-traffic areas with geo-targeted social media ads can reinforce your message across touchpoints. These can be booked programmatically to appear at optimal times, ensuring maximum exposure. These strategic placements helps in capturing the attention of a large audience, improving the effectiveness of your awareness efforts.

## Traffic

Traffic can be driven by combining traditional media exposure with digital call-to-action. Search engines like Google Ads allow for targeted search results. Social media platforms drive clicks through engaging content. Email marketing directly targets existing customers or leads with links to your website.

For example, using targeted email or printed ad campaigns with links (in the form of QR-Codes, for example) to new blog posts can drive interested readers to your website, improving traffic metrics. This approach leverages the direct nature of email marketing and the traditional reach of printed ads to boost site visits and improve engagement. For radio spots, podcasts and online radio you can mention easy-to-remember URLs.

## Conversions

Conversions can be improved by creating a consistent customer journey (check Chapter 13) across media types achieved through various channels. Ecommerce platforms utilize shopping ads and inventory ads to facilitate direct purchases. Affiliate marketing leverages connections with influential bloggers or review sites. Social media platforms like Pinterest or Instagram support direct shopping features.

For example, an Instagram shopping campaign where users can purchase products directly through the app streamlines the conversion process from discovery to purchase. This approach simplifies the buying journey, making it easier for customers to complete their transactions within the platform. In-store displays can promote app-based purchases and you can use URL-shorteners and specific tracking codes on printed media.

## Engagement

Engagement can be improved by coordinating online and offline interactions. Social media is effective for creating interactive content or polls on platforms like Twitter or Facebook. Interactive web content, such as quizzes or games, can also relate to your brand or products.

For example, For example, live events can feature social media walls displaying real-time audience participation, while TV shows can incorporate hashtag campaigns to bridge traditional and digital engagement.

## Brand Loyalty

Brand loyalty can be build through synchronized traditional and digital touchpoints. Email campaigns provide regular updates and exclusive offers for existing customers. Loyalty apps offer rewards or points for repeat purchases.

For example, physical loyalty cards can link to mobile apps, while in-store experiences can trigger personalized digital follow-ups. This integration creates a seamless brand experience across channels. You can also use a mobile app that tracks customer purchases and rewards points redeemable for discounts or free items that strengthens brand loyalty. This approach encourages repeat business by providing tangible incentives for continued engagement with the brand.

## Advocacy

Advocacy can be amplified by connecting offline experiences with digital sharing opportunities. Social media is effective for encouraging shares and testimonials. Review platforms are useful for engaging with reviewers and fostering positive reviews.

For example, creating a campaign that incentivizes customers to share their positive experiences on social media, potentially with a hashtag linked to the campaign, can enhance advocacy. This approach leverages the power of word-of-mouth and personal recommendations to build a stronger brand presence. Another example are In-store displays that encourage social media sharing, while print magazines feature customer stories that link to expanded online content.

## Lead Generation

Lead generation can also be done by creating bridges between traditional and digital media. Webinars use educational content to gather sign-ups. LinkedIn is effective for B2B lead generation through targeted professional networks.

For example, hosting a series of webinars on current industry topics that require registration can provide valuable leads who have shown a direct interest in your field. This approach educates the audience and captures potential leads for further engagement. An example of bridging traditional and digital media are Trade show interactions that can be followed up with targeted digital content, while print advertisements can include QR codes for immediate digital engagement.

# Understanding Campaign Types and Their Risks Across Media

Managing multiple media types requires understanding how each contributes to campaign success. While digital media provides immediate metrics, traditional media's impact often requires different measurement approaches. Consider these differences when allocating budget and assessing performance. Here's how different media can alter the risk distribution.

*Awareness* and *engagement* through social media and billboards offer more exposure but higher risk. Costs are not directly tied to results. These channels increase visibility, but the financial risk is high because engagement and conversions are not certain.

*Traffic* through email and search engines has moderate risk. These channels drive focused traffic with measurable engagement. Costs align more with user interaction, balancing investment and return.

CHAPTER 29  INTEGRATING TRADITIONAL AND DIGITAL MEDIA FOR MARKETING CAMPAIGNS

*Conversions* via ecommerce platforms and social shopping features have lower risk. Expenses are linked to actual sales conversions. This ensures that spending matches tangible results, reducing uncertainty.

## Summary

I've discussed how to leverage various networks and media channels for different marketing goals, enhancing your campaigns to be more holistic and integrated:

- Use digital and traditional media strategically to align with specific marketing objectives, from raising awareness on billboards to driving engagement via social media.

- Programmatic buying has broadened the scope of traditional media, integrating these into more dynamic and responsive campaign planning.

In the next chapter, I will dive into ad formats. Having already discussed channels and advertiser channel providers, I will now explore which formats are best suited for specific campaign goals. For example, should I use display ads for awareness campaigns, or are search ads a better option? What about traffic campaigns?

# CHAPTER 30

# Format Recommendations for Digital Marketing Campaigns

Understanding the diverse landscape of advertising formats and how they work is really important. Not only does the choice of the format and its characteristics impact the delivery of your message, but it also influences audience engagement and campaign performance. In this chapter, I will dive deeper into understanding the characteristics of various ad formats suitable for different marketing goals. I'll outline how these characteristics align with specific marketing objectives, enhancing the effectiveness of your campaigns.

## Introduction to Ad Format Characteristics

Ad formats in digital marketing extend beyond mere aesthetics; they encompass functionalities and have unique technical requirements, creative possibilities and user interaction patterns that can make or break your campaign objectives. Hence, selecting the right format is an important decision to take for targeting your audience effectively and fulfilling your marketing goals. Remember to check Chapter 22 for a detailed overview of the different formats.

# Understanding Various Ad Formats and Their Characteristics

Each ad format comes with its own set of features which can influence various aspects of a marketing campaign, from visibility, engagement to conversion. Here's how to choose the best formats based on your specific campaign goals.

## Awareness

Recommended formats include video ads, display ads, billboards, and virtual and augmented reality experiences. These formats are visually engaging and can convey messages quickly and memorably. They are perfect for capturing attention and leaving a lasting impression. Video ads require attention to length, resolution, and sound design. Display ads need clear visual hierarchies and responsive layouts. Virtual and augmented reality experiences demand specialized 3D assets and interactive elements.

For example, a company launching a new soft drink might use dynamic video ads on social media to stir excitement and curiosity. They could leverage catchy music and vibrant visuals to create buzz and draw attention to the new product.

## Traffic

Recommended formats include clickable display ads, sponsored content, and search engine ads. These formats feature direct and clear call-to-actions (CTAs) and are optimized for clicks, guiding users directly to your landing pages. Clickable display ads need clear call-to-action, placement and response tracking. Text ads require concise messaging and keyword optimization.

For example, an online retailer promoting seasonal sales might utilize search engine marketing with clear CTAs like "Shop Now" to drive immediate traffic to its online store. This strategy helps to attract potential customers and increase site visits effectively.

## Conversions

Recommended formats include shoppable posts, lead generation forms, and retargeting ads. These formats are highly targeted, often personalized, and feature direct paths to purchase or sign-up. Shoppable posts require product feed integration and mobile-optimized layouts. Lead forms need field validation and data collection setup. Retargeting ads demand cookie implementation and audience segmentation capabilities.

For example, a fitness app could use Instagram shoppable posts that allow users to sign up for a premium subscription directly from an inspiring fitness transformation post. This strategy makes it easy for users to convert from interest to action, boosting subscription rates.

## Engagement

Recommended formats include interactive ads, quizzes, and social media stories. These formats are designed to be interactive, encouraging users to spend time engaging through polls, games, or immersive experiences. Interactive ads need user input handling and response tracking. Quizzes require scoring logic and result displays. Stories formats demand vertical layouts and progress indicators. Each interactive format has specific technical requirements for user engagement.

For example, a brand launching a new cosmetic line might use social media stories with polls like "Choose Your Favorite Color" to engage users and make them feel a part of the product experience. This approach fosters a sense of involvement and connection with the brand.

## Brand Loyalty

Recommended formats include email newsletters, customer rewards ads, and app notifications. These formats are personalized and provide ongoing communication with existing customers to reinforce relationships and encourage repeat business. Email newsletters require responsive templates and personalization fields. Reward program displays need point system integration. App notifications demand scheduling and targeting capabilities.

For example, a coffee shop might send monthly newsletters to its patrons featuring special offers and loyalty rewards to enhance customer retention and loyalty. This strategy helps maintain a strong connection with customers and encourages them to return frequently.

## Advocacy

Recommended formats include hashtag challenges, testimonial ads, and referral incentives. These formats encourage sharing and user-generated content, fostering a community of brand advocates. Hashtag campaigns need tracking and aggregation features. Testimonial formats require social proof elements and sharing capabilities. Referral systems demand unique code generation and tracking.

For example, a pet food brand could encourage happy customers to share their pet's photos with a specific hashtag, offering a chance to win a year's supply of pet food. This approach motivates customers to advocate for the brand and creates a sense of community.

## Lead Generation

Recommended formats include webinars, gated content, and ebook downloads. These formats provide educational or valuable content behind a data capture form, attracting high-intent users. Webinar formats need registration systems and attendance tracking. Gated content requires form integration and content delivery automation. Download tracking demands file hosting and access control.

For example, a software company may offer free webinars on industry insights, requiring participants to register, thus capturing potential leads. This method helps in identifying and engaging with users who have a genuine interest in the industry or product.

## Choosing the Right Mix of Formats

When planning your digital marketing campaign, consider using a mix of formats that support each other to effectively reach and resonate with your audience across different stages of the marketing funnel. Moreover, select networks that support these formats effectively to ensure a correct campaign execution.

For example, for a holistic campaign aimed at both educating and converting users, you might start with an engaging video to draw interest (Awareness), follow up with interactive webinars (Engagement), and ultimately drive sign-ups through targeted lead generation forms (Conversion). Remember that different formats have varying technical requirements and implementation timelines. Consider these requirements when planning your content creation and development schedules. You can check Chapter 22 for more details on formats and Chapter 31 for more on schedules and working with partners.

## Summary

In this chapter, I explored different ad formats and their characteristics across different marketing goals. What you should remember is

- Choosing the correct ad formats based on their characteristics, creative possibilities and technical requirements can significantly improve your campaign.
- Aligning format choice with marketing objectives makes use of each format's potential.
- Integrating multiple formats into a cohesive strategy can provide a seamless consumer experience.

You already understand what you want, how, and where. Now comes a crucial point: how to communicate this. That's where briefings come into play. A briefing does not have to be a lengthy, endless document, but it should answer the most important questions. The next chapter is all about the briefings you need to prepare before your campaign starts, and at the latest, communicate in the initial meetings with your service partners.

# CHAPTER 31

# Digital Marketing Brief

In the realm of digital marketing, the importance of a comprehensive brief cannot be overstated. A well-crafted digital marketing brief ensures that all parties involved in the campaign are aligned with your objectives, goals, and expectations. This chapter delves into how to construct an effective digital marketing brief that serves as a roadmap for your marketing efforts, guiding providers and stakeholders through the complex landscape of digital marketing.

## Crafting a Comprehensive Digital Marketing Brief

When developing a digital marketing brief, you're essentially communicating your campaign vision to your service providers. This document should clearly outline what you aim to achieve or your campaign objectives, detail the product or service in focus, define who you're competing against, and delineate the campaign's timeline.

Campaign objectives involve a clear description of what the campaign intends to achieve. This section should explicitly state your goals and the desired outcomes. It helps align the service providers with your vision and ensures everyone works toward the same targets.

Product or service details include comprehensive information about what you're promoting. This part of the brief should explain the features, benefits, and unique selling points of your product or service. Providing this information allows your service providers to craft messages and strategies that highlight your offerings effectively.

Competition analysis offers insights into who you are competing against. Understanding your competitors is crucial for positioning your product or service. This section should analyze their strengths, weaknesses, and strategies, helping you identify opportunities and threats in the market.

The timeline outlines detailed start and end dates, including any key milestones. It ensures the campaign progresses as planned and helps manage expectations. A well-defined timeline keeps everyone on track and allows for timely adjustments if necessary.

You can find template briefings with examples in the Annexes 1, 2, 3 and 4 of the book. They are also available to download on the book page. These resources provide practical guidance and can serve as a useful reference when creating your digital marketing brief.

## Structuring Your Digital Marketing Briefings

*As a rule of thumb, you need at least four Briefings, even if they are for the same provider.*

You need to prepare at least four types of briefs, even if they are for the same provider. This structured approach ensures that each aspect of your campaign is meticulously planned.

If you are working with a marketing expert (agency, freelancer, or similar), it is perfectly fine to ask for their feedback based on their experience, but they need an entry point to provide their suggestions. Based on that, you can write in specific sections that you expect suggestions and that you don't have an answer yet.

The four briefings I mention are

1. Digital Marketing Brief for Campaign Settings
2. Digital Marketing Brief for Campaign Creatives

3. Digital Marketing Brief for Campaign Monitoring
4. Digital Marketing Brief for Campaign Landing Page

Let's explore them one by one.

## Digital Marketing Brief for Campaign Settings

A digital marketing brief for campaign settings covers everything from target groups and chosen advertising channels to the geographical focus and landing page details (if it already exists). This document ensures that all aspects of your campaign are aligned with your overall marketing strategy and objectives.

For example, you might specify using Google Ads to target young professionals in urban areas for a campaign promoting a new business software tool. This specification helps in creating settings that resonate with the intended audience and ensures that the advertising efforts are concentrated in areas with the highest potential impact.

**Identifying target groups** is important for any campaign. This section should describe the demographics, interests, and behaviors of the people you want to reach. Understanding your audience allows you to create messages and select channels that effectively engage them.

**Chosen advertising channels** should align with where your target audience spends their time. Whether it's social media platforms, search engines, or display networks, selecting the right channels ensures your ads are seen by the right people. For instance, if your target group consists of young professionals, platforms like LinkedIn and Google Ads might be the most effective.

The **geographical focus** of your campaign helps in localizing your efforts. By specifying urban areas, you can concentrate your resources on regions where your target audience is most likely to be found. This focus can improve the relevance of your campaign.

**Landing page** details are essential for converting visitors into leads or customers. This section should outline the key elements of the landing page, including the headline, value proposition, and call to action. A well-designed landing page tailored to your campaign can significantly improve conversion rates and understanding the landing page structure will help you or your service provider define better settings for your campaign.

By covering these elements in your digital marketing brief, you provide a clear roadmap for your campaign. This ensures that all stakeholders understand the campaign settings and work toward achieving the defined objectives efficiently.

Now let's move to the creative's briefing.

## Digital Marketing Brief for Campaign Creatives

A digital marketing brief for campaign creatives focuses on the creative assets such as copy, images, and overall design. This document should outline which assets are already available and which need to be developed. Providing a clear inventory of existing assets and identifying gaps helps streamline the creative process and ensures that all necessary materials are ready for the campaign.

For example, if your campaign is about promoting a new fashion line, you'd specify whether you have existing high-quality images of your products or if you need the creative team to produce these.

The section on available assets should detail what you currently have, including high-resolution images, video content, logos, brand guidelines, and any previous ad copies. Attaching these assets allows the service provider to evaluate them and determine their suitability for the specific advertising channels you intend to use. This evaluation helps avoid issues where assets might not meet the requirements of certain platforms, ensuring a smoother campaign launch.

Next, the document should specify the assets that need to be developed. This might include new product photos, promotional videos, graphic designs, and copywriting. Clearly outlining these needs helps the creative team understand the scope of their work and plan accordingly. For instance, if high-quality product images are missing, the brief should detail the types of images required, the style, and any specific angles or features to highlight.

Additionally, the overall design guidelines should be included in the brief. This covers aspects like color schemes, typography, and brand voice. Ensuring consistency with your brand identity across all creative assets is vital for a cohesive campaign.

By providing a comprehensive digital marketing brief for campaign creatives, you ensure that your service providers clearly understand what is available and what needs to be developed. This clarity facilitates a more efficient and effective creative process, ultimately leading to a more successful campaign.

---

**Note** I've stated this before, but you don't have to have all the information. Stating the missing part is also part of the process, and your service provider should be able to help you where information is missing.

---

## Digital Marketing Brief for Campaign Monitoring

A digital marketing brief for campaign monitoring outlines how the campaign's performance should be monitored and reported. This document specifies the expectations for adjustments and reporting frequency, ensuring that all stakeholders are aligned on how success will be measured and managed throughout the campaign.

For example, for an ecommerce campaign, you might require weekly performance reports and give the provider the authority to adjust CPC bids to optimize the campaign. This approach ensures that the campaign remains agile and responsive to real-time data and trends.

Firstly, the brief should detail the key performance indicators (KPIs) that will be used to measure the campaign's success, or at least the information you would like to receive.[1] These metrics might include metrics such as click-through rates (CTR), conversion rates, cost per acquisition (CPA), impressions, placements, and anything else. Clearly defining these metrics and your expectations helps in setting clear objectives and benchmarks for the campaign.

Next, the brief should specify the frequency of performance reports. For an ecommerce campaign, weekly reports might be necessary to keep track of the campaign's progress and make timely adjustments. These reports should provide insights into the campaign's performance against the defined KPIs, highlighting areas of success and opportunities for improvement.

In addition to reporting frequency, the brief should outline the format and content of the reports. This might include detailed analytics dashboards, summaries of key metrics, and actionable insights. Providing a clear template for these reports ensures consistency and helps in making the data more accessible and understandable for all stakeholders.

The brief should also specify the expectations for adjustments. For instance, giving the provider the authority to adjust CPC bids allows for real-time optimization based on performance data. This flexibility is crucial for maximizing the efficiency and effectiveness of the campaign. Additionally, the brief might outline processes for other adjustments, such as changing ad creatives, reallocating budget across channels, or targeting different audience segments.

---

[1] Check Chapter 12 for an overview on metrics and Chapter 24 for an overview of analytics.

Finally, the brief should define the communication protocols for campaign monitoring. This includes specifying who will receive the reports, how feedback should be communicated, and the process for making significant campaign adjustments. Clear communication protocols help in maintaining transparency and ensuring that all parties are informed and aligned throughout the campaign.

By providing a comprehensive digital marketing brief for campaign monitoring, you ensure that the campaign's performance is closely tracked and optimized and meets your expectations.

Now let's move to the last briefing, the one for landing pages. I've written a lot about landing pages in this book already (Chapter 23 is all about landing pages), so I hope that by this point you understand how important they are.

## Digital Marketing Brief for Campaign Landing Page

A digital marketing brief for a campaign landing page details the required elements such as copy, design, and tracking implementations. This document ensures that the landing page aligns with the overall campaign strategy and enhances user experience, ultimately driving conversions and a great user experience.

For example, if the campaign promotes an exclusive webinar, the brief would detail the landing page's registration form, design aesthetics to match the webinar's theme, and integration of tracking codes to measure sign-ups. Providing this information ensures that the landing page effectively supports the campaign's goals.

Firstly, the brief should outline the copy[2] requirements for the landing page. This includes the headline, subheadings, body text, and call-to-action (CTA) statements. The copy should be clear, compelling, and aligned with the campaign's messaging. For a webinar promotion, the copy might highlight the benefits of attending, the topics covered, and the credentials of the speakers.

---

[2] I discussed copy, messages, and creatives in Chapter 16 and in Chapter 23.

Next, the brief should specify the design elements. This includes the overall layout, color scheme, typography, and images or graphics to be used. The design should be visually appealing and consistent with the campaign's theme and branding. For instance, the landing page for a webinar should have a professional look, with visuals that reflect the webinar's subject and branding.

Additionally, the brief should detail the required functionalities and features. This might include a registration form, social sharing buttons, and a countdown timer. The registration form should be easy to use and only ask for essential information to minimize friction for users. Integrating social sharing buttons can help increase the reach of the campaign, while a countdown timer can create a sense of urgency.

Tracking implementations is also important for measuring the success of the landing page. The brief should specify the tracking codes and analytics tools to be used. This might include Google Analytics, Facebook Pixel, or other conversion tracking tools.[3] These implementations help monitor user behavior, measure sign-ups, and assess the overall performance of the landing page.

Making the creatives (or the information that will be on them) available to the service provider is a good practice. This ensures that the landing page makes sense with the ads, copy, and other campaign assets. Consistency across these elements enhances ad quality and improves user experience, leading to higher conversion rates. If you don't provide access to the landing page, you cannot be surprised if the creatives and the landing page have not so much in common and your if Ad Quality is low.[4]

By providing a detailed digital marketing brief for the campaign landing page, you ensure that all necessary elements are considered and aligned with the campaign's objectives.

---

[3] I wrote about conversions in Chapter 18.
[4] I wrote about ad quality in Chapter 11.

CHAPTER 31  DIGITAL MARKETING BRIEF

**Note** You can, of course, provide all four briefings to each of your providers. That way they will get the details of the work they have to do and a general overview of your campaign.

Figure 31-1 shows a summary of the four briefings along their main components.

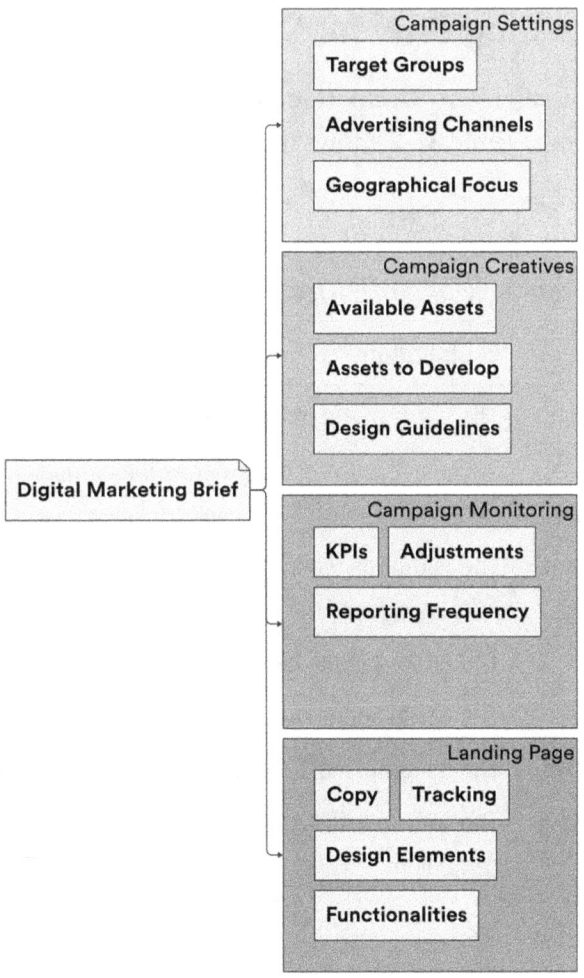

*Figure 31-1. Summary of digital marketing briefings*

CHAPTER 31   DIGITAL MARKETING BRIEF

# Details of the Four Digital Marketing Briefings

Now that you understand the importance of the four briefings, let's go into the details. I understand briefings as a profile or a technical sheet. It should contain everything I've discussed distilled to the bone and should serve as a quick reference for you and your partners.

Let's start with the campaign settings.

## Digital Marketing Brief for Campaign Settings

Table 31-1 shows all my recommended minimum fields for a brief on campaign settings. Table 31-2 shows the same table but already filled with an example.

*Table 31-1.* Structure of a briefing for campaign settings

| Field | Explanation |
|---|---|
| Campaign name | The name of the marketing campaign |
| Target group or marketing personas | The specific group or personas the campaign aims to reach |
| Advertising channel provider(s) to use | The platforms where the ads will be placed (e.g., Google Ads, Facebook Ads) |
| Formats to use | The ad formats to be utilized (e.g., text, image, video) |
| Creatives | The visual and textual content for the ads |
| Geographic location | The geographical area where the ads will be targeted |
| Landing page | The URL or details of the landing page associated with the campaign |

*(continued)*

## CHAPTER 31 DIGITAL MARKETING BRIEF

*Table 31-1.* (*continued*)

| Field | Explanation |
|---|---|
| Which accounts to use for the campaign | The account credentials for the ad platforms (e.g., Facebook Page, Google Ads Account) if needed or state that this is the responsibility of the service provider. Please check Chapter 2 on digital assets before taking this decision |
| Start date | The date when the campaign will begin |
| End date | The expected end date and the maximum possible end date for the campaign. This is important in case of optimizations |
| Contact person for questions | The individual to contact for any questions about the campaign. Name, phone number, and email should be the minimum |
| Competition brand and offer | Information on competing brands and their offers that the service provider should check or research. This is important for the keywords[5] and targeting |
| Awareness level of the target customer | The level of awareness the target audience has about the product or service[6] |
| Missing information | Instructions on whether the provider should proceed without certain information or include it in their proposal |

Of course, you can improve that structure anyway you want, but in my experience those fields are a must and will prevent many misunderstandings.

Now let's make this more tangible. Table 31-2 has the same structure with the same example as in the previous section.

The example was a campaign promoting a new business software tool through Google Ads for young professionals in urban areas.

---

[5] Check Chapters 14 and 19 on keywords and competitors.
[6] Check Chapter 4 for an overview of awareness levels in digital marketing.

*Table 31-2.* *Example of a briefing for campaign settings*

| Field | Example |
| --- | --- |
| Campaign name | New Business Software Launch |
| Target group or marketing personas | Young professionals in urban areas |
| Advertising channel provider(s) to use | Google Ads |
| Formats to use | Text and image ads |
| Creatives | High-quality images of the software interface, engaging ad copy |
| Geographic location | Urban areas |
| Landing page | www.example.com/software-launch |
| Which account to use for the campaign | Use the provider's Google Ads Account |
| Start date | 2024-09-01 |
| End date | Expected: 2024-12-01, Maximum: 2024-12-31 |
| Contact person for questions | Diego Carrasco (diego+example@diegocarrasco.com) |
| Competition brand and offer | Competitor XYZ offering similar software at a lower price. The main differences are A, B, C. |
| Awareness level of the target customer | Low awareness |
| Missing information | Provider should include research and development in their offer if information is missing after a follow-up meeting with Diego |

With such a campaign profile, a service provider will be able to make the right questions should he need additional information.

Now let's move to the briefing for creatives.

## Digital Marketing Brief for Campaign Creatives

Table 31-3 shows the fields I recommend for a basic briefing for creatives. Depending on the service provider, they might require additional information and, if so, they will ask for it.

*Table 31-3. Structure of a briefing for campaign creatives*

| Field | Explanation |
|---|---|
| Name of the campaign | The title or name of the marketing campaign |
| Contact person for this project | The individual responsible for overseeing the project |
| Target group or marketing personas | The specific group or personas the campaign aims to reach |
| Which advertising channel providers and formats will be used | The platforms and ad formats to be used, or if suggestions from the provider are needed |
| Do you have reference material? Where can that be downloaded? | Availability of reference material and its download location |
| Are you expecting a suggestion from your provider? | Whether suggestions from the service provider are expected |
| Do you already have the copy (texts)? Where are they available? Should they be adapted? | Availability and location of the copy and whether it needs adaptation |

(*continued*)

*Table 31-3.* (*continued*)

| Field | Explanation |
| --- | --- |
| Do you already have the images? Where are they available? Should they be adapted? | Availability and location of the images and whether they need adaptation |
| Due date for all the creatives and expected follow-up meetings | The deadline for the creatives and the schedule for follow-up meetings |
| Should the landing page be checked? Where is it available? Should it be adapted? | Whether the landing page needs to be checked (recommended), its location, and if it needs adaptation |
| Awareness level of the target customer | The level of awareness the target audience has about the product or service |
| Which creatives? | The specific types of creatives needed for the campaign. Image Ads for Facebook, RSA for Google, L-Format Image for ATV? |

Same as before, let's make this more tangible with the previous example in Table 31-4: a campaign promoting a new fashion line.

*Table 31-4.* *Applied structure of a briefing for campaign creatives (example)*

| Field | Example |
|---|---|
| Name of the campaign | New Fashion Line Promotion |
| Contact person for this project | Your name (john.smith@example.com) |
| Target group or marketing personas | Young adults interested in fashion |
| Which advertising channel providers and formats will be used? | Instagram image ads, Facebook carousel ads, or suggestions from the provider |
| Do you have reference material? Where can that be downloaded? | Yes, available at www.example.com/references |
| Are you expecting a suggestion from your provider? | Yes |
| Do you already have the copy (texts)? Where are they available? Should they be adapted? | Yes, available at www.example.com/copy. Adaptation required |
| Do you already have the images? Where are they available? Should they be adapted? | Yes, available at www.example.com/images. Adaptation required |
| Due date for all the creatives and expected follow-up meetings | 2024-08-15, follow-up meetings every two weeks |
| Should the landing page be checked? Where is it available? Should it be adapted? | Yes, available at www.example.com/landing-page. Adaptation required |
| Awareness level of the target customer | Medium awareness |
| Which creatives? Image Ads for Facebook, RSA for Google, L Image for ATV? | Image Ads for Facebook, responsive search ads (RSA) for Google, large images for ATV |

CHAPTER 31   DIGITAL MARKETING BRIEF

Specifying the formats already tells a lot to a service provider, as most of the requirements such as quality and size are already online. Understanding the organizational aspects of the project, such as due dates and follow-up meetings, helps your partner to plan accordingly and understand your expectations.

Now let's move to monitoring.

## Digital Marketing Brief for Campaign Monitoring

*Table 31-5.* *Structure of a briefing Four digital marketing briefings campaign monitoring for campaign monitoring*

| Field | Explanation |
|---|---|
| Name of the campaign | The title or name of the marketing campaign |
| Contact person for monitoring regarding updates and decisions | The individual responsible for overseeing monitoring and making updates or decisions |
| Can that person make decisions? | Whether the contact person has the authority to make decisions. If not, who should be contacted |
| Can the provider change some settings if the campaign is not running as expected? | Whether the service provider is allowed to make changes to the campaign settings if issues are identified |
| Is the service provider expected to deliver any sort of reports? | The requirement for the service provider to deliver reports, including frequency and key questions to be answered |
| Should the service provider check or review the landing page? | Whether the service provider should review the landing page as part of the monitoring process |
| Other important fields for monitoring agreement | Any additional fields important for agreeing on monitoring procedures |

## CHAPTER 31  DIGITAL MARKETING BRIEF

As before, let's make this more tangible with Table 31-6 by using the example, an ecommerce holiday promotion campaign; having Sarah Johnson as the main contact for updates and Michael Lee for final decisions ensures clarity in communication. Allowing the provider to adjust CPC bids and ad placements helps maintain optimal performance.

*Table 31-6.* *Example Structure of a Briefing for Campaign Monitoring*

| Field | Example |
|---|---|
| Name of the campaign | Ecommerce Holiday Promotion |
| Contact person for monitoring regarding updates and decisions | Sarah Johnson (`sarah.johnson@example.com`) |
| Can that person make decisions? | No, contact Michael Lee (`michael.lee@example.com`) for decisions |
| Can the provider change some settings if the campaign is not running as expected? | Yes, the provider can adjust CPC bids and ad placements |
| Are we as a service provider expected to deliver any sort of reports? | Yes, weekly performance reports. Reports should answer: What are the conversion rates? What is the cost per acquisition? Are there any emerging trends? |
| Should they check or review the landing page? | Yes, the provider should review the landing page for consistency and performance |
| Other important fields for monitoring agreement | Ensure all tracking codes are properly implemented and functional |

This brief should include information on the campaign name, the contact person for monitoring, and their decision-making authority. It should also specify whether the service provider can make changes to the campaign settings if necessary.

Finally, let's move to the landing page.

CHAPTER 31 DIGITAL MARKETING BRIEF

# Digital Marketing Brief for Campaign Landing Page

Table 31-7 shows the structure of the briefing for a landing page with my recommended fields.

*Table 31-7. Structure of a briefing for a Landing Page*

| Field | Explanation |
|---|---|
| Name of the product, service, or campaign | The title or name of the product, service, or campaign being promoted |
| Creative assets | The visual and textual content to be used on the landing page |
| Platform | The platform where the landing page will be hosted |
| Tracking codes | The tracking codes to be implemented for monitoring performance |
| Copy (texts) | The written content to be included on the landing page |
| CTA (call-to-action) | The specific call-to-action phrases or buttons on the landing page |
| Design (if done internally or by another third party) | Information on whether the design is done internally or by a third-party designer |
| Awareness level of the target customer | The level of awareness the target audience has about the product or service |

Again, let's give this form with an example as shown in Table 31-8: a webinar promotion.

***Table 31-8.*** *Example structure of a briefing for campaign landing page*

| Field | Example |
|---|---|
| Name of the product, service, or campaign | Exclusive Webinar Promotion |
| Creative assets | High-quality images, promotional video, logo |
| Platform | WordPress |
| Tracking codes | Google Analytics, Facebook Pixel |
| Copy (texts) | Engaging headline, webinar details, speaker bios, registration information |
| CTA (call-to-action) | "Register Now" button |
| Design (if done internally or by another third party) | Design by internal team |
| Awareness level of the target customer | High awareness |

With that, I've covered the four types of briefings. You may need more if your campaign should run across many advertiser channel providers, involves the development of a mobile app, or has other requirements, but with these four briefings you should be covered for most of the cases.

1. Now let's move on to what providers need to know and understand to help you reach your goals.

CHAPTER 31   DIGITAL MARKETING BRIEF

# What Your Providers Need to Know

For your providers to effectively meet your campaign's needs, they must fully understand your goals, the campaign's context, and specifics. Misunderstandings can lead to misaligned efforts and wasted resources. Clear and detailed briefs help prevent these issues by providing an overview of your campaign's requirements and goals.

## Understanding Your Campaign Goals and Expected Outcomes

Your overall campaign goals and the specific outcomes you expect are the foundation of your brief. These should be articulated clearly so that your service providers know exactly what success looks like. For instance, if the goal is to increase webinar sign-ups by 50%, this target guides all subsequent decisions and actions.

## Level of Involvement and Strategic Input

Define the level of involvement you desire from your providers. Do you want them to simply execute your plan, or do you expect strategic input and creative suggestions? Clear expectations ensure providers know whether they should follow directives or contribute ideas.

## Building or Setting Up

Clarify if you expect your providers to build or set up something specific, like a new landing page or ad creatives. This helps them understand the scope of their tasks and allocate resources accordingly.

## Providing Suggestions

State explicitly if you expect your providers to offer suggestions. This can be particularly important in areas where they have expertise that you may not, such as new advertising channels or creative strategies.

## Periodic Meetings and Status Updates

Specify if you expect periodic meetings and status updates. Regular check-ins ensure that the campaign stays on track and any issues are addressed promptly. This fosters collaboration and keeps all stakeholders informed.

## Collaboration with Other Providers

Indicate if you expect them to work with other providers. Coordination between multiple partners requires clear communication and defined roles to avoid overlap and ensure aligned efforts and results.

## Important Dates for Projects

Highlight the important dates for you and your projects. These could include start and end dates, key milestones, and any significant events that impact the campaign. Providing this timeline helps in planning and prioritizing tasks.

## Deliverables for Team, Boss, and Stakeholders

Detail what you need to deliver or present to your team, boss, or stakeholders as a result of this project. Understanding these expectations helps your providers tailor their deliverables to meet your needs and ensure stakeholder satisfaction. This also means less work for you because you won't need to adapt the results on your own.

CHAPTER 31   DIGITAL MARKETING BRIEF

# Real-Life Scenarios of Misunderstandings

We have all been there. You got out of a meeting with a great feeling, knowing that in two weeks you will get some results. After three weeks, you still haven't heard from your partner, and you start to wonder what happened.

Misunderstandings happen, and the only way you have to prevent them is to set clear expectations. Here are some not-so-fictional scenarios where a good briefing could have made the difference.

## Scenario A: Mismatched Campaign Goals

Let's take the following situation: A company wanted to increase brand awareness but didn't specify this goal clearly in the brief. The provider, misunderstanding the primary objective, focused on generating immediate sales instead. Consequently, the ads created were too sales-oriented and failed to build the desired brand recognition. Given that the brand was new and not well-known, the clicks-count was rather low, explained as well because of the sales-oriented ads and the wrong selection of the bidding strategy. If the brief had clearly outlined the primary goal of brand awareness, the provider would have been guided to create content that aligned with this objective, resulting in a more effective campaign.

## Scenario B: Lack of Strategic Input

Imagine a project where you expected strategic suggestions from your provider, but did not explicitly state this in the brief. As a result, the provider merely executed the provided plan without offering any improvements or optimizations. The problem is that the plan was only an idea of yours, and you actually expected them to improve on it based on their know-how. The campaign, therefore, underperformed, missing out on potential improvements that the provider's expertise could have brought. Including a request for strategic input in the brief would have encouraged the provider to suggest valuable optimizations, leveraging their expertise to improve the campaign's effectiveness.

## Scenario C: Unclear Deadlines

Consider a project with multiple phases, but the brief did not specify deadlines for each phase. This lack of clarity led to the provider missing key milestones, ultimately delaying the overall project because other partners had to wait longer to get some assets. Clearly defined milestones and deadlines in the brief would have helped the provider manage their time and resources more effectively, ensuring timely progress and completion of each project phase. This would have kept the project on track and met your expectations.

By addressing these potential misunderstandings in your briefs, you ensure your providers have a clear and better understanding of your needs. This clarity fosters better collaboration, efficient execution, and ultimately more successful campaigns (and less headaches for your).

## Expected Outcomes from a Digital Marketing Brief

Upon receiving your digital marketing brief, providers should deliver a confirmation that shows you they understood. This can be in the form of an email, a formal document, a meeting, or a phone call. The main point is to be sure they understood everything and nothing is missing for them to help you make your campaign great. This assures you that they understood the campaign requirements and outlines their approach to achieving your goals.

For example, for the campaign settings, you should receive a brief description of the campaign, the contact person in charge to whom you can make questions, the planned settings (which also serves as backup), the initial keywords, bidding strategies, and other settings for you to review or have as a reference.

For the creatives, receiving a confirmation regarding the time frames, the formats with their specifics, the assets they will use, and those that they will build, as well as the general settings of the campaign, such as target group, landing page, goals, and awareness levels, will tell you if your partner understood at least your main requirements.

In monitoring, receiving a document with the template of the report or a demo of the dashboard will help you understand if that is what you were expecting. Usually, receiving this before the campaign starts is a great way to confirm that you will receive what you are expecting.

Finally, receiving an initial wireframe or sketch of the landing page with its main elements, a list of the assets to be used, and the tracking codes, tools, and platforms will help you confirm that there is no missing point.

You can explain, if the service provider is hesitant to deliver such a confirmation, that it benefits both parties. For you, it ensures they fully understand your requirements. For them, it acts as a backup document that, once approved by you, prevents any misunderstandings and last-minute undocumented changes. This confirmation serves as the definitive reference.

## Summary

In this chapter, I've covered four briefings that, in my own experience, are the most important ones when planning a digital marketing campaign. I explained their base components and the importance of detailed communication between you and your providers. You should at least remember that

- A clear digital marketing brief sets expectations, aligns objectives, and facilitates effective campaign management.

- Confirmation of your providers' understanding of your brief is crucial and should be confirmed in written form when possible.

Now you have everything you need for your partner to start working on your campaign. Next, I will focus on what happens when the campaign begins. What should you know? What are the processes, structures, and policies you should be aware of? In the next chapter, I will give you an overview of the role of famous bots, what they do, and why a perfectly good campaign might be paused, canceled, or take longer to be approved. This will also help you understand those situations where changes in your campaign settings don't immediately show results.

# PART III

# Execution | During-Campaign Management |

## Managing Your Campaign As It Runs: Tips for Monitoring and Improving Your Marketing Efforts in Real Time

In this part of your digital marketing journey, you're moving from planning to action. While the groundwork lays the foundation, the real test begins once your campaign goes live. This segment of the book focuses on managing your campaign during its active phase, ensuring that you're equipped to monitor and optimize in real time (or at least make the right questions at the right time).

The emphasis here is on understanding the importance of staying engaged with your campaign even after it's been launched. Although you might work with specialists who handle the day-to-day management, having knowledge about what to look at, what to expect, and when to make strategic changes is vital. This ensures you're not just passively observing but actively participating in steering the campaign toward success.

PART III   EXECUTION | DURING-CAMPAIGN MANAGEMENT |

# Real-Time Monitoring and Adjustments

Once your campaign is live, the landscape can shift quickly. User behavior, competitive actions, and market changes all influence the effectiveness of your digital marketing efforts. This means that the targeting you prepared might need to be adjusted, live. This is completely different from traditional print ads and sometimes makes the advertiser (you) think everything is possible. It is not, but there are lots of options to improve a running campaign and even stopping it midway.

This part of the book provides guidance on how to keep your finger on the pulse of your campaign, making data-informed decisions that enhance performance and mitigate risks.

You'll learn about tools and techniques for monitoring key performance indicators, and I'll guide you in interpreting the insights you gather. This section ensures you're never in the dark about how your campaign is performing and what steps you can take to improve its trajectory.

Your service provider might be an expert, but most likely manages several customers and campaigns in parallel. If you have ideas on optimizations or insights as to what can be improved, that's completely ok. You have a far better understanding of your customers and market than any provider you might have. What's important is that your service provider is willing to hear you and do the required changes, if possible and within budget, or for the provider to be able to explain why your suggestions might not be the best way to move forward. Remember, one thing is to have ideas and insights, and another is for them to be feasible and good.

PART III EXECUTION | DURING-CAMPAIGN MANAGEMENT |

# Chapters Covered in This Part

This part of the book includes several short chapters that delve into different aspects of during-campaign management:

- **Verification Bots from Ad Channel Providers**: Understanding the influence of nonhuman validations and verifications from the advertising channel provider, for example, creative validation, account verification, and business verification and how to account for it.

- **The Learning Phase in Digital Ads**: What happens when your campaign first goes live? This chapter explains the initial learning phase that digital platforms go through and how it affects your ad delivery and your potential optimizations.

- **How Budget Works in Digital Campaigns**: An essential guide to managing your budget effectively during the campaign. It covers how costs are calculated and what you can do to ensure you maximize your investment. It also covers some small policies you might ignore if you are not careful.

- **Real-Time Campaign Optimizations**: Actions you can take to tweak and improve your campaign based on real-time data.

- **Changing Settings Mid-Campaign**: Sometimes, strategic shifts are necessary mid-flight. This chapter discusses how and when to make significant changes without disrupting the momentum of your campaign.

# Understanding the Role of Reports and Feedback

Even if your campaign is being handled by experts, insist on regular reports and updates (if in the scope of your agreed services). This will allow you to understand how your campaign is behaving.

Be mindful of what "regular" reports mean. If your service provider makes automatic reports available, those might be enough; if not, depending on the campaign and its duration, one short report per week or every two weeks might suffice. It all depends on your individual use case.

The journey through this part of the book prepares you for active and informed participation in your digital marketing campaigns, ensuring you're not just observing but also adding to the process with your insights.

# CHAPTER 32

# Verification Bots from Advertising Channel Providers: Navigating Campaign Approvals and Pauses

As you embark on running a digital marketing campaign, one of the crucial steps involves the review and approval process conducted by advertising channel providers like Google Ads or Facebook Ads. This chapter delves into what happens after you've set up your campaign and submitted your creatives for approval and why sometimes, even when everything seems perfect, your campaign might not run as expected.

## The Approval and Learning Phase

Once you submit your campaign for activation, the next step is the review of your campaign creatives by the advertising channel provider. This is usually where the platform checks if your creatives, targeting, and landing page comply with its policies.

CHAPTER 32  VERIFICATION BOTS FROM ADVERTISING CHANNEL PROVIDERS: NAVIGATING CAMPAIGN APPROVALS AND PAUSES

## Creative Approval

Advertising channel providers review submitted media and text to ensure they comply with their policies. While some providers may approve creatives by default and later disapprove if issues arise, others might take a few hours to a few days to give the green light.

If creatives are disapproved, you or your service provider might need to address the flagged issues or file a complaint if the disapproval seems erroneous. This is particularly common on platforms like Facebook, where specific images or text can trigger false positives.

**Example**

Imagine you have an ad with an image that Facebook initially approves, but later flags and pauses your campaign because the image is mistakenly identified as promoting prohibited content. In such cases, filing a quick appeal explaining the context of the image can resolve the issue.

## Learning Phase

Post-approval, most ads enter what is known as the "learning phase." This period lasts around 4 to 6 days on average but can vary based on the advertising platform. During this phase, the provider's algorithms analyze your settings and perform trial-and-error tests to optimize the ad's performance (what's commonly advertised as machine learning).

**Example**

Your new campaign targeting young entrepreneurs might take a few days under Facebook's learning phase to fine-tune whom within that group the ad resonates with the most, based on interactions, views, and clicks.

# Common Reasons for Campaign Pauses

Despite a smooth start, campaigns can sometimes be paused or stopped automatically due to several factors identified by the provider's verification bots.

## Issues with Creative Approval

Even if initially approved, an ad might later be disapproved due to policy changes or additional scrutiny by the advertising platform.

In this case, you might file a complaint and have your ad be re-checked, but this does not always work. In those cases, creating a new campaign (by duplicating it) usually works if the reason for disapproval was really not founded. If there was a good reason, you will get your creative disapproved again.

## Landing Page Errors

Campaigns can get paused if the landing page becomes unavailable or dysfunctional, as the bots continually verify the accessibility and functionality of the Landing Page provided.

## Malware on the Landing Page

The presence of malware detected on the landing page can trigger an immediate pause to protect users from potential harm.

## Target-URL Modifications

Changes in the target URL that lead to different content than initially verified can result in campaign pauses to ensure user experience and safety.

**Example**

If your campaign directs users to a promotional landing page and that page unexpectedly goes down, Google's bots will detect this and might pause your campaign to prevent a poor user experience.

## Handling False Positives

Verification bots, while essential for maintaining the quality and safety of ads across platforms, are not infallible. They can sometimes flag content incorrectly, leading to what we call "false positives."

If you encounter a situation where your campaign is unjustly paused or disapproved, the immediate step is to contact the advertising channel provider for a review. Providing additional context or rectifying overlooked errors can often quickly solve these issues.

**Example**

In a scenario where your campaign for a health supplement is paused due to the erroneous detection of prohibited drug content, providing certificates or proof of compliance can help quickly reinstate your campaign.

## Moving Forward

Understanding the role of verification bots and the common reasons for campaign pauses prepares you to respond effectively to such situations. Always be prepared to interact with the support channels of your advertising platforms to resolve issues promptly.

In the cases of working with service providers, you should understand that sometimes they handle all these cases in the background because this is more common than what you would think.

In the next chapter, I will briefly explain what learning phases are and why they might have a significant impact on your changes.

# CHAPTER 33

# Understanding the Learning Phase in Digital Marketing Campaigns

In this chapter, I go into the concept of the learning phase, an important but often misunderstood period of time during a digital campaign. This phase sets the base for the performance of your campaign (from the advertiser channel provider side), as it helps the algorithms of the advertising platform optimize based on your chosen settings and assets. I'll explain what triggers a learning phase and what this means for your ongoing campaigns.

## What Is a Learning Phase?

The learning phase is the initial period when the advertising channel provider's algorithm tests various configurations to establish the most effective way to run your ad. This phase is driven by the data it gathers from real-time interactions with your target audience, allowing the system to learn which approaches yield the best results.

CHAPTER 33   UNDERSTANDING THE LEARNING PHASE IN DIGITAL MARKETING CAMPAIGNS

**Detailed Insights**

During the learning phase, the system may try different ad placements, audience segments, and times of the day to see where and when your ads perform best. This is aimed at maximizing your return on investment by honing in on the most cost-effective strategies.

---

**Note**   In most walled-garden platforms, what happens in this phase is more of a black-box. You won't have the tools to check what's going on besides your usual KPIs and normal analytics. In some cases, such as Google Ads, the result of the learning phase might be to not participate in auctions at all, a situation you will identify because your campaign is active but not getting any results (no or little impressions, clicks, or anything else). In this case, you have to make a big-enough change to reactivate your campaign by triggering a new learning phase. My recommendation is to duplicate the Ad Group (in the specific case of Google Ads) or just duplicate the campaign. This will trigger the algorithm to run again.

---

# Events Triggering a Learning Phase

Certain adjustments to your campaign can prompt the algorithm to re-enter the learning phase. Understanding these triggers helps you manage your campaign more effectively by anticipating and planning for potential periods of optimization and by not making those changes at the end of your campaign.

## Budget Adjustments

Significant changes to your overall budget or daily spending limits can initiate a learning phase. This is because the algorithm needs to reassess how to allocate your new budget effectively across available ad opportunities.

**Example**
Imagine you've launched a campaign for a new product line, and midway through, you decide to increase your daily budget significantly. The algorithm will need time to learn the most effective ways to spend this additional budget, potentially altering your ad's delivery pattern.

## Asset Changes

Modifying key assets such as banners or images can also trigger a learning phase. This is because visual elements play a substantial role in ad performance, and the algorithm must understand how these changes affect user engagement. (Check Chapter 11 on Ad Quality for more details.)

# Navigating Changes During the Learning Phase

While it's possible to make changes during the learning phase, it's essential to do so with caution. Frequent changes can prolong this phase, impacting overall campaign performance.

**Plan Ahead**
Try to anticipate major changes early in the campaign design to minimize disruptions during the learning phase. By planning ahead, you can create a more stable environment for your campaign to optimize effectively.

### Limit Frequent Adjustments

Avoid making repeated substantial changes that could reset the learning phase unless absolutely necessary. Frequent adjustments can confuse the optimization algorithms and delay reaching peak performance.

### Strategic Modifications

If changes are essential, ensure they are strategic and based on solid data or extensive experience to justify the potential reset of the learning phase. Strategic modifications should aim to improve campaign performance significantly and be well thought out.

It's also acceptable to make such changes to learn how they impact your campaign, but be conscious about doing so. Understanding the effects of such modifications can provide valuable insights, but it's important to weigh the benefits against the potential delays in optimization.

## Summary

This chapter has given you some insights into the learning phase of digital campaigns. The key takeaways are

- The **learning phase** is when the ad-serving algorithm tests various settings to find the most effective way to deliver your ads.
- Significant **changes to your campaign**, such as budget adjustments or updates to key assets, can trigger a new learning phase, affecting the ad delivery strategy.
- **Strategically manage changes** during this phase to optimize the campaign's performance without unnecessary disruptions.

Your campaign has started, your briefings are great, and communication with your partner is going smoothly. But what are daily budgets and lifetime budgets all about, and why might it be possible for my campaign to overspend on some occasions? That's the topic of the next chapter.

# CHAPTER 34

# Understanding How Budgets Work in Digital Marketing Campaigns

Managing your budget effectively in digital marketing is just as important as adapting your strategy for different platforms. In this chapter, I'll explore how budgets are handled across various advertising channels, focusing on the nuances that can impact your financial planning. Knowing how to set and manage your day and campaign budgets will ensure more controlled spending and better alignment with your campaign goals.

## Introduction to Digital Marketing Budgets

A digital marketing budget can be defined in two ways: as a day budget and as a campaign or lifetime budget. Each type serves a different strategic purpose and is handled differently by various advertising platforms.

## Day Budget

A day budget is the maximum amount you allocate for spending within a single day on a specific campaign. This budget type allows for daily expenditure control and is typically used in channels where traffic and engagement patterns might vary significantly day by day. By setting a day budget, you ensure that your spending remains consistent and controlled, which is particularly useful for campaigns with fluctuating daily performance.

Campaign Budget (Also Known As **Lifetime Budget**)

A campaign budget, or lifetime budget, refers to the total sum you intend to spend over the entire duration of the campaign. This budget type is useful for long-term planning and ensures that your spending is capped at a certain figure for the entire campaign period. It allows for a more strategic allocation of funds over time, accommodating for periods of high and low engagement without exceeding the total budget.

Both budget types are essential tools in digital marketing, offering flexibility and control to match the specific needs and goals of your campaigns. By understanding and utilizing day and campaign budgets effectively, you can optimize your spending and achieve better results across different advertising platforms.

# How Different Advertising Providers Handle Budgets

Different platforms have their unique rules and systems for managing budgets, and it's essential to understand these to optimize your spending.

CHAPTER 34   UNDERSTANDING HOW BUDGETS WORK IN DIGITAL MARKETING CAMPAIGNS

# Google Ads Budgeting

Google Ads has a flexibility clause where it can spend up to double your day budget on a given day. However, it ensures that in a given running calendar month, the total does not exceed what it calculates as your monthly maximum expendidure—30.4 times your daily budget. This clause allows for spending acceleration on days when your ad might be performing exceptionally well, without increasing your overall budget ceiling.[1]

**The keyword here is running calendar month**, from 1st until the end of the month.

In Google Ads, campaign budgets are typically reserved for Video Ads campaigns. For other types of campaigns, daily budgeting is the norm.[2]

**Example**

If you set a daily budget of $100 on Google Ads, on certain high-traffic days, the system might spend up to $200, anticipating lower spending on other days to keep the monthly expenditure within the $3,040 limit.

**Facebook Ads Budgeting**

Facebook also offers the flexibility to choose between a daily budget and a lifetime budget. Unlike Google, this choice is available across all types of campaigns, providing more versatility in how you manage your finances.

With Facebook's daily budget, there's a minimum spend threshold which you need to meet. This ensures that your ads gain sufficient exposure to reach campaign objectives effectively.

**Example**

For a Facebook campaign promoting a special event, using a lifetime budget might be more suitable, as it allows you to allocate a set amount to spend from the campaign start date up to the event date.

---

[1] https://support.google.com/google-ads/answer/2375454?hl=en and https://support.google.com/google-ads/answer/6385083?hl=en
[2] As of July 2023.

CHAPTER 34   UNDERSTANDING HOW BUDGETS WORK IN DIGITAL MARKETING CAMPAIGNS

## Summary

In this chapter, I've covered the available budget alternatives of the digital advertising platforms Facebook Marketing (Meta) and Google Ads. Key points include

- The difference between day budgets and campaign budgets and how they influence financial control
- Specific budgeting features and norms of major platforms like Google Ads and Facebook Ads

In the next chapter, I will discuss usual optimizations you can apply on running campaigns.

CHAPTER 35

# Understanding and Implementing Campaign Optimizations

In this chapter, I dive into optimizations while running digital marketing campaigns. I will focus on which changes can you or your service partner do to improve the campaign results. These adjustments are made while the campaign is running, with the goal of improving performance based on real-time data analysis. I will explore the most common optimizations used by service providers, and I will introduce additional strategies that are significant for your toolkit.

## Introduction to Campaign Optimizations

Optimizations in digital campaigns refer to ongoing adjustments made by marketing professionals to various campaign aspects, from targeting to creative elements. The importance of these adjustments changes depending on the goals and specifics of your campaign, and they are not only for achieving desired results but also for ensuring that your budget is utilized efficiently.

I will classify the optimization you can do to any campaign into four categories:

- Budget adjustments
- Keyword management
- Creative adjustments
- Targeting adjustments

Let's walk through them and understand their significance and characteristics. But first, let's discuss why should you or your service partner optimize a campaign at all.

## Why Optimize a Campaign

The primary reason to optimize a digital marketing campaign is to improve its performance in achieving set goals, whether they involve increasing engagement, driving more conversions, or improving specific metrics like the frequency (refer to Chapter 12 on Metrics and Chapter 15 on Campaign Types).

Optimizations allow you to adjust strategies based on audience behavior, market conditions, and the effectiveness of different elements of the campaign. This ensures that your campaigns remain dynamic and capable of adapting to changing conditions. But why would you need to adjust your campaign to market conditions? Because, although you may work with a partner that did research the targeting settings properly, markets are dynamic and change continuously. For example, your competition might launch a product you were not aware of, which may change the way you communicate with your customers. It may also

CHAPTER 35   UNDERSTANDING AND IMPLEMENTING CAMPAIGN OPTIMIZATIONS

happen that your inventory is running low on some product colors, and you need to remove them from your creatives, or that there is a new law in your region you need to comply with.

There are just too many reasons why you would want to optimize your campaign, and it is important that you understand what is possible.

# Common Optimizations and Their Applications

Let's dive into the most commonly implemented optimizations categories, describing each one, its purpose, practical examples, potential impact, and the associated risks.

Please keep in mind that each category can consider several adjustments. For instance, in Keyword Management, you can remove or add keywords, but also change their match type, adjust the CPC per keyword, create approve and disapprove lists, add specific landing pages for specific keywords, and a lot more. I will just use some examples and the main characteristics of each category to give you an overview of them. This is by no way a detailed guide to campaign adjustments.

## Budget Adjustments

Budget Adjustments means adjusting the campaign's budget—either the overall limit or the allocation per day or per keyword. This is a common optimization that helps align spending with your campaign goals and market response and to control how you want to manage your finances regarding the campaign.

### Why Do This

If certain aspects of the campaign are performing exceptionally well, increasing the budget allocation can capitalize on this success, potentially leading to better results.

On the other side, if the campaign is not getting enough results, adjusting the budget may allow it to participate in more auctions and win better placements.

*Example*
Suppose an ad group promoting a new product line is achieving high conversion rates. Increasing its daily budget could amplify its reach and conversions, making full use of its current success.

*Potential Impact*
Improve campaign performance by leveraging successful elements to a greater extent.

*Risks*
Increased spending without guaranteed proportional returns, especially if market conditions change or if the initial success does not scale linearly.

## Keywords Management

Optimizing the keywords involved in your campaign. This includes, for example, adding new relevant keywords, removing underperforming ones, or adjusting bids for current keywords.

*Why Do This*
Keeping your keywords relevant ensures that your ads continue to reach the right audience and adapt to changes in market behavior and competitor strategies.

*Example*
Mid-campaign, you might identify emerging trends or seasonal changes that introduce new relevant keywords. Incorporating these into your campaign could capture additional traffic and engagement.

*Potential Impact*
Maintain or enhance the relevance and effectiveness of the campaign.

*Risks*
Potential disruption of established keyword performance and temporary inefficiency during the adjustment period.

## Creative Adjustments

Updating the creative elements of your ads, such as images, videos, or ad copy, to maintain the audience's interest and respond to performance analytics.

*Why Do This*
Refreshing creatives can re-engage viewers and improve interaction rates, especially if original elements become less effective over time.

*Example*
If ad fatigue is observed—where the CTR of an ad begins to decline—introducing new visuals or tweaking the message could revitalize its performance.

*Potential Impact*
Renewed engagement and interaction with your target audience.

*Risks*
New creatives might not resonate as expected, requiring further iteration and testing.

## Targeting Adjustments

Refining the targeting parameters of your campaign, such as demographic details, geographic locations, or user behaviors, to better align with your audience.

*Why Do This*
Effective targeting ensures that your ads reach the most appropriate and responsive segments of your audience, maximizing impact and efficiency.

### Example

You may discover that a particular demographic subset is responding more positively to your ads. Focusing more of your budget on this group could yield better results.

### Potential Impact

Increased efficiency and effectiveness of ad spend.

### Risks

Narrowing the focus might exclude potential customers who fall outside the adjusted targeting parameters but could still convert.

## Summary

In this chapter, I've explored several key optimizations that can significantly influence the success of your digital marketing campaigns. Properly implementing these optimizations, and understanding when and which ones to implement, will have an important impact in dynamically adapting to campaign data (data you get from your service partner or your advertisement channel providers) and achieving optimal results. Remember, the agility to respond to real-time feedback and data is one of digital marketing's most significant advantages.

In the next chapter, I will discuss timings and access for making these changes, as everything depends on your contracts with your service providers and how you manage your digital assets.

CHAPTER 36

# Campaign Settings Adjustments: Timing and Access

In this chapter, I will explore the aspects related to modifying the settings of your digital marketing campaign. Regardless of whether your campaign is yet to launch, is currently running, or is paused, understanding when and how you can make changes is essential for effective campaign management.

## Understanding When You Can Change Campaign Settings

Modifying the settings of your digital marketing campaign can be done at different stages, each with specific considerations and potential implications.

**Before It Runs**
The ideal time to make changes is before the campaign launches. Adjustments made at this stage ensure that the campaign starts with the most accurate settings aligned with your goals. The biggest part of the settings should be set before it runs. While you may need to make changes

based on data and feedback from the advertiser channel provider and your service partners, having a solid foundation before launching minimizes disruptions and optimizes initial performance.

**While It Is Running**

Changes can be made while the campaign is running, but it's important to be cautious. Significant modifications might trigger a new learning phase, which could temporarily affect the performance of your ongoing campaign. This period of adjustment is necessary for the system to recalibrate and optimize the new settings, so plan these changes strategically and only when necessary.

**When Paused or Live (Not Removed)**

As long as a campaign has not been permanently removed or deleted, it can be reactivated and adjusted. This flexibility allows you to pause a campaign, tweak settings, and resume it with new parameters. This stage is useful for making substantial changes without impacting the campaign's historical data and performance metrics.

---

**Note** Changes made during a campaign must be handled with care to avoid triggering extensive learning phases unnecessarily (refer to Chapter 33 on Learning Phases for more details).

It is important to note that I wrote "when a campaign is paused or live". Any campaign that is not removed triggers a series of processes on the side of the advertising channel providers that can lead to accounts getting closed, creatives being disapproved, and other consequences. This is because, for an advertiser channel provider, a campaign that can run (i.e., not deleted) should always comply with their policies. That means that any landing pages, inventory or product feeds, videos, and other assets related to them should be available and comply with their policies.

---

CHAPTER 36   CAMPAIGN SETTINGS ADJUSTMENTS: TIMING AND ACCESS

# Where to Change the Settings of Your Campaign?

The ability to alter campaign settings depends heavily on your arrangements with service providers and the ownership of the advertising account.

**Using a Full-Package Service**

In scenarios where the advertising provider or your service partner manages everything, you will need to communicate with your provider to discuss potential changes. Often, direct access to make changes might not be available. You will rely on your provider to implement any adjustments, so clear communication and detailed briefings are crucial to ensure your needs are met.

**Advertisement Account Owned by Your Provider**

If modifications are allowed under your agreement, discuss with your provider how these should be implemented to align with your new requirements. This typically involves coordinating with your provider to ensure that changes are made correctly and promptly. You may refer to Chapter 2 on digital assets and Chapter 31 on briefings for more information in this regard. Understanding your provider's policies and procedures for making changes can help streamline this process and avoid misunderstandings.

**Account Owned by You**

If you own the account, you typically have the freedom to change settings directly. This ownership allows for more immediate and flexible adjustments to campaign settings. However, it is advisable to consult your marketing team or hired experts to ensure that those changes support your strategic goals. You should easily access the management interface for your advertising platform, allowing you to implement changes as needed while maintaining alignment with your overall strategy.

CHAPTER 36   CAMPAIGN SETTINGS ADJUSTMENTS: TIMING AND ACCESS

# Which Changes Impact Campaign Timing?

Certain adjustments, particularly those affecting the financial aspects of your campaign like the day budget or cost-per-click (CPC) limits, can reintroduce a learning phase. Understanding why this matters and how to manage these changes can significantly impact your campaign's performance.

**Learning Phase Considerations**
Changes that initiate a learning phase can cause temporary performance dips as the system recalibrates to optimize your campaign with the new settings. Understanding which changes necessitate this can help you plan alterations judiciously, minimizing disruption to ongoing operations. Please refer to Chapter 33 on Learning Phases for more details.

# Summary

I have discussed the timings and required access to optimize your campaigns. The main key takeaways you should remember are

- Timing, cautious approach, and information are key when adjusting settings of your digital marketing campaigns to avoid triggering unnecessary learning phases.

- Depending on who manages the advertising account, your access to make changes can vary. This can be discussed with the briefing.

- Recognize the potential impacts of mid-campaign adjustments, particularly those that affect budget settings, to better manage expected learning phases and resultant performance shifts.

In the next chapter, I will discuss the analysis of your digital marketing campaign, including what you should expect, how to conduct the analysis, and why it's important.

# PART IV

# Campaign Analysis

As your digital marketing campaign reaches its conclusion, the focus shifts to understanding its performance. In this part of the book, we'll delve into the critical final stage: campaign analysis. With the groundwork laid, the campaign executed, and adjustments made along the way, it's now time to evaluate the results.

Campaign analysis isn't just about looking at numbers; it's about interpreting the data in a way that provides actionable insights. However, this part will not teach you how to analyze the data yourself. Instead, it will guide you through what to expect from the reports provided by your service providers. Understanding these reports is key to recognizing which metrics truly matter and which might be misleading or purely cosmetic.

In the next chapter, you'll learn how to navigate the structure of digital marketing reports, avoid common misinterpretations, and identify vanity metrics that might cloud your judgment. By the end, you'll have an idea of what to expect of your service providers regarding reportings, and you will understand why the initial briefing is so relevant for this stage, ensuring that your marketing efforts align with your business goals and that you can communicate effectively with your digital marketing partners.

CHAPTER 37

# Navigating Digital Marketing Reports at Campaign Completion

In this chapter, I'll explore the essentials of digital marketing reports, guiding you through understanding, interpreting, and utilizing these reports effectively. As your campaign wraps up, these reports provide insights, not just on the campaign's performance, but also on how you can leverage this data for future marketing success.

## What Should a Report Look Like

Digital marketing reports can vary significantly in structure depending on the company or expert you work with and the kind of campaigns you are running. However, an effective report should be clear, concise, and relevant to your campaign's specific goals.

## Key Elements of an Effective Digital Marketing Report

A well-rounded digital marketing report comprises several key components that collectively provide a comprehensive view of a campaign's performance. The common components are

1. Executive summary
2. Campaign overview
3. Performance metrics
4. Channel-specific metrics
5. Insights and recommendations
6. Visualizations
7. Conclusions
8. Annexes (optional)

Let's explore each one.

First, the executive summary provides a snapshot of the campaign's performance. It highlights key metrics, results, and critical insights or recommendations. This section gives readers an overview, setting the tone for more detailed analysis. This section is also the first one you should read, and sometimes the only one. All the other sections are there to provide the data and explanations for the highlights in the executive summary. Reading this section, you should, in one or two pages, get all the information you need to understand what was done, the main results of the campaign, and how to move forward.

## CHAPTER 37  NAVIGATING DIGITAL MARKETING REPORTS AT CAMPAIGN COMPLETION

Next, the campaign overview details the campaign's objectives, target audience, employed messaging, and the channels utilized. This section establishes the context, helping readers understand the foundation upon which the report and its metrics are built.

The performance metrics section includes essential metrics such as impressions, clicks, conversion rates, and cost per conversion. These metrics are selected based on their relevance to the campaign goals—stated in the previous section of the report—offering clear insights into the campaign's results. This section is important for assessing how well the campaign met its objectives.

Channel-specific metrics provide a breakdown of metrics by channel for campaigns utilizing multiple platforms. This section shows click-through rates, conversion rates, and costs per conversion for each channel. Such detailed analysis aids in identifying the most effective channels, guiding future investments and strategy adjustments.

Based on the data, the insights and recommendations section offers strategic advice for optimizing future campaigns and adjusting current strategies to enhance performance. This section translates raw data into actionable strategies, providing a roadmap for improvement.

Visualizations, such as charts, graphs, and tables, are important for making complex information more digestible and are a great asset for you as a marketer to explain the results of the campaign to your stakeholders. They present the data in a way that is easier to understand at a glance, aiding quick decision-making and comprehension.

Finally, the conclusions section summarizes the key findings and outlines actionable next steps based on the campaign results. This section consolidates the report's insights, ensuring that readers walk away with a clear understanding of what has been learned and what actions should follow.

Additionally, some reports include one or several annexes with raw data, tables, research, and other information that might be relevant to understand the report. This is optional.

CHAPTER 37   NAVIGATING DIGITAL MARKETING REPORTS AT CAMPAIGN COMPLETION

---

**Note**   The report you receive might have another structure, but it should contain the mentioned elements. It also depends on your briefing[1] and what you agreed with your service provider. Remember that reports take time and might mean additional costs.

---

## What Data Should My Provider Make Available

The data a service provider should provide during or after a campaign varies depending on several factors, such as what you agreed upon in the briefings, the type of service they are providing (whether it's a full all-inclusive service or something else), the kind of campaigns you are running, and the questions you want to answer, provided this was previously discussed.

Your provider should disclose detailed cost metrics like clicks, impressions, cost per click, cost per impression, and cost per conversion, unless all these services are bundled into a complete package. When dealing with a "complete package," it's important to recognize that this often includes a set number of clicks and impressions. These packages generally encompass not only the core services but also additional charges like service fees, monitoring, and optimization expenses, all wrapped into one consolidated price.

The data your provider should make available depends on what you agreed upon before starting the campaign and on the goals you set for the campaign. For example, if your main goal was to increase the awareness of a product, then the metrics "Impressions," "Frequency,"

---

[1] Check Chapter 31 on digital marketing briefings for digital marketing campaign monitoring. If the analysis of the campaign is not done by the same provider as the monitoring, you might want to create a fifth briefing based on that one.

"CTR," and "Clicks" will most likely help you understand that. If, for instance, your goals were to generate sales using shopping ads, you will want to understand how much each sale cost, using metrics like cost per conversion or cost per click. Remember that I discussed important metrics depending on your marketing goals in Chapter 27. You might want to refer to that chapter for further insights.

It is important to agree on the metrics you will want to receive during the briefing stage before the campaign starts. Some metrics are only available with additional settings, such as conversions, and if not communicated, they may not be available at the end of the campaign. Therefore, clear communication and agreement on the specific metrics needed are crucial for accurately measuring and understanding the campaign's success.

## Frequency and Timing of Reporting

The frequency and timing of reports should align with the duration and dynamics of your campaign. For short campaigns, a mid-campaign check-in and a final report might suffice, while longer campaigns might require weekly or biweekly updates to keep all stakeholders informed and enable timely adjustments. This also completely depends on what you agreed upon in your briefings.

## Understanding Pitfalls, Misinterpretations, and Vanity Metrics

Beware of common pitfalls such as overemphasis on vanity metrics that may not necessarily correlate with business objectives or misinterpretation of data due to lack of context. It's vital to approach data with a critical mind, in context and in consultation with your digital marketing specialist to discern actionable insights from mere data points.

For instance, if your primary goal is for your ad to be viewed by as many people as possible, metrics like clicks and CTR may be irrelevant, but frequency and impressions will be highly relevant.

Vanity metrics are not always bad. Sometimes, stakeholders give a lot of importance to such metrics because that is how they are evaluated or because that is what is understood as success within their companies. My personal recommendation in this case is to not overthink it. Prepare all the vanity metrics they want and need, but make your decisions and improve your future marketing initiatives based on the data you know you need.

Understanding these pitfalls ensures you can navigate through the data landscape effectively. By critically analyzing the data and contextualizing it within your campaign goals, you can avoid common misinterpretations and focus on metrics that truly reflect your business objectives. This balanced approach allows you to present necessary data to stakeholders while making informed decisions to enhance your marketing strategies.

# Summary

In this chapter, I gave you an overview of reportings in digital marketing. This chapter builds on all the previous chapters related to metrics, marketing goals, campaign types, and analytics and serves as a way to link all the concepts and elements you learned in them.

The main takeaways you should remember are

- Effective digital marketing reports are clear, concise, and structured to highlight the most relevant information for decision-making.

- Ensure your provider offers transparency in reporting and data provision, especially concerning costs and performance metrics, but consider your agreements at the start of the campaign. Don't ask the impossible if there was no clear understanding of the deliverables

## CHAPTER 37  NAVIGATING DIGITAL MARKETING REPORTS AT CAMPAIGN COMPLETION

and expectations in the beginning. Finally, it is your responsibility to communicate what you want, and the briefing is a great tool for that.

- Regular and appropriately timed reports can significantly enhance your ability to manage and adjust your digital marketing strategies effectively if that is what you agreed. A good service partner will most likely communicate with you if they discover any issues or make adjustments if that was agreed on in the briefing.

The next chapter will be the first of five chapters where I will elaborate on recommendations regarding the structure of digital marketing campaigns. I will start with how to structure your marketing efforts regarding campaigns, ad groups, and ads.

# PART V

# Recommendations

With the completion of your campaign and analysis in hand, it's time to look forward and refine your digital marketing approach. In this part, I'll focus on providing tailored recommendations to help you make strategic decisions that align with your business's unique needs. Whether you're a small company just getting started or an established brand with multiple locations, this section offers insights into structuring your campaigns and evaluating the advice you receive from service providers.

This part will guide you through the nuances of organizing your digital marketing efforts, whether you're managing multiple campaigns, ad groups, or individual ads. The goal is to help you optimize your structure to maximize efficiency and effectiveness. Additionally, you'll learn how to critically assess recommendations from your providers, ensuring that their advice aligns with your specific objectives.

I'll also explore digital marketing strategies tailored to different business models. Whether you own all your locations or operate through a network of independently owned partners, these chapters will provide actionable strategies to enhance your digital presence. By the end of this section, you'll be equipped with practical recommendations that can be immediately applied to your ongoing and future digital marketing campaigns.

CHAPTER 38

# Structuring Digital Marketing Efforts: Multiple Campaigns vs. Multiple Ad Groups vs. Multiple Ads

In this chapter, I will explore how to effectively structure your digital marketing efforts. The configuration you choose can significantly impact the performance and manageability of your campaigns. It is important to understand the differences between running multiple campaigns, dividing a single campaign into multiple groups, or using multiple ads within those groups.

## Introduction to Campaign Structuring

Structuring digital marketing campaigns involves deciding whether to create multiple campaigns, utilize multiple groups within a single campaign, or run multiple ads within those groups. Each approach has its benefits and challenges, which can affect not only the campaign's performance, but also how easily you can manage and optimize your marketing efforts and budget.

## Why Structure Matters

Choosing the right structure for your campaign can help you better allocate your budget, target more effectively, and gain clearer insights from your analytics. It enables you to customize your approach based on specific target audiences, products, or marketing goals. The structure you decide on also depends on the advertising channel provider you will use. For instance, Meta Ads can optimize a budget in one campaign for many Ad Sets (groups of ads). This means Meta's algorithm can move budget from one Ad Set to another depending on their performance. Google Ads can optimize multiple Ads in an Ad Group, prioritizing those with better performance.

---

**Note** Please keep in mind that these are just examples and are not descriptions of the full capabilities of each platform. Once you understand why is the structure relevant, you will be able to discuss this in detail with your service provider and your digital marketing expert. Giving you an overview and enough information to understand the relevance of these concepts is the goal of this chapter.

---

## Campaign Structure Overview

To better understand the implications of each structuring option, let's define and compare them. Multiple Campaigns involve setting up separate campaigns for different targets or objectives. Each campaign can be tailored with its own settings, budgets, and goals. On the other hand, Multiple Groups in a Campaign, also known as ad sets on some platforms, allow for grouping different ad types under a single campaign umbrella. This provides flexibility to target different demographics or test various creative strategies within the same campaign. Within each group or ad set, you may choose to run Multiple Ads to test variations in messaging, imagery, or CTA to see which performs best.

It is important to note that there are settings that apply only to specific levels. Refer to Chapter 6 on targeting for more details.

## Multiple Campaigns

Using Multiple Campaigns has several advantages. First, each campaign has its own budget, allowing you to allocate funds more precisely to different product lines, services, or target audiences. Second, campaign-level settings such as location targeting, language, and ad scheduling can be customized for each campaign, providing more granular control. Third, you can choose different ad formats (e.g., Search, Display, Video) and networks (e.g., Google Search Network, Google Display Network) for each campaign. Fourth, performance data is isolated for each campaign, making it easier to analyze and optimize specific segments without cross-campaign interference.

However, there are disadvantages to using Multiple Campaigns. Managing multiple campaigns can become complex and time-consuming, especially if you have a large number of products or services. Additionally, there may be overlap in targeting, which could lead to competition between your own campaigns, potentially driving up costs.[1]

Multiple campaigns are best suited for large-scale operations where distinct markets or objectives are targeted. They are particularly effective for organizations with diverse product lines or services that

---

[1] Check Chapter 7 on cannibalization for details.

cater to different customer segments. For instance, a company selling both software and hardware products can create separate campaigns for software promotions and hardware sales. This allows the company to tailor its marketing messages and strategies to resonate specifically with each product's audience, optimizing engagement and conversion rates.

## Multiple Ad Groups in a Single Campaign

Using Multiple Ad Groups in a Single Campaign has its own set of advantages. It is easier to manage and monitor compared to having multiple campaigns, especially for smaller accounts or those with fewer products or services. A single budget is shared across all ad groups, which can simplify budget management but may also require careful monitoring to ensure even distribution. Campaign-level settings apply to all ad groups, ensuring consistent targeting and scheduling. It is also easier to manage negative keywords at the campaign level to prevent overlap and irrelevant clicks.

However, using Multiple Ad Groups in a Single Campaign also has disadvantages. There is less granular control over budget allocation, as all ad groups share the same campaign budget. Performance data is aggregated at the campaign level, which can make it harder to isolate and analyze the performance of individual ad groups.

This approach is great for campaigns targeting similar audiences with varied interests, or for marketers who wish to test different advertising strategies under a single budget. For example, a tourism agency runs a campaign promoting a destination with different ad groups targeting families, solo travelers, and adventure seekers. Each group receives tailored ads that resonate with their specific interests, all under the same campaign aimed at boosting tourism.

CHAPTER 38   STRUCTURING DIGITAL MARKETING EFFORTS: MULTIPLE CAMPAIGNS VS. MULTIPLE AD GROUPS VS. MULTIPLE ADS

# Which One to Choose

When deciding which approach to choose, use Multiple Campaigns if you need distinct budgets for different products, services, or target audiences. This approach is also beneficial if you require different targeting settings, ad formats, or networks for each segment or if you want to isolate performance data for more precise analysis and optimization. Use Multiple Ad Groups if you prefer a simpler structure that is easier to manage, if you wish to share a budget across similar products or services, or if you need consistent targeting and scheduling settings across all ad groups.

# Multiple Ads

Using multiple ads offers several advantages. First, it allows you to conduct A/B testing by using different ad copy, headlines, and calls-to-action to see which performs best, improving overall campaign performance over time. Different ad variations can appeal to different segments of your target group, potentially increasing overall engagement and conversion rates. Multiple ads enable you to create more specific and relevant messages[2] for different keywords or product categories within an ad group, potentially improving quality scores[3] and ad performance. With multiple ads, you have more data points to analyze and optimize, allowing for continuous improvement of your campaigns.

However, there are potential drawbacks to using multiple ads. Managing and monitoring multiple ads can be more time-consuming and complex, especially for larger campaigns. You will need to ensure that your budget is distributed effectively across multiple ads, which may require more careful management. If not managed properly, having multiple ads

---

[2] Check Chapter 16 on messages for more details.
[3] Check Chapter 11 on ad quality.

could lead to inconsistent messaging or branding across your campaigns. Additionally, it may take time for the ad platform's algorithms to gather enough data to optimize performance across multiple ads effectively.

This strategy is useful for optimizing ad performance within a specific target group or demographic, especially when trying to refine messages or visual elements. For example, a beverage brand runs multiple ads within the same group to test different taglines and images. One ad features a tagline focusing on health benefits, while another emphasizes taste. The brand measures engagement and conversion to determine which message appeals more effectively to its target audience.

## When to Use Multiple Ads

When deciding whether to use multiple ads, consider the size and complexity of your campaign, your available resources for management and optimization, the diversity of your product offerings or target audience segments, and your goals for testing and improving ad performance.

## Recommendations for Structuring Your Digital Marketing Efforts

Table 38-1 outlines the advantages and disadvantages of each approach and when each is most applicable.

CHAPTER 38  STRUCTURING DIGITAL MARKETING EFFORTS: MULTIPLE CAMPAIGNS VS. MULTIPLE AD GROUPS VS. MULTIPLE ADS

*Table 38-1.* *Comparison table of different campaign structures*

| Strategy | Description | Advantages | Disadvantages | Ideal Usage |
|---|---|---|---|---|
| Multiple Campaigns | Separate campaigns are each targeted to distinct objectives or audiences | • Tailored strategies per campaign<br>• Easier budget allocation | • Higher complexity in management<br>• Potential for higher costs | Best for large-scale operations targeting distinctly different markets or objectives |
| Multiple Groups in a Campaign | Multiple ad groups under a single campaign, each targeting different segments | • Centralized management of budget<br>• Flexibility in targeting and testing | Shared campaign settings might limit some customization options | Great for campaigns targeting similar audiences with varied interests or testing different ad strategies |
| Multiple Ads in a Group | Several ads within a single group, each differing slightly in design or copy | • A/B testing of creative elements<br>• Quick insights from performance variations | Can dilute focus if too many variations are tested at once | Useful for optimizing ad performance within a specific target group or demographic |

CHAPTER 38   STRUCTURING DIGITAL MARKETING EFFORTS: MULTIPLE CAMPAIGNS VS. MULTIPLE AD GROUPS VS. MULTIPLE ADS

# Planning Your Campaign Structure

When planning your campaign structure, you should first consider your overall marketing goals. Next, analyze your audience to determine whether distinct campaigns or grouped strategies will effectively meet their needs and interests. Finally, reflect on your management resources to decide if a simpler or more complex structure is sustainable based on your team's capacity and expertise. This careful planning ensures that your campaign structure aligns with both your strategic objectives and operational capabilities.

Remember to use what you learned about Awareness Levels (check Chapter 4) and Target Groups (check Chapter 9).

# Summary

In this chapter, I gave you an overview of different structures for digital marketing campaigns, stating their advantages, disadvantages, and some recommendations.

You should remember that

- Structuring your campaigns correctly can substantially impact their effectiveness and manageability.

- Multiple campaigns offer customization at the highest level, multiple groups provide flexibility within a campaign, and multiple ads allow for detailed performance testing.

- Choose the structure that best aligns with your marketing goals, audience characteristics, and resource availability.

In the next chapter, I will offer another perspective on advertiser channel provider recommendations—the suggestions you see on their platforms. I will explain why sometimes these recommendations are designed not for your benefit, but to enhance the efficiency of their own systems.

CHAPTER 39

# Evaluating Provider Recommendations in Digital Marketing Campaigns

In this chapter, I explore the nuanced area of acting on recommendations given by advertising channel providers. It's crucial to approach these recommendations judiciously, considering both your campaign goals and the underlying motivations of the providers. Here, you'll learn how to discern which suggestions might genuinely benefit your campaign and which might primarily serve the provider's interests.

## Should I Implement All the Recommendations from My Provider

When you receive recommendations from your advertising channel provider, such as those offered by Google Ads or Meta Ads, it's important to critically assess their applicability to your specific marketing objectives and campaign structure. The right answer is "It depends," and in this chapter I will explain why.

CHAPTER 39   EVALUATING PROVIDER RECOMMENDATIONS IN DIGITAL MARKETING CAMPAIGNS

## Understanding Provider Recommendations

Advertising channel providers often provide recommendations to optimize your campaigns. While many of these suggestions can be beneficial, improving campaign performance and efficiency, they can sometimes lean toward maximizing the provider's revenue while not actually helping you.

# Weighing the Benefits and Risks of Advertiser Channel Provider Recommendations

Consider these aspects when evaluating provider recommendations.

## Alignment with Campaign Goals

When evaluating provider recommendations, first assess how well these suggestions align with the objectives of your campaign. For example, if your primary goal is to increase brand awareness, recommendations that focus solely on driving conversions might not be suitable. You should ensure that any recommended strategies contribute directly to achieving your specific marketing goals.

## Technical Feasibility and Expertise

Next, consider the technical feasibility of implementing the recommended changes. Some suggestions might involve technical adjustments, such as adding new tracking codes to your website or integrating advanced analytics features. It is important to evaluate whether you possess the technical expertise to implement these changes, or if you need to seek additional resources. Ensuring you have the necessary permissions and capabilities to make these adjustments is crucial for effective implementation and viability of a recommendation.

## Cost Implications

Finally, understand the cost implications of adopting the provider's recommendations. Often, recommendations might involve increasing your advertising spend or opting for more expensive strategies. It is vital to analyze whether the potential increase in costs is justified by the expected benefits. Be wary of suggestions that might inflate your budget without offering guaranteed proportional returns, or recommendations that might increase your maximal CPC without considering the margin you have from your products and services. Analyze how these cost changes align with your budgetary constraints and overall marketing strategy.

## Practical Example

Consider a scenario where your advertiser channel provider recommends switching from a CPC (Cost-per-Click) model to a CPM (Cost-per-Mille) model to supposedly boost visibility. Before making this change, you would need to assess whether this aligns with your goal of driving more targeted traffic rather than just increasing impressions. Additionally, evaluate if your team can adjust the campaign settings accordingly and if the increased expense fits your budget without straining your resources.

CHAPTER 39   EVALUATING PROVIDER RECOMMENDATIONS IN DIGITAL MARKETING CAMPAIGNS

## Example: Google Ads Conversion Recommendations

Let's take a closer look at a common recommendation: using conversion tracking in Google Ads. While tracking conversions can provide invaluable insights into campaign effectiveness, it might not be suitable for all campaign types. For an awareness campaign, where the focus is on reaching a broad audience rather than driving specific user actions, conversion tracking might not be the best tool.

**Adopting Recommendations with Caution**

Always consider how implementing these recommendations could impact your overall strategy and whether they provide clear benefits that justify any additional costs or efforts.

# Summary

This chapter is meant to make you doubt the recommendations you get from the platforms you use. You should not blindly follow everything a provider says, and you should always consider your marketing goals. You should at least remember that

- Not all provider recommendations will align perfectly with your campaign goals. It's essential to analyze each suggestion critically.

- Balancing the benefits of recommendations with their cost implications and their relevance to your campaign aims is crucial.

- Ensure you have the necessary resources and knowledge to implement suggested changes effectively.

In the next chapter, I will explain the important considerations for small companies regarding digital marketing.

# CHAPTER 40

# Digital Marketing Strategies for Small Companies

In this chapter, I explore which important points in digital marketing strategies should you consider as a small company. Small businesses often operate under constraints such as limited budgets, resources, or in-house expertise. Therefore, choosing the right strategies and understanding how to manage digital marketing efforts efficiently are paramount.

For small companies, digital marketing presents an invaluable opportunity to enhance visibility, engage with customers, and drive growth. However, the approach to digital marketing must be strategic and well-informed to maximize results without overextending resources.

## Key Considerations for Small Companies in Digital Marketing

Implementing a digital marketing initiative involves several considerations.

## Budget Allocation

Small companies must carefully consider their budget allocation when implementing digital marketing initiatives. Limited resources require a focus on cost-effective strategies. It is crucial for small companies to prioritize spending on campaigns that promise the highest return on investment. They should start with small, targeted campaigns that can be scaled up based on performance. Depending on the budget, you may also need to consider spending an important part of your budget on a service partner or experimenting yourself (which sometimes may cost even more). I recommend, if you don't have any experience, to look for a partner that also explains how he does things. Then you can work with him on a consulting basis, lowering your fixed costs of managing the campaign.

## Choice of Campaign Types

With limited budgets, these companies benefit most from focusing on campaigns that align closely with their immediate business goals. For example, if the goal is brand awareness, social media campaigns might be more beneficial than expensive search engine marketing.

## Selection of Advertiser Channel Providers

The selection of advertiser channel providers should be based on the specific needs and budget constraints of the small company. It is important to choose providers that offer scalable solutions and transparent pricing models. Small businesses should look for platforms that allow them to start with a modest budget and increase their spending as they see results. The providers of their choice should also be flexible to change and pause the campaigns.

## Structure and Functionality of the Company Website

The structure and functionality of the company website plays a critical role in the success of digital marketing efforts. For small companies, the website must be user-friendly and optimized for conversions. This includes having a clear call to action, an easy navigation system, and ensuring the website is mobile-friendly, as these elements are essential for turning visitors into customers. If the site does not comply with the minimum requirements of the advertising channel providers, then the campaign will most likely underperform. In this case, getting a partner to improve your website or your landing page should be the priority. It is also important to check if you have access to your website and which changes can you do. It is not surprising to find out that many small businesses do not have proper digital presences because of time, resources, or knowledge. Refer to Chapters 2 (Digital Assets) and 23 (Landing Pages) for more details.

## Availability and Quality of Landing Pages

The availability and quality of landing pages are crucial for capturing leads and achieving conversions (Refer to Chapter 11 (Ad Quality) and Chapter 23 (Landing Pages) for more information). Small companies should focus on creating landing pages that are directly relevant to the ads they are running. These pages should provide the necessary information and incentives for visitors to convert, such as sign-up forms, contact information, or special offers.

## Practical Example

Consider a small local bakery looking to increase foot traffic through digital marketing. The bakery allocates a modest budget to a Facebook advertising campaign targeting local residents. The campaign uses ads that link to a well-designed landing page offering a discount for first-time customers. The simplicity and directness of this approach make it manageable within their limited resources and help track the effectiveness of their ad spend.

## Choosing Between Agency, Freelancer, or Self-Learning

When it comes to managing digital marketing, small companies typically have three primary options:

- Hiring an agency
- Engaging a freelancer
- Adopting a self-learning and hands-on approach

### Agency or Freelancer

When deciding between working with an agency or a freelancer, the specific needs and budget constraints of your business play a crucial role. Each option offers different benefits and limitations, depending on what your business requires from its digital marketing efforts.

Please consider that defining the goals and context of your campaign will still be your responsibility. Here a good preparation of the brief will help enormously (refer to Chapter 31 on briefings).

Also consider that both agencies and freelances require an investment of time on your part to understand your requirements and take decisions, unless you agree on a hands-off approach, where you basically treat your partner as a marketing department in a long-term relationship, providing them enough information to make decisions.

## Working with an Agency

Working with an agency provides a comprehensive suite of services along with access to a team of experts, making it ideal for businesses that seek full-service marketing solutions. Agencies bring a broad skill set to the table, offering more resources and scalable services that can grow with your business needs. Equipped to handle a wide range of tasks, from strategic planning to creative execution and analytics, agencies can provide a holistic approach to marketing.

However, there are disadvantages to consider. Working with an agency is generally more expensive than hiring a freelancer. The structured nature of agencies can also mean less flexibility in terms of project customization, as they may have standard approaches that they apply across clients. This can sometimes limit the ability to tailor strategies to the unique needs of your business.

## Hiring a Freelancer

Choosing a freelancer is suitable for targeted projects or when you need expertise in a specific area of digital marketing. Freelancers are typically more cost-effective and offer high flexibility, adapting quickly to your specific project requirements. This adaptability makes them ideal for businesses with precise needs or smaller budgets.

However, the scope of work a freelancer can handle is limited to their individual skills, and availability can be an issue if they are juggling multiple clients. This can affect the consistency and reliability of your digital marketing efforts. Therefore, it is particularly important to set expectations at the beginning of the conversations. If you expect them to be available every day, for example, this is one of the points that both parties should agree on to ensure a smooth working relationship.

## Practical Example

Imagine a small startup looking to establish its brand identity. Hiring a freelancer who specializes in branding and graphic design might be more economical and allow for direct collaboration on the brand's visual style. Conversely, a larger company planning a comprehensive marketing campaign that spans various channels might find that an agency, with its diverse team and resources, can more effectively manage such a complex undertaking.

## Courses, Self-Learning, and Experimentation

For small companies with extremely tight budgets or those aiming to build in-house expertise, self-learning and experimentation stand out as highly viable options. These methods allow businesses to gain practical experience and refine their marketing strategies over time.

Please note that, if you choose this alternative, you will make mistakes and hopefully learn from them. Also, please understand that just taking one course will most likely not be enough. Most digital marketing experts have many courses and years of experience under their belt, and thus will make decisions for which you will need at least some iterations and mistakes to learn.

## Digital Marketing Courses

Digital marketing courses are a great resource for understanding both the basics and more advanced concepts of digital marketing.

Almost every advertising channel provider offers their own courses and certifications. In such cases, please be aware that those courses and certifications are optimized for their own platforms. Refer to Chapter 39, where I explain a similar point regarding their recommendations.

Other platforms such as Udemy, Coursera, EDX, and other Massive Online Courses Platforms (MOOCs) also have free or low-cost courses with great and well-structured content.

## Benefits of Digital Marketing Courses

These courses, offered by many online platforms, can help you quickly come up to speed on the latest digital marketing techniques and trends without the need for expensive consultants or agencies.

In context, as I wrote before, a digital marketing specialist has done more than one course. Thus, when I write "quickly," I mean several tens of hours of learning. For instance, if you take a normal course on Coursera, dedicating 2–4 hours a week, it will take you a couple of months to finish.

> **Note** By the way, if you read this book, you have done a lot of work already, and you have a basis to understand almost any course in digital marketing.

## Practical Example

A local bakery owner enrolls in a digital marketing course on a popular online learning platform. The course covers essential topics such as SEO, PPC advertising, and social media marketing, empowering the owner to implement these strategies effectively to increase the bakery's online visibility and sales.

# Self-experimentation

Managing campaigns in-house can provide valuable hands-on experience and more profound insights into what marketing strategies work best for your business.

I recommend experimenting first with low-cost campaign types such as awareness campaigns and then diving deeper into more specific campaigns.

## Benefits of Self-experimentation

This approach allows you to directly apply what you've learned in real-world scenarios, adjusting tactics based on immediate results and feedback. It fosters an in-depth understanding of digital marketing dynamics specific to your market.

In this case, you will have to analyze and react to the data your advertiser channel provider gives you, and will mean, most of the time, a big time investment.

## Practical Example

A small tech startup decides to handle its Google Ads campaigns internally rather than outsourcing. Through trial and error, the team learns to optimize ad spend, discovering which keywords and ad formats yield the highest ROI. This hands-on experience proves invaluable in scaling their marketing efforts effectively and will help them later when working with other partners.

## Combining Learning and Practice

Integrating both structured learning through courses and practical application through self-experimentation offers a balanced approach. It provides theoretical foundations and immediate practical experiences, ideal for small companies seeking to maximize their digital marketing efficacy while controlling costs.

## About Creatives and Settings

The creation of advertising materials, known as creatives, and the configuration of campaign settings are important elements that can significantly impact the success of your digital marketing efforts. Effective management of these elements can enhance your campaign's reach and effectiveness.

In this case, you can make use of the features to build your creatives based on your landing page, or use online tools and templates and use them as base to create your own versions. I will elaborate on this after discussing the settings of the campaign.

## Default vs. Custom Settings

Choosing between default and custom settings involves a strategic decision based on your specific business goals and audience.

## Understanding Default Settings

Default settings offer a quick setup option that may save time, but might not be optimized for your specific campaign goals. Some advertising channel providers offer predefined campaigns or functionalities that take some parameters, such as geographical region and a landing page, and generate a campaign based on that information. The quality of those campaigns is directly related to the quality of the input, and most of the time may serve as a good initial campaign for you to run and modify.

In one sentence: Default Settings help you get started quickly.

## The Value of Custom Settings

Customizing settings to align with your business goals and target audience can greatly enhance the effectiveness of your campaigns. It allows for greater control over how your ads are targeted, displayed, and managed.

This also involves investing in research and configurations.

## Practical Example

Consider a small ecommerce store that adjusts its Facebook ad settings from the default to custom by focusing on demographic factors like age and interests relevant to its products. This customization leads to a higher engagement rate compared to when using the platform's default settings.

## Quality of Creatives

The quality of the creatives used in your campaigns is paramount, as we saw in Chapters 11 (Ad Quality) and 22 (Ad Creatives and Copy).

## Importance of High-Quality Creatives

Creatives, encompassing both visual and textual elements, must be professional, align with your brand, and resonate with your target audience. High-quality creatives attract attention and contribute to the overall effectiveness of your marketing messages.

In some cases, you may start running a campaign using the assets you already have at your disposal, such as your logo, website copy, product images, and so on. Some advertising channel providers have AI-Powered Creatives (check Chapter 22 on creatives) and can use those assets and your website to create the required creatives. In the case of Copy (i.e., Text Ads), they do an impressive job (which can be further improved by you), but in the case of Display Ads, it all depends on your assets.

## Practical Example

A small fitness studio wants to run ads for their new trainings, which starts in 2 weeks. They don't have a designer, and hiring one is outside their budget. They decide to take some good pictures of their trainings, use their logo and their website, and run responsive search ads and responsive display ads in Google Ads, thus leaving the Creative creation to Google's AI. That way they can quickly run a basic digital marketing campaign, setting a basic geographical targeting and get a campaign based on their assets and website content. With the results of that campaign, they can later improve future initiatives.

CHAPTER 40    DIGITAL MARKETING STRATEGIES FOR SMALL COMPANIES

# Leveraging Consultancy Services from Advertiser Channel Providers

Many advertising platforms offer consultancy services that can help you optimize your campaigns. These services can be particularly beneficial for small businesses that lack in-depth marketing expertise but still want to ensure their campaigns are set up for success.

Some consultants do a fantastic job, while others don't put much effort. I recommend taking their suggestions with a grain of salt and, if possible, contact them when you have specific questions. In those cases, you will notice that, as long as you speak their "language" (check Part 1), you will get additional information and great suggestions.

# Summary

In this chapter, I discussed some of the most important points for a small company when deciding how to run a digital marketing campaign. You should at least remember that

- Small companies need to carefully choose their digital marketing strategies based on budget, expertise, and resources.
- Options include hiring agencies or freelancers, engaging in self-learning, or a combination of these.
- Understanding and leveraging the right tools, consultancy services, and campaign settings are crucial for achieving effective results.

In the next chapter, I will explain what's important and provide some recommendations for companies with many self-owned locations.

# CHAPTER 41

# Digital Marketing for Companies with Multiple Locations They Own

In this chapter, I delve into digital marketing for organizations managing multiple physical locations, such as retail chains, hotel groups, and restaurant franchises. Marketing multiple locations presents unique challenges. Tailoring your approach to fit the specific context of each location can significantly enhance the effectiveness of your digital marketing efforts.

## Tailoring Your Approach

What do I mean by tailoring your approach to the specific context of each location? It involves understanding and utilizing the unique characteristics of each location to develop specific targeting criteria. This means recognizing that each location might appeal to different aspects of your market and should therefore be approached with strategies designed to capitalize on these unique features.

CHAPTER 41  DIGITAL MARKETING FOR COMPANIES WITH MULTIPLE LOCATIONS THEY OWN

# Key Considerations for Multi-location Marketing

The way people search for a brand and the targets available per location varies significantly. The choice of advertising channel providers, demographics, and network selection also shifts depending on whom you aim to reach at each location.

## Options for Structuring Campaigns

When structuring your campaigns for multiple locations, you have several strategic options. One approach is to create a campaign per location, which allows for maximum customization, aligning marketing efforts with the specific local audience's preferences and behaviors. This strategy provides the greatest flexibility and precision but can be resource-intensive to manage.[1]

Another option is to create a campaign per region. This strategy is useful for grouping locations with similar market dynamics, streamlining campaign management while still allowing for regional customization. It balances the need for localized marketing with the efficiencies of managing fewer campaigns.

Creating a campaign per country is a broader approach that works well for national branding strategies. This ensures consistent messaging across all locations within a country, making it easier to manage while maintaining some level of customization for national nuances.

For global brands, creating a campaign per continent (while considering language differences) might also be an option. This strategy focuses on continental differences in consumer behavior and market conditions, allowing for large-scale management with attention to broad regional characteristics.

---

[1] Check Chapter 38 on the structure of digital marketing campaigns.

Alternatively, creating a campaign per language targets linguistic groups specifically, which is particularly effective in multilingual regions or countries. This approach ensures that language-specific preferences and cultural nuances are addressed, enhancing the relevance and impact of your marketing efforts.

Lastly, creating a campaign per target focuses on specific demographic or psychographic segments across various locations. This strategy tailors messages to meet the characteristics of each target group, providing personalized marketing that can drive engagement and conversions.

Each of these structuring options offers different benefits and challenges, depending on the scale of your operations, the diversity of your target markets, and the resources available for campaign management. Choosing the right strategy involves considering these factors to align your marketing efforts effectively with your business goals and audience needs.

## Detailed Campaign Structuring

Within each campaign structure you create, whether by continent, country, or any other classification, you can incorporate various ad groups, ads, creatives, and copy. This structure primarily serves to organize your marketing efforts efficiently, acting as a framework within which more detailed decisions about advertising elements are made.

Extending strategy directives across locations involves passing down the main directives of a broad strategy to define each location's specific campaigns. For example, you might decide on a continent-based strategy and then tailor each location's campaigns to target specific groups that resonate with the broader directive. This approach ensures consistency in your overall strategy while allowing for localized adaptation.

For instance, if your business operates in Europe and Latin America, you could tailor your continent-wide strategies to reflect regional nuances. In Europe, you might emphasize the multicultural aspects of each country and how these influence your business. For example, highlighting how your brand caters to diverse tastes and preferences can resonate well with a European audience. In Latin America, the focus could shift to highlighting the vibrant "Latin passion" and unforgettable experiences associated with your brand. Emphasizing cultural celebrations, local traditions, and the emotional connection with your brand can enhance engagement in Latin American markets.

This structure should be viewed as a guideline to help define other aspects of the campaign under the same strategic umbrella. It ensures that while each campaign retains a degree of autonomy to target its specific audience effectively, it still aligns with the overall strategic goals and themes of the organization. By using such structured guidelines, you ensure that your marketing efforts are both coordinated and locally relevant, enhancing the overall impact of your digital marketing initiatives. This approach maximizes efficiency and strengthens the coherence of your brand message across different markets.

## Adapting Campaign Criteria for Each Location

Adapting campaign criteria for each location will help you maximize the relevance and impact of your digital marketing efforts. You may choose to adapt one or more criteria based on your specific needs and objectives. Remember, there is no one-size-fits-all solution, and you will gain experience and insights as you test different approaches. Generally, the more specific your targeting is, the smaller and more precise the group of people you can reach. Conversely, broader targeting can increase your reach but may show your ad to less relevant audiences. Striking a balance is key.

## CHAPTER 41  DIGITAL MARKETING FOR COMPANIES WITH MULTIPLE LOCATIONS THEY OWN

Geotargeting is essential, especially for businesses like restaurants, hotels, and retail stores that rely on local foot traffic. Geotargeting helps you reach people in the immediate vicinity of your location or in places your customers are interested in. For example, you might target similar cities to the one your hotel is in because your target audience is searching for experiences rather than specific cities, and they might change their destination if they find a better offer. This strategy is vital for businesses dependent on local customers.

You can set geotargeting parameters to encompass the area around your location, specific locations you are interested in, or exclude specific locations where you don't want your ad to be shown. Proper use of geotargeting can significantly improve offline conversions and increase foot traffic to your stores, especially in Search Ads (SEM). However, consider potential challenges such as VPN use or location settings on user accounts, which may cause discrepancies in the geolocations targeted.

Tailoring your keywords based on the location can improve the relevance and effectiveness of your campaigns. For businesses like restaurant chains, incorporating the city name or specific locality into your keywords can capture more targeted searches. For instance, targeting "restaurant in <city>" can attract users with intent to dine in that particular city.

Adapting your creatives based on the geographical characteristics of each location can make your campaigns more appealing. For example, a hotel chain might use images of the beach for ads targeting coastal locations, while using mountain imagery for ads aimed at properties near mountainous regions. This customization ensures that the creatives resonate well with the specific attractions of each location.

Custom landing pages for each location enhance user experience and campaign effectiveness by matching the context of the ad with that of the landing page. By adapting the content and images on the landing page to match each location, you deliver more value to the user and enhance their journey from ad to purchase. For example, a hotel's landing page for a beach location might highlight local beach activities and offer relevant promotions, whereas a mountain location's page might focus on hiking and outdoor adventures. This specificity improves user engagement and conversion rates.

Targeting specific demographics based on location-specific interests will also help you to maximize the relevance and impact of your campaigns. For example, in a city known for both family-friendly activities and nightlife, a hotel might target families with ads promoting babysitting services, while targeting young couples with ads highlighting nightlife and entertainment options.

Automation can streamline the creation and management of campaigns, especially for businesses operating in multiple locations. Tools like Google Ads Editor and scripts can automate the setup of campaigns, ad groups, and ads. Most advertising channels provide APIs to facilitate these processes, although implementation complexity can vary. While many aspects of campaign setup can be automated, the initial definition of target groups, core messaging, and main content of landing pages require human input.

Even when using AI tools to generate creatives and copy, it is crucial to ensure that the output aligns with your brand's values and marketing goals. Always review automated outputs to ensure they meet your standards. By combining automated processes with human oversight, you can maintain quality and relevance in your campaigns.

## Summary

Effectively adapting your digital marketing strategies to fit the unique characteristics of each location can significantly improve the performance of your campaigns. In this chapter, I provided practical examples and guidelines to help you tailor your digital marketing efforts according to the specific needs of different locales.

Here are the key takeaways you should remember:

- **Geotargeting Is Essential**: It is crucial for businesses that rely on local foot traffic, like restaurants and hotels. Geotargeting helps attract nearby customers, improving offline conversions and foot traffic.

- **Tailor Keywords to Location**: Incorporating specific geographical identifiers in your keywords can significantly increase the relevance and effectiveness of your campaigns.

- **Customize Creatives and Landing Pages**: Adapting your creatives and landing pages to reflect the local environment or attractions can improve engagement and conversions by resonating more effectively with the target audience.

- **Demographic-Specific Campaigns**: Crafting campaigns that cater to the specific demographics of each location can maximize campaign relevance and impact, especially in diverse areas with varied interests and needs.

- **Automation Can Streamline Processes**: While many aspects of campaign setup can be automated, such as the creation of campaigns and ad groups, human oversight is crucial to ensure that all elements align with your business goals and brand identity.

- **Human Oversight Is Imperative**: Despite the benefits of automation, the definition of target groups, core messaging, and the creation of landing page content require careful human consideration to ensure they meet the strategic goals of your marketing efforts.

In the next chapter, I will elaborate on the challenges and opportunities of digital marketing for companies with many independently owned locations and partners.

# CHAPTER 42

# Digital Marketing for a Company with Many Independently Owned Locations and Partners

You are a company with many independently owned distributors, like an auto brand and car dealerships, an insurance company and its agents, a bike brand and bike stores, and so on. Your marketing efforts have to be CI-conformant[1] and should adapt to the realities and context of your distributors.

---

[1] CI-conformant in marketing refers to elements or activities that are in line with and adhere to a company's Corporate Identity (CI) guidelines.

CHAPTER 42  DIGITAL MARKETING FOR A COMPANY WITH MANY INDEPENDENTLY OWNED LOCATIONS AND PARTNERS

# Key Considerations for Independently Owned Locations

Independently owned locations have their own requirements and goals, besides selling your products or services. There are many locations that are multi-brand or that base their business on their own brand. In many cases, they want to also market their own brand, name, and offers, and not just your centrally decided ones.

You should also consider that local partners and locations know more about their context (in most cases) than your central marketing agency or department, and your role is mainly to guide them and provide them with resources to run great campaigns that make their business and your brand grow. No one wants to run a campaign and spend resources just for the sake of it.

## Understanding Local Context

The way people search for a brand and the targets available per location can vary significantly. Choosing the right advertising channel provider, understanding the demographics, and selecting the appropriate network are all crucial according to whom you want to reach.

Regardless of the specifics for each location and partner, your central marketing strategy and message (not copy nor creatives) does not change.

## Practical Example

In Latin America, certain social networks may be more popular compared to those in Europe or the United States. It is sensible to align your social media strategies with the platforms that are most engaged by your target audience in each region and adapt your assets and copy to those realities, maintaining your main message.

Another example involves search ads in multilingual countries like Switzerland. Here, it is necessary to target French, German, and Italian speakers, using alternative product descriptions, keywords, and creatives tailored to each language group.

## Geotargeting: Adjustments Based on Location

Geotargeting must be finely tuned to match the characteristics of the location, especially for partners in rural areas.

In rural areas, a larger geotargeting radius may be required due to low population density. Older demographics might mean that social networks targeting younger audiences are less effective. Limited Internet bandwidth could necessitate the use of bandwidth-friendly creatives and landing pages, avoiding heavy content like videos.

## Customizing Campaign Elements: Adapting Campaign Criteria for Each Location

Now that you understand why adapting your campaign to the reality of each location is important, let's dive into what possibilities are there.

## Location/Partner-Specific Keywords

Tailoring keywords to reflect the unique characteristics of each location and the local audience's search habits is crucial. For instance, a bike brand might use "mountain bikes in [City]" for locations near mountainous regions and "city bikes in [City]" for urban areas, ensuring relevance and targeted traffic. You may also target location-specific competition using keywords such as "better bikes than [Other Brand]."

## Practical Example

An automobile brand could use specific model names combined with location-specific terms, such as "2024 [Model] sedan in [City]" to attract buyers looking for the latest models within their vicinity and show creatives with local landmarks or famous characters in each location.

# Location/Partner-Specific Creatives

Creatives should resonate with the local demographic while highlighting the unique selling propositions that appeal to that area. This might involve highlighting specific product features that meet the local climate or geographical needs.

## Example of Creative Adaptation

For an insurance company, creatives in regions known for natural disasters might focus on policies offering comprehensive coverage for flood or earthquake damage, using imagery and language that conveys protection and security, while the same company advertising in a city known for using bikes as main mean of transport can highlight insurances covering bikes.

# Location/Partner-Specific Landing Pages

Each landing page should address the specific services, promotions, or products available at that location, while maintaining overall brand consistency. It should link seamlessly with the creatives used in campaigns to enhance user experience.

It is important to use specific landing pages for each campaign, specially in this case where you don't always control your locations or partners' websites. Having an Ad link to a landing page that shows other products as advertised can be taken as fraud and get the ad account closed.

## Practical Example

For bike brands, a landing page for stores in urban areas might highlight the availability of commuter bikes and related gear, including maps of local cycling routes and testimonials about biking in the city, as well as replacement bikes in case of malfunctioning. In contrast, locations near trails or rural areas could emphasize adventure bikes and offer information on local biking events or group rides.

## Demographics

Understanding and targeting the demographics specific to each location allows for more precise and effective marketing. This might involve segmenting your audience by lifestyle preferences, age groups, or typical needs based on the locality's characteristics.

### Example of Demographic Targeting

An automobile brand might target families in suburban areas with ads for SUVs and minivans that emphasize safety and space, whereas in urban areas, they might focus on eco-friendly hybrids and compact cars that appeal to single professionals and younger consumers.

# Supporting Partners and Privately Owned Locations

The central brand can significantly enhance local marketing efforts by providing marketing assets, training, and support that maintain brand consistency while allowing for local adaptation. The central brand can supply a range of marketing assets, such as high-quality images, brand logos, detailed product information, and campaign templates that partners can localize to fit their markets. By providing these assets, the central brand enables partners to tailor resources to meet local needs while ensuring brand coherence.

Training partners to effectively use these assets and execute campaigns ensures that local advertising is both effective and consistent with the brand. For instance, an automobile brand could provide its dealerships with access to an online portal containing advertising templates,[2] detailed guides on car models, and promotional material. Dealerships could use these resources to create local ads that reflect regional preferences and promotions while maintaining brand consistency. This approach ensures that local marketing efforts are well-supported, cohesive, and aligned with the overall brand strategy.

## Customizing Marketing Elements to Local Needs

Customizing marketing elements to local needs is crucial. I've written about the requirements of each location, but there are also challenges for the central marketing efforts when managing and dealing with location-specific initiatives. In this case, you can suggest specific criteria and, depending on the business relation with your locations and partners, they can use them or dismiss them. Let's dive into what you, as the central marketing division for a brand, can offer.

Keywords tailored to partner locations can significantly enhance the relevance of your campaigns. For example, an insurance company might suggest region-specific keywords focusing on particular local needs or regulations, such as "earthquake insurance in [City]" or "flood insurance coverage in [Region]." This approach ensures that the keywords are directly relevant to the target audience in each specific location.

---

[2] Commonly known as a marketing automation platform or marketing management system.

## CHAPTER 42   DIGITAL MARKETING FOR A COMPANY WITH MANY INDEPENDENTLY OWNED LOCATIONS AND PARTNERS

Creatives adapted for local markets are another effective strategy. A bike brand might allow dealers to customize provided creatives to highlight relevant products, such as urban commuter bikes or mountain bikes, based on the local market focus. This customization ensures that the advertising resonates with local consumer preferences and needs.

Landing pages customized locally can greatly enhance user engagement. The central brand can offer landing page templates that partners can personalize with local details like contact information and customer testimonials. This personalization improves local relevance and customer engagement, making the marketing efforts more effective.

Demographic-specific ad targeting is also crucial. Guiding partners on targeting ads based on local demographics, such as suburban families or urban professionals, can make advertising more effective and tailored. This targeting ensures that the ads reach the most relevant audience segments in each location.

Automating marketing support for partners can save time and ensure consistency across all locations. Using marketing portals and resource management tools helps you distribute tailored content efficiently, ensuring that each partner receives materials that are customized yet consistent with the brand's standards. In this case, the choice of a system that fulfills your requirements is extremely important, as the system will help you reach your goals or prevent you from doing so if it does not allow you to do what you need.

An example of automated distribution can be seen in an insurance company's central office using automated tools to distribute promotional campaigns to agents. This ensures that all materials comply with both local regulations and brand standards. However, it's important to note the limits of automation. While many aspects of campaign setup can be automated, the initial briefing, the definition of the main message, and the marketing strategy to be implemented cannot be automated. Once these elements are defined, you may automate part of the implementation, creative creation, copy, and keywords, depending on your provider's capabilities.

CHAPTER 42   DIGITAL MARKETING FOR A COMPANY WITH MANY INDEPENDENTLY OWNED LOCATIONS AND PARTNERS

## Summary

In this chapter, I covered the essential considerations for digital marketing in companies with many independently owned locations and partners. I have explored how the central brand can support local marketing efforts, enhance the effectiveness of campaigns through localized customizations, and utilize automation to streamline processes while maintaining the integrity and coherence of the brand, as well as which targeting criteria can be adapted.

The main takeaways for you to remember are

- **Support from the Central Brand**: It is crucial for the central brand to provide comprehensive marketing assets, training, and support to empower partners to tailor local marketing efforts effectively.

- **Local Customization of Marketing Elements**: Adapting marketing assets such as keywords, creatives, and landing pages to local markets enhances the relevance and effectiveness of campaigns.

- **Automation Benefits**: Employing automation tools can help in efficiently managing and distributing marketing materials across various locations, ensuring consistency and brand compliance.

- **Human Element**: Despite the advantages of automation, the human element remains essential, particularly in defining campaign strategies and engaging with customers to ensure that each campaign resonates with the local audience.

- **Maintaining Brand Integrity**: While allowing for local customization, it is important that all marketing efforts adhere to the central brand's guidelines to maintain a cohesive brand image across all locations.

In the next chapter, I will give you a broad overview of social media, what is it, and some key concepts and considerations generally applicable.

# PART VI

# Overview of Social Media

As we move into other topics in digital marketing, social media is a must. This part of the book will provide an overview of how to navigate and leverage these powerful platforms for your digital marketing strategy. Social media is not just a channel; it's a dynamic ecosystem that requires careful planning, active engagement, and continuous adaptation.

In this section, I'll explore what social media is and why it's essential for businesses today. I'll discuss the strategic decisions involved in selecting the right platforms, managing your brand's presence, and ensuring consistency across various networks. Additionally, you'll learn about the importance of social listening and reputation management, which are relevant for maintaining your brand's image in an increasingly connected world.

Content creation, influencer partnerships, and crisis management are also key components of a successful social media strategy, and I'll give you an overview of each of these areas to help you develop a well-rounded approach. Finally, I'll touch on the emerging trends in social media and how to prepare for the future, ensuring your strategy remains relevant and effective as the digital landscape evolves.

By the end of this part, you'll have a basic understanding of how to craft and manage a social media strategy that aligns with your business goals, engages your audience, and strengthens your brand's online presence.

# CHAPTER 43

# Social Media Overview: What Is Social Media and Social Media Activity?

Social media encompasses every post, reaction, and interaction made within a social network. It forms an interactive space where individuals and organizations can share, co-create, discuss, and modify user-generated content.

Social media is interactive, dynamic, and poses many possibilities and challenges. In this chapter, I elaborate on some of the challenges you should be aware of as well as the differences between social media, social advertising, and digital marketing. I also provide an overview of the most used social media networks as well as some of the less known niche ones.

CHAPTER 43   SOCIAL MEDIA OVERVIEW: WHAT IS SOCIAL MEDIA AND SOCIAL MEDIA ACTIVITY?

# The Decision to Have a Specific Social Media Account

The decision to have a specific social media account requires careful consideration. Many companies focus on managing and enhancing their social media presence with various automation tools. However, it's crucial first to ask whether your company or brand should be on social media at all, and if so, which platforms are most suitable.

## Owning Brand Handles

One perspective suggests that securing as many social media handles related to your brand as possible can prevent misuse by others. This approach focuses on protecting your brand identity across various platforms, and it is also one approach I recommend, as long as the proper information is added to each profile.

## Selective Presence

Conversely, being "present" on social media means actively engaging with your audience. This involves answering questions, interacting with customers, and maintaining brand consistency across channels. It's often more manageable and effective to focus on a few key networks where your audience is most active. While it's wise to reserve handles on other platforms, you can use those accounts to inform customers and users of your primary communication channels. By doing this, you guide your audience to the platforms where they can find active engagement with your brand.

In line with maintaining your brand voice and promise, it's essential to select channels that align with your brand's strategy and audience. Inform your customers where you are most active and guide them to these platforms for reliable interactions. This approach ensures that your social media presence is strategic and manageable.

As a rule of thumb, it's better to control what customers find about your brand online than to let chance dictate their buying decisions. You should decide how, where, and what information they encounter. This approach ensures that accurate and compelling details influence their choices.

## Control Over Digital Assets

Consider the control you relinquish when operating on platforms owned by others. As discussed in Chapter 2 on digital assets, the importance of backing up your content and maintaining control over your digital presence cannot be overstated. Investing heavily in a platform without safeguards can jeopardize your brand's digital assets. Therefore, having a strategy to secure and manage your digital presence is essential for long-term brand protection and engagement.

Now that you understand the importance of control and presence in social media, let's move to an overview of the available networks.

## Overview of Social Media Networks

This section outlines the main social media channels available, highlighting their primary uses, audience types, and particular strengths. Understanding the landscape can help you choose the most suitable platforms for your brand's needs. Remember that social media is highly dynamic, and their audiences change over time. For instance, Facebook initially emerged as the social network for young people, but it is now seen as a network for adults by younger generations. It is important to continuously research where your target group is most active.

CHAPTER 43   SOCIAL MEDIA OVERVIEW: WHAT IS SOCIAL MEDIA AND SOCIAL MEDIA ACTIVITY?

## Facebook

Facebook offers extensive reach across diverse demographics, making it particularly suitable for detailed market segmentation. The platform allows for targeted advertising and the creation of community pages that can engage specific groups of users. Its broad user base enables brands to connect with a wide variety of audiences, from teenagers to seniors. Users interact with content through likes, comments, and shares, providing valuable feedback and engagement metrics. Facebook's parent company is Meta, which also owns Instagram and other services.

## X/Twitter

X, formerly known as Twitter, is best known for its real-time engagement and is a favored platform for conversations, often revolving around current events, customer service issues, and breaking news. Its fast-paced nature demands quick responses from brands, making it a critical channel for public relations and customer interaction if used. Brands use X to post updates, respond to customer queries promptly, and engage with trending topics, which can significantly boost visibility and brand relevance. Users on this platform expect quick responses.

## Instagram

Instagram is a highly visual platform, ideal for brands that can showcase strong visual content such as fashion, food, travel, and art. The platform supports various content types like photos, videos, stories, and reels, each offering unique ways for brands to engage with audiences. Instagram's features, like shoppable posts, also allow for direct sales, making it a powerful tool for driving visual marketing strategies and enhancing user engagement through aesthetic content.

## LinkedIn

LinkedIn serves as a professional network that is excellent for B2B interactions and building industry authority. Companies use LinkedIn to share industry-related content, network with professionals, recruit employees, and establish thought leadership. The platform facilitates professional content sharing, including articles, company updates, and professional achievements, making it a crucial part of any B2B digital marketing strategy.

## TikTok

TikTok has rapidly become a favorite among younger audiences with its short-form video content. The platform's algorithm favors high-engagement content, pushing videos that receive more interactions quickly to a broader audience. Brands on TikTok often create fun, engaging, and sometimes viral content that resonates with a youthful demographic, utilizing trends and challenges to maximize their visibility and engagement.

## Pinterest

Pinterest is particularly useful for brands with strong visual appeal, such as those in the DIY, fashion, food, and home decor sectors. The platform allows users to create and manage theme-based image collections around events, interests, and hobbies. Brands can utilize Pinterest to drive purchase intent by linking images directly to product pages, making it an effective platform for influencing buying decisions and driving traffic to ecommerce sites.

## Less Known But Niche, Regional, and Decentralized-Alternative Social Media Networks

Exploring a wide range of social media platforms provides opportunities for targeted engagement within specific cultural, geographical, or interest-based communities. Here are some less-known social networks that target specific audiences.

### Vero

Vero caters to users and brands valuing privacy, offering a platform without ads and data tracking, which appeals to a growing demographic concerned with digital privacy. (www.vero.co/)

### Ravelry

Ravelry is a niche platform focusing on knitting and crocheting, providing a direct channel for craft brands to engage enthusiasts with specific interests. (www.ravelry.com/)

### Nextdoor

Nextdoor connects neighbors, making it essential for local businesses aiming to build a community presence and engage with a geographically targeted customer base. (www.nextdoor.com/)

### Xing

Xing is particularly relevant for brands with a presence in German-speaking countries, offering networking and recruitment opportunities similar to LinkedIn. (www.xing.com/)

## WeChat

WeChat is crucial for brands operating in China, integrating messaging, social media, and payment functionalities into one platform, thus essential for engaging with the vast Chinese market. (www.wechat.com/)

## LINE

Popular in Japan, Taiwan, and Thailand, LINE allows brands to communicate directly with users in these regions, offering unique marketing opportunities through its messaging and service integrations. (https://line.me/)

## Discord

Discord supports vast community building, originally centered around gaming but now encompassing various hobbies and interests, making it suitable for brands looking to engage deeply with specific communities. (https://discord.com/)

## Reddit

Reddit's vast network of communities based on interests provides a rich ground for targeted advertising and deep engagement, especially for brands looking to interact directly with niche audiences. (www.reddit.com/)

## Twitch

Twitch, the leading platform for live-streaming, mainly in the gaming sector, offers brands a dynamic way to engage with audiences in real time, enhancing interactivity and brand visibility. (www.twitch.tv/)

## Decentralized Social Networks

Open-alternative networks are relevant for brands whose value proposition includes transparency, user control, and data privacy, resonating with a growing user base skeptical of traditional social media practices.

### Mastodon

Mastodon provides a decentralized alternative to traditional social media, aligning with values of transparency and user empowerment, ideal for brands advocating for Internet freedom and data privacy. It is usually seen as an alternative to X/ Twitter. (`https://mastodon.social/`)

### Lemmy

Lemmy, similar to Reddit but decentralized, offers privacy and control, suitable for engaging with users who prioritize open source values and community-led platforms. (`https://join.lemmy.ml/`)

# Differences Between Social Media, Social Ads, and Digital Marketing

Understanding the distinctions and relationships between social media, social ads, and digital marketing is essential for implementing effective online strategies.

**Social Media**
Social media refers to platforms where users create, share, and interact with content. It serves as a channel for brand presence and engagement, community building, and customer service. Through social media, brands can connect directly with their audience, foster a community around their products or services, and respond to customer inquiries and feedback in real time.

## CHAPTER 43  SOCIAL MEDIA OVERVIEW: WHAT IS SOCIAL MEDIA AND SOCIAL MEDIA ACTIVITY?

### Social Ads

Social ads are paid advertisements placed on social media platforms. These ads are targeted based on user behavior and demographics, making them highly effective for reaching specific audiences. By leveraging the detailed targeting options provided by social media platforms, brands can ensure their ads reach the most relevant users, thereby increasing the likelihood of engagement and conversion. It is important to consider data privacy when doing social media ads, as some areas limit the amount of data the networks can save and use.[1]

### Digital Marketing

Digital marketing encompasses a broader range of online marketing activities beyond social media, including SEO, PPC, email marketing, content marketing, and more (as seen in this book). It integrates various strategies to reach audiences across the digital landscape. Each component of digital marketing works together to create a cohesive online presence, driving traffic, engagement, and conversions.

### How Everything Is Related

Social media serves as the engagement layer in digital marketing, providing a direct way to interact with users and strengthen brand presence. Social ads amplify this interaction by targeting specific user segments, enhancing visibility and driving specific marketing goals. Together, they form integral components of a comprehensive digital marketing strategy, each supporting the other to maximize online presence and impact. By understanding how social media, social ads, and digital marketing interrelate, brands can create more effective and cohesive online marketing strategies.

---

[1] Check Chapter 26 on the legal landscape in digital marketing for more details.

# Other Aspects of Social Media You Should Consider

Above, I outlined the basic concepts you should know about social media, but there are many other aspects and areas to consider. Here, I provide an overview.

## Influencer Partnerships

Influencer partnerships effectively leverage the credibility and dedicated audiences of well-known social figures to boost your brand's outreach and authenticity. The core of these collaborations involves carefully selecting influencers whose public persona and audience demographics align closely with your brand values and target market.

**Challenges**
One of the primary challenges in influencer partnerships is ensuring the authenticity of the collaboration. The partnership must feel genuine to both the influencer's audience and your own customer base to avoid perceptions of mere transactional endorsements. Additionally, aligning both parties' expectations regarding the campaign goals, content creation, and compensation can be complex and requires clear communication.

**Opportunities**
The main opportunity in influencer partnerships lies in the ability to engage with an already engaged and loyal audience. Influencers who have established trust with their followers can effectively sway opinions and encourage interactions, significantly boosting your brand's visibility and credibility. This can lead to increased brand awareness, higher conversion rates, and direct access to niche markets that might be otherwise challenging to reach.

## Related Tools

Several tools can facilitate effective influencer partnerships. Examples include the following.[2]

BuzzSumo helps identify influential content creators based on topics relevant to your brand. Hootsuite allows for managing and monitoring social media interactions associated with influencer campaigns. AspireIQ connects brands with potential influencers and manages the end-to-end process of influencer collaboration.

## Practical Examples and Use Cases

For instance, a skincare brand might partner with influencers who focus on organic living to promote their new line of eco-friendly products.

By collaborating on content that highlights the natural ingredients and eco-conscious packaging, the influencer can authentically introduce the products to their audience. This partnership could include sponsored posts, story takeovers, and even live demonstrations of the product use, all coordinated to maximize engagement and drive traffic to the brand's website or ecommerce store.

## What You Should Remember

Influencer partnerships, when managed well, offer substantial benefits for brands looking to expand their reach and credibility rapidly. By choosing the right influencers, setting clear goals, and utilizing appropriate tools for management and analysis, companies can maximize the impact of these collaborations.

---

[2] The author mentions these platforms as examples, and there is no link whatsoever between him and the platforms.

## Social Listening and Reputation Management

Social listening encompasses the process of monitoring digital conversations across various platforms to gauge public sentiment about your brand and industry. This proactive approach is crucial not only for responding timely to customer feedback, but also for steering your brand's public perception in a positive direction.

**Challenges**

The primary challenge in social listening is the overwhelming volume of data generated across social media, blogs, forums, and other digital platforms. Filtering this data to extract actionable insights without getting lost in the noise requires the right tools and a strategic approach. Another challenge is distinguishing between noise and meaningful conversations that require engagement or intervention. The use of sentiment analysis and big data analysis is a suitable approach in this area.

**Opportunities**

Social listening offers substantial opportunities to engage directly with customers and manage potential issues before they escalate into crises. By actively engaging with both positive and negative feedback, a brand can manage its reputation and strengthen customer loyalty. This direct engagement helps humanize the brand and can transform general feedback into valuable insights for improving products or services.

**Related Tools**

Several tools can aid in effective social listening and reputation management. Brandwatch provides analytics to track and analyze online conversations about your brand, offering insights into public sentiment and emerging trends. Sprout Social offers social media management capabilities, including monitoring, engagement metrics, and response management tools. Hootsuite Insights allows for real-time social media monitoring and sentiment analysis to understand audience feelings toward your brand at scale.

### Practical Examples and Use Cases

Consider a consumer electronics company that monitors online discussions to quickly identify issues users are experiencing with a new device. By using social listening tools, the company can detect common complaints about a specific feature and address them in real time by providing troubleshooting tips through social media channels and directly engage with customers to solve their issues. Additionally, the insights gained can inform future product updates or changes, demonstrating a commitment to customer satisfaction and continuous improvement.

### What You Should Remember About Social Listening

Social listening and reputation management are vital for maintaining a positive brand image and fostering customer loyalty. By leveraging cutting-edge tools to monitor and engage with digital conversations, brands can not only preemptively address potential issues but also deepen their relationship with customers, turning everyday interactions into loyalty and trust.

## Content Strategies

Developing a strategic approach to social media content is important for engaging and retaining your audience effectively. This strategy must strike a balance between promotional material and content that educates, entertains, or informs, providing tangible value to your audience.

### Challenges

The main challenge in content strategy is the need for continuous innovation in content creation to stand out in a saturated market. Marketers must consistently produce fresh and relevant content that captures the interest of their audience while also aligning with brand goals. Ensuring content relevance and freshness can be demanding given the rapid evolution of user interests and competitive content.

# CHAPTER 43  SOCIAL MEDIA OVERVIEW: WHAT IS SOCIAL MEDIA AND SOCIAL MEDIA ACTIVITY?

## Opportunities

However, this challenge presents significant opportunities to establish your brand as a thought leader and a reliable source of valuable information. By delivering content that consistently meets the needs and interests of your audience, a brand can build a loyal following, enhance engagement, and ultimately drive conversions. Effective content strategies attract new followers and deepen existing customer relationships, promoting higher engagement rates and encouraging social sharing.

## Related Tools

Several tools can support effective content strategies. For example, **Buffer** simplifies the scheduling and posting of content across multiple social media platforms, allowing for consistent content delivery. **BuzzSumo** helps identify trending topics and content types that resonate with your target audience, facilitating the creation of relevant and engaging content, and **Canva** provides easy-to-use design tools for creating visually appealing graphics that can enhance the impact of your content.

## Practical Examples and Use Cases

Imagine a technology company that uses educational content to explain complex products to a non-technical audience. By creating video tutorials, infographics, and blog posts that simplify these concepts, the company can position itself as an expert in the field. This approach helps in demystifying technology and engages users who are looking for easy-to-understand information, leading to increased trust and loyalty.

## You Should Remember

A well-thought-out content strategy is fundamental to successful social media marketing. By continuously providing valuable, relevant, and engaging content, brands can effectively attract and retain audiences, turning social media platforms into powerful tools for building brand authority and driving business growth.

CHAPTER 43 SOCIAL MEDIA OVERVIEW: WHAT IS SOCIAL MEDIA AND SOCIAL MEDIA ACTIVITY?

# Social Media Analytics

Social media analytics play an important role in evaluating the effectiveness of your marketing efforts. By systematically analyzing metrics such as engagement rates, reach, and conversion metrics, you gain the ability to discern which aspects of your strategy are working and which are not.

**Challenges**

A significant challenge in social media analytics is selecting the appropriate metrics that truly reflect the success of your strategies. The abundance of available data can be overwhelming, and focusing on misleading metrics can divert attention from what truly matters. Moreover, correctly interpreting complex data sets to derive actionable insights requires both skill and experience.

**Opportunities**

However, the challenges are accompanied by substantial opportunities. The strategic use of analytics allows for the optimization of your social media campaigns based on real, measurable user feedback and behaviors. This data-driven approach enables continuous refinement and improvement of strategies, leading to more efficient and effective marketing efforts.

**Related Tools**

To effectively manage and interpret social media analytics, several tools are indispensable. Some examples of such tools are **Google Analytics and Matomo to p**rovide comprehensive insights into website traffic and user behavior after clicking through from social media.[3]

**Emplifi o**ffers detailed analytics and benchmarking tools that help brands to understand their social media performance in comparison to competitors. **Sprout Social** integrates analytics and engagement tools that allow for tracking and improving campaign performance across multiple social platforms.

---

[3] For more on Analytics, check Chapter 24.

CHAPTER 43   SOCIAL MEDIA OVERVIEW: WHAT IS SOCIAL MEDIA AND SOCIAL MEDIA ACTIVITY?

**Practical Examples and Use Cases**

Consider a retail brand that uses analytics to track the performance of a new product launch on social media. By analyzing engagement rates and conversion metrics from promotional posts, the brand can identify which messages and visuals resonate best with their audience. This insight allows them to adjust their content and promotional strategies in real time, focusing more on the most effective tactics to maximize impact and sales.

**What You Should Remember About Social Media Analytics**

Social media analytics are important for brands aiming to capitalize on their online presence in social media. By effectively employing these tools to monitor, analyze, and act on social media data, marketers can enhance their understanding of audience behavior, refine their marketing strategies, and achieve superior results in their digital marketing endeavors.

## Social Media and SEO

The intersection of social media and search engine optimization (SEO)[4] has become increasingly relevant for enhancing web traffic and online visibility. While it is established that social signals such as likes, shares, and comments do not directly influence search engine rankings,[5] the indirect effects of these activities can significantly enhance a brand's exposure and drive more traffic to its website.

You should also remember that the factors that influence SEO and rankings are constantly evolving, and this may change in the future.

---

[4] Check Chapter 23 on landing pages.

[5] www.semrush.com/blog/social-signals-seo/, www.searchenginejournal.com/ranking-factors/social-signals-rankinng-factor/, www.seedingup.com/blog/the-influence-of-social-signals-on-offpage-seo/, https://seobase.com/do-social-signals-directly-influence-rankings, and www.searchenginejournal.com/ranking-factors/social-signals-rankinng-factor/

## Challenges

The primary challenge lies in creating content that not only engages but also encourages sharing among users. High-quality, shareable content can naturally extend your brand's reach and visibility online, which indirectly benefits SEO by generating more inbound links and traffic. However, consistently producing content that resonates with both social media audiences and aligns with SEO can be demanding.

## Opportunities

The opportunity in integrating social media with SEO strategies lies in leveraging social platforms to amplify your content reach, which can lead to increased site visits and, potentially, higher page rankings. By promoting content through social media channels, you can attract more viewers, which encourages further sharing and interaction. This cycle of sharing and visiting can lead to greater organic search visibility over time.

## Related Tools

Several tools can help synchronize social media and SEO efforts. For instance, **BuzzSumo can help you** discover content that performs well in social media, which can inform content creation for SEO, **Hootsuite** allows for scheduling posts that drive traffic to optimized landing pages, helping to increase social sharing and inbound links, and **SEMrush** offers features to analyze the SEO impact of your social media traffic, showing how social interactions contribute to your website's search engine performance.

## Practical Examples and Use Cases

Imagine a company that specializes in eco-friendly products publishing an informative blog post about the benefits of sustainable living. By using social media to highlight key points from this article and engaging influencers to discuss and share the content, the company can significantly increase its visibility. As the content gets shared and linked to from various external sources, it drives direct traffic and improves search rankings due to increased organic engagement and inbound links.

## You Should Remember
Understanding the synergistic relationship between social media and SEO is relevant for modern digital marketing strategies. By creating content that leverages social engagement for SEO benefits, brands can enhance both their social media effectiveness and search engine visibility, leading to a comprehensive digital marketing success.

# Crisis Management on Social Media

Handling crises on social media requires a proactive strategy to monitor and manage your brand's reputation effectively. The initial challenge in managing a crisis on these platforms involves responding swiftly and appropriately to negative feedback or public mishaps.

## Challenges
The immediate challenge in crisis management on social media is the speed at which information spreads. Quick, thoughtful responses are crucial to mitigate damage and manage the situation effectively. The difficulty lies in crafting responses that address the concerns raised without escalating the situation further. Maintaining a balance between prompt replies and ensuring that the information is accurate and in line with your brand's values is essential.

## Opportunities
Effectively managing crises on social media presents an opportunity to demonstrate your brand's dedication to customer satisfaction and transparency. Handling issues competently can enhance your brand's reputation and strengthen customer trust. Successful crisis management can transform potential negatives into powerful demonstrations of your brand's reliability and responsiveness.

## Related Tools
Several tools can aid in the swift management of social media crises. Some examples of such tools are **Sprout Social** that offers monitoring tools that alert you when there are spikes in mentions, which could

indicate a brewing crisis and **Brandwatch that d**elivers insights into social sentiments and trends, allowing you to understand the context of crises and strategize effectively.

**Practical Examples and Use Cases**

Consider a scenario where a product defect has led to customer complaints spreading on social media. By monitoring these discussions early through tools like Brandwatch, your company can quickly assess the situation and respond. Publishing a well-prepared statement addressing the issue, explaining the steps being taken to rectify it, and apologizing for any inconvenience can help mitigate the crisis. Further, direct engagement with affected customers to resolve their issues can reinforce a positive brand image.

**You Should Remember**

Proactive crisis management on social media is vital for protecting and enhancing brand reputation. By employing effective monitoring tools, preparing for potential crises, and responding swiftly and strategically, companies can navigate these challenges successfully and even turn them into opportunities for brand enhancement. This is closely related with social listening and reputation management.

# Emerging Trends and Future Outlook

Staying at the forefront of emerging trends in social media such as augmented reality (AR), virtual reality (VR), and artificial intelligence (AI) can significantly enhance your brand's position in digital marketing innovation. These technologies promise to transform the ways audiences interact with content, offering more immersive and engaging experiences.

**Challenges**

The primary challenge associated with these emerging technologies is keeping pace with the rapid rate of technological advancements. Integrating AR, VR, and AI into existing marketing strategies without alienating your current audience requires careful planning and execution. It's crucial to introduce new technologies in a way that adds value to user interactions rather than overwhelming them with novelty.

**Opportunities**

The opportunity to engage a tech-savvy audience with these innovative tools is immense. AR can enhance the shopping experience by allowing customers to visualize products in their own space before purchasing, while VR can create completely immersive brand experiences that are impossible in physical reality. AI's potential lies in its ability to personalize interactions at scale, predict user behaviors, and automate routine tasks, thus increasing efficiency and personalization.

**Related Tools**

Several tools and platforms can help integrate these technologies into your social media strategy. Some examples include **Snapchat Lenses that** offers AR capabilities that brands can use to create interactive experiences directly on consumer smartphones; **Oculus Rift,** a VR platform that can be used for creating deeply immersive virtual experiences that showcase products or services; and **Chatbots powered by AI with** tools like ManyChat or Chatfuel that allow brands to implement AI-driven chatbots on social media platforms, enhancing customer service and engagement.

**Practical Examples and Use Cases**

A fashion retailer might use AR to let customers try on clothes virtually through an app integrated with their social media platforms, increasing engagement and potentially boosting sales. A travel company could use VR to offer virtual tours of exotic destinations, captivating potential travelers with immersive previews of their possible next vacation. Meanwhile, AI chatbots can be used on platforms like Facebook to provide instant customer support and personalized shopping advice, making the social media experience more interactive and responsive.

**You Should Remember**

Emerging technologies like AR, VR, and AI hold the potential to revolutionize social media marketing by creating more engaging, personalized, and immersive experiences. By embracing these technologies, brands can enhance user engagement and stay ahead in the competitive digital marketing landscape. Understanding and adapting to these trends will be crucial for brands aiming to maintain relevance and appeal to future generations of consumers. But you should also remember that AI and trendy latest technology comes with its challenges.

# Key Points to Consider for Your Social Media Strategy

In this chapter, I highlighted the diverse components that need consideration when developing a robust social media strategy. By understanding and addressing these various aspects, marketers can optimize their social media presence and prepare for future challenges and opportunities in the digital landscape.

## General Social Media

- **Consistency Across Platforms**: Ensure your brand voice and messaging are consistent across all platforms where you maintain a presence.

- **Engagement Over Broad Presence**: Focus on platforms where you can actively engage with your audience, rather than spreading your efforts too thinly across many networks.

- **Backup and Control**: Always have a strategy for backing up your content and maintaining control over your digital assets to avoid dependency on a single platform.

# Influencer Partnerships

- **Challenge**: Ensuring authenticity and aligning expectations.
- **Opportunity**: Leveraging the influencer's audience for enhanced brand credibility and reach.
- **Action**: Select influencers who align with your brand values and negotiate clear, mutually beneficial agreements.

# Social Listening and Reputation Management

- **Challenge**: Filtering vast amounts of data to find actionable insights.
- **Opportunity**: Proactively managing your brand's reputation and enhancing customer loyalty.
- **Action**: Implement tools like Brandwatch and Sprout Social to monitor and respond to social conversations effectively.

## Content Strategies

- **Challenge**: Continuously creating fresh and relevant content.
- **Opportunity**: Establishing your brand as a thought leader and go-to resource.
- **Action**: Develop a balanced content strategy that educates, entertains, and informs, using tools like BuzzSumo to identify trending topics.

## Social Media Analytics

- **Challenge**: Choosing the right metrics and interpreting data accurately.
- **Opportunity**: Data-driven optimization of social media campaigns.
- **Action**: Use analytics tools like Google Analytics and Matomo to measure effectiveness and adjust strategies accordingly.

## Crisis Management on Social Media

- **Challenge**: Responding quickly and appropriately to negative feedback.
- **Opportunity**: Demonstrating brand reliability and responsiveness.
- **Action**: Prepare for potential crises by setting up alert systems and having response plans in place.

## Emerging Trends and Future Outlook

- **Challenge**: Keeping pace with rapid technological advancements.

- **Opportunity**: Captivating a tech-savvy audience with innovative marketing techniques.

- **Action**: Stay informed about new technologies like AI and VR to integrate them into your social media strategy effectively.

In the next chapter, I will give you an introduction to the use of artificial intelligence in digital marketing, its main concepts, and why it is something you should know about.

# PART VII

# Artificial Intelligence in Digital Marketing

Artificial intelligence (AI) is rapidly reshaping how digital marketing campaigns are structured, analyzed, and implemented. This chapter delves into AI, demystifying its capabilities and exploring its role in marketing strategies.

**Understanding Artificial Intelligence in Marketing**
AI encompasses systems or machines that mimic human intelligence to perform tasks and can iteratively improve based on the information they collect. In the realm of digital marketing, AI's ability to process large volumes of data and make informed decisions is invaluable.

**Why AI Matters in Marketing**
For marketers, grasping the potential of AI is important as it transforms raw data into actionable insights, automates and optimizes processes, and personalizes customer interactions. These capabilities lead to increased efficiency and effectiveness in campaign execution.

**Evaluating AI in Marketing**
Understanding the strengths and limitations of AI is essential for its effective implementation. AI excels at processing and analyzing vast amounts of data, delivering personalized marketing at scale. It supports predictive analysis, anticipating customer behaviors and enabling proactive campaign adjustments. However, AI's performance is heavily

dependent on the quality and quantity of data available. Insufficient or poor-quality data can significantly impair its effectiveness. Additionally, over-reliance on AI may lead to a reduction in personal touch in customer communications, and there's a risk of opaque decision-making processes within AI systems, which may not always align with a brand's unique context or ethical standards.

In the next chapters, I will elaborate on the impact of artificial intelligence in several areas in digital marketing.

# CHAPTER 44

# Enhancing Targeting with AI

AI's ability to sift through massive datasets and identify valuable patterns empowers marketers to significantly refine their targeting strategies. In this chapter, I explore how AI improves the precision of marketing campaigns through advanced targeting techniques.

## Understanding AI-Driven Targeting

AI targeting utilizes machine learning algorithms to analyze customer data and identify behavioral patterns. This analysis enables marketers to segment audiences more precisely and tailor marketing efforts effectively, increasing the relevance of campaigns to each audience segment.

Nowadays, AI is also used by agencies and marketers to generate list of keywords, campaign settings, and definition of target groups. The quality of these is completely dependent on the quality of the data fed to the AI and the context. Without proper context, the AI will give a result that may not be aligned with your goals or with your brand promise.

> **Tip** Here the briefings come also to help. By providing the briefing to AI, you will get better answers that have better chances of aligning with your overall strategy. If you additionally provide a well-structured landing page, the results will be better. Check Chapter 23 on landing pages, specifically the section on AI and landing pages, to get more details on how AI can use it.

## Why AI Targeting Matters to Marketers

There are at least two faces to AI targeting. On one side is the use of AI by the advertiser channel providers to manage bids and decide who sees which ad, and on the other side is the use of AI in the definition of target groups and targeting criteria by the advertisers.

For the first case, you should understand that, while AI can analyze and act on big data fast and efficiently, the process behind its decisions is in a black box most of the time. This means you have to trust that the machine is taking the best decisions given the data it has. And this point is important. It requires quality and clean data, which means that what you feed the AI will have a great impact on the results.

For the second case, you need to understand your target group, your brand promise, and your products and services to be able to efficiently use AI in the definition of your briefings and settings. The AI will not do your work nor replace your experience and insights, but it will help you get your work done more quick. If you know what you have to do and how, you can get AI to help you get the results, but if you don't have any idea of what you are doing, you won't be able to evaluate the results of the AI and thus be at the mercy of chance.

AI is most helpful for those who already know what they are doing, and those who can explain clearly what they need and why.

CHAPTER 44    ENHANCING TARGETING WITH AI

# Evaluating the Implications of AI Targeting

Understanding the advantages and potential drawbacks of AI targeting is essential for its effective application.

AI targeting offers several advantages. When used correctly, it enables better allocation of marketing resources by focusing efforts on the most promising leads and customer segments. This targeted approach enhances customer engagement and can lead to higher conversion rates, provided the AI systems are fed with high-quality data. By leveraging AI, marketers can gain more in-depth insights into customer preferences and behaviors, allowing for more personalized and effective marketing strategies.

However, there are also significant drawbacks to consider. One of the primary concerns is potential privacy issues, as customers may be wary of how their data is being used. This concern requires a careful and transparent approach to data handling to maintain customer trust. Additionally, the effectiveness of AI targeting is heavily dependent on the quality of the data fed into the systems. Poor-quality data can lead to inaccurate predictions and suboptimal marketing outcomes. Furthermore, AI algorithms require ongoing updates to keep pace with changing consumer behaviors and market trends. Finally, there is a need for expertise in using AI models and tools to ensure they are applied effectively and ethically.

In summary, while AI targeting can significantly enhance marketing efforts through better resource allocation and improved customer engagement, it also poses challenges related to privacy, data quality, algorithm maintenance, and the need for specialized knowledge. Balancing these advantages and drawbacks is key to leveraging AI targeting successfully.

CHAPTER 44 ENHANCING TARGETING WITH AI

# Expectations Regarding Digital Marketing Service Providers

When working with service providers, expect a responsible use of AI that respects data privacy and utilizes advanced algorithms to enhance their work. Don't expect an AI to replace your service partner, but expect AI to enhance their work and response speed.

While some resources may suggest that AI can replace humans, this is only possible in cases where the process, results, and inputs are well known and highly tested. I don't mean AI can't get there, but once you start using AI for digital marketing, you will quickly notice its limitations, such as lack of control in the output, lack of consistency, or lack of quality and clean data to use it.

You cannot just throw a lot of data to an AI and expect a solution to your problem as a result. AI is a technology, and you have to understand and learn how to use it. This is true for machine learning, large language models, and anything in between. If you throw garbage to a model, garbage will come out, but with a better presentation.

# Summary and Key Takeaways

In this chapter, I explored how AI enhances marketing strategies. By analyzing massive datasets, AI helps marketers refine their targeting, making campaigns more precise and tailored to each audience segment. I discussed the dual aspects of AI targeting: one used by advertiser channel providers to manage ad delivery and the other by advertisers to define target groups and criteria. Both uses demand a deep understanding of AI's capabilities and limitations to fully leverage its potential in digital marketing.

1. **Dual Roles of AI in Targeting**: AI targeting operates in two main capacities within digital marketing. Advertiser channel providers use AI to optimize ad bids and delivery, requiring trust in the AI's black-box processes. On the other hand, advertisers use AI to define target groups and targeting criteria, which necessitates a clear understanding of the brand, market, and AI capabilities.

2. **Data Quality and Context Are Critical**: The effectiveness of AI in targeting heavily depends on the quality and context of the data provided. Marketers need to ensure that the data fed into AI systems is high-quality and contextually relevant to achieve desired outcomes. Poor input leads to poor output, which can misalign with campaign goals and brand promises.

3. **AI Augments, Not Replaces, Human Expertise**: While AI can significantly accelerate and refine the process of targeting, it does not replace the need for human expertise and insights in marketing. Effective use of AI requires a deep understanding of both the technology and the marketing objectives. Marketers must be adept at specifying what they need from AI to ensure it complements their strategies effectively.

In the next chapter, I will elaborate on content optimization with AI and why it is important for you.

# CHAPTER 45

# Content Optimization with AI

Artificial intelligence (AI) is significantly transforming content creation in digital marketing. This chapter delves into how AI enhances, rather than replaces, the roles of professionals in copywriting, design, and creative fields and addresses the challenges of maintaining brand voice and authenticity.

## Enhancing, Not Replacing, Professional Creativity

AI tools in digital marketing are often misconceived as replacements for human creativity. However, their true value lies in enhancing the work of professionals. AI accelerates the creative process by generating initial drafts and ideas that professionals can refine and enrich, ensuring that the final content reflects the nuanced understanding that only humans possess.

In some specific cases, you can also use the output of AI with good results, such in the generation of the copy for Search Ads and other creatives, but you have to feed the AI with the right message, your target audience, and your brand promise, as well as your product and services. That input does not come from an AI, but from you and your team and experience.

CHAPTER 45  CONTENT OPTIMIZATION WITH AI

## Challenges in Maintaining Brand Voice

While AI can generate content quickly, maintaining consistency in the brand's voice remains a challenge. It is crucial for content, whether generated by AI or humans, to resonate with the brand's personality and speak in a voice that engages and relates to customers. Ensuring that AI-generated content does not sound mechanical but instead reflects the brand's unique style and tone is essential for authentic engagement. This also requires the evaluation of the content to check if it matches the brand standards, which sometimes takes more time than doing it manually.

AI is still evolving, and this will surely change in the future, but you will notice that in numerous instances you need to make plenty of corrections to actually use automated generated content or make several iterations and fine-tuning to get it right. Often, the whole process of using AI for content is an interesting experience, but your realize that its development, while great, is not there yet. Using AI as support technology is, on the other side, a different experience, as you don't expect ready-to-use outputs but rough drafts you can work on.

## Recognizing and Penalizing AI-Generated Content

Recent advancements in technology have led to better recognition of AI-generated content by many platforms like Medium.com. Many now penalize such content by lowering its ranking or even prohibiting it, due to concerns over authenticity and quality. This development makes it vital for marketers to use AI tools judiciously, ensuring that content remains high-quality and indistinguishable from human-generated material.

## The Need for Expert Configuration

The default settings of AI content creation tools are often not sufficient to produce optimal results on the first—and even second or third—try. Successful application of AI in content creation requires expert configuration and regular evaluation of the output. Marketers must apply their experience and judgment to tailor AI outputs, ensuring they meet the brand's standards and campaign objectives.

## Understanding AI to Utilize It Effectively

To leverage AI effectively in digital marketing, a deep understanding of both the technology and its implications for content strategy are necessary. Marketers must be adept at interpreting AI-generated content and integrating it seamlessly with human-created elements. Without a solid understanding of what AI can and cannot do, there is a risk of misaligned content that fails to meet strategic goals.

## Summary and Key Takeaways

In this chapter, I explored the supportive role of artificial intelligence in enhancing the creativity and efficiency of digital marketing professionals. It emphasizes that AI tools are designed to augment, not replace, human expertise in creating compelling digital content. The chapter also addresses the challenges of maintaining a consistent and authentic brand voice, the implications of AI content detection by digital platforms, and the importance of expert oversight in AI content generation.

1. **AI As an Enhancer, Not a Replacer**: AI tools are best used to support and enhance the work of content creators, providing a foundation upon which professionals can build to produce high-quality, engaging content. AI should be viewed as a collaborative tool that amplifies the creative capabilities of marketing teams.

2. **Maintaining Brand Voice and Authenticity**: While AI can streamline content creation, it often struggles to fully capture the nuances of a brand's voice. It is crucial for marketers to review and refine AI-generated content to ensure it aligns with the brand's personality and maintains authenticity in customer interactions.

3. **Navigating AI Detection and Penalties**: With advancements in technology, digital platforms have become adept at detecting AI-generated content, which can lead to penalties such as lower search rankings. Marketers must use AI judiciously and ensure content meets platform standards to avoid negative impacts on SEO and visibility.

4. **Expertise Is Essential for Effective AI Use**: Effective use of AI in content creation requires a deep understanding of both the technology and the strategic goals of marketing campaigns. Marketers must configure AI tools expertly and continually evaluate their output to ensure alignment with campaign objectives and brand ethos.

In the next chapter, I will elaborate on managing expectations and elaborate, in my opinion, when AI is not the answer.

# CHAPTER 46

# Managing Expectations: When AI Is Not the Answer

While AI brings great advantages to digital marketing, it is vital to recognize its limitations and identify scenarios where traditional methods or human intervention might be more effective. This chapter delves into situations where AI may not provide the best solution and discusses how to balance AI applications with human insights for optimal outcomes.

## Understanding AI's Applicability and Limitations

Knowing when and where to deploy AI is crucial for leveraging its strengths, but recognizing its limitations is equally important, especially in tasks that require nuanced human judgment, high levels of creativity, or complex ethical decision-making.

Not every problem is a problem to be solved by AI. Sometimes, simple systems and simple solutions have a better ROI than implementing AI.

For instance, processes that need reliability and consistency in their results are a bad match for Large Language Models—LLM (in most cases)—but may be a great case to use more traditional solutions such as classifiers. Although Large Language Models are a trend right now, there are many older models which are stable and reliable, and that may be the solution to your problem.

Let's take the challenge of showing relevant products and articles to your sites visitors based on previous behavior and preferences. In that case, a Recommender System is a way better solution than an LLM and a lot cheaper as well.

Being aware of AI's limitations helps prevent an overreliance on technology that can lead to suboptimal strategies, customer dissatisfaction, or missed opportunities.

# Evaluating AI's Role in Marketing

A comprehensive understanding of both the benefits and the drawbacks of AI is important for its effective application in marketing. This balanced perspective enables marketers to strategically deploy AI where it adds the most value while being cautious of its limitations.

## Benefits of AI in Marketing

AI significantly enhances marketing efficiency by automating routine tasks, allowing marketing teams to focus on more strategic activities, like defining target groups, personas, and new products and services. It excels in processing and analyzing large volumes of clean and high-quality data, which is needed for developing insights into customer behavior and market trends. When trained with accurate data, AI can predict consumer behaviors and market developments with remarkable accuracy. This capability allows for more targeted marketing efforts and better allocation of resources, leading to increased ROI.

CHAPTER 46   MANAGING EXPECTATIONS: WHEN AI IS NOT THE ANSWER

## Drawbacks of AI in Marketing

Despite its advantages, AI has notable limitations that must be carefully managed. One of the primary drawbacks is AI's inability to fully understand complex contexts and interpret nuanced human emotions. These limitations become particularly evident in tasks that require a deep understanding of cultural subtleties or ethical considerations. Furthermore, an overreliance on AI can lead to depersonalized customer experiences, as AI may not always align perfectly with the human aspects of customer service and brand interaction. This misalignment can harm customer relationships and brand reputation if not monitored and corrected.

## Navigating AI's Challenges

To mitigate these drawbacks, it is crucial for marketers to not solely depend on AI for all aspects of marketing. Integrating human oversight into AI-driven processes ensures that the output remains aligned with the brand's ethical standards and customer expectations. Human marketers are essential for interpreting AI-generated data and making nuanced decisions that AI alone might not handle effectively.

By understanding these benefits and drawbacks, marketers can make informed decisions about where and how to integrate AI into their marketing strategies, ensuring that AI serves as a powerful tool to enhance, not hinder, their marketing efforts.

## Practical Examples

AI's integration into marketing strategies offers substantial benefits, but it's important to recognize scenarios where it might not be the ideal solution. This understanding helps in effectively balancing the use of technology with human insights.

For instance, handling complex customer service issues is a domain where AI often falls short. Although AI-powered chatbots can manage routine inquiries efficiently, they typically struggle with complex issues that require empathy and a deep understanding of nuanced human emotions. For instance, in situations involving customer complaints that escalate due to emotional distress or require delicate negotiations, human agents excel by providing the necessary empathy and personalized attention that AI systems are currently unable to replicate.

Similarly, when driving creative campaigns, the initial generation of ideas may be supported by AI to speed up brainstorming processes and data analysis. However, the creation of truly original and emotionally resonant campaign concepts often requires human creativity. AI tools might suggest themes based on data trends, but the subtleties of crafting a message that deeply connects with an audience—incorporating cultural nuances, humor, and storytelling elements—are best handled by human marketers. An example of this is in advertising campaigns intended to evoke strong emotional responses or align with specific cultural moments, where human touchpoints are crucial for authenticity and depth.

In both cases, while AI provides a starting point or handles mundane tasks, the critical elements that require human judgment, empathy, and creative insight ensure the effectiveness of the overall strategy. Marketers must therefore judiciously use AI where it adds value, and rely on human skills for aspects that AI cannot yet manage effectively.

## Business Challenges of Implementing AI

Implementing AI within business operations presents several challenges that organizations must navigate to effectively leverage this technology without compromising the quality of customer interactions and internal processes.

## CHAPTER 46   MANAGING EXPECTATIONS: WHEN AI IS NOT THE ANSWER

The risk of over-automation is a significant concern, particularly in customer-facing roles. While AI can streamline processes and improve efficiency, relying too heavily on automation can lead to a reduction in the personalization and engagement that customers expect. This can ultimately harm your brand's perception, as customers might feel they are interacting with a machine rather than a caring human. For example, when customer service becomes fully automated, the lack of human empathy and understanding can frustrate customers, especially during complex or highly personal service requests.

Skill gaps present another challenge. As AI technologies evolve, there is a continuous need for upskilling and training teams to ensure they can effectively integrate AI tools into their workflows. The pace of technological change demands ongoing education and adaptation. Organizations must invest in training programs to keep their workforce adept at using new AI tools, ensuring the technology enhances rather than hinders their capabilities.

Complex integration of AI into existing processes also poses a challenge. For AI to truly be effective, it must complement rather than replace human input, requiring seamless integration into the current workflows. This integration often demands substantial time and resources, including redesigning existing processes and ensuring that AI systems can communicate effectively with other digital tools in use. This complexity can be resource-intensive, not just in terms of financial outlay, but also in the allocation of human capital to manage and maintain the integration.

Addressing these challenges requires a balanced approach where AI is seen as a tool to enhance human work, not replace it. By maintaining this balance, businesses can mitigate the risks associated with AI implementation and maximize the benefits of this powerful technology.

CHAPTER 46   MANAGING EXPECTATIONS: WHEN AI IS NOT THE ANSWER

# Additional Considerations

Incorporating AI into business strategies requires careful consideration to ensure it improves rather than complicates processes. Two critical aspects must be continuously managed: balancing technology with human interaction and the regular evaluation of AI's impact.

Balancing technology and human interaction is vital, particularly in areas where human touch significantly adds value. AI should support, not replace, human capabilities, especially in direct customer interactions, creative endeavors, or situations requiring ethical judgment. For example, while AI can guide customer service by providing initial responses or directing queries, the final and more complex decisions should often be handled by humans who can understand subtleties and offer empathy. Similarly, in creative processes, AI can assist with preliminary designs or content drafts, but the final creative touches that resonate with audiences on a deeper level should ideally be crafted by human professionals.

Continuous evaluation of AI implementations is another important consideration. Regularly assessing how AI tools perform and impact business outcomes is necessary to ensure they are truly beneficial. This involves not just measuring performance against KPIs, but also gathering feedback from users and customers to understand their experience with AI-driven processes. Adjustments should then be made based on this feedback to enhance the synergy between AI applications and human insights, ensuring that AI remains a valuable tool in the organizational arsenal.

These considerations require ongoing attention and adaptation. By actively managing the integration of AI and ensuring it complements human efforts, organizations can leverage AI to its fullest potential while maintaining the quality and humanity of their services.

## Summary

In this chapter, I offered my personal view on the limitations of AI in digital marketing, identifying specific scenarios where AI may not be the optimal solution. I discussed the importance of recognizing when traditional methods or human intervention is more effective, particularly in areas requiring deep human insight or ethical judgment. The discussion emphasizes balancing AI application with human expertise to achieve the best outcomes and avoid potential pitfalls of overreliance on technology.

1. **Recognize AI Limitations**: It's essential to understand that AI is not suitable for all marketing tasks, especially those requiring nuanced human judgment, creativity, or ethical considerations. Acknowledging this helps prevent the inefficiencies that might arise from an overreliance on AI.

2. **Balance AI with Human Insight**: Integrating AI should not exclude human intervention. Human oversight is crucial in areas like customer service and creative campaign development, where empathy and deep understanding play significant roles. AI should be used to enhance these processes, not replace the human elements that are critical to success.

3. **Evaluate AI Appropriately**: Continuous evaluation of AI's role and its impact is necessary to maintain an effective balance between technology and human input. Regular assessments help ensure that AI tools are being used appropriately and are genuinely augmenting marketing efforts, rather than undermining them.

4. **Manage Business Challenges**: Successfully implementing AI involves addressing significant challenges such as the risk of over-automation, skill gaps, and the complexities of integrating AI into existing workflows. Effective management of these issues requires ongoing training, resource allocation, and careful planning to ensure that AI supports rather than detracts from business goals.

5. **Maintain Ethical Standards**: As AI becomes more prevalent, maintaining ethical standards in its application is paramount. Service providers and marketers alike should prioritize transparency, customer privacy, and the integrity of brand messaging to foster trust and sustain customer relationships.

Understanding when AI is not the answer is as, if not more, important than knowing how to leverage it effectively.

# CHAPTER 47

# Closing Words

I started this book with the goal of making it compact and practical, but as I wrote and checked with colleagues, friends, family, and beta readers, it became apparent that I had to delve deeper into the basics to help as many people as possible. Each chapter was developed by mixing theory and praxis, allowing some deviations from pure theory based on my experience. There are many situations where adapting theory into practice is necessary. I've made many learnings and aimed to spare you as many headaches as possible.

I am fully aware that there are some topics I may have dug too deep into, and others where I may not have gone too deep. Nonetheless, I hope this book provides a comprehensive overview of digital marketing and how to manage campaigns with several partners. The structure, with several short (and some not so short) chapters, is designed to allow you to use the book as a reference.

Digital marketing is constantly evolving and changing along with trends and our audiences, so we must stay up-to-date one way or another. This book is my contribution to help make this journey a little lighter. Please check the book's website for updates on this and other topics on digital marketing, and contact me on LinkedIn if you find any errors or if you would like additional topics covered in the future.

That said, here is a quick summary of what you have learned with this book.

## CHAPTER 47   CLOSING WORDS

First, I introduced a new definition of digital marketing to explicitly communicate the importance of viewing it as a continuous process rather than a one-time marketing initiative. Then, we covered a lot of jargon and concepts, from digital assets, advertiser channel providers, and awareness levels to walled gardens and the open Internet. We also elaborated on more specific concepts such as targeting, cannibalization, placements, and inventory. I explained the differences between commonly confused terms such as target groups, audiences, and personas, and we delved into bids, ad quality, and digital marketing metrics. You also got a brief overview of the customer journey and how digital marketing can help you enhance it.

Then, we moved on to the specific elements of digital marketing. You learned about the different types of digital marketing campaigns, how ad accounts work, and got a brief introduction to conversions, a term broadly used in the industry. With all that, I mentioned why a competitor analysis is important and explained the main differences between traditional and digital marketing initiatives.

After establishing that base knowledge, we explored the different channels, formats, and creatives available in digital marketing, and I explained what landing pages are and why they are an essential part of your campaign. Then we moved to analytics, marketing specialists, and the legal landscape—topics that are important but usually handled by others. You just need to understand what they are and how to check if others are doing their jobs.

Having learned all the jargon and concepts, I finally explained how a campaign is set up and run. Parts 2, 3, and 4 are shorter mainly because all the concepts and topic details are explained in the first part, and I build on them. Here we started with defining campaign goals, selecting advertising channel providers, channels, and formats, and delved into briefings. I tried to give you practical examples which, although simplified, are more detailed than many I've received in recent years. That means you can use them and the templates in the annexes as a base to create your own. I sincerely expect that, just by using them, you will prevent yourself many headaches.

## CHAPTER 47 CLOSING WORDS

Then we moved forward to how a campaign runs, focusing on common processes that usually run in the background but have a significant impact on the results and may make you wonder why some things are not working if you do not know of their existence. Understanding the learning phase, how budgets work, and how you or your partners can optimize and adjust a campaign, as well as the consequences of doing so, will also prevent misunderstandings between you and your stakeholders.

Finally, in a short chapter, I explained what you should expect from a campaign analysis in terms of deliverables and data, and how these results are completely dependent on the briefings you prepared.

Then, in an effort to make all that you learned more tangible, I elaborated on five different situations with examples and recommendations, which you can use as a base to define your digital marketing initiatives.

Additionally, because they are tightly related to digital marketing campaigns, I gave you an overview of social media and my take on artificial intelligence in digital marketing, highlighting where you should be careful, what you should be aware of, and where AI is just not the answer.

I hope this book has allowed you to get up-to-date on the important topic of digital marketing, that it serves as a practical and theoretical reference when you forget something or have questions, and that it helps you prevent headaches.

To your marketing efforts being effective and your campaigns successful.

May the ads be with you.

# ANNEX 1

# Digital Marketing Brief for Campaign Settings

This document outlines the foundational settings for your upcoming digital marketing campaign. It ensures all parties involved clearly understand the strategic framework, targeting details, and operational parameters.

| | |
|---|---|
| **Campaign name** | "Launch of Eco-Luxe Skincare Line" |
| **Campaign objective** | Increase brand awareness and drive pre-orders |
| **Target group or personas** | Millennials interested in sustainable beauty products |
| **Advertising channel provider(s)** | Google Ads, Facebook Ads |
| **Formats to use** | Display ads, video ads |
| **Geographic location** | United States, primarily urban areas |
| **Landing page URL** | "https://example.com/skincare-launch" |
| **Account usage** | Use the brand's existing advertising accounts |
| **Start date** | July 1, 2023 |
| **End date** | July 31, 2023 (*expected*), August 15, 2023 (*max*) |

(*continued*)

ANNEX 1   DIGITAL MARKETING BRIEF FOR CAMPAIGN SETTINGS

| | |
|---|---|
| **Contact person** | Jane Doe, Marketing Coordinator |
| **Competition brands** | Other luxury organic skincare brands |
| **Customer awareness level** | Moderate awareness, with recent exposure through social media |

*This is a Template Brief for Digital Marketing Campaign Settings. You can use it as is, or change it according to your needs.*

# ANNEX 2

# Digital Marketing Brief for Campaign Creatives

This brief example focuses on the creative elements of your campaign. It specifies the visual and textual content to be used, ensuring alignment with the campaign's goals and the brand's identity.

| | |
|---|---|
| **Advertising channel providers and formats** | Chosen based on the campaign settings document |
| **Reference material available** | Yes, previous campaign images and videos (attach them or add a link to download them) |
| **Expectations from provider** | Suggestions for innovative ad formats |
| **Copy available** | No, requires development |
| **Images available** | Yes, from previous photo shoots |
| **Due date for creatives** | June 15, 2024 |
| **Landing page review needed** | Yes, to ensure alignment with new creatives |
| **Contact person** | John Smith, Creative Director |

ANNEX 2   DIGITAL MARKETING BRIEF FOR CAMPAIGN CREATIVES

*In this brief, the focus is on gathering and organizing all creative assets needed for the campaign. Clear communication with the creative team is crucial to ensure that all materials align with the campaign's objectives. You may use it as is or change it according to your needs. If you need many creatives, I recommend to use one page per creative.*

# ANNEX 3

# Digital Marketing Brief for Campaign Monitoring

## Digital Marketing Brief for Campaign Monitoring

This document outlines how the campaign will be monitored and which metrics are relevant for assessing its performance. It ensures that there is a plan in place for responding to data and making necessary adjustments.

| | |
|---|---|
| **Adjustments authorization** | Yes, the provider may adjust bid strategies based on performance |
| **Report expectations** | Weekly performance reports required |
| **Landing page monitoring** | Yes, ongoing review to optimize conversion rates |
| **Contact person for this project** | *Provide contact details of the person responsible for overseeing the landing page development. This facilitates clear communication and prompt feedback* |

ANNEX 3　DIGITAL MARKETING BRIEF FOR CAMPAIGN MONITORING

*This document is important for setting expectations on how the campaign will be monitored and optimized. It involves deciding who has the authority to make changes and how often reports should be generated for review.*

# ANNEX 4

# Digital Marketing Brief for Campaign Landing Page

## Digital Marketing Brief for Campaign Landing Page

Creating an effective landing page is crucial for the success of your digital marketing campaign. This brief will ensure your landing page aligns well with your campaign goals and optimizes the user experience to maximize conversions.

ANNEX 4   DIGITAL MARKETING BRIEF FOR CAMPAIGN LANDING PAGE

| Element | Description |
| --- | --- |
| Product/service/ campaign name | Specify the name of the product, service, or campaign this landing page is promoting. This ensures clarity and consistency in messaging |
| Creative assets | List all creative elements such as images, videos, and graphical assets that need to be included on the landing page |
| Platform | Identify which platform the landing page will be hosted on, such as WordPress, Shopify, or a custom solution |
| Tracking codes | Specify any tracking codes that need to be integrated for analytics and performance monitoring, such as Google Analytics or Facebook Pixel |
| Copy | Provide or outline the textual content for the landing page. This includes headlines, product descriptions, and call-to-action texts |
| CTA (call-to-action) | Clearly define the call-to-action for the page. What is the one action you want users to take? This could be "Sign Up," "Buy Now," or "Learn More." |
| Design | Outline any specific design requirements or provide guidelines to ensure the landing page adheres to your brand's aesthetic |
| Contact person for this project | Provide contact details of the person responsible for overseeing the landing page development. This facilitates clear communication and prompt feedback |
| Awareness level of target customer | Describe the assumed awareness level of the target customer. Are they completely new to the brand, or do they have prior exposure? This helps in tailoring the content's complexity and depth |

Consider this template brief as a base document to guide the development of your landing page. You can extend and change it according to your requirements. It's designed to streamline communication and ensure all team members are aligned with the vision and requirements of the project.

# Index

## A

ABM, *see* Account-based marketing (ABM)
Accelerated Mobile Pages (AMP) banners
    advantages, 206
    disadvantages, 206
    recommendations, 205
    related concepts, 205
    relevant channels, 206
    requirements, 206
    use case, 206
Account-based marketing (ABM), 137
Acquisition, 279, 280
Ad accounts
    advertising platforms, 146
    Facebook Ads, 147
    Google Ads, 146
    integrations and extensions, 148
    multiple functions, 145
Adaptation, 444
Ad copy, 88, 97, 98, 122
Addressable TV (ATV), 181, 182
Ad formats, 142, 143, 167, 169, 171, 173, 175, 177, 180, 183, 186, 189, 194, 316
    awareness, 340, 341
    characteristics, 339, 340
    conversions, 341–343
    overview, 201–203
    right mix of formats, 343
    traffic, 340, 341
Ad message, 88
Ad placements, 55, 78, 85, 94, 99, 102, 105, 112, 115, 361
Ad platforms, 59
Ad position, 89, 90
Ad providers, 82
    practical insights, 82
Ad quality, 92, 95, 102, 104, 168, 170, 352
    ad providers, 82
    ad text, 84
    advertiser and provider, 79
    consequences, 86
    customer's view, 81
    diagram, 88
    digital marketing, 79
    effects, 85
    high-quality ads, 80
    low-quality ads, 80
    ranking, 83, 85
    score, 83

INDEX

Ad quality (*cont.*)
  score explanation, 84
  tracking, 80
Ad rank, 89
Ad relevance, 86, 88, 100, 103
Ad sets, 410
Advertiser-channel-provider
    policies, 17, 46
Advertisers, 10, 25, 27, 40–42, 46,
    54, 60, 64, 65, 69, 79, 99,
    135, 203, 210, 221, 245
  ad quality, 83
  channel providers, 422, 432
  CPC model, 70
  in CPI, 73
  CPM model, 71
  CPV, 72
  eCPC, 73
  example scenario, 83
  ROAS, 74
  verification, 305
Ad visuals, 88
Advocacy, 320, 336, 342
Ahrefs, 157
AI, *see* Artificial intelligence (AI)
Allowlisting, 51
Amazon Ads, 39
AMP banners, *see* Accelerated
    Mobile Pages (AMP)
    banners
Analytics, 273, 274
  comparative table, 274–277
  comparison table, 290–293
  first-party, 273

  in marketing, 293
  third-party, 273
  *See also* Tracking
App install ads, 202
  ad formats, 243
  advantages, 244
  bypassing, 243
  challenges, 244
  considerations and
      requirements, 244
  effectives, 243
  fitness mobile application, 243
  mobile and tablet, 242
  relevant channels, 244
AR, *see* Augmented reality (AR)
Artificial intelligence (AI), 10, 266,
    271, 471
  additional considerations, 494
  applicability and limitations,
      489, 490
  benefits, 490
  brand, 486
  business challenges,
      492, 493
  drawbacks, 491
  effectively in digital
      marketing, 487
  evaluation, 481, 482
  expert configuration, 487
  implications, 481, 482
  marketers, 480
  in marketing, 481, 490
  navigation, 491
  practical examples, 491

510

professional creativity, 485
recognizing and penalizing, 486
service providers, 482
targeting, 479
ATV, *see* Addressable TV (ATV)
Auction, 82, 85, 96
Audiences, 60, 61, 63, 65, 71, 86, 88, 92, 139–141, 164, 165, 205, 207, 259, 278, 282
   analysis, 60
   attention, 80, 98
   engagement, 94
   interactions, 255
   performance data, 213
   preferences, 102, 137
   target, 77
   tech-savvy, 233
   understanding, 59
Audio ads, 202
   advantages, 220
   challenges, 220
   commercials, 216
   considerations and requirements, 219
   crafting, 216, 217
   digital marketing, 216
   execution, 217, 218
   importance, 216
   visual elements, 218, 219
Augmented reality (AR), 471
Augmented reality (AR) ads, 188–190
Authenticity, 486, 488
Automation, 438, 439

Awareness, 402
   ad formats, 340, 341
   goals, 328
   levels, 416
   marketing goals, 317
   network selection, 334

# B

Bids, 63, 85, 88, 92, 108, 350, 361
   audience, 71
   cost per click (CPC), 70
   in digital marketing, 63, 64
   risk strategies, 65, 66
Black boxes, 39
Blockchain, 193, 194
Blocklisting, 50, 52
Brand, 486
   equity, 16, 17
   loyalty, 319, 336, 342
   protection, 306–309
Briefings, digital marketing
   campaign creatives, 348, 349
   campaign landing page, 351–354
   campaign monitoring, 349–361
   campaign settings, 347, 348
   competition analysis, 346
   expert, 346
   product/service, 345
Broad match, 123
Budgets, 126
   adjustments, 389, 390
   allocation, 422
   campaign budget, 384

INDEX

Budgets (*cont.*)
   day budget, 384
   Google Ads, 385
   impacts, 46–49
BuzzSumo, 463

## C

California Consumer Privacy Act (CCPA), 301
Call-to-actions (CTAs), 87, 140, 213, 217, 260, 262, 292, 351
Campaign approvals
   creatives, 376
   learning phase, 375–377
Campaign budget, 384
Campaign criteria, 436–438
Campaign elements
   location/partner-specific creatives, 444, 445
   location/partner-specific keywords, 443
   location/partner-specific landing pages, 444
   practical example, 444
Campaign goals, 498
Campaign pauses
   creative approval, 377
   landing page errors, 377
   malware, 377
   target-URL modifications, 378
Campaigns, 289
Campaign settings
   account owned, 395
   advertisement account, 395
   advertising channel providers, 394
   before it runs, 393, 394
   full-package service, 395
   paused/live, 394
   is running, 394
Campaign structuring
   brand, 436
   guideline, 436
   options, 434, 435
   strategic goals, 436
   strategy directives, 435
Cannibalization, 45, 46, 498
   addressing, 47
   budget impacts, 46–49
   risk of, 47
Carousel ads, 231
   advantages, 233
   challenges, 234
   considerations and requirements, 233
   effectiveness, 232
   fashion retailer, 232
   formats, 232
   relevant channels, 233
CCPA, *see* California Consumer Privacy Act (CCPA)
ChatGPT, 266
Cinema ads, 184, 185
Clarity, 81
Clicks in digital marketing
   connections, 96
   importance, 96

# INDEX

mechanics, 96
performance, 97
practical example, 97
user interaction, 97
Click-through rates (CTR), 54, 82, 84, 350
   in campaign optimization, 98
   in digital marketing, 97
   on digital marketing, 99
   importance, 98
   improving, 100
   marketing metrics, 99
   practical example, 99, 100
   working, 98
Comparative table, 195–200
Competitor, 155, 156
   integrating tools, 159, 160
   landing pages, 158
   tools and techniques, 156–158
Connected TV (CTV), 179–181
Consultancy services, 432
Content marketing, 136
Content strategies, 475
   challenges, 465
   opportunities, 466
   practical examples, 466
   related tools, 466
   social media marketing, 466
Contextual advertising, 121, 122
Contextual matching, 86
Conversion optimization, 83
Conversion rate, 102
   connection, 103
   on digital campaigns, 103
   importance, 102
   improving, 104
   practical example, 104
   working, 103
Conversions, 149, 150, 164, 188, 271, 281, 287, 292
   Exit Links, 285
   goals, 329
   marketing goals, 318
   network selection, 335
   recommendations, 420
   recommended formats, 341–343
   tracking, 263, 264
Conversion tracking
   codes, 150
   Google Ads, 150
   Google analytics, 151
   working, 150
Copy, 140, 169, 171, 211, 362
Copy consistency, 86
Core channels, 168
   display ads, 168–170
   mobile and in-app ads, 178–180
   native ads, 173, 174
   Search ads (SEM ads), 170–172
   social media ads, 173–175
Cost efficiency, 83
Cost implications, 419
Cost per acquisition (CPA), 350
Cost per action (CPA), 64, 71
   e-commerce site, 72
   risk bearing, 71

INDEX

Cost-per-click (CPC), 54, 64, 396, 419
    bidding strategies, 92
    click-through rates, 92
    definition, 70
    digital advertising, 91
    high-competition keywords, 93
    and implications, 125
    improving, 94
    keywords, 125
    mechanics, 92
    practical example, 93
    risk bearing, 70
    use case example, 71
Cost per impression (CPM), 64
Cost per install (CPI), 73
    mobile gaming company, 73
    risk, 73
Cost-per-mille (CPM), 71, 110, 419
    advertising strategies, 110
    company launching, 71
    connections, 111
    impacts, 111
    importance, 110
    managing, 112
    practical example, 111
    risks, 71
Cost per view (CPV), 72
    in bidding strategies, 95
    connections, 95
    importance, 94
    mechanics, 94
    reducing, 95, 96
    risk bearing, 72
    tech company, 72
    video ad, 95
Country-specific taxes
    in Asia, 305
    in Europe, 304
    in North America, 304
    in South America, 305
Coursera, 427
CPA, *see* Cost per acquisition (CPA); Cost per action (CPA)
CPC, *see* Cost-per-click (CPC)
CPM, *see* Cost per impression (CPM)
CPV, *see* Cost per view (CPV)
Creative approval, 376
Creatives, 145, 166, 169, 170, 179, 203, 348, 349, 503–505
    adjustments, 391
    audio messaging, 220
    description, 140
    digital marketing brief, 357–360
    requirements, 142, 143
    and settings, 429
    types, 141
Crypto ads, 193, 194
CTAs, *see* Call-to-actions (CTAs)
CTR, *see* Click-through rates (CTR)
CTV, *see* Connected TV (CTV)
Customer awareness
    diagram and interactions, 35
    identifying and understanding, 29
    "most aware" customers, 33
    oversights, 30

# INDEX

pain/problem aware, 34
product aware customers, 33
products/services, 29
solution aware customers, 33
strategy, 34
strategy details, 35
unaware completely, 34
visualization, 30–32
Customer interactions, 35
Customer journey, 115
    checkout, 117
    digital marketing, 116
    follow-up feedback, 117
    start stage, 117
    visit site, 117
Custom landing pages, 437
Custom settings, 430

# D

Data privacy, 274
Data privacy legislation, 300
    on digital marketing, 303
    regulations in Asia, 302, 303
    regulations in Europe, 300
    regulations in North America, 301
    regulations in South Africa, 301
    regulations in South America, 301
Data quality, 483
Default settings
    *vs.* custom, 429, 430
    understanding, 430

Demographics, 445
Digital advertising
    ecosystem, 75, 76
    advertising channel providers, 24–26
    development and planning, 23
    diagram, 25
    four pillars, 27
    structure, 26
Digital assets, 34, 455
    brand equity, 16, 17
    email template, 19, 20
    nonaggressive way, 19
    rule of thumb, 17, 18
    tangible and intangible, 15
Digital campaigns, 11, 91, 103, 139, 165, 166, 264
    categories, 322–325
    creatives, 503–505
    landing page, 507–508
    monitoring, 505–507
    objectives, 345
    risks, 325
    settings, 501, 502
    types, 133–136
    *See also* Digital marketing
Digital marketing, 19, 23, 25, 28, 49, 53, 56, 57, 60, 62, 94, 95, 115, 119, 125, 126, 130, 131, 133, 137, 145, 204, 216, 248, 257, 258, 264, 271, 272, 461, 497
    advantages and disadvantages, 10–12

# INDEX

Digital marketing (*cont.*)
  bids, 63, 64
  campaign categories, 322–325
  cannibalization, 45–48
  channels, 194
  comparative table, 164, 165
  conversion, 149
  country-specific taxes, 303
  courses, 427
  creation, execution and analysis, 4
  customer awareness, 29–37
  definition, 3–5, 498
  digital channels, 9
  elements, 498
  get up-to-date, 499
  message, 5
  multiple digital channels and formats, 4
  open web, 40
  process, 4
  protecting, brand, 306–309
  reaction times, 9
  return on ad spend (ROAS), 74
  service providers, 482
  set of traget groups, 5
  specialist types, 295, 296
  stages, 6–9
  strategies, 36
  targeting, 41
  *vs.* traditional, 163, 164
  walled gardens in advertising, 39

Digital out-of-home (DOOH), 167, 182–184
Digital services tax (DST), 304
Digital tracking, 112, 113
Discord, 459
Display ads, 168–170
DOOH, *see* Digital out-of-home (DOOH)
DST, *see* Digital services tax (DST)
Dynamic ads, 202, 239
  advantages, 242
  algorithms, 240
  challenges, 242
  considerations and requirements, 241
  e-commerce platform, 240
  other formats, 240
  real-time data, 240
  relevant channels, 241

# E

EcoGlow, 267
eCPC, *see* Enhanced cost per click (eCPC)
Email marketing, 176–178
Emerging trends, 471–473, 476
Engagement, 319, 335, 341
Engagement variability, 59
Enhanced cost per click (eCPC), 73
  online retailer, 74
  risk, 73
Entry Links, 284

## INDEX

ePrivacy Directive, 300
ePrivacy Regulation, 300
Events, 286, 287
Exact match, 123
Exit Links, 285
Extensions, 59, 148

## F

Facebook, 23, 39, 59, 68, 69, 82, 83, 101, 130, 233, 252, 253, 456
    Ads, 147, 263, 305, 318, 375, 385
    Carousel Ads, 5
    pixel, 151
False positives handling, 378
Fixed bidding, 65
Flexibility, 10, 27, 182, 215
Flexibility in costs, 164
Four digital marketing briefings
    campaign creatives, 357–360
    campaign monitoring, 360, 361
    campaign settings, 354–357
    landing page, 362–364
Frequency, 106, 403
    connections, 107
    impacts, 107
    importance, 106
    management, 107
    in marketing strategies, 106, 107
    practical example, 107
    working, 106

## G

GDPR, *see* General Data Protection Regulation (GDPR)
General Data Protection Regulation (GDPR), 300
General targeting, 43, 45, 46
Geotargeting, 437, 439, 443
Goals, 288, 316
Google Ads, 4, 11, 20, 23, 24, 39, 59, 68, 69, 83, 85, 92, 96, 99, 126, 134, 146, 150, 157, 206, 212, 225, 236, 248, 252, 259, 263, 305, 347, 355, 375, 380, 410
    budgeting, 385
    conversion tracking, 420
    diagram, 26
    graphics, 26
Google analytics, 151
Google Video Ads, 5

## H

High-quality ads, 80
High-quality creatives, 431
HTML banners
    advantages, 205
    description, 203
    disadvantages, 205
    mockup example, 203
    recommendations, 204
    related concepts, 204
    relevant channels, 204
    use cases, 204

# INDEX

HTML structure
   ecommerce platform, 270
   elements of, 269, 270
   LLM, 267, 268
   transitioning, 270

## I, J

Image ads, 201
Impressions, 350
   on campaigns, 101
   connection, 101
   importance, 101
   optimizing, 102
   tracking, 102
   working, 101
Independently-owned locations
   local context, 442
   practical example, 442, 443
   supporting partners, 445
Influencer partnerships, 474
   challenges, 462
   oppurtunities, 462, 463
   practical examples, 463
   related tools, 463
   substantial benefits, 463
Informational intent, 130
Innovation, 27, 133, 181, 221, 283
Instagram, 456
Intangible digital assets, 15, 16
Integrations, 148, 151, 159, 160
Interactive content, 191-193
Interstitial ads, 202, 234
   advantages, 236
   challenges, 236
   comparing, 235
   considerations and
      requirements, 236
   mobile gaming app, 235
   relevant channels, 236
   temporarily pause user
      interaction, 234
   user engagement, 235
Inventory, 49, 50, 498
Inventory ads, 202, 226, 230
   advantages, 228
   considerations and
      requirements, 228
   disadvantages, 228
   effective, 226
   implementation, 226
   online retailer, 226, 227
   relevant channels, 227

## K

Key performance indicators (KPIs),
   317, 350
Keywords, 141, 171, 207-209, 389
   ad copy, 122
   alignment, 86
   budgeting, 126
   comparative table, 160, 161
   Contextual advertising, 121, 122
   costs and CPC, 125
   intent, 130, 131
   landing pages, 122
   long-tail, 128

management, 390, 391
matches, 123, 124
match types, 124
optimization strategies, 127, 128
positive and negative term, 120
research tools and techniques, 126, 127
selection, costs, and budgeting, 125
strategic use, 124
trends and seasonality, 129
user behavior, 130, 131
KPIs, *see* Key performance indicators (KPIs)

# L

Landing pages, 84, 89, 97, 102, 104, 122, 158, 256, 271, 277, 439, 507–508
advertising channel provider, 258
annotated elements, 262
availability and quality, 423
campaign, 257
campaign brief, 351–354
conversion tracking, 263, 264
correlation with ads, 259
design and content, 257
errors, 377
four digital marketing briefs, 362–364
homepage, 258, 259
known brand, 258

location/partner-specific, 444
malware, 377
quality, 86
significance, 259
specificity and context, 260
structure, 261
visual hierarchy, 260–262
Large language models (LLMs)
comprehension, 267, 268
HTML role, 266
optimization, 269, 270
Lead ads, 202, 223
advantages, 225
challenges, 225
considerations and requirements, 225
crafting, 223
importance, 223
LinkedIn, 223
mockup example, 224
relevant channels, 225
Lead generation, 337, 343
Learning phase
algorithm, 380
asset changes, 381
budget adjustments, 381
considerations, 396
creative approval, 376
detailed insights, 380
navigating changes, 381, 382
post-approval, 376
real-time interactions, 379
Lemmy, 460
LINE, 459

INDEX

LinkedIn, 223, 457
LinkedIn Ads, 306
LLMs, *see* Large language models (LLMs)
Local keywords, 130
Long-tail keywords, 128
Low-quality ads, 80

## M

Manager Account, 146
Marketers, 166, 193, 194, 200
Marketing elements, 446, 447
Marketing goals, 316
    advocacy, 320
    awareness, 317, 328
    brand loyalty, 319
    categories, 316, 317
    conversions, 318, 329
    engagement, 319
    lead generation, 320–322
    traffic, 318, 328, 329
Marketing objectives, 40, 70, 137, 246, 247, 255, 256, 317
    clarification, 316, 317
    *See also* Marketing goals
Massive Online Courses Platforms (MOOCs), 427
Mastodon, 460
Matomo, 157
Media assets, 88
Message delivery, 83
Messages, 140, 169, 171, 174, 211
Meta Ads, 410

Metadata, 265, 266
Mobile and in-app ads, 178–180
Mobile gaming ads, 73
    ad placement strategy, 55
    impact exploring, 54
    thumb-clicks, 53
MOOCs, *see* Massive Online Courses Platforms (MOOCs)
Multi-location marketing, 434
Multiple Ad Groups, 412
Multiple ads, 413, 414
Multiple campaigns, 410
Multiple groups, 411

## N

Native ads, 173, 174, 202, 237
    advantages, 239
    aesthetic integrity, 237
    challenges, 239
    considerations and requirements, 239
    crafting, 237
    lifestyle blog, 237
    other formats, 237
    relevant channels, 238
NatureCare, 268
Navigation, 491
Navigational intent, 130
Network policies, 306
Network risk profiles
    evaluating, 330
    marketing, 329

# INDEX

Network selection
   across media, 334
   advocacy, 336
   awareness, 334
   brand loyalty, 336
   conversions, 335
   engagement, 335
   lead generation, 337
   traffic, 334, 345
Nextdoor, 458

# O

Open-alternative networks
   Discord, 459
   Lemmy, 460
   LINE, 459
   Mastodon, 460
   Nextdoor, 458
   Ravelry, 458
   Reddit, 459
   Twitch, 459
   Vero, 458
   WeChat, 459
   Xing, 458
Open web, 40
Optimizations in digital campaigns
   budget adjustments, 389, 390
   creative adjustments, 391
   keywords management, 390, 391
   marketing professionals, 387
   performance, 388
   strategies, 388
   targeting adjustments, 391, 392

# P

Page Fold, 287, 288
Page Views, 283
Partners supporting, 445
Password Managers, 19
PDPA, *see* Personal Data Protection Act (PDPA)
PDPL, *see* Personal Data Protection Law (PDPL)
Performance-based bidding, 65
Perplexity, 266
Persona, 61
Personal Data Protection Act (PDPA), 302
Personal Data Protection Law (PDPL), 302
Personal Information Protection Act (PIPA), 302
Personal Information Protection and Electronic Documents Act (PIPEDA), 301
Personalized marketing, 481
Phrase match, 123
Pinterest, 457
Pinterest Ads, 306
PIPA, *see* Personal Information Protection Act (PIPA)
PIPEDA, *see* Personal Information Protection and Electronic Documents Act (PIPEDA)
Placements, 49, 50, 76, 85, 350, 498
   blocklisting URLs, 52
   monitoring, 52

Placements (*cont.*)
   tools and analytics, 52
   URLs, 51
   *See also* Ad placements
Podcast ads, 190, 191
POPIA, *see* Protection of Personal Information Act (POPIA)
Pop-up ads, 203
   ad formats, 249
   advantages, 250
   advertisements, 248
   advertising formats, 251–254
   considerations and requirements, 250
   crafting, 249
   in digital marketing, 248
   e-commerce website, 249
   relevant channels, 250
   types, 248
Print ads, 185, 186
Print advertising, 112, 113
Product aware customers, 33
Programmatic buying, 76, 77
   cinema ads, 184, 185
   print ads, 185, 186
Protection of Personal Information Act (POPIA), 301
Providers, 364
   alignment with campaign goals, 418
   benefits and risks, 418
   buiding/setting up, 364
   campaign goals, 364
   collaboration, 365
   cost implications, 419
   critical milestones/deadlines, 364
   important dates, 365
   level of involvement, 364
   periodic meetings, 365
   practical example, 419
   recommendations, 417
   status updates, 365
   suggestions, 365
   team, boss/stakeholders, 365
   technical feasibility, 418
   understandings, 418

## Q

Quality assessment, 82
Quality of creatives, 430
Quality score, 85, 259

## R

Ravelry, 458
RDA, *see* Responsive Display Ads (RDA)
Reach, 104, 179, 182, 184
   connections, 105
   enhancing, 105
   importance, 104
   measuring, 105
   working, 105
Real-life scenarios
   expected outcomes, 367, 368
   lack of strategic input, 366

# INDEX

mismatched campaign goals, 366
unclear deadlines, 366
Real-time bidding (RTB), 147, 184
Real-Time Visitors, 277, 278
Reddit, 459
Referral marketing, 136
Relevance, 81
Reports
    campaign overview, 401
    campaigns, 399
    channel-specific metrics, 401
    components, 400–402
    data provider, 402
    frequency, 403
    metrics, 403
    performance metrics, 401
    pitfalls, misinterpretations, and vanity metrics, 403
    recommendations, 400
    timing, 403
Resource efficiency, 27
Responsive Display Ads (RDA), 4, 202, 213
    application, 213
    challenges, 215
    channels, 215
    flexibility, 215
    key features, 214, 215
    manual intervention, 216
    multiple assets, 213
    significance, 213
Responsive Search Ads (RSAs), 210
    advantages, 212

considerartions and requirements, 212
disadvntages, 212
dynamic approach, 210
elements, 210
headlines and descriptions, 211
importance, 211
related channels, 211
travel agency, 211
Retargeting campaigns, 136
Return on ad spend (ROAS), 74
    alternatives, 76, 77
    calculation, 75
    in digital marketing, 74
    example, 75
    importance, 76
    luxury watch brand, 74
    programmatic buying, 76
    risks, 74
Return on investment (ROI), 125
Right strategy, 67–70
Risks, 79, 325, 329
    bidding strategies, 67–70
    managing, 66
    media, 334
    providers, 418
    right strategy, 67–70
    *See also* Network risk profiles
ROAS, *see* Return on ad spend (ROAS)
ROI, *see* Return on investment (ROI)
RSAs, *see* Responsive Search Ads (RSAs)
RTB, *see* Real-time bidding (RTB)

523

INDEX

# S

SEA, *see* Search Engine Advertising (SEA)
Search ads (SEM ads), 170–172, 437, 485
Search Engine Advertising (SEA), 266
Search Engine Friendly (SEF), 265
Search Engine Marketing (SEM), *see* Search ads (SEM ads)
Search Engine Optimization (SEO), 265, 266, 468
Search engine results pages (SERPs), 127, 196
SEF, *see* Search Engine Friendly (SEF)
Self-experimentation, 428
Self-learning, 426
SEM ads, *see* Search ads (SEM ads)
SEMrush, 156
SEO, *see* Search Engine Optimization (SEO)
SERanking, 127
SERPs, *see* Search engine results pages (SERPs)
Service partners, 141, 142, 166, 168, 177
Share of impressions, 108
    connections, 109
    impacts, 109
    importance, 108
    in marketing, 108
    optimizing, 109
    practical example, 109
    working, 108
    *See also* Impressions
Shopping ads, 202, 228
    advantages, 231
    challenges, 231
    channels, 230
    considerations and requirements, 231
    high-quality, 229
    importance, 229
    inventory ads, 230
    online electronics store, 229
Small companies
    advertiser channel providers, 422
    agency/freelancer, 424
    benefits, 427
    budget allocation, 422
    campaign types, 422
    company website, 423
    constraints, 421
    courses, self-learning, and experimentation, 426
    default *vs.* custom settings, 429, 430
    freelancer hiring, 425, 426
    learning and practice, 429
    practical example, 424, 426, 428
    working with an agency, 425
Social ads, 461
Social listening, 474
    challenges, 464
    crisis management, 470, 471

# INDEX

opportunities, 464
practical examples, 465
related tools, 464, 465
Social media, 454, 460, 473
    account, 454
    analytics, 475
    brand handling, 454
    challenges, 469
    crisis management, 475
    influencer partnerships, 462, 463
    online visibility, 468
    opportunity, 469
    practical examples, 469, 470
    related tools, 469
    selective presence, 454, 455
    *See also* Social media networks
Social media ads, 173–175
Social media analytics, 467, 468
Social media networks, 455
    Facebook, 456
    Instagram, 456
    LinkedIn, 457
    Pinterest, 457
    TikTok, 457
    Twitter, 456
Solution aware customers, 33
Specialists, digital marketing, 295, 296
    choosing, 297
    knowledge and experience, 296, 297
    working place, 296
Specific targeting, 43, 45–48, 67, 105, 106

Speed, 164
Sponsored content
    ad formats, 246
    advantages, 247
    advertiser, 245
    brand's values, 245
    challenges, 247
    considerations and requirements, 247
    crafting, 245
    culinary blog collaboration, 246
    effective, 245
    relevant channels, 247
Spotify, 218
Strategic advantage, 27
Structuring digital marketing
    analysis and optimization, 413
    campaign-level settings, 411
    large-scale operations, 411
    multiple campaigns, 411
    planning, 416
    recommendations, 414–416
    service provider, 410

# T

Tailoring, 433
Target groups, 57, 58, 61, 96, 101, 106, 169, 171, 174, 416
    ad platforms and targeting options, 59
    audience, 60
    digital marketing, 60
    identification, 58

## INDEX

Target groups (*cont.*)
    persona, 60
    utilization, 58
Targeting, 56, 63, 69, 76, 93–95, 97, 100, 112, 118–120, 130, 141, 147, 170, 205, 207, 208, 215, 227, 244, 259, 273, 350, 355, 438, 498
    adjustments, 391, 392
    artificial intelligence (AI), 479
    contextual advertising, 121, 122
    criteria, 45
    definition, 42
    in digital marketing, 41
    dual approach, 43
    messages and creatives, 42
    options, 59
    preferences, 47
    settings and criteria, 42
    settings and parameters, 41
    strategies, 59
    types, 43
Text ads, 201
    advantages, 209
    audiences, 209
    creating, 207
    description, 207
    disadvantages, 209
    matter, 208
    relate concepts, 208
    related channels, 208
    requirements, 209
    usage reccomendations, 208
    use cases, 208

Thumb-clicks, 53, 92, 178
    identifying, 54
    impacts, 54
    monitoring, 54
TikTok, 457
Tracking
    codes and privacy, 161
    and data privacy, 274
    goals, 288
    impressions, 102
    Page Views, 283
    parameters, 152, 274
    QR codes, 164
    User IDs, 280
    visitors, 264
Trade Desk platform, 147
Traditional marketing
    comparative table, 164, 165
    *vs.* digital, 163, 164
Traffic
    ad formats, 340, 341
    goals, 328, 329
    marketing goals, 318
    network selection, 334
Transactional intent, 131
Transactional keywords, 131
Twitch, 459
Twitter, 456
Twitter Ads, 306

## U

Udemy, 427
Unique Page Views, 282, 283

Unique Visitors, 278, 279
URLs management, 51, 112, 152
User behavior, 130, 131, 190, 239, 244, 280
User experience, 55, 70, 80, 95, 99, 103
User Flow, 287, 288
User IDs, 280, 281
User intent, 131, 212, 270
User Journey, 287, 288
UTM codes, 152

# V

Vanity metrics, 12, 403
Vero, 458
Video ads, 202
    advantages, 222
    advertising format, 220
    challenges, 222
    compelling, 221
    considerations and requirements, 222
    effective, 221
    relevant channels, 222
    smartphone, 221
Virtual reality (VR), 471
Visit Duration, 281, 282
Visual hierarchy, 260–262
Visualizations, 401
Voice search ads, 187, 188
VR, *see* Virtual reality (VR)

# W

WeChat, 459

# X, Y, Z

Xing, 458

GPSR Compliance

The European Union's (EU) General Product Safety Regulation (GPSR) is a set of rules that requires consumer products to be safe and our obligations to ensure this.

If you have any concerns about our products, you can contact us on

ProductSafety@springernature.com

In case Publisher is established outside the EU, the EU authorized representative is:

Springer Nature Customer Service Center GmbH
Europaplatz 3
69115 Heidelberg, Germany

www.ingramcontent.com/pod-product-compliance
Lightning Source LLC
LaVergne TN
LVHW010332260326
834688LV00036B/670